GAY IS GOOD

GAY IS GOOD

The Life and Letters
of Gay Rights Pioneer **Franklin Kameny**

Edited by **Michael G. Long**

SYRACUSE UNIVERSITY PRESS

∞ The paper used in this publication meets the minimum requirements of the American National Standard for Information Sciences—Permanence of Paper for Printed Library Materials, ANSI Z39.48-1992.

For a listing of books published and distributed by Syracuse University Press, visit www.SyracuseUniversityPress.syr.edu.

ISBN: 978-0-8156-1043-4 (cloth)   978-0-8156-5291-5 (e-book)

Library of Congress Cataloging-in-Publication Data
Kameny, Frank, 1925–2011.
  Gay is good : the life and letters of gay rights pioneer Franklin Kameny / edited by Michael G. Long. — First edition.
     pages cm
  Includes bibliographical references and index.
  ISBN 978-0-8156-1043-4 (cloth : alk. paper) — ISBN 978-0-8156-5291-5 (ebook)
1. Kameny, Frank, 1925–2011—Correspondence.   2. Gay men—United States—Correspondence.   3. Political activists—United States—Correspondence.   4. Gay rights—United States.   5. Gays—United States.   I. Long, Michael G.   II. Title.
  HQ75.8.K35A4 2014
  323.3'264—dc23   2014037582

Manufactured in the United States of America

that the law of good be,

published with grant by
Figure Foundation

Gay is good.
　　—Franklin E. Kameny

Michael G. Long is an associate professor of religious studies and peace and conflict studies at Elizabethtown College and is the author or editor of several books on civil rights, religion and politics, and peacemaking in mid-century America, including *Beyond Home Plate: Jackie Robinson on Life after Baseball* (Syracuse University Press); *Martin Luther King, Jr., Homosexuality, and the Early Gay Rights Movement* (Palgrave Macmillan); *I Must Resist: Bayard Rustin's Life in Letters* (City Lights); *Marshalling Justice: The Early Civil Rights Letters of Thurgood Marshall* (Amistad/HarperCollins); and *First Class Citizenship: The Civil Rights Letters of Jackie Robinson* (Times Books). Another of Long's books, *Christian Peace and Nonviolence*, focuses on international peacemaking efforts by Christian activists and scholars. Long's work has been featured or reviewed in the *New York Times*, the *Washington Post*, the *Los Angeles Times*, the *Boston Globe*, *USA Today*, CNN, *Book Forum*, *Ebony/Jet*, and many other newspapers and journals. Long blogs for the Huffington Post and has appeared on C-Span and NPR. His speaking engagements have taken him from the National Archives in Washington, DC, to the Schomberg Center of the New York Public Library in Harlem, and to the City Club of San Diego. Long holds a PhD from Emory University in Atlanta and resides in Highland Park, Pennsylvania.

Contents

List of Illustrations   *xi*

Acknowledgments   *xiii*

Introduction: *Making Society Change*   *1*

1. **"The Winds of Change Are Blowing"**
1958–1962   *24*

2. **"Genocide Is the Word That Must Be Used"**
1963–1964   *49*

3. **"We Have Outgrown the 'Closet-Queen' Type of Approach"**
1965   *83*

4. **"The Lunatic Fringe"**
1966   *117*

5. **"We Are People; We Are Not Specimens or Inanimate Objects"**
1967   *138*

6. **"Gay Is Good"**
1968   *150*

7. **"Without Our Demonstrations . . . Stonewall Would Not Have Happened"**
1969   *181*

8. **"Psychiatry Is the Enemy Incarnate"**
1970–1971   *216*

9. "The Ground Rules Have Changed"

1972   237

10. "VICTORY!!!! WE HAVE BEEN 'CURED'!"

1973   256

11. "So Much to Feel Satisfied, Content, Victorious, and Enthusiastic About"

1974   287

12. "I Have Brought the Very Government of the United States to Its Knees"

1975   307

Conclusion: *Jefferson, Lincoln, King—and Kameny*   326

Notes   337

Location of Letters   359

Index   365

Illustrations

Following page 168

1. Kameny in World War II
2. Kameny at Harvard University
3. Kameny's petition to the U.S. Supreme Court
4. Macy's letter to Kameny
5. Jack Nichols and Kameny
6. The march on Independence Hall
7. Delivering a gay rights letter to the White House
8. Kameny offering counsel to a prisoner
9. *The Homosexual Citizen*
10. Christopher Street Gay Liberation Day March
11. Kameny in front of the Capitol
12. "Gay, Proud, and Healthy" educational exhibit
13. Crank mail
14. Kameny at the Smithsonian
15. Kameny's signature

Acknowledgments

I am deeply grateful to the following individuals and institutions: Frank Kameny, who, with encouragement from Charles Francis, generously donated his papers to the Library of Congress; the Estate of Dr. Franklin E. Kameny; Charles Francis and Bob Witech of the Kameny Papers Project; Randy Wicker; Andrew Tobias; Syracuse University Press, especially Jennika Baines, Mona Hamlin, Kay Steinmetz, and Kelly Lynne Balenske; copy editor Jessica LeTourneur; the staff at the Manuscripts Division of the Library of Congress; Tal Nadan and Philip Heslip of the Manuscripts and Archives Division of the New York Public Library; Thomas Lisanti of the Permissions and Reproduction Services of the New York Public Library; Stacey Chandler and Stephen Plotkin of the John F. Kennedy Presidential Library; archivists at the presidential libraries of Dwight Eisenhower, Richard Nixon, Jimmy Carter, and Ronald Reagan; the staff at High Library of Elizabethtown College, especially Sylvia Morra and Louise Hyder-Darlington; Kathleen Murphy; Michael Key of the *Washington Blade*; Elizabethtown College, especially Dean Fletcher McClellan, for financial support, and Carol Ouimet; first-rate anonymous reviewers of the manuscript; independent researcher Marc LaRocque; freelance writer and editor Elaine Tinari Benedetti; the cool kids—Jackson Griffith Long and Nathaniel Finn Long; and their strong mom, Karin Frederiksen Long. Special thanks to my dear friend Sharon Herr for proofreading the manuscript and preparing it for delivery.

GAY IS GOOD

Introduction

Making Society Change

Gay rights pioneer Franklin Kameny was pleased as he sat down to type a letter on June 3, 1972. "Dear Mother," he wrote. "The past two weeks have been among the most gratifying I have experienced in a very long time, and I thought I'd share them with you."[1] He was not exaggerating. Kameny had just seen phenomenal results from his innovative and longtime advocacy for gay rights. The Washington, DC, school board had approved a policy of nondiscrimination in the hiring and promotion of homosexuals. The DC government had signed a legal agreement with the American Civil Liberties Union (ACLU) stating that the district's sodomy law did "not apply and cannot be applied to private consensual acts involving adults."[2] A federal court had ruled that the practice of homosexuality did not constitute sufficient grounds for the U.S. government to deny security clearances to individuals working with classified information. And a DC superior court judge had decided that the district's statute prohibiting solicitation for "lewd and immoral purposes"—a law that had long fueled police harassment against gay men and lesbians—was unconstitutional.[3] "These things represent many years of work for me and many hundreds of thousands of typed words," he explained to his mother.[4]

Stacks upon stacks of papers surrounded him as he typed in the small office in his redbrick home in northwest Washington—news clippings, letters, and articles. His black metal files overflowed, and space was at a premium. But however cluttered his office was, Kameny himself was crystal-clear as he reflected on the approach he had adopted in his longtime crusade. "Some 32 years ago," he typed, "I told you that if society and I differ on anything, I will give society a second chance to convince me. If it fails, then I am right and society is wrong, and if society gets in my way, it will be society which will change, not I. That was so alien to your entire approach to life that you responded with disdain. It has been a guiding principle of my life. Society was wrong. I am making society change."[5]

This book is the story of Franklin Kameny's pioneering efforts to help change society so gay men and lesbians could at last enjoy their constitutional right to pursue happiness without harassment or discrimination. An old black typewriter was his preferred weapon as he battled for civil rights and liberties for homosexuals.[6] Kameny shot off hundreds of thousands of words, many of them dripping with sheer contempt for the anti-gay attitudes and policies he was targeting. He typed feverishly day and night, and sometimes into the early hours of the next morning, and then he typed some more, striving in letter after letter to win first-class citizenship for men and women long characterized as sick, immoral, and sinful.

By wielding letters as his favorite weapon, Kameny could and did gain entrée into places that would otherwise have been closed to him—some of the most powerful offices in Washington, DC, and across the country. He sneaked into these guarded offices through the open mailbox, and once safely inside he landed with a thud on the stately desks, shouting at the top of his lungs for justice long denied. With an eye toward changing the social fabric, Kameny wrote to many of the leading personalities and institutions in both political and civil society—to Presidents John F. Kennedy and Richard Nixon, Ann Landers and Johnny Carson, the American Psychiatric Association and the Department of Defense—and usually more than once. If his first letter to a policy- or opinion-maker did not prompt a satisfactory reply, he sent another and then another. No one in the early gay rights movement came close to Kameny in producing the quantity of letters he composed in his relentless campaign for equality.

Because he wrote so many letters, this book focuses on a limited period—from 1958, just after he was fired from the federal government, to 1975, when he was appointed as commissioner on the District of Columbia's Commission on Human Rights. Arguably the most important time in his life, this seventeen-year period witnessed Kameny's evolution from a victim of law to a vocal opponent of law to a voice of law. "I AM the law," he wrote just after becoming a commissioner for human rights.[7]

This book allows Kameny to tell his own story. His early gay rights letters construct a lively and colorful narrative, often with him as its main character, of the politicization of the gay and lesbian movement in the United States—its controversial adoption of protest politics as well as its later transition into electoral politics. Throughout his life, Kameny tended to depict the homophile movement, at the time he became an activist, as a small number of groups quietly dedicated to two main tasks: educating gay men and lesbians about their homosexuality, usually by relying on studies penned by heterosexual psychotherapists, and offering them related social services such as individual counseling.[8] This was not an entirely accurate description, and recent books in LGBT studies have shown the early move-ment for gay and lesbian rights to be much more diffused and politically engaged than Kameny ever granted.[9] Nevertheless, although he was not a lone wolf crying in the wilderness of pre–Stonewall America, Kameny did indeed play a major and national role in setting forth public critiques of homophile strategies limited to education and counseling and in pushing reticent parts of the homophile movement to become more militant in advocating for social change on issues such as the mental health and civil rights of gay men and lesbians.

As they tell this story, Kameny's letters reveal some of the radical roots of the modern LGBT movement. Contrary to popular notions, today's LGBT movement did not begin with the Stonewall riots in 1969. Long *before* Stonewall, there was Franklin Kameny, encouraging gays to embrace homosexuality as moral and healthy, publicly denouncing the federal gov-ernment for excluding homosexuals from federal employment, openly fighting the military's ban against gay men and lesbian women, debating psychiatrists who depicted homosexuality as a mental disorder, identify-ing test cases to advance civil liberties through the federal courts, acting as counsel to countless homosexuals suffering state-sanctioned discrimi-nation, and even organizing marches for gay rights on the White House and other public institutions. Kameny's historically rich letters thus reveal some of the early stirrings of today's politically powerful LGBT movement.

These letters are lively and colorful because they are in Kameny's inimitable voice—a voice that was consistently loud, echoing through such places as the Oval Office, the Pentagon, and even the British Parliament, and often shrill, piercing to the federal agency heads, military generals, and media personalities who received his countless letters.[10] Kameny's voice was also wide-ranging, speaking about everything from the variety of his sex life to lavender-colored gay rights buttons to the belief that homosexuality is caused environmentally. At times he seemed quite conventional, counseling activists to wear suits or dresses to a post-Stonewall march, while at other times he was unabashedly militant, characterizing psychiatrists as a bunch of quacks waddling around with shoddy studies in tow.

Kameny's booming and meandering voice evolved by leaps and bounds through the years, transforming from tones of personal desperation to principled fury. His evolution from pathetic to prophetic is dramatic; so too is the way he adapted to the tide of gay liberation in the period following Stonewall. Kameny's mature voice helped to bridge the yawning gap between the homophile movement and the gay liberation era.

Finally, Kameny also had an effective voice. In tandem with others, he shouted down the American Psychiatric Association's diagnosis of homosexuality as a mental disorder, shattered the U.S. Civil Service Commission's policy against hiring homosexuals for federal employment, and won gay men and lesbians the right to security clearances. In August 1975, Kameny highlighted his effectiveness in yet another letter to his mother:

> Another victory. On Thursday morning the Pentagon phoned me and surrendered. They have withdrawn their appeal in the major security clearance case which I have been fighting for years (the one which took me to California just a year ago) and are issuing the clearance, totally on OUR terms; AND they are reversing their traditional policy of denial of security clearance to gays. . . .
>
> During the past month, I've been receiving a torrent of congratulations and applause from one end of the country to the other—phone calls, letters, personal comments—for my victory over the Civil Service Commission.
>
> I have brought the very government of the United States to its knees, after a long and difficult fight.[11]

Kameny's lengthy battles earned him torrents of criticism. Much of the scolding, in private and public, came from within the homophile movement itself. In the early 1960s, some homophile leaders found his emphasis on the health of homosexuality too dismissive of scientific studies depicting gays as stunted in their psychosexual development. In the mid-1960s, some activists, especially those in the Daughters of Bilitis, characterized his direct-action approach as destructive to the wider homophile movement. And at the end of the 1960s, gay militants formed in the crucible of the Stonewall riots denounced his efforts to gain entrance into the government as far too reformist; they preferred overthrowing the government rather than serving as its employee.

What fueled him through all this?

Franklin Edward Kameny was born in New York City's borough of Queens, in Richmond Hill, on May 21, 1925. He was reared by his Jewish parents: Emil, an electrical engineer whose family had migrated from Poland, and Rae, who left her job as secretary to be a homemaker to Franklin and his younger sister Edna. Although the Depression caused financial strain within the household, his parents worked to make sure that the family enjoyed a comfortable and stable middle-class home.

By his own account, he did not have an absent father and a smothering mother—the type of parents that psychiatrists often identified as a primary cause in the psychosexual development of homosexuals. Rather, both parents actively created a nurturing environment for young Franklin, especially when they noticed that he was learning how to read at the tender age of four.[12] Just three years later he expressed interest in becoming an astronomer.

By the time he was fifteen Kameny had jettisoned his Jewish faith in favor of devotion to scientific study, with a special interest in astronomy. It was around this same time, according to his own account, that Kameny first told his mother that if he was right and society was wrong, society would be the one to change. Although his mother had "expressed disdain" at such sentiment, Kameny normally found his parents to be liberal in outlook and "very permissive." "They wouldn't have dared be otherwise!" he later told his friend Kay Lahusen. "I was always a free spirit intellectually."[13]

With an IQ of 148, Kameny excelled as a student at Richmond Hill High School, skipping two grades because of his high aptitude in science and math and founding the school's astronomy club. After graduating at the age of sixteen, he enrolled as a commuter student at Queens College in September 1941, with a declared intent to earn a degree in physics, but just three months after he began his college studies Japanese pilots bombed Pearl Harbor. "Nothing was the same after that," he later reflected.[14]

Kameny enlisted in the U.S Army two years later, three days before his eighteenth birthday, hoping to win enrollment in a special training program in engineering. At the time of his enlistment he was asked, as all other potential enlistees were, whether he had homosexual tendencies. "I did, and I was well aware of them," he recalled. "As a healthy, vigorous 17- or 18-year-old, things had gone somewhat beyond mere tendencies.[15] And I lied, as everyone did on this subject in those days."[16] But Kameny did not have second thoughts about lying to the U.S. Army. "I knew . . . what the culture of the day demanded and what the Army demanded and what you had to do if you wanted to go anywhere."[17]

He got what he wanted, too, at least for a while. Kameny was called to active duty on September 20, 1943, and after basic training at Fort Benning in Georgia he found himself traveling to the University of Illinois for specialized studies in mechanical engineering. But Congress, much to Kameny's chagrin, canceled the Army Specialized Training Program before he could complete it. "The rug was just pulled out from under us," he remembered, "and so one day I was sleeping in the Sigma Chi fraternity house . . . and the next day I was sleeping . . . in a sodden field in Louisiana."[18] The Army had quickly transferred Kameny to Camp Polk, designating him as an eighty-one-mm mortar crewman in the 58th Armored Infantry Battalion of the Army's 8th Armored Division, and by October 1943 he was heading to Europe, where he would soon engage in frontline combat in the Battle of the Bulge. He quickly learned to distinguish the different sounds whizzing about his head during the battle. "If you hear the whistle of a shell and then the explosion, you're O.K. But if the whistle stops suddenly, before the explosion, you're in grave danger of being hit."[19] Death always felt close. "I came within a hair's breadth of losing my life several times," Kameny recalled.

Kameny earned a combat medal for his service at the Battle of the Bulge, but the free-spirited intellectual found few other pleasures in the military. The highly regimented life of a Private First Class in the U.S. Army, with its demands of obedience and submission, was far from the permissive home he had grown up in and not even close to his idea of the good life. He "would submit to the military only up to a point and no further. I was known as a nonconformist," he said.[20]

His sex life was virtually nonexistent. Although other soldiers had noted his sexuality and had even made passes at him, Kameny was still rather sexually naïve and did not pursue his suitors. But he did enjoy one memorable encounter during his years in the Army, with a young man from New Hampshire. "It was done very quietly in a garden behind a house, a block or so up from the house where we were staying" in Germany, he remembered. "That was the only actual gay experience I had in the military."[21]

Discharged from the Army on March 24, 1946, Kameny headed back to the classrooms and laboratories at Queens College, wrapping up his degree in physics in less than two years. His native intelligence and strong work ethic earned him academic success, and he graduated with honors, even winning admission to Harvard University's graduate program in astronomy. Kameny's professional path was nicely laid out before him, and his social life also kicked into high gear. At first he dated heterosexually at Harvard, just as he had done in high school and college, feeling unsteady about fully embracing his emerging gay sexuality. But while undertaking doctoral research at the University of Arizona, he began to explore Tucson's underground gay culture, and on his twenty-ninth birthday, May 21, 1954, he and a sexually experienced seventeen-year-old undergraduate made love on a moonlit night in the desert outside the city.

The Harvard doctoral student and his new lover enjoyed "a golden summer" together.[22] For Kameny, it was a period of awakening that extended far beyond issues of sex; it was also his time to come out publicly as a gay man. When he first stepped into Tucson's gay bar, he recalled, "it was my first actual introduction . . . to the gay community—my coming out." Kameny began learning the ways of a gay culture that had eluded him in earlier years—its roles, practices, and language. "That's when I first heard the word 'gay,'" he stated. "I had never heard it before."[23]

Out of the closet, Kameny embraced his identity as a gay man during and after his summer in Tucson. "I took to it like a duck to water, as if it were made for me and I for it!" he said.[24] Following his stint at the University of Arizona, Kameny took off for a job and additional research at Armagh Observatory in Northern Ireland, where it did not take long for him to become known as the "gay American."[25] He often spent his evenings at a gay bar in Belfast, and his Irish friends frequently made the trek to visit him for star-filled nights at the observatory. The gay life in Belfast was short-lived, however, lasting only a year, and in October 1955 Kameny returned to Harvard to complete the last year of his doctoral program.

The newly out doctoral student did not let the demands of a rigorous Harvard program interrupt his budding life as a gay man. While dividing his time between writing his thesis and frequenting gay bars in Cambridge and Boston, both of which enjoyed a lively gay culture, he nevertheless remained focused enough to finish his degree by June 1956, and successful enough to land a job as a research associate at Georgetown University in Washington, DC.

Kameny discovered a small but growing and vibrant gay culture in the nation's capital, and he sought to immerse himself in it as deeply as he could, going out to the popular gay bars almost every night (Carroll's on Ninth Street, the Redskin Lounge on L Street, and the Chicken Hut at H and 18th). He attended weekly parties and even scheduled getaway weekend trips to Fire Island in New York for him and his gay friends. His social life was flourishing in ways that had been unimaginable to him as a college student, and his work at Georgetown University was also proceeding apace without any problems.

But then a jolting event occurred on August 29, 1956, while he was attending meetings of the American Astronomical Society in San Francisco. On that day Kameny was arrested at Key Terminal, an area locally known as a prime spot for gay cruising. Two police officers from the city's vice squad had witnessed Kameny and another man engaging in sexual contact in a men's room inside the bus terminal and consequently arrested both on charges of "lewd and indecent acts."[26]

Like countless other gays arrested in similar circumstances, Kameny did not choose to fight the charges. He wanted them to go away as quickly and quietly as possible, so he pled guilty, paid his fifty-dollar fine, and received a six-month probation requiring him to mail in a monthly form. After successfully completing the terms of his probation, he received written acknowledgement stating that California had formally changed his record to "not guilty: complaint dismissed."[27]

Almost a year after his arrest, Kameny switched jobs. The U.S. government had recruited him to be an astronomer with the Army Map Service (AMS), and in July he accepted a full-time job, seeing it as a possible route to a position within the flourishing U.S. space program. Although Kameny enjoyed his work as a federal astronomer, even dreaming of one day becoming an astronaut, his position with AMS lasted only five months. At issue was his earlier arrest.

The police record of Kameny's 1956 arrest had found its way into the hands of investigators within the U.S. Civil Service Commission (CSC), and in October 1957, while conducting fieldwork in Hawaii, he received a letter instructing him to return to his home base in Washington for administrative matters. There he soon found himself in an intense meeting with CSC investigators seeking details of the arrest and additional information about his sexuality. They asked him to comment especially on evidence suggesting he was a homosexual. But the civil libertarian Kameny, according to his own account, "refused to answer on grounds which amounted to stating that these matters are a citizen's own business, and are not the proper concern of the CSC [Civil Service Commission] or the US government."[28]

AMS fired Kameny on December 20, 1957, on charges that he had provided a false statement on his application form. When applying for federal employment, Kameny had written "disorderly conduct" in answer to the application's question about details of past arrests; AMS ruled that Kameny should have noted his arrest on charges of "lewd and indecent acts" (even though his record had been expunged). But the AMS firing was not all that Kameny had to endure. On January 15, 1958, the CSC informed him that because of his "immorality" he had also been debarred from federal employment.[29] The CSC decision was professionally devastating, making Kameny an undesirable not only in the federal government but also among private government contractors and universities working with the federal government.

The firing and debarment of a federal employee for reasons related to homosexuality was not uncommon in 1957. As historian David Johnson has expertly shown, "a Lavender Scare—a fear that homosexuals posed a threat to national security and needed to be systematically removed from the federal government—permeated 1950s political culture."[30] The Scare began in earnest in 1950, shortly after John Peurifoy, the deputy undersecretary of the State Department, told a congressional committee that his department had fired individuals considered to be security risks, including ninety-one homosexuals. Peurifoy's comments sparked national outrage about homosexuals in federal government, and the ensuing Scare saw the purging of thousands of individuals from their governmental positions.

The Scare also gained significant traction when President Eisenhower issued a new national security order—Executive Order 10450—stating that individuals disqualify themselves from federal employment by undertaking "any behavior which suggests the individual is not reliable or trustworthy." The order listed specific examples of such behaviors, and "sexual perversion," a code word for homosexuality, appeared on the list, marking the first time that the federal government officially sanctioned the identification of homosexuality as a behavior threatening to national security.[31] With Executive Order 10450 as their mandate, federal agency heads increased efforts to purge their agencies of homosexuals.

Kameny's firing might have been standard fare in the Lavender Scare, but it also posed new and unforeseen problems for the officials charged with purging homosexuals from the federal government. Typically, gay men and lesbians who lost their governmental positions during the Scare retreated into the private sector without officially or publicly protesting their dismissals. But Kameny was rarely typical, and he decided to appeal his firing through the governmental chain of command, starting with the AMS and CSC hierarchy, continuing on to congressional committees with oversight of federal employment practices, and ending with the Supreme Court and President John F. Kennedy, with several other stops along the way.

At first, his intent was to get his job back by asking his superiors to treat him as an individual, as one trustworthy Franklin Kameny, not as another nameless homosexual among countless other nameless homosexuals. He made this particular case especially in a June 1959 letter he sent to Defense Secretary Neil McElroy:

> I ask to be considered not as a faceless statistic, but as an individual person—as one expects to be considered in a democracy, as distinguished from a totalitarian state. I ask that you consider ME, and not just a disconnected fact or two about my background. . . . No one has examined *ME*—the matter has been handled as if I were an inanimate, insensate object, to be talked about, but not talked . . . with.[32]

Kameny's analysis was indeed accurate: The U.S. government had treated him not as a distinct individual but merely as part of a class of homosexuals unworthy of federal employment. A letter from John Hanes Jr. of the Department of State's Bureau of Security and Consular affairs, joined a host of others in making this point clear:

> You are equally aware as I of the reasons why the Department of State does not hire homosexuals and will not permit their employment. I am quite prepared to agree that a substantial amount of the reason behind this policy results from the attitude of our society in general toward any behavior which it considers undesirable and which it does not accept. Homosexuality is one such behavior.
>
> So long as this is the attitude of our society—and you are well aware that it is, as expressed both formally in laws, regulations and ordinances, and informally in the average reaction of people toward homosexuals—the homosexual is automatically a security risk because of the social and emotional pressures to which he is subject from society, and because of the ever-present risk that such pressures can be utilized by hostile elements to coerce him into activities other than those which he would undertake of his own free will. Also because of the prevailing mores of our society, the homosexual frequently becomes a disruptive personnel factor within any organization.[33]

Kameny grew livid, and also hungry and desperate. During the period of unemployment immediately following his firing, he often lived on twenty cents worth of food a day, just enough for two hot dogs and mashed potatoes. He sometimes turned to the Salvation Army for material assistance, and if he had a few extra coins on hand, he would put a spoonful of butter on his potatoes. Disinclined to suffer in silence, Kameny shared his sense of desperation with his former superiors, especially Harris Ellsworth, the chair of the Civil Service Commission:

> In two weeks, Mr. Ellsworth, my unemployment compensation will run out. Largely through your actions, I have no prospect of a suitable job. My financial resources are completely exhausted. At that time, therefore, I plan to cease eating entirely, and to starve to death; as you enjoy your Christmas dinner, you might keep in mind that, through your actions, one of your fellow human beings will be about to die. I hope you enjoy the role of executioner.[34]

But Kameny was not about to let Ellsworth play the roles of jury, judge, and executioner without facing a fierce legal counterattack, and beginning in June 1959 he pleaded his case before the federal courts. The results were predictable: By the end of the year, a federal judge dismissed Kameny's formal complaint, and in June 1960 a three-judge panel of the U.S. Court of Appeals for the District of Columbia agreed with the earlier decision, finding that the Army Map Service had acted according to regulations and that because the AMS had responded appropriately there was no need to revisit the CSC debarment.

Equally predictable, Kameny was not deterred and set out on a campaign to generate funding and support for his ongoing legal battles. Up to this point, he had not been a member, active or inactive, of the homophile movement in the United States. He had once visited the headquarters of *ONE* magazine while traveling on business, but homophile activism had not appeared in his life before his debarment from federal employment.[35] But he desperately needed money for his legal fight, and though he enjoyed no contacts in the homophile movement, he turned to its leading organizations with a request for funds. He put his plea in detailed letters to the Mattachine Society in San Francisco, the Mattachine Society in New York City, and *ONE*, explaining the nuances of his arrest, the grounds on which he was arguing his case, and the possibility that his "test case" would "set valuable precedents" benefitting many homosexuals. The fieriest part of his letter centered on his commitment to the flourishing of his rights:

> I am not a belligerent person, nor do I seek wars, but having been forced into a battle, I am determined that this thing will be fought thru to a successful conclusion, come what may, and that as long as any recourse exists, I will not be deprived of my proper rights, freedoms and liberties, as I see them, or of a career, profession, and livelihood, or of my right to live my life as I choose to live it, so long as I do not interfere with the rights of others to do likewise.[36]

Kameny was indeed determined and, despite his own self-assessment, fiercely belligerent. He had hired an attorney, Byron N. Scott, to steer his legal campaign through the federal court system, but after the U.S. Court of Appeals had ruled in favor of the government, Scott withdrew from the case, leaving his client with a copy of the Supreme Court rules. A motivated self-learner, Kameny decided to study the copy and write and file his very own petition. He studied other sources as well, taking inspiration and instruction from Alfred Kinsey's studies of human sexuality, as well as contemporary books on homosexuality.

Writing his own petition to the Supreme Court was a bold move for a man with no legal training. It was also a historic move, marking the first such petition advocating for the recognition of homosexuals as a minority group suffering from government-sanctioned discrimination. Representing a marked evolution in Kameny's own thought, the brief focused not only on his rights as an individual, as distinct from other homosexuals, but also on the second-class citizenship of all homosexuals in the United States.

Kameny filed his landmark petition for a writ of certiorari with the Supreme Court on January 27, 1961.[37] He began the petition by pleading with the court to consider his case in full, arguing that it addressed "matters never before examined by the courts" and that it was "one of extreme importance to a very large number of American citizens." Using a thick didactic style, he claimed that homosexuals made up "10% of our population at the very least—perhaps, at least some 15,000,000 people" (14). Although the 10 percent figure was not commonly accepted at the time,

Kameny explained that he was drawing it from Kinsey's documented claim that 10 percent of all males "were more or less exclusively homosexual" (34).

More importantly, without admitting or conceding that he was gay, Kameny then made the case that the country's large group of homosexuals comprised an oppressed minority unable to enjoy basic constitutional rights. While drawing connections between prejudices suffered by homosexuals and those experienced by African Americans, Catholics, Jews, and others, he also argued that, unlike other minority groups, homosexuals confronted a government that actually "intensified" prejudice directed against them (15). "In fields of anti-Negro, anti-Semitic, anti-Catholic, and other prejudice, the government has indeed recognized, and is playing fully and admirably, its role as a leader of changes in attitude," he wrote. "In regard to the homosexual, the government is following—and following abjectly—an example of prejudice of the least admirable kind, with no effort to change its own attitude, much less to stimulate changes of attitude elsewhere" (50).

In addressing the details of his particular case, Kameny accused the government of a denial of due process. The decision to fire and debar him, he stated, relied on inaccurate facts related to his arrest and reflected a failure to follow established procedures (his superiors, after all, never provided him with exact information about his "immoral conduct"). But Kameny added a critical point: that even if the government had used correct facts and proper procedures, the CSC regulation citing "immoral conduct" as a basis for dismissal was "too broad and vague to have legal weight . . . or be implementable except in a totally arbitrary and capricious manner" (28). Even worse, he stated, the vague regulation was unconstitutional.

On the issue of sexual morality Kameny was a civil libertarian, quick to point to the First Amendment in defense of his right to create his own sexual ethics. "Any decision as to morality and immorality is a matter of a citizen's personal opinion and his individual religious belief," he wrote (28). The commission's classification of homosexuals as immoral was a blatant "attempt to tell the citizen how to think and how to believe." In effect, it was "tantamount to its establishing certain religious beliefs . . . and to setting up an implicit religious test"—actions clearly proscribed by the First Amendment. The government thus had no constitutional right to define sexual morality or to punish citizens for not conforming to such federal morality. "The explicit substance and fabric of our government are written law, not morality . . . and it is within the framework of legality and illegality, not morality and immorality, that the government must actually function," he argued (29).

Kameny also sketched his own moral perspective on homosexuality, partly to let the justices know that the vague phrase "immoral conduct" meant one thing to the government and quite another to him. "Petitioner asserts, flatly, unequivocally, and absolutely uncompromisingly," he wrote, "that homosexuality, whether by mere inclination or by overt act, is not only not immoral, but that, for those choosing voluntarily to engage in homosexual acts, such acts are moral in a real and positive sense, and are good, right, and desirable, socially and personally" (26). Kameny did not detail his reasons for holding this view, but the direct effect of his positive characterization of homosexuality was to allow him to deny that his actions in San Francisco were in any way "immoral."

As a secular rationalist, Kameny was not content merely to point out that his version of sexual morality differed from the government's, and so he also turned to the classical tool of reason to argue that the CSC policy discriminating against homosexuals was "neither reasonable, rational, realistic, consistent with other policy, nor in the national good or in the interest of the general welfare" (33). Rather than rational, the policy was "a reflection of ancient primitive, archaic, obsolete taboos and prejudices . . . an incongruous, anachronistic relic of the Stone Age carried over into the Space Age—and a harmful relic!" (33–34).

Kameny mustered several interrelated arguments for advancing the notion that the CSC policy was irrational, and one of them appealed to Kinsey's claim that 30 percent of all males engaged in a homosexual experience between the ages of sixteen and fifty-five. Relying on this figure, Kameny informed the justices that CSC policies could conceivably be invoked against 600,000 employees in federal service—a figure so large that government would be brought to its knees if the CSC executed its regulation with any sense of efficiency or comprehensiveness. It was a good thing, Kameny noted, that the CSC was so ineffective in routing out homosexuals.

A second argument focused on the heterogeneity of homosexuals within U.S. society and culture. Because homosexuals were "completely heterogeneous," sharing no "distinguishing characteristics" (physical, intellectual, emotional, or vocational) other than their homosexuality, the government had wasted massive amounts of time and money "trying to ferret out these people" (36).

For obvious reasons, Kameny drew special attention to the issues of mental health and moral character, taking direct issue with the diagnosis that homosexuals were mentally disordered and morally untrustworthy. "The average homosexual is as well-adjusted in personality as the average heterosexual," he wrote. "There are those who are among the most stable members of the community, and those who are neurotic and psychotic, and a majority who fall somewhere in between, as with the population at large" (37). The same was true in matters of moral character. Homosexuals are "as honest and as dishonest . . . as is the citizenry at large" (38). It was thus irrational for the government to suggest that all homosexuals were mentally unstable and morally vulnerable—unworthy of federal employment. In an amusing jab, Kameny even added that it was CSC polices, not homosexuals, that were psychopathic:

> Not only are the Civil Service Commission's policies on homosexuality not pervaded by a discernible thread of reason, but they seem pervaded by a thread of madness. In their complete negation of the realities around us, they remind the observer of an excerpt from a nightmare of the lunatic asylum. In their form and in their practice, they border upon, if they do not actually overstep the bounds of the psychopathic (33).

But Kameny's creative redirection of the charge of madness was a mere side point in this section. His main task was to argue that CSC policies, lacking any rational basis for lumping all homosexuals together as deficient and unworthy of employment, represented "nothing more than the prejudices of the officials in the Civil Service Commission (and, perhaps, elsewhere in government)" (39). The CSC was prejudiced against homosexuals, pure and simple, and its ban of homosexuals was blatantly discriminatory. Just as dominant society had once treated African Americans, Catholics, and Jews with prejudice and discrimination lacking any rational or constitutional grounds, so too did the CSC treat homosexuals. And such prejudicial treatment was illegal in its very essence. "The Commission's policies against the employment of homosexuals," Kameny wrote, "constitute a discrimination no less illegal and no less odious than discrimination based upon religious or racial grounds" (56).

But the discriminatory ban of homosexuals in federal employment not only violated the due process clause of the Fifth Amendment; it also undermined government's very reason for existence:

> Our government exists to protect and assist *all* of its citizens, not, as in the case of homosexuals, to harm, to victimize, and to destroy them. Unfortunately, much of that portion of our present-day Federal government . . . has lost sight of this . . . Insensately single-minded, they pursue their narrow, savage, backward policies, paying no heed to the needless havoc wrought upon the hapless citizens who are their victims (49).

Kameny could not quite contain his passion as he summarized his arguments for the court. "Respondents' case is rotten to the core," he wrote.

> The government's regulations, policies, practices and procedures, as applied in the instant case to petitioner specifically, and as applied to homosexuals generally, are a stench in the nostrils of decent people, an offense against morality, an abandonment of reason, an affront to human dignity, an improper restraint upon proper freedom and liberty, a disgrace to any civilized society, and a violation of all that this nation stands for (59).

Kameny's petition was historic. Although he was not the first to hold that homosexuals were an oppressed minority, that the government had acted unconstitutionally in its treatment of homosexuals, that homosexuals should enjoy equal treatment under law, or even that homosexuality was moral, Kameny was certainly the first to place these ideas before the nation's highest court and demand not only an official hearing on them but also legal action ensuring that homosexuals could finally enjoy the fruits of first-class citizenship.[38] But however historic it was, the petition did not sway the justices. The Supreme Court denied Kameny's petition on March 17, 1961 and, as was its custom, offered no public reasons for denying cert.[39]

But Kameny still did not surrender, and less than two months after the Supreme Court decision, he sat down and typed a letter to President John F. Kennedy. Kameny appreciated the new president's progressive vision and was hoping that the New Frontier might blaze a trail for the civil liberties of homosexuals. "In World War II," he wrote, "I willingly fought the Germans, with bullets, in order to preserve and secure my rights, freedoms, and liberties, and those of my fellow citizens. In 1961, it has, ironically, become necessary for me to fight my own government, with words, in order to achieve some of the very same rights, freedoms, and liberties for which I placed my life in jeopardy in 1945. This letter is part of that fight."[40] Kameny pleaded his case, as well as the case of all U.S. homosexuals, but the Kennedy administration did not reply. The New Frontier, it seemed, would not welcome homosexuals.

As the final door slammed in his face, Kameny knew he would no longer be a professional astronomer quietly working to support the hopes and dreams of the U.S. government, let alone to fulfill his own dream of working in the space program. After an initial period of unemployment, he landed a job as a physicist at various optics laboratories in the DC area, but none of these positions ever turned into anything resembling a career.[41] Having suffered so many failures in his personal campaign to win back his federal job and employment rights for other homosexuals, Kameny had become "radicalized." As he later explained this to historian Eric Marcus, "You don't hear that word much now, but it describes exactly the process I and many others have experienced. I have handled many cases over the years of people who were meek, mild, and unassertive, who just wanted to go about doing their work, and then, suddenly they were hit hard. They were trampled upon with a hobnailed boot, and it radicalized them."[42]

In Kameny's understanding, this is exactly what had happened to him. He had been hit hard, and the intense pain of losing his job and then all of his appeals had turned him into a political radical committed to winning not only his own personal rights but also the rights of all other homosexual citizens in the United States. Thanks to the U.S. government—the AMS, the CSC, Congress, the Supreme Court, and the Kennedy administration—Kameny had transitioned from a quiet government employee into an angry gay militant determined to battle anything, however powerful, that dared to suggest that homosexuals were second-class citizens. The only remaining question was: how to battle?

Kameny did not become just any radical; the hobnailed boot had not turned him into an anarchist or a violent revolutionary intent on blowing up the government. He was not about to don a mask, agitate police horses, and throw flammable canisters at government buildings. But he was prepared to put on a respectable jacket and tie and organize like-minded individuals in nonviolent campaigns to win homosexuals their constitutional rights. This indeed was Kameny's version of radical politics—organizing for a civilized fight against political and civil societies aligned against homosexuals. "Given the realities and problems of fighting the government on my own, the time had come to fight collectively," he stated.[43]

So less than three months after he typed his letter to President Kennedy, Kameny and a new friend, Jack Nichols, took steps to organize a collective fight in Washington, DC. Nichols had first introduced himself to Kameny at an after-hours party after hearing him speak favorably about Donald Webster Cory's *The Homosexual in America*. Cory's groundbreaking book had inspired Nichols as a teenager to claim his homosexual identity with pride. "He helped me to see poor self-images not as a product of homosexuality, but as a result of the prejudices internalized," he stated. "At that moment, I was determined to stand outside the condemning culture, and with the healthy pride of a teen, to claim my rightful place as an individual."[44] As for Kameny, he appreciated Cory's argument that homosexuals constituted "a minority, not only numerically, but also as a result of caste-like status in society," and that the minority status of homosexuals was

> similar, in a variety of respects, to that of national, religious, and other ethnic groups: in the denial of civil liberties; in the legal, extra-legal and quasi-legal discrimination; in the assignment of an inferior social position; in the exclusion from the mainstreams of life and culture; in the development of the protection and security of intra-group association; in the development of a special language and literature and a set of moral tenets within our group.[45]

Kameny found Cory's book to be an excellent case for homosexual rights and had drawn from it liberally when writing his own Supreme Court petition. Perhaps most inspiring to the vocal Kameny, however, was

Cory's criticism of the "conspiracy of silence" that existed among homosexuals wrongly denied their civil rights.[46]

After bonding over their appreciation for Cory, Nichols and Kameny exchanged phone numbers, and a few days later the two new friends met together in Frank's untidy apartment on Columbia Road and resolved to jumpstart a grassroots movement focused on securing civil liberties for homosexuals. For advice and counsel, they contacted the Mattachine Society of New York (MSNY), whose leaders, Curtis DeWees and Al de Dion, readily agreed to strategize with Kameny, Nichols, and other interested parties on August 1, 1961, at the Hay-Adams Hotel in Washington. Louis Fouchette, who spearheaded the DC Police Department's Morals Division, infiltrated this organizational meeting—but not for long. Kameny blew the officer's cover in front of the assembled group, and Fouchette stormed out of the meeting before it ended.

The August 1 meeting led to more sessions, and on November 15, 1961, Kameny and Nichols joined at least three others at the first official meeting of what would become the Mattachine Society of Washington (MSW)—an independent entity within the existing homophile movement. Kameny was not in favor of the Mattachine name, wanting instead "something that was more explicit and expressive," but he was outvoted by the assembled group.[47] Nevertheless, the group did elect Kameny as its president, and under his leadership MSW adopted a statement of purpose that committed the new organization "to act by any lawful means" in order "to secure for homosexuals the right to life, liberty, and the pursuit of happiness, as proclaimed for all men by the Declaration of Independence, and to secure for homosexuals the basic rights and liberties established by word and the spirit of the Constitution of the United States."[48]

This historic statement fashioned MSW as an activist organization within the wider homophile movement. It was radical, in Kameny's understanding, because it would not limit itself to the work traditionally undertaken by much of the movement: education and social services. Kameny believed that relying on education alone would never successfully scale the high walls of prejudice against homosexuals, and that undertaking social services was helpful for addressing short-term problems (like egos destroyed by abusive parents) but ultimately wrongheaded as a tactic for making the type of lasting social and cultural changes that can be wrought only by the guarantee of civil liberties. In formulating these pragmatic points for his homophile colleagues, Kameny claimed inspiration from the modern civil rights movement. It was not until African Americans adopted direct-action campaigns designed to secure constitutional rights, he said, that they began to transform society's stance toward racial prejudice.[49]

Although it charged MSW with employing an activist approach, the statement of purpose also clearly set parameters to its politics. Kameny represented the *conservative* radicals of U.S. social movements, those devoted to transforming society only through means deemed legal by the U.S. democratic system. Protesting unjust laws was fine and good, as long as the means of protest were "lawful"; any attempt to use illegal means, especially violence, he deemed irresponsible and dangerous to the goal of the movement.

MSW's approach was also limited by its goal of securing constitutional rights and liberties for homosexuals within the U.S. political system. Like Roy Wilkins and Martin Luther King Jr., Kameny was a patriotic militant, wholly committed to the principles of freedom and democracy, as expressed in the Declaration of Independence and the U.S. Constitution, and to the roles, practices, and institutions that gave life to freedom and democracy within political and civil societies. As a patriotic American, he stood opposed to revolution from within or without.

If a revolutionary is one who is committed to overthrowing the major institutions of political and civil society, Kameny was no revolutionary. The thousands of letters he typed as a leader of the early gay rights movement expressed no desire to rid society of government, universities, mainstream media, places of faith, or professional associations, no matter how anti-gay they seemed. In this sense, Kameny was a reformist or, better stated, a political transformist; he dedicated these early years to transforming social roles, institutions, and practices from being anti-gay into accepting homosexuals as equal in value to heterosexuals. He did this not so much for the sake of making society a paragon of virtue, but primarily to give homosexuals the choices they deserved in their pursuit of happiness.

As an American gay, Kameny also refused to entertain any approach that struck at the heart of "one nation . . . indivisible, with liberty and justice for all." Again like King and Wilkins, Kameny was a thoroughgoing integrationist; he was insistent on integrating homosexuals, with all of the constitutional rights enjoyed by heterosexuals, into mainstream U.S. society. The thought of establishing separate spaces or communities for homosexuals was completely foreign, indeed anathema, to Kameny's unwavering commitment to integration in mainstream America.[50] He had fought too long and too hard in World War II to consider fracturing US citizens one from another as a viable option.

Kameny flourished in his role as MSW president. No longer a lowly PFC or an unemployed astronomer, he was now Franklin E. Kameny, PhD, president of the Mattachine Society of Washington, the nation's first homophile organization formally devoted to securing civil liberties for homosexuals. Armed with years of experience in battling the federal government, Kameny was well poised to become the general of MSW's campaign; he was bright and brash, assiduous and abrasive, focused and fierce. If he lacked anything, it was certainly not confidence. Even though he had lost every battle along the way, he was utterly convinced that he could and would make society change for the better—that he could and would make society recognize that "gay is good."[51]

To the surprise of his countless critics, Kameny was at least partly right. In tandem with many others in the rising gay and lesbian rights movement, he would play an important role in helping to mastermind and create a massive shift in social attitudes and practices. One letter at a time, the gay rights pioneer would seek to bend society to his will. It would take a while, but he had lots of paper—and no other job to fill his time.[52]

A final note: Although this book focuses on Franklin Kameny, it does not claim that he was the One Great Man who singlehandedly transformed the homophile movement and changed U.S. society and culture. The early gay rights movement was a collective effort, the lifework of numerous individuals and groups, some well known to scholars and others simply lost to history. As suggested earlier, Kameny himself did not always grasp this point sufficiently. He sometimes took sole or primary credit for achievements in which many other individuals or groups were involved, and he frequently depicted himself as the most important leader of the early gay rights movement—the one person who could legitimately speak for the entire gay population. Kameny did not suffer from a small ego, and he was inclined to tout his importance at the expense of many others who were fighting similar battles in the early gay rights movement. Thus, at some points in his own telling, Kameny appears to be the One Great Man who forced history to change in relation to gay rights. I will try to let Kameny speak for himself in the pages ahead, but I hope readers will rush to consult recent works by scholars and writers, especially Michael Bronksi's *A Queer History of the United States*, to help better understand the dangers of claiming too much importance for any one individual in the early gay rights movement, including someone as important as Franklin E. Kameny, PhD.

1

"The Winds of Change Are Blowing"

1958–1962

Kameny to CSC Chairman Harris Ellsworth

Kameny sketched his 1956 arrest in a written statement he sent to the American Civil Liberties Union as part of a wider pitch for legal assistance:

> On August 29, 1956, in the San Francisco area, where I was attending meetings of the American Astronomical Society, I was approached while in a public men's room, and, for less than 5 seconds, was sexually molested by another man. There was neither solicitation nor invitation on my part, nor was there any physical, emotional, sexual, or other response of any sort. I brushed him aside, adjusted my clothing, and was departing, alone, when I was arrested by two plainclothes policemen who had witnessed the incident through an overhead grillwork.
>
> The trial took place the following morning. I was informed that were I to plead "not guilty," I would be required to remain in San Francisco for several days until the case would be disposed of, whereas a plea of "guilty" would result in a quick disposition of the matter. I already had hard-to-get plane reservations to New York (it was just before Labor Day), I was expected there and elsewhere in the East, and so, for much the same reasons as those for which one might plead "guilty" to a traffic violation which, technically, one should and would like to fight, I pled "guilty" here. I was fined $50 and given six-months probation, the conditions of the probation being satisfied by my mailing in a form on the first day of each month.
>
> At the end of the period of probation, by provision of California law, and upon proper application by me, the plea and verdict were officially and

formally changed, on the record, to "not guilty: complaint dismissed," and I received from the State of California a document so stating.[1]

Typically, homosexuals purged from governmental positions did not protest their dismissals. But Kameny appealed his firing through the governmental chain of command, starting with the Army Map Service (AMS) and the Civil Service Commission (CSC). Following is one of several letters he sent to CSC Chair Harris Ellsworth. Of special note is Kameny's desperate tone, as well as his characterization of homosexuality as a sexual "irregularity."

NO DATE (1958)

Mr. Ellsworth:

Your letter of October 27, 1958 is completely inadequate as a reply to mine of October 2. As a citizen, rather than as an appellant, I raised a number of points in that letter, and I request a proper reply to them—as it is my right so to request and to receive—and promptly so. . . .

In two weeks, Mr. Ellsworth, my unemployment compensation will run out. Largely through your actions, I have no prospect of a suitable job. My financial resources are completely exhausted. At that time, therefore, I plan to simply cease eating entirely, and to starve to death; as you enjoy your Christmas dinner, you might keep in mind that, through your actions, one of your fellow human beings will be about to die. I hope you enjoy the role of executioner. I am not being melodramatic, nor am I exaggerating the situation; I see absolutely no other course of action except for that indicated two paragraphs below . . .

When you people seek to destroy a citizen, you do it with a most relentless thoroughness!! You are apparently about to succeed with your destruction—in the most literal sense—in this case.

There is only one alternative to complete starvation, which I have thus far been able to discover—one which has been recommended to me by a number of completely loyal citizens. It is an alternative, however, which I find most repugnant and distasteful. Since, to all intents and purposes, the US government has declared me persona non grata, it has been suggested that I offer my services to other governments. As disagreeable as this course of action may be, I must confess that a stomach which has only occasionally been properly filled in the past eight months, and which has before it only the prospect of total and permanent emptiness, is a powerful incentive toward overcoming even such formidable obstacles as learning the Russian or some other language. . . .

I write, from here on, as a citizen, rather than as an appellant. As such, I demand prompt and complete answers to my questions regarding the CSC's policies in the matters here—specific and detailed replies, not a group of vague generalities and platitudes; replies which do not "pass the buck" to other branches or agencies of the government. . . .

(a) By what right does the CSC or any agency or branch of government interfere in the purely religious matter of defining, for the individual citizen, what is and is not moral? This would seem to be a violation of the First Amendment to the Constitution, restricting the government's role in the establishment and control of religion.

(b) How does the CSC defend its dispensing with the services of a competent scientist, in a field of critical shortage, on trivial irrelevant and immaterial grounds, and doing so in a manner which renders him unavailable and unable to contribute his abilities and training elsewhere? As a citizen and a taxpayer, who is aware of the widely publicized need, in this country, for trained scientific personnel, and whose taxes are going to pay for various educational programs designed to fill that need, I demand to have justified to me your action in "killing off" one already-trained scientist on superficial, trivial, irrelevant, immaterial grounds.

(c) What justification does the CSC have for its overall policy toward those who evince some evidence of sexual or other irregularity in their personal, private backgrounds? On what grounds, and by what *logical, rational* chain of reasoning does the CSC deduce that these people are unfit for, or unsuitable for government employment?

I demand a clear, *rigidly logical* answer to the last two questions.

(d) How does the CSC justify its practice of allowing one single minor facet of an employee's personality or background which is deemed undesirable, to outweigh all others, no matter how desirable those others may make him, *as a whole person*? You surely do not consider that all your federal employees, by any standards at all, are examples of complete perfection in every respect; every human being has his failings and faults.

(e) I suggested and pointed out the need for a re-approach to, a reexamination of, and a reappraisal of this whole problem, either within the government service or by private firms, and with frightening rapidity, I am reaching a state where I will not have the wherewithal to supply myself with food, shelter, and clothing. As I stated above, I *wish* to be of use to the country; I *can* be of service to the country. I need only to be allowed to be so! . . .

Most sincerely and desperately yours,

Franklin E. Kameny

Kameny was also irritated by CSC's refusal to detail the specific reason for charging him with immorality. He highlighted this in the following section of his "sworn appeal" to the CSC:

> *To deprive a citizen of his livelihood, his profession and his reputation, and, effectively, to ruin his life, on the basis of vaguely formulated allegations, without informing him of the explicit circumstances of the specific acts of which he is accused, is quite in keeping with what we expect of the USSR and expected of the famous Nazis and others of their ilk. It is not the sort of procedure we expect of the United States government . . . One does not, in the American tradition, punish a man . . . without giving him full details of that for which he is being penalized, before he is penalized.*
>
> *It is a long-established, deeply rooted American tradition that a man is innocent until proven guilty, and not vice versa. This means that the full burden and onus of proof of guilt lie with the accusers; not the burden of proof of innocence with the accused. I don't have to prove myself innocent; you have to prove me guilty. I do not have to prove my moral conduct; you have to prove my alleged immoral conduct. It is not enough for you merely to accuse me of misconduct, and ask me to prove my innocence. In the American tradition, you must prove me guilty. You have not done so. You have not even begun to do so. You have not even stated what it is, except in the most vague and general way, that you are alleging me to be guilty of. This is the way things are done in the USSR. This is not the American way!*[2]

Kameny to Chief Justice Earl Warren and Associate Justices

The Eisenhower Administration's industrial security program identified "sex perversion" and "immoral" behavior as grounds for denying security clearances to employees in both the public and private sectors.[3] *Without a clearance, Kameny found it difficult to land the type of job for which he had been trained at Harvard. "Meanwhile," he later remembered, "my unemployment compensation ran out, and so, in January, February, March . . . and April, and again in June, July, and August of 1959, I lived on 20 to 25 cents (and a borrowed 20 cents, at that) worth of food per day, while rent and other bills piled up."*

A few months before Kameny wrote the following letter, the Supreme Court had agreed to hear yet another case involving a citizen who had lost his job in the private sector as a result of being deemed a security risk by the government. When commenting on the case, the Washington Post—*a newspaper that Kameny read closely—stated: "It is cause for worry when even one loyal American not only may lose his job but also may bear an inescapable stigma under a system which lacks the safeguards of due process so basic to American justice."*[4] *Unfortunately, only the first page of the following letter survives.*

APRIL 6, 1959

Gentlemen:

I write as a private US citizen who is interested in and who (extremely highly indirectly) has an interest in the outcome of the cases currently before you involving the Defense Department's industrial security program.

I am writing to suggest, respectfully, that in the interest of the welfare of this country, anything which you can do by your decisions to weaken the security program, as it presently exists and is presently administered, will be much to the good.

You are familiar—much more so, I am sure, than am I—with the provisions and administration of the program in regard to issues of so-called "loyalty." There is another side to the program, however, which is less publicized, but which needlessly victimizes an appalling number of competent, valuable, often talented and highly trained people, and which represents a far greater threat to this nation's security and freedom than would any possible disclosure of the secret information involved.

Under the security program, anyone is considered as a risk whose personal life—in thought, idea, and action, all—would not have pleased Queen Victoria at her dreariest, or the Puritans at their "purest."

Whatever one may believe about the virtues and merits of our present social system, as it is ideally supposed to exist, it is surely the right of an American citizen to dissent and, provided that he neither harms nor interferes with others, not to conform. This is implicit in the Declaration of Independence's guarantee of the right to the pursuit of happiness. The security system does not grant this, however—particularly in the area of sexual preferences.

By a kind of "Alice-in-Wonderland" reasoning, which sounds logical at first, but which bears little if any relationship to the reality around us and to the real rather than to the theoretical people whom the Defense Department conceives us to be, any departure from "rulebook" conventionality is supposedly something of which one is deeply ashamed, and which, therefore, makes one subject to all kinds of pressures to disclose information. That the most conventional of people might, in many cases, disclose information upon the slightest threat, while the nonconformist might feel strong enough in his nonconformity and, in any case, might take seriously his commitment not to disclose information, is not considered. In the whole administration of the program, the individual, as such, is never taken into account. A totally arbitrary unrealistic set of definitions has been set up, specifying who is a "security risk." These are followed slavishly and ritualistically, with no slightest regard to the individual himself. . . .

Kameny to Defense Secretary Neil McElroy

After the CSC denied his appeal, Kameny conducted a letter-writing campaign that sought assistance from, among others, President Eisenhower,[5] key White House staff members, and chairs of the civil service committees in the U.S. House and Senate.[6] The following letter is a request for assistance that Kameny sent to Secretary of Defense Neil McElroy. At this point, Kameny makes his case not by appealing to the civil liberties of all homosexuals but by asking that the government treat him as a distinct individual.

JUNE 1, 1959

Dear Mr. McElroy:

As a citizen, I am appealing to you, as the appropriate government official, for assistance in a matter in which I feel that I am being unjustly and improperly treated by your department, to the detriment of the nation as well as of myself; a situation of which I have been able to obtain no rectification at lower level. . . .

Let me say, first of all, that this is not a matter involving the loyalty provision of the security system, in any sense or aspect whatever. No slightest question has been raised on that issue, and I have, in fact, been given a "clean bill of health" in that regard.[7]

The entire matter centers around a minor, trivial, totally unimportant, and insignificant incident in my personal background; an incident having nothing to do with my competence as an astronomer, or as a scientist; one having nothing to do with my qualities as a "security risk," or with my ability to safeguard, properly, any information entrusted to me. It involves a purely ritualistic, unreasoning, irrelevant, needless insistence upon harsh and rigid interpretation of not completely rational regulations.

It seems illogical and ridiculous, to put it mildly, that one minor, trivial, and totally unimportant incident in a man's life should be permitted, on a purely formalistic basis, to stand in the way of his being allowed to put much-needed and hard-to-find abilities, interests, and technical training to the use of nation and society.

The country needs astronomers. The need exceeds the entire supply by a factor of several hundred percent. There are positions open at Cape Canaveral and elsewhere which I seem almost tailor-made to fill, and for which the number of qualified candidates is well-nigh nil; positions for which I am very much wanted. But, because of this rigid, undeviating, rule-bound insistence upon adhering to the letter of unreasonable and unnecessary regulation, I find myself, at present, barely able to keep body and soul together, doing a job which could be done by anyone with a good high-school education. Is this the best manner in which we can utilize our available, technically-trained manpower?!

What I ask in this case is what any citizen of this country should feel that he is entitled to: to be considered *as an individual*. I ask that someone authorized to do so, with sufficient flexibility of personality and psychology, and with adequate discretionary powers, consider whether I am a security risk—NOT whether, under precisely the same circumstances, John Doe or James Smith would be security risks, but whether Franklin

E. Kameny *is* a risk. I ask to be considered not as a faceless statistic, but as an individual person—as one expects to be considered in a democracy, as distinguished from a totalitarian state. I ask that you consider ME, and not just a disconnected fact or two about my background.

One would hardly expect a doctor to make a valid diagnosis upon the basis of a few scattered, irrelevant facts about his patient, without a personal examination; nor would we expect an automobile mechanic to provide reliable information about the expected manner of function of an engine, without an inspection of the engine itself. Yet this is exactly what is being done here, in the case of the incomparably more complex and subtle human psyche. A very few irrelevant "facts" about my background have been assembled, and on the basis of these, it has been decided that I ought not to be entrusted with classified information, and, therefore, in effect, that I may not work. No one has examined *ME*—the matter has been handled as if I were an inanimate, insensate object, to be talked about, but not talked with. No one has attempted to determine whether I am capable to safeguard properly information entrusted to me. I ask that this be done. I ask that you consider *not* whether the rulebooks say that I *might* be a poor risk, but whether, in fact, I *am* a poor risk. You will find that I most emphatically am *not*. And I ask that this determination be made by considering me, personally, as a living, individual human being, and not in the impersonal manner in which these matters are usually handled. I am not a machine!

I ask for a chance to convince, personally, those empowered to make the decision, that I am entitled to a clearance. I ask that I have a chance to be considered by men who have not made up their minds in advance, men of flexible minds who are about to, and who are high up enough in the hierarchy to be empowered to and unafraid to judge and to decide a case on its merits rather than on the rigid letter of the regulation.

I am NOT a security risk; I AM entitled to as high a clearance as is required for a job for which I am qualified; I am as good a risk as anyone liable to be hired anywhere, and far better than most.

I *can* be of service to this country as an astronomer; the country *needs* my services; I *wish* to be of service; I need only to be allowed to be of service. A word from you will enable me to be so.

I realize that the normal procedure in these matters is for the potential or actual employer of a bona fide job applicant or jobholder to apply for the necessary clearance. In this case, however, that has proven to be of no avail. I have been an applicant for a number of positions; my potential employers in these positions very much wanted me, but found themselves not permitted to employ me. I am thus appealing to you to resolve this impasse; at this stage, only you can. If this should be contrary to your normal procedure then, since your normal procedures have had the objectionable and universally harmful results which they have had in this case (results harmful to nation, science, society and individual; results helpful only to the USSR), in this case at least, if not in all, your procedures should be changed.

I ask, therefore, that you, or someone else possessing the proper authority discuss the matter *with me personally*, assess whether *I*, specifically, as an individual, judged upon a logical, rational, sensible, reasonable, and, above all, a realistic basis, am entitled to a clearance, regardless of what the regulations may say about statistical masses of people, and issue me the clearance necessary for me to be able to make my contribution and to be useful to country, to society, to science, and to self.

I look forward to hearing from you promptly and constructively on this matter, and trust that, to the advantage of all, and to the disadvantage of none, arrangements leading to the issuance of the necessary security clearance will quickly be forthcoming.

Thank you.

Most sincerely yours,

Franklin E. Kameny

Around this same time, Kameny had also been corresponding with John Hanes Jr., the administrator of the Department of State's Bureau of Security and Consular Affairs. In one of his replies, Hanes offered several arguments in favor of retaining the policy that identified all homosexuals as security risks. "The homosexual," he wrote, "is automatically a security risk because of the social and emotional pressures to which he is subject from society, and because of the ever-present risk that such pressures can be utilized by hostile elements to coerce him into activities other than those which he would undertake of his own free will. Also because of the prevailing mores of our society, the homosexual frequently becomes a disruptive personnel factor within any organization."⁸ With blanket responses like this one in hand, Kameny began to focus less on the demand that he be treated as an individual, as distinct from other homosexuals, and more on the second-class citizenship of all homosexuals in the United States. He made this transition of thought most definitively in the historic petition he filed with the U.S. Supreme Court in 1960.

Kameny to President John F. Kennedy

Less than two months after the Supreme Court denied his petition, Kameny turns to his "court of last appeal"—President John F. Kennedy. Using Kennedy's call for "The New Frontier" and sacrificial service to country, Kameny implores the president to ensure the protection of civil liberties for homosexuals.⁹ Indeed, this letter, coupled with his Supreme Court petition, is the best evidence of this period for showing Kameny's broadening and deepening interest in the civil rights of all homosexuals in the United States.

MAY 15, 1961

Dear President Kennedy:

I write to you for two reasons: (1) To ask that you act as a "court of last appeal" in a matter in which I believe that you can properly act as such; and (2) perhaps much more important, to bring to your attention, and to ask for your constructive action on, a situation involving at least 15,000,000 Americans, and in which a "New Frontier" approach is very badly needed. These people are the nation's homosexuals—a minority group in no way different, as such, from the Negroes, the Jews, the Catholics, and other minority groups. . . .

In World War II, I willingly fought the Germans, with bullets, in order to preserve and secure my rights, freedoms, and liberties, and those of my fellow citizens. In 1961, it has, ironically, become necessary for me to fight my own government, with words, in order to achieve some of the very same rights, freedoms, and liberties for which I placed my life in jeopardy in 1945. This letter is part of that fight.

The homosexual in the United States today is in much the same position as was the Negro about 1925. The difference is that the Negro, in his dealings with this government, and in his fight for his proper rights, liberties, and freedoms, has met, at worst, merely indifference to him and his problems, and, at best, active assistance; the homosexual has met only active hostility from his government.

The homosexuals in this country are increasingly less willing to tolerate the abuse, repression, and discrimination directed at them, both officially and unofficially, and they are beginning to stand up for their rights and freedoms as citizens no less deserving than other citizens of those rights and freedoms. They are no longer willing to accept their present status as second-class citizens and as second-class human beings; they are neither.

Statistics on the sharply rising numbers of homosexuals who are fighting police and legal abuses, less-than-fully-honorable discharges from the military, security-system disqualifications, and who are taking perfectly proper and legal advantage of military policies and prejudices and draft-board questions to escape the draft, etc., will, I believe, bear me out.

The winds of change are blowing. A wise and foresighted government will start NOW to take *constructive* action on this question.

Your administration has taken a firm and admirable stand, and has taken an active interest in the maintenance of the civil liberties of minority groups, and in the elimination of discrimination against them. Yet the federal government is the prime offender in depriving the homosexual of his civil and other liberties, and in actively discriminating against him. May I suggest that the homosexual is as deserving of his government's protection and assistance in these areas as is the Negro, and needs that protection at least as much—actually much more? The abuses, by constituted authority, of the person, property, and liberties of American homosexuals are flagrant, shocking, and appalling, and yet not only is not a finger raised by the government to assist these people, but the government acts in active, virulent conspiracy to foster and perpetuate these abuses.

This is an area in which a sophisticated, rational, and above all, a civilized approach is badly needed. Short of a policy of outright extermination (and, economically, personally, and professionally, the government's actions are often tantamount to this), the government's practices and policies could not be further removed from such a sane approach. We are badly in need of a breath of fresh air here, Mr. Kennedy—a reconsideration of the matter, divorced from the old, outworn clichés, discredited assumptions, fallacious and specious reasoning, and idle superstition. The traditional new broom, with its clean sweep, is badly needed.

Under present policies, upon no discernible rational ground, the government is deprived of the services of large numbers of competent, capable citizens—often skilled, highly trained, and talented—and others are forced to contribute to society at far less than their full capacity, simply because in their personal, out-of-working-hours lives they do not conform to narrow, archaic, puritan prejudice and taboo.

In my own case, extensive technical training—a Harvard Ph.D. in Astronomy—is going completely to waste, entirely as a result of the government's practices and policies on this question. While the nation cries out for technically trained people, I, two years ago, as a result of the government's acts and policies, was barely surviving on twenty cents worth of food per day. Is this reasonable?

You have said: "Ask not what can your country do for you, but what can you do for your country."[10] I know what I can best do for my country, but my country's government, for no sane reason, will not let me do it. I wish to be of service to my country and to my government; I am capable of being of such service; I need only to be allowed to be so. Thus far, my government has stubbornly and irrationally refused to allow me to be so, and has done its best to make it impossible for me ever to be so. This is equally true, actually or potentially, of millions of homosexuals in this country— well over 10% of our adult population. Not only the society in which they live, but the government under which they live, have steadfastly and stubbornly refused to allow them to serve and to contribute. . . .

Action by the government, on this question, is needed in four specific areas (listed here in no particular order) and a fifth general one. These are: (1) the law, and the mode and practices of its administration and enforcement, and the abuses thereof; (2) federal employment policies; (3) the policies, practices, and official attitudes of the military; (4) security-clearance policies and practices in government employment, in the military, and in private industry under government contract; and (5) the education of the public and the changing of their primitive attitudes. No constructive action has ever been taken in any of these areas.

Yours is an administration which has openly disavowed blind conformity. Here is an unconventional group with the courage to be so. Give them the support they deserve as citizens seeking the pursuit of happiness guaranteed them by the Declaration of Independence.

You yourself said, in your recent address at George Washington University, "that (people) desire to develop their own personalities and their own potentials, that democracy permits them to do so."[11] But your government, by its policies certainly does not permit the homosexual to develop his personality and his potential. I do not feel that it is expecting too much to ask that governmental practice be in accord with administration verbiage.

At present, prominently displayed at the entrance to each of the Civil Service Commission's buildings is an excerpt from another statement of yours, in which you said, "let it be clear that this Administration recognizes the value of daring and dissent."[12] I have demonstrated that I have the daring to register public and official dissent in an area wherein those directly involved have never before dared register with dissent. May I ask that my government show equal daring and dissent in "coming to grips" with this question in a proper and constructive fashion. Let more than mere lip service be given to laudable-sounding ideals!

I can close in no better fashion than by quoting Thomas Jefferson:

> I am not an advocate for frequent changes in laws and constitutions. But laws and constitutions must go hand in hand with the progress of the human mind. As that becomes more developed, more enlightened, as new discoveries are made, new truths discovered, and manners and opinions change, with the change of circumstances, institutions must advance also to keep pace with the times. We might as well require a man to wear still the coat which fitted him when a boy as civilized society to remain ever under the regimen of their barbarous ancestors.[13]

His words could not be more aptly quoted in this regard. Let us, as we advance into the Space Age, discard the policies and attitudes, and "laws and constitutions," the customs and institutions of the Stone Age. . . .

Thank you for your consideration of the matters presented here. I look forward to your reply.

Most sincerely yours,
Franklin E. Kameny

Kennedy did not reply.[14]

Kameny to CSC Chairman John Macy Jr.

John Macy Jr. became chairman of the Civil Service Commission at the beginning of the Kennedy administration and continued in the position until the end of the Johnson administration in 1969. Kameny was a constant presence in Macy's professional life, arguing in one case after another that CSC's policies toward homosexuals were unconstitutional. Following is one of Kameny's earliest letters to his archrival. Like his May 15 letter to President Kennedy, this one shows Kameny's preference for using a public servant's own words when criticizing government-sanctioned discrimination against homosexuals.

JUNE 5, 1961

Dear Mr. Macy:

I am writing in regard to remarks which you made in public speeches on or about May 10, and June 1, 1961.

In the first speech, you stated that manpower shortages could best be met by policies that do not ignore the abilities of minority groups; that you could think of no better way to meet the expected manpower shortage of the 1960's than by non-discriminatory personnel policies.[15] You have reinforced this in other public utterances.

In the second speech you asked that personnel administrators "assure equal opportunity to all groups for entry and advancement by rejecting discriminatory standards such as race, creed, color, sex, or *other non-quality measures*" (emphasis mine); that they "assure advancement in service only on merit and through demonstrated ability, and not through . . . conformity"; and that they "develop a climate for high quality, productive effort, dedicated to the public interest and with respect for the worth and dignity of every man and woman rendering such service."[16]

I could not agree more fully. However, I should like to point out that, in regard to one minority at least, your own Civil Service Commission practices discrimination of the most vicious and virulent sort; that it is not assuring equal opportunity for entry and advancement without regard to non-quality measures; that it is insisting upon the strictest of conformity; that it is acting with no slightest regard for the individual worth and dignity of the men and women serving.

The minority group to which I refer is our nation's homosexuals— a minority in no slightest way different, as such, from other minority groups, such as the Negroes and the Jews. . . .

There is not one single argument which can be advanced against the employment of homosexuals which does not have its parallel in the invalid arguments of segregationists, anti-Semites, and the like, against the objects of their prejudices and hatreds, and which arguments are not, therefore, equally invalid, degrading, and disgraceful to what considers itself to be a civilized country.

Your commission's policies on the employment of homosexuals represent an attempt to impose conformity of just the type which you have disavowed. They represent an attempt to limit entry and advancement by standards based upon non-quality measures. They represent a blatant disregard for the worth and dignity of the individual citizen.

Your commission's treatment of the homosexual is not significantly different from the fanatical southern racist's treatment of the Negro; from the Afrikaner's treatment of the South African native; or (short, possibly of the ovens and gas chambers) from the Nazi's treatment of the Jew—and with no more justification than any of those groups has.

You object to discrimination and prejudice and all that go with them, but through your own commission's policies, there has grown up and become entrenched in your Civil Service Commission, and elsewhere throughout the government, a corps of professional, rabid, fanatical "queer" hunters and "queer" haters, many of whom, if not actually psychopathic on this question, are not far from it, and who (except for the objects of their vicious hatred and malice) are in no way different from the professional Jew-baiters and Negro-baiters found in the Nazi party and in the Ku Klux Klan. Your commission has long ago lost all sense of proportion and perspective on this question, and has taken to treating homosexuals in a fashion comparable with murderers. A return to sanity is badly needed. . . .

I realize, fully, that this is a very "touchy" subject. I also realize, fully, that while it is currently fashionable (and also politically expedient) to defend the rights of Negroes, Jews, and a few other minorities, it is unfashionable (and probably politically inexpedient) to defend the rights of homosexuals—or, in fact, not to persecute them vigorously. However, in light of the principles enunciated by President Kennedy in the course of setting forth his very welcome philosophy of the New Frontier, such considerations of fashion and political expediency should carry no weight. . . .

The winds of change are blowing, Mr. Macy. These fifteen or more million Americans are not going to stand, indefinitely, for the type of discrimination, persecution, suppression, and oppression which they have been receiving at the hands of your commission and other constituted authority, any more than the Negroes have been willing to. The homosexual in this country is in the position that the Negro was in about 1925, when he first began to fight, in a coordinated fashion, for his proper rights.

A wise and foresighted administrator will realize these things, and will begin NOW to take *constructive* (as distinguished from mere repressive) action, while he can still do so in his own fashion, rather than to wait until forced to do so by the courts, as you will surely be, in time, since your policies of discrimination against the homosexuals are patently unconstitutional (as well, of course, as being plainly against the national interest).

I wish to know (and I expect a specific reply) how you can justify your basically indefensible policies on the employment of homosexuals. . . .

> Most sincerely yours,
> Franklin E. Kameny

Unlike President Kennedy, Macy actually replied to Kameny's pointed letter. His June 22 reply stated his case in terse language:

> *The Civil Service Regulations include the following as a disqualification for employment in the Federal service: "Criminal, infamous, dishonest, immoral, or notoriously disgraceful conduct."*

The Commission's policy, based on impartial consideration of many cases involving all aspects of human behavior, is that homosexuals or sexual perverts are not suitable for federal employment.

On considering the representations in your letter of June 5, 1961, I find no basis for changing this policy.[17]

Kameny to Attorney General Robert F. Kennedy

Two months after receiving Macy's letter, Kameny and his new friend Jack Nichols took historic steps to organize a grassroots movement focused on winning civil rights and liberties for homosexuals. The FBI was watching.[18] *After it learned about the organizational meeting held at the Hay-Adams Hotel on November 5, 1961, the FBI conducted interviews of the hotel staff and gathered other information on Kameny's budding organization. It did not take long for Kameny to discover FBI efforts to embed an informant within the Mattachine Society of Washington (MSW) and to obtain lists of its members and contacts. Kameny and MSW were not the first or only gay activists to be targeted by the FBI; the bureau had already conducted surveillance of the Daughters of Bilitis, other chapters of the Mattachine Society, and One, Inc. The following letter is Kameny's letter of protest to Attorney General Robert F. Kennedy.*

JUNE 28, 1962

Dear Mr. Kennedy:

I write in regard to recent actions on the part of investigators of the Federal Bureau of Investigation, and the direction which some of their questioning has taken. . . .

. . . While our purposes are highly controversial, and while you may, personally, very well not agree with them, nevertheless they are perfectly and fully lawful and proper; no slightest imputation of illegality has been directed against us, nor is there any slightest ground for such imputation.

Nevertheless, in the course of FBI interrogations, recently, citizens were asked what they knew of the Mattachine Society of Washington. They were asked for the names of members and for membership lists (which, of course, were not supplied). They were asked if particular people belonged to the group. They were asked about the location of meetings. One was even asked to act as an informer for the FBI, to gain and to pass on to them the names of members and other information about the Society and its activities.

We look upon this as grossly improper and offensive. As long as our purposes and activities are lawful, neither our members nor our activities are proper material for investigation by the United States Government, or by any branch, agency, office, or officer thereof, under any circumstances whatever.

We look upon these actions by the FBI as being equivalent, de facto, even if, perhaps, not de jure (although possibly that too) to improper harassment and intimidation. We have discussed these matters with the American Civil Liberties Union, and they are substantially in agreement with us on this.[19]

We feel that American citizens have the right to band together for lawful and orderly achievement of any lawful and orderly purpose, however unpopular, however controversial, and however much at odds with existing official policy, without making themselves the objects of official interrogation, harassment, and intimidation, and without making themselves the objects of official inquiry, infiltration, and informants.

I hardly need remind you of the U.S. Supreme Court decision in the case of *Alabama v. the NAACP*, in regard to the supplying of membership lists.[20] The precise details and circumstances may be somewhat different here, but the difference is purely legal sophistry; the principle is precisely the same, and the parallel is close.

Therefore, we formally request that, in regard to the Mattachine Society of Washington, such inquiries and investigations as to membership and other facts, and other similar acts by the FBI and by investigative agents and agencies throughout the Federal government be brought to a halt immediately.

We will be pleased to discuss these and related matters with you personally, should you wish it.

Your early reply is requested.

Thank you.

Sincerely yours,
Franklin E. Kameny

Kameny's letter ended up at the FBI, where an agent denied that the FBI had harassed MSW and recommended that Kennedy not acknowledge the letter.[21] *The attorney general did not reply.*

Less than a month later, Kameny wrote another attorney in federal government—Supreme Court Justice Hugo Black—with an invitation to speak before an MSW meeting, even suggesting that the justice address the question of whether the government should be "forbidden to intercede" in areas of morality, especially those involving homosexuality.[22] *Black did not accept the invitation.*[23]

Around this same time, Kameny did receive a reply from a letter he had written to nationally syndicated columnist George Sokolsky. The New York–based writer gave Kameny his first significant exposure in the national media by mentioning him, though not by name, in his July 27 column on the susceptibility of homosexuals to blackmail:

> *It is generally maintained by police officials that apart from the morals involved, the practitioners of various homosexual methods are subject to blackmail. In fact, if caught at their activity, they are usually arrested. They are therefore unfit for service in sensitive areas of government, such as the State or Defense departments.*
>
> *A correspondent from Washington writes me to challenge such a statement:*
>
> *"By what authority or knowledge do you presume that all homosexuals are so ashamed of their state and activities that they are subject to blackmail on that account? I know many hundreds of homosexuals, and I know that these people are not all subject to blackmail, by any means."*

Kameny did not succeed in convincing Sokolsky, but the columnist conceded that the problem of blackmail would cease if the country passed laws "recognizing homosexuality as a permissible way of life," and called upon the State and Defense departments to "accept the challenge and uncover what the truth is."[24]

Kameny to the Director of the U.S. Public Health Service

As president of MSW, Kameny began what would turn out to be a long and concerted campaign against health-care officials, public and private, regarding their understanding and treatment of homosexuality. His main point in the following letter—that homosexuality is not a disease—offers a foretaste of much longer arguments he advanced in later years. Kameny sent this critical letter to the head of the U.S. Public Health Service—the main division of the U.S. Department of Health, Education, and Welfare.

AUGUST 3, 1962

Dear Sir:

As the enclosed formal statement of purpose indicates, the Mattachine Society of Washington is a group dedicated to improving the status of the homosexual minority in our nation, by all lawful means. For the homosexual, we are what the NAACP is for the Negro.

In light of the preceding, we wish to protest the item in Question 20, on your Form 89, Report of Medical History, which asks: Have you ever had, or have you now, homosexual tendencies?

We feel that this question is as improper, and as irrelevant, to any proper governmental inquiry as (and in precisely the same fashion as) would be a question as to whether the examinee were or had been a Jew, a Negro, or a Catholic; or whether he were part of the minority which preferred pork to beef.

We deny any relationship or relevance, whatever, between homosexuality, whether overt, or merely by inclination, and fitness for government or other employment.

We insist firmly that homosexuality is merely a matter of personal taste and preference, if a minority one, and is not, in any sense, whether physical or psychological, a disease, illness, ailment, or malfunction.

We feel that, under no circumstances whatever, are a citizen's sexual tastes and orientation the proper concern of any branch, agency, agent, office of officer of the U.S. government—no more so than are a citizen's race or religion.

The question is, in function, quite as discriminatory, and quite as unjustifiably so, as are questions on race and religion, and serves merely to allow the prejudiced to indulge their prejudices.

We feel that the question is indefensible, and that no rationale can be shown for its presence on this or any other form.

Accordingly, we formally request that the question on homosexual tendencies, and all other questions on homosexuality, be deleted from the Form 89, and from any other forms on which such questions may appear. . . .

Thank you.

Sincerely yours,

Franklin E. Kameny

Kameny did not receive a reply, and Joe Parker, the acting director of security for the Department of Health, Education, and Welfare, forwarded a copy of Kameny's letter to FBI director J. Edgar Hoover.[25]

Kameny to Admiral Laurence Frost

On August 28, 1962, Kameny sent an MSW letter of introduction to all members of Congress and other top government officials. The letter, as well as an enclosed news release, described the purposes of MSW and asked for assistance in the campaign to fight discrimination against homosexuals. "If we can get even one mildly sympathetic reply from one member of Congress, we will have broken a hitherto impenetrable wall, and will have gained immeasurably," Kameny wrote a fellow activist at the time.[26]

Kameny customized some of the letters, and in the following letter to Laurence Frost, the director of the National Security Agency (NSA), he refers to the case of two NSA defectors. On September 6, 1960, William Martin and Bernon Mitchell, mathematicians in NSA's cryptology department, appeared in Moscow to announce that they had defected to the Soviet Union because U.S. intelligence methods, especially the use of intelligence reconnaissance missions, were "dangerous to world peace."[27] *A few days later, Representative Francis Walter of Pennsylvania—chairman of the House Un-American Activities Committee (HUAC)—publicly claimed that the two defectors were "poor, unfortunate homosexuals" whom the government should never have entrusted with state secrets. Even "common gossip," Walter stated, had identified one of the two defectors as a "notorious homosexual."*[28]

AUGUST 28, 1962

Dear Admiral Frost:

Enclosed, for your interest and information, is a formal statement of the purposes of the Mattachine Society of Washington, a newly formed organization devoted to the improvement of the status of our country's 15,000,000 homosexuals.

Included, also, is a copy of our news release, which was submitted to the Washington newspapers, and to the various press services.

The question of homosexuality, and of the prejudice against it, both personal and official, is a serious one, involving, as it does, more than one out of every ten American citizens, including roughly a quarter-million in each the Federal Civil Service, the Armed Forces, and security-sensitive positions in private industry, and a number of your own employees—numbers which have not in the past been reduced by measures of exclusion which were taken, and which will not be reduced in the future.

We feel that the government's approach is archaic, unrealistic, and inconsistent with basic American principles. We feel, in addition, that it is inexcusably and unnecessarily wasteful of trained manpower and of the taxpayers' money.

We are very well aware of the arguments which would make security risks of all homosexuals. These arguments are based largely upon myth, folklore, ignorance, and superstition, plus the usually erroneous feelings, impressions, and deductions of those who are not homosexual, as to what the homosexual feels and fears, the pressures to which he is subject, and the degree to which he is subject to them. We are sure that a careful look at the statistics on the number of breaches of security actually involving homosexuality as an element in the breach, combined with the knowledge that screening procedures have made no extensive inroad into the number of homosexuals now holding clearances, the country over, and are not likely to, will lead you to agree with us.

We know, of course, of the acute and special problems, in this regard, with which the Martin-Mitchell incident presented you. We feel that their allegedly being homosexuals had no more demonstrable connection with their defection than did their being mathematicians; you did not fire all mathematicians after their defection; nor, in the same vein, did the government refuse to grant clearances to Jews after the Rosenberg and Soblen cases.[29] It is not American to penalize the very many for the sins of the very few.

We realize that this area presents you with many potential problems, some of them extremely subtle and touchy ones of politics and public relations, and that they are not always subject to easy solution, but policies of repression, persecution, and exclusion will not prove to be workable ones in the case of this minority, any more than they have, throughout history, in the cases of other minorities. This is a problem which must be worked with, constructively, not worked against, destructively, as is now the case. A fresh approach by the federal government is badly needed.

We would very much like to cooperate with you in these matters, if you will enable us to work with you, but in any case, we are determined that this question will be brought out into the open, and that present government policy and practice will be reconsidered.

We welcome any comments which you may have on this subject.

We will be pleased to meet with you personally, at your convenience, to discuss these and related matters.

Thank you for your consideration of our position. We would appreciate your reply.

Sincerely yours,
Franklin E. Kameny

Kameny also sent a letter of introduction to Secretary of Defense Robert McNamara. The customized section of this letter represents one of Kameny's earliest efforts to combat discrimination in the U.S. military:

In regard to members of the Armed Forces, we feel, first, that homosexuals are no less suitable for military service than are heterosexuals. Rather more than a million served well and honorably in World War II. The Army, the Navy, the Air Force, and the Marine Corps, made up today of over 10% homosexuals, function with no inefficiency or other ill effect on this account.

However, second, even if, for various reasons of prejudice, it should be felt that homosexuals are unsuitable for service in the Armed Forces, then those discovered should be discharged with fully honorable discharges. Reason, justice, and fairness call for no less. The present practice of giving less-than-fully-honorable discharges is needlessly vicious, and causes much totally unnecessary suffering and hardship. If you do not want a man, then let him go, but do not blight the remainder of his life in the process.[30]

Within two months of writing this letter, Kameny found himself inside the Pentagon, lobbying for security clearances for homosexuals. Walter Skallerup Jr., deputy assistant secretary of defense for security policy, had scheduled the meeting after an exchange of letters between Kameny and the Defense Department. Three MSW representatives, including Kameny, met with Defense officials on October 23, 1962. "The conference lasted for about 2 ¾ hours," Kameny wrote shortly afterwards. "To the best of our knowledge and belief, this is the first time that official representatives of any section of the federal government have ever consented to meet with spokesmen of the homosexual community, as such."[31]

Kameny and his fellow MSW members did not persuade the defense officials to change their policy, but Kameny saw the meeting as nevertheless productive: "The directly and immediately constructive results of the conference were few. It served primarily as the firm opening of a door which we are keeping open—as a curtain raiser—and as a means for both sides to present, and to clarify to each other, their positions and views." The meeting also afforded Kameny the opportunity to gain some insight into the department's reasons for denying clearances. "The Department of Defense seems to be deemphasizing the blackmail threat as the rationale for denial of clearances to homosexuals," he wrote. "They base their present position upon the assertion that ALL homosexuals, per se, are unstable and, therefore, cannot be entrusted with classified information. This position allegedly stems from the advice of psychiatrists whom they have consulted."[32]

Kameny's letter of introduction to the MSW also earned meetings with the respective staffs of two liberal Democrats—William Fitts Ryan of New York City and Robert Nix Sr., of Philadelphia. Not all members of Congress were so positive in their replies, though. Democratic Representative Paul Johnson of Missouri handwrote this response: "I am unalterably opposed to your purposes and cannot see how any person in his right mind can condone the practices which you would justify. Please do not contaminate my mail with such filthy trash."[33] Republican Representative Charles Chamberlain of Michigan claimed that "in all my six years of service in the United States

Congress I have not received such a revolting communication."[34] And Democratic Representative Joe Kilgore of Texas forwarded his letter to J. Edgar Hoover, asking the FBI director whether there was "any truth" to Kameny's claims about homosexuals in federal agencies. Kilgore also wanted to know "what steps are being taken to remove such described types from the area of government service."[35] Kameny had already sent a letter of introduction to Hoover, and the director had also received copies that Kameny had mailed to Secretary of Defense McNamara and Navy Secretary Fred North.[36]

As Kameny sought to reach out to federal officials, he and MSW took other significant steps. On November 14, for example, he and MSW members met with health officials in the District of Columbia to "discuss means and methods of cooperating in an attack" on the problem of venereal disease among homosexuals. MSW and health officials agreed to work together "in the writing and distribution of a leaflet on VD aimed specifically toward the homosexual community." The meeting also saw MSW urging health officials to ensure "absolute anonymity . . . for all those attending the District's VD clinics."[37]

MSW members were also establishing "close liaison" with the newly formed American Civil Liberties Union [ACLU] chapter in Washington, DC.[38] In November 1961 Kameny had helped to found the National Capital Area affiliate of the American Civil Liberties Union (NCACLU), and in May 1962 he had sent the national ACLU a letter suggesting that "the entire area of law, policy, practice and procedure, federal, state, and local, in regard to the homosexual, is one which is ripe for action by civil liberties groups such as the ACLU."[39] In an effort to align with the ACLU, Kameny and MSW members became members of NCACLU's various committees with the intent of bringing "our problems to the fore," as he put it. By the end of 1962 Kameny was directly pitching NCACLU to take legal action "on questions of discrimination against the employment of homosexuals."[40]

2

"Genocide Is the Word That Must Be Used"

1963–1964

Kameny to Vice President Lyndon B. Johnson

On May Day 1963, Vice President Johnson offered a public statement on the need to provide equal federal employment opportunities for all "national-origin minority groups" (for example, Puerto Ricans, Mexicans, and Native Americans).[1] Even though Johnson focused on national origin, Kameny uses the principles behind Johnson's pronouncement to call for the end of discrimination against homosexuals in matters of employment and citizenship rights. Part of the driving force behind this letter was a landmark statement ("Discrimination Against the Employment of Homosexuals"), referred to in the following letter, that Kameny had drafted for and presented to the Subcommittee on Equal Employment Opportunities of the D.C. Advisory Committee of the U.S. Civil Services Commission on February 28.[2]

Kameny also refers to another legal challenge to the Civil Service Commission. This particular case was partially rooted in the 1947 arrest of Bruce Scott, an employee of the Department of Labor, on charges of loitering in Lafayette Park, just across the street from the White House. Scott was forced to resign in 1956, when an upgrade of security clearances in his office resulted in the discovery of his 1947 arrest. After several years of underemployment, Scott learned of early efforts to start MSW, quickly became a charter member and officer, and with encouragement and counsel from Kameny, soon reapplied for a position in the federal government, this time with full intention to fight any denial. The government played its role perfectly, denying

49

him employment because of his arrest, and Scott filed suit in April 1963. His attorney, David Carliner, was from the National Capital Area Civil Liberties Union (NCACLU); both Kameny and Scott were also charter members of NCACLU, and Kameny had arranged for Carliner to act as Scott's counsel.

Also significant is Kameny's report that the "first picketing of the White House, to protest federal policy and practice toward homosexuals, has just occurred." There was no major media coverage of this historic event.[3]

MAY 4, 1963

Dear Mr. Johnson:

We are writing in regard to statements which you made on May 1, 1963, and which were reported in the *Washington Post* of May 2.

You said that there are other minority groups in the United States beside the Negro, and they often face the same barriers in their quest for jobs and full citizenship rights.

You said: "Just as with Negroes, the capabilities and talents of our other minority citizens stand as a high asset in the ledger book of our national strength. We must see that they are receiving full opportunity to contribute on the basis of individual merit. . . ."

"To see that all minority groups receive the same opportunities for employment and advancement in the federal service as are afforded any of our citizens is part of the challenge to our leadership."[4]

We agree fully and wholeheartedly. However, we represent and speak for a minority, the members of which, when known as such, are excluded from employment—federal as well as private—to a degree never dreamed of by the Negro in his worst nightmares.

We represent the largest minority group in this country, after the Negro—15,000,000 American citizens—a minority larger than any of those discussed by you in your remarks of May 1.

We represent a minority against whom the federal government is the most persistent, recalcitrant, and flagrant of offenders.

We represent a large minority who are treated as second-class citizens, consistently and as a matter of course, and in favor of whose rights not a single official voice has thus far been raised.

We represent the homosexual minority in this country—some 10% of the citizenry.

We realize that our position may, perhaps, be unorthodox. We are aware, too, of the difficult political implications which this question raises. Nevertheless, we feel that the homosexuals are a minority group, no different, as such, from the Jews, the Negroes, or any others, and deserve the same consideration from their government.

While we have no slightest desire to embarrass anyone, or to create a difficult situation, just for the sake of the embarrassment and the difficulty—in fact, quite to the contrary—we must point out that this problem is not going to vanish if it is ignored. It will become increasingly more evident and more intractable.

The second case challenging federal policies on the employment of homosexuals has just entered the courts. Others are on their way. The first picketing of the White House, to protest federal policy and practice toward homosexuals, has just occurred (with, let us emphasize, no connection with the Mattachine Society of Washington). It is safe to predict that increasing numbers of increasingly vigorous protests against federal disorientation toward homosexuals will occur.

You have seen the unfortunate results which have occurred and are occurring when the South refused to cope constructively with the Negro problem. It is about time that constructive action started to "take this particular bull by the horns."

If you and others in the administration really mean what you say in regard to equality of opportunity, elimination of prejudice, equality of rights, non-existence of second-class citizenship in this country, etc., then we feel justified in asking that you demonstrate your sincerity by taking constructive action in regard to federal and other discrimination against the homosexual citizen.

We enclose herewith, a statement recently presented by us to the Sub-Committee on Equal Employment Opportunities of the D.C. Advisory Committee of the U.S. Commission on Civil Rights. As American citizens, presenting our viewpoint to our public officials, on a matter of importance to us, to a very large number of other citizens, and to the nation, we respectfully request that you, personally, give it a careful, open-minded, receptive reading.

We will be pleased to discuss these matters with you personally.

We respectfully request a reply, and will look forward to its early receipt.

Thank you.

Sincerely,

Franklin E. Kameny

Around this same time, Kameny won a meeting with Lieutenant General Lewis Hershey, director of the Selective Service System, to discuss the confidentiality of information provided by homosexuals registering with the Selective Service. Kameny had written Hershey on March 31, 1963, that MSW was "receiving a steadily increasing number of requests for guidance from homosexuals who (although they know, correctly, that they are as capable as other citizens of giving honorable and effective service, and desire, neither more or less than other citizens, to do so) wish not to perjure themselves, and wish to give an honest, truthful, affirmative answer to your questions about homosexuality."[5] In their meeting with Hershey, Kameny and MSW members sought to receive assurance that such information would be kept confidential and thus not shared with other federal agencies. Hershey refused their request.[6]

Kameny to Theodore Sorensen

By 1963 the FBI had successfully recruited a PCI (potential criminal informant) within the MSW network, and J. Edgar Hoover received the following report on June 10:

> PCI was advised he was recently contacted by an individual named "RANDY," who claimed to be a leader of a homosexual group in New York City. "RANDY" told PCI he was bringing approximately fifty homosexuals to Washington, D.C., in August, 1963, to picket the White House and they were planning to carry placards enscribed with slogans criticizing the government for discriminating against homosexuals in government employment.[7]

Although it had not yet fully identified him, the FBI was referring to Randy Wicker, founder (and the only member) of the Homosexual League of New York (HLNY). Wicker, whose real name was Charles Hayden Jr., had started HLNY after becoming frustrated with the failure of the Mattachine Society of New York (MSNY) to give him free reign in, among other things, attracting the attention of local and national media. By the time Hoover received the aforementioned report, Wicker had helped to place articles about homosexuals in publications such as Harper's *magazine and the* New York Post. *In June 1963, the* Nugget, *a popular men's magazine, character- ized Wicker as the Martin Luther King Jr. of the homosexual rights move- ment.*[8] *It is likely that in the following letter to Ted Sorensen, special counsel to President Kennedy, Kameny had Wicker and his militant followers in mind when writing about "others who are far more extreme [than MSW], far less responsible, and certainly not willing to cooperate."*

JUNE 21, 1963

Dear Mr. Sorensen:

On March 6, 1963, we wrote to you in regard to administration policy toward homosexuals. In well over three months which have elapsed, we have had neither response nor even acknowledgement.

We are sure that were the NAACP to write to you in regard to problems of the Negro community, or the B'nai B'rith Anti-Defamation League, in regard to problems of the Jewish community, prompt, meaningful, con- structive answers would have been forthcoming. Unless you are content to have your actions give the lie to pious words denying the existence of second-class citizenship in this country, we deserve as much consideration as do spokesmen for other major groups. In any case, as citizens and as taxpayers, we deserve proper replies to our letters to our public officials, at any level.

Our problems are real ones and our complaints are valid ones. They will not vanish if you look the other way long enough; when you look back, they will be right there awaiting your constructive action. The South found that out in regard to the problems of the Negro. And you will discover, in regard to this problem, as the South discovered in regard to segregation, that the problem will intensify and will become increasingly intractable with the passage of time, if it is not properly attended to, in a constructive fashion. . . .

You have seen what happened in Mississippi, in Alabama, and in many other places in the nation, when constituted authority refused to consider coming to terms with, or even to meet with, an oppressed minority. We fail to see any difference between the discreditable stand taken by Governors Barnett and Wallace, and certain officials of the cities of Birmingham, Alabama, and Jackson, Mississippi, on the one hand, and the equally discreditable position, down to refusals even to so much as reply to a letter, taken by the administration here in Washington.

Differences of opinion on this question are understandable. Refusal by our government even to communicate with us is unforgivable.

The lack of communication between the two sides in the South has been deplored, not least by the federal government. Yet the same government has completely shut down all channels of communication with us. We have offered to confer and to discuss, in an attempt to resolve these matters. More often than not, we have not even received the common courtesy of a reply to our letters.

The Attorney General recently stated, in regard to the Negro community, that: "The Negroes in this country cannot be expected, indefinitely, to tolerate the injustices which flow from official and private discrimination. As the years pass, resentment increases. The only cure for resentment is progress."[9] Our resentment, too, is increasing, and we, too, are losing patience with a total and complete lack of progress.[10]

We are informed that the first picketing of the White House, in protest against federal policy toward homosexuals, took place recently. We are also informed that those responsible for the picketing are planning more and larger demonstrations. (Let it be emphasized that the Mattachine Society of Washington had no part in that picketing, and were only informed of it after it occurred.)

The first challenge to Civil Service Commission policy on homosexuality went to the Supreme Court, quietly, about two years ago. The second challenge entered the lower courts, with much publicity, and with the sponsorship of the American Civil Liberties Union, about two months ago. . . .

It is indeed to the shame and discredit of the government of the United States of America, with all that this country stands for, that it should find itself arrayed against the side of personal liberties, rather than for them, and that it should force its citizens to go to the courts in order to bring an end to an odious and unreasonable discrimination which the government itself should be taking the initiative to end.

Given Kinsey's statistics on the prevalence of homosexual activity; given the Civil Service Commission's, the security-clearance authorities', and the Armed Forces' policies of rigorous exclusion of anyone having had any such experience, and the well-nigh total ineffectiveness of those policies in practice, with no ill-effects; given the increasingly public and vociferous protest against federal policy on this subject; given the innumerable statements by high federal officials in regard to freedom, utilization of manpower, minority rights, civil rights, elimination of prejudice, elimination of second-class citizenship, etc., etc.; and given the failure of the concerned areas of the government—and, in fact, of the administration—to respond reasonably, convincingly, or at all, to searching questioning on this matter, from several quarters, it becomes obvious that the government is rapidly backing itself into a totally untenable position—into a morass of inconsistencies and contradictions from which it will become increasingly difficult to extricate itself without severe embarrassment. We do not desire such embarrassment; we are sure that you do not.

We are a reasonable group, taking a moderate position, and willing to work in intelligent, knowledgeable cooperation with you, with full cognizance of the political and other subtleties and realities of the situation. There are others who are far more extreme, far less responsible, and certainly not willing to cooperate. They are beginning to stir, and, if something is not done to remedy the present situation, they will take the initiative and will make themselves known, very publicly, in manners which you will find as unpalatable as the South found the methods of the extremists who were forced into action by Southern recalcitrance.

The homosexual community will not put on as spectacular a display as the Negro community is now putting on. Nevertheless, feelings are quite as strong and are quite as near the breaking point. You can no longer rely upon the continued supine acceptance, by the homosexual community, without resistance or fight, of the wrongs meted out to them. The lessons being taught by the Negro are being learned elsewhere.

Correctly or incorrectly, it was recently alleged that the Attorney General failed utterly to comprehend the mood and feeling of the Negro community. Be informed that the resentment of the homosexual community toward what it feels increasingly to be a hypocritical federal government is real, deep, highly justified, and no less strong than that of the Negro toward the governments in the South and elsewhere—and these feelings are growing rapidly.

We know, as fully and as correctly as the Negro and the Jew know, that in these matters of discrimination and prejudice, we have right and morality on our side. We wish, in a responsible and friendly fashion, to work out a difficult situation with you, to the benefit of all concerned, and of this nation. Are you going to allow us to do so, or must these problems be worked out over your continued opposition and total noncooperation, to the detriment of all? They WILL be worked out, with your cooperation or without it. We very much prefer the former; we think that you should too. . . .

Once again, we ask for a reply to the questions: Does the Administration plan to take any constructive action in regard to present highly discriminatory federal policies and practices in regard to homosexuals? If so, what and when? If not, why not?

Once again, we request a conference with you and other appropriate White House and government officials on these related matters.

We look forward to an early and constructive reply.

Thank you.

Sincerely yours,

Franklin E. Kameny

A month after Kameny wrote the aforementioned letter, Wicker sent Kameny a short note including news about plans for picketing: "Quite honestly I am in a quiet period so far as organizational activity is concerned. My next major effort will be picketing the White House this fall—so far I have 12 to 20 pickets; heterosexuals included—could be a bombshell."[11] The FBI was paying attention to Wicker's plans, and on August 30, 1963, just two days after the March on Washington for Jobs and Freedom, J. Edgar Hoover informed Robert Kennedy about "homosexuals planning to picket

the White House." Hoover then followed up with the attorney general on
September 11, noting that an informant had offered the FBI "information
that approximately 100 members of the New York City Mattachine Society,
who will be joined by members of the Washington, D.C., Chapter of the
Mattachine Society, plan to picket the White House on October 25, 1963.
The source indicated that the purpose of the demonstration is to protest the
United States government's discrimination against homosexuals in federal
employment."[12] On September 5, 1963, Hoover also informed Robert F. Ken-
nedy that the FBI "had received information that homosexuals may picket
the Department of Justice on Friday, September 6, 1963," in order to "protest
the FBI's discrimination against homosexuals." The FBI had received this
information from an anonymous male caller. "The caller refused to identify
himself or furnish the names of any participants."[13]

Kameny to Chief of Police Robert Murray

Kameny devoted considerable time to fighting police harassment of homo-
sexuals in the District of Columbia. He became a vocal leader in this battle
shortly after he had heard reports of a particularly brutal police raid at the
Gayety Buffet on 9th Street—a favorite meeting place for local gays. Kameny
obtained affidavits of the arrested men, some of whom claimed verbal and
physical abuse, and recounts the raid and arrests in the following letter of
complaint to Robert Murray, the District's chief of police.

JUNE 26, 1963

Dear Mr. Murray:

We are writing in regard to what seems to us to be a case of abuse of
police power, of severe irregularity in procedure, and of violations of the
rights of citizens, which recently occurred in the District of Columbia.

On May 25, 1963, at about 10:30 PM, six men, apparently selected at
random, and without cause, were arrested in the Gayety Buffet at 511 9th
Street, N.W. Each was charged with disorderly conduct, the details of the
alleged conduct having implications of homosexuality.

Among the violations occurring were:

1. (a) Arrest without probable cause.
   (b) Use of a "dragnet" type of arrest.

2. (a) Refusal by police to make a prompt statement of the reasons for the arrest, even when repeatedly requested to do so by the persons being arrested.

(b) Threatening the manager of the establishment with arrest when she inquired as to the reasons for the arrest of her patrons.

3. Police brutality, occurring unprovoked during an interrogation at police headquarters and leading to the brief hospitalization of the man struck.

4. (a) Charges concocted by the police and not related to fact.

(b) Statements placed upon arrest records without being shown to the accused.

(c) Basing of charges upon alleged acts which are not violations of law.

5. Illegal confiscation, by a police officer, of property of one man arrested.

In addition, on at least one occasion a policeman stated that the police intended to close the Gayety Buffet. The police department exists to carry out, in lawful and orderly fashion, the orders of appropriate branches and agencies of government, not to originate those orders. It is not for the police to decide that a particular business establishment is to be closed, nor is it within the proper scope of police activity for the police department to harass an establishment or otherwise put it out of business, because the police happen to look upon it with disfavor.

Finally, we must protest the use by the police, toward homosexuals, of contempt, derision, and ridicule.[14] You would not officially tolerate your men calling a Negro a "nigger," a Jew a "kike," or an Italian a "wop." Furthermore, you would not allow your men, whatever their personal, private feelings might be, to show open contempt, derision, or ridicule to members of any of these minority groups simply because they are so. The only correct term to use in these cases is "homosexual," NO other. Coarse and crude language and insults are no more fittingly addressed to the arrested homosexual citizen than to any other. Indeed we wish to make it perfectly plain that homosexuals are first-class citizens, in full possession of the rights of all other citizens, and are due from their public officials not one whit less respect for themselves and for their dignity than are all other citizens.

We have no wish unnecessarily to embarrass the police department, or to cause difficulties for you. Therefore we shall not—at this time—create any publicity on these matters, or bring them to the attention of higher authority. We reiterate, however, that homosexuals, like all other citizens, are not to be subjected to arbitrary arrest and improper police action.

We are very well aware of the flagrant abuses of this sort which are perpetrated by the police of other cities. Thus far, except for this instance, Washington has been largely free of such abuses. We assume that the situation will remain so henceforth, and that homosexuals arrested under other circumstances will also be properly treated.

We have obtained sworn affidavits from several of the people involved in the matters discussed above. Copies of these affidavits have been sent to the National Capital Area Civil Liberties Union. We have consulted with them on this matter, and have been assured of their full support and backing in the position that we have taken, and in action necessary.

We request a constructive reply from you. We will be pleased to meet with you to discuss these and related matters. A reply from or meetings with your subordinates in the Morals Division will not be acceptable.

Thank you.

Sincerely yours,

Franklin E. Kameny

This was not the first time Kameny took direct action against the police department.

"When I came to Washington," he later remembered, "Lafayette Park was the prime, outdoor cruising spot in this city." There was a men's room on the H Street side. There was a two-way mirror that served very nicely as a mirror if you wanted to look into it. If you weren't in the know, you never thought of it one way or another. So one day—this has become a classic story among people who know me—I went in there and measured the mirror's wooden frame. I got a piece of plywood and pre-nailed it, then went back with the plywood and hammer and covered the mirror. Bang, bang, bang, it was done. I don't know how long it stayed there, but for a while that mirror wasn't functional anymore.[15]

Nor would the aforementioned letter be his last communication with the DC police. It was merely the formal beginning of a protracted campaign that would last until 1975, when the DC police's Morals Division lost its funding.

Kameny to Randy Wicker (Charles Hayden Jr.)

Kameny was deeply concerned about the public image of homosexuals. Indeed, not long before mailing this letter, he and the MSW executive committee had asked MSW secretary Bruce Schuyler to communicate this urgent message to the editors of ONE *magazine in Los Angeles:*

> *The Executive Board of the Mattachine Society of Washington has directed me to express unequivocally to you its utter shock and disgust that you would waste valuable space to reproduce an ordinary and artistically and socially unredeeming drawing of a nude sailor defecating. The drawing does not . . . have a place in a magazine which is intended to correct the public image of homosexuals.*
>
> *Our president and vice-president have just done much to dispel some of the popular misconceptions of homosexuals by their comportment and their testimony before Subcommittee 4 of the House District of Columbia in hearings on Congressman Dowdy's bill, H.R. 5990.*[16]

Schuyler was referring to Democratic Representative John Dowdy of Texas—a social conservative—who had introduced a bill designed to revoke a permit allowing MSW to raise funds to combat prejudice against homosexuals. At summer hearings held by the House's subcommittee on the District, Dowdy charged that granting MSW a fundraising permit was nothing less than "a security problem." "If these people are a charitable organization, I've grown up in the wrong generation," he added. Kameny testified at the hearing, becoming the first openly homosexual individual to testify at a congressional hearing. Defending MSW as "a civil liberties organization," he stated: "We are a reputable, responsible group, working seriously in an area where much work is needed and very little is being done."[17] *With Kameny's testimony in mind, Schuyler added the following in his letter to* ONE:

> *The hearings were well and objectively reported by the Washington newspapers and by a TV broadcast.*

Now along comes your magazine with a drawing which Congressman Dowdy can wave at his colleagues in the House of Representatives and shout: "What did I tell you? These unnatural people are not interested in educating others except to their own unnatural lusts!" Let me make it perfectly clear: the Congressman has not yet said this, but your drawing certainly now has provided him with the opportunity, if he wants to take it.[18]

Dowdy's bill passed the House but failed to win enough support in the Senate.[19] With its fundraising ability intact, MSW emerged as victor in its first open campaign in the U.S. Congress—and as the recipient of positive coverage in the national media.

As he basked in the attention of the media, Kameny remained hypervigilant against any methods within the homophile movement that would undermine his efforts to present homosexuals as respectable and acceptable to heterosexual America. In the following letter, he expresses this attitude when writing about gay-friendly buttons that he had ordered from Wicker (Kameny did not appreciate their lavender color), and about the wisdom of undertaking a campaign targeting aggressive police actions against homosexuals cruising public toilets.

SEPTEMBER 8, 1963

Dear Charlie:

. . . While I will grant that the lavender buttons didn't look as bad as I'd expected—primarily because the lavender color isn't as apparent as I'd thought it would be—my basic reaction remains the same. Whether you like it or not—and, perhaps, more fundamental, whether it's rational or not—the prejudiced connotations in regard to lavender vis a vis homosexuality and effeminacy DO exist ("effeminacy" is a simplification of a subtle complex of reactions relating to that color in this context, as I'm sure you're well aware). You don't attempt—at least you don't, if you hope to be successful—to overcome one prejudice by exacerbating another. One almost automatic reaction of those who are prejudiced and whose prejudices are being attacked is to make fun of the prejudice-attackers. The fun usually isn't on a rational basis, either, but in the minds of the prejudiced it serves as a thoroughly effective shield against the entrance of any sort of rational argument to dispel or lessen the prejudice, and, often, will serve to reinforce the prejudice. That is just the kind of reaction you'll get here. In a good many instances where a plain, black-and-white button might arouse some anger (which sometimes leads to constructive thought) or just some startled re-thinking, the use of lavender will elicit a snickering "what can you expect of a bunch of pansies," and a reinforcement of old prejudices. The reaction may not be logical, but it'll be there, nonetheless.

Furthermore, even if I accept your argument that we'll educate and enlighten ONLY those people mentally free enough to absorb education and who have a personal tolerance for "difference," it should be kept in mind that those among that group who already are not on our side are usually very well aware of, and very sensitive to, the attitudes around them. They need to be made to feel at ease in accepting the new (for them) attitudes in question. They need to be made to feel that they aren't going TOO far out (socially, at least). Lavender buttons will not give them the ease of mind which will be conducive to a receptive attitude for the ideas which you want to promulgate.

I won't belabor this point further. I think that I've made my position clear.

In regard to the three points which you mention in your next paragraph. First, I feel that it just simply is NOT true that the reason for the promiscuity of many homosexuals is the fact that they live in a male-dominated culture. I think the reason is that THEY, as individuals, each one separately, is a male, and males are naturally promiscuous. . . .

I quite agree with you in regard both to public toilet cruising, as seen from the viewpoint of our group and the cruiser, and in regard to police activity. The picture is not entirely one-sided, however, as I'm sure you realize. First of all, if the police were to do as you suggested, they would soon become totally ineffective, and things would rapidly get out of hand; places just would not cease to be pick-up places, but would become places in which overt activity would take place in increasing amounts. Unfortunately, in any context, there will always be enough people to abuse any freedom which they are given so that things will be spoiled for the rest of us. . . .

However, in this regard, once again, you get into a matter of strategy and regard for the feelings of the people with whom you are dealing.

Entirely aside from the reactions of much of the public to homosexuality in general, the whole image of the homosexual as one who hangs around public toilets—with the general distaste which the public feels for toilets, public or private—is even greater. To many of them, ALL homosexuals are people who hang around public toilets. When you discuss this, in a public talk, as a (in your mind) major source of the injustices against us, you are only reinforcing already existing distastes and prejudices. The public is NOT going to take up the cause of making toilet-cruising safe for homosexuals, no matter how it is presented, and presenting it at all, outside of homosexual circles, will only make the public shun taking up ANY aspect of our cause.

Now, on your insistence on the truth—unadulterated, and unsifted. This I think is a mistake, and a great one. I have had the same discussion with Cory. If we were presenting these questions to a scientific audience, hearing them as scientists, in an unemotional, intellectual manner, then I'd say "Fine, let's present them with as complete, unslanted a picture as we can." However, we're not dealing with science—we're dealing with politics.

We are dealing with down-to-earth, grass-roots politics, in the fullest sense of those terms. We are dealing not with people who will or even who can look at these things unemotionally and intellectually, but with prejudiced people who will look at them that way. If you present such people with nine strong points on your side, and one weak point which agrees with their prejudices, the nine points will slide off their minds like water off a duck's back, and they will respond to the tenth by saying "See, he's one of THEM, and even he agrees with me" and they'll leave with their prejudices stronger than ever.

Therefore . . . all that is true should certainly NOT be said, except to VERY, VERY, VERY carefully chosen audiences.

I am no politician—although sometimes I wonder (with some dismay) if I'm not in process of becoming one—but I think that, in principle, any politician will agree with my basic premises here.

Don't give your opponents ammunition to use against you—and in these matters, THEY and THEIR prejudices, NOT you, determine what is and what is not ammunition. You are quite correct, when you say that "there are a thousand techniques of opinion manipulation, etc." I don't think that the presentation of the plain, bold, unvarnished truth to popular audiences is such a technique. . . .

Returning—because you did—again to the question of the turn which the movement is taking, away from "truth" and toward "image making"—that all goes back to what I said above. The movement is maturing and becoming sophisticated enough to realize that it is engaged in a political battle, and in a battle to change people's opinions, and that it is naïve to the point of foolishness to expect or to believe that the plain, unvarnished, full truth is going to gain the ends expected. It never will. We are very conscious of public image in Washington, and we feel, correctly so. We intend to continue to operate in that fashion. It is not a move away from truth, but a move toward a selected presentation of truth—something which, as a scientist, arouses my revulsion, BUT I have to recognize that in this context I am NOT functioning as a scientist, and that to attempt to do so would be the gravest of errors. . . .

Frank

Not long before he wrote the aforementioned letter, Kameny and Nichols had assembled a small group of gay marchers—seven DC Mattachine members—for the historic March on Washington for Jobs and Freedom.[20] Identifying themselves as a gay contingent would have gone against the rules of the March,[21] but Kameny later recalled that he "held a gay rights sign."[22] The day had a profound effect on the Mattachine members. As Nichols listened to King sharing his dream with the nation, he thought to himself that someday gays would have to march for their own civil rights.[23]

Randy Wicker (Charles Hayden Jr.) to Kameny

Wicker continues the wide-ranging discussion of tactics and philosophy, arguing for an approach less accommodating to cultural constraints than Kameny's. Of particular interest here is Wicker's expression of frustration with mental-health-care professionals dealing with homosexuality, including New York psychoanalyst Edmund Bergler, who had described homosexuals as "essentially disagreeable people, regardless of their pleasant or unpleasant manner . . . [which includes] a mixture of superciliousness, false aggression, and whimpering." Bergler had also depicted homosexuals as "subservient when confronted with a stronger person, merciless when in power, unscrupulous about trampling on a weaker person . . . What is most discouraging, you seldom find an intact ego . . . among them."[24] *Wicker also refers to psychologist Albert Ellis, whose clinical work had led him to conclude that exclusive homosexuality was both a phobic reaction to members of the opposite sex and a neurotic fixation on the same sex, and that psychotherapists could help reverse homosexuality in individuals.*[25]

NO DATE [SEPTEMBER 1963]

Frank—

A hurried note in answer to your letter. First of all, our discussion of the lavender button bit is moot in a very real way. At the point where others in the movement choose to be effective politicians and start mapping out a program to educate the public "selectively"—at that point I find myself to be a free-thinker and critic of my fellow crusading homophiles. Maybe in this particular instance I have unearthed a really amazing truth about myself—MAYBE CHARLIE HAYDEN IS A UTOPIAN AFTER ALL . . .

I am OUT of the movement for good. . . .

I cancelled my book contract. Sent them the money back and filed the work I had done in a dusty drawer. I just couldn't get enthused or busy on a book concerning homosexuality. I am sick of the subject for present. Maybe after a few months or years of rest the old concern, drive, vision, and flame will burn brightly once more. Right now I have developed the feelings of "FUCK THIS STUPID WORLD AND THE PEOPLE IN IT WHO THINK STUPIDLY ABOUT SOMETHING AS BASICALLY SIMPLE AS HOMOSEXUALITY." I have a life to live. I want to spend it learning and living with the enlightened, the informed, even the "hippies." I don't want to spend agonizing hours in publishers' offices, magazine offices, pleading like dirt for the right to advertize or trying to rile them into giving something legitimate publicity. I JUST DON'T WANT TO BE BOTHERED. I DON'T WANT TO FIGHT CITY HALL. I WANT TO EAT, SLEEP, FUCK, LIVE! I also want to try writing.

I have come to feel rather strongly that homosexuality is not a problem in itself. It is just one flaw in the defective fabric of a defective society. For instance, last winter *Harper's* magazine ran a terrible article by a psychologist named Arthur Cain on Alcoholics Anonymous. In this piece he criticized AA for being "anti-professional." He went to lengths to show how AA considered itself the only valid authority on alcoholism to the point that he felt it "hampered" legitimate research and its pronouncements became "law" in the field. As I read I couldn't help but think of all us in the homosexual movement who put up with the insipidness of professional men like Bergler, Ellis, etc. (the others are not so colorful but just as uninformed and stupid as a rule).

I had been to a Gambler's Anonymous meeting and was impressed by the same attitude about psychiatrists. No one had been helped by them; those who spoke as authorities usually didn't know what they were talking about; no really valuable research was being done at present. The result was an idea I am pursuing at haste right now. A radio show for WBAI and an article on "THE DOCTOR AND THE SOCIAL PROBLEM: SOMETHING'S WRONG SOMEWHERE!" The panel would consist of Dr. Wainwright Churchill, a member of GA, of Narcotics Anonymous, of A.A. and of Mattachine discussing what the social scientist must do to correct his presently faulty approach in these emotionally laden areas. I think it will be a shocker! . . .

By the way, one thing I would probably like to write some day is the blueprint of the homosexual revolution . . . I mean attempt a type of sexual "Mein Kampf," "Communist Manifesto," etc. No one to my knowledge has yet undertaken it. . . . However, such a book would have to be mimeographed and passed from hand to hand. It would be a bad PR piece for the movement when gotten hold of on the outside . . . For instance, one of its basic assumptions would probably be that homosexuality is a legitimate and rewarding erotic endeavor of the human animal; either as simple physical pleasure or as a new horizon of communication homosexual behavior should be encouraged universally— . . . which would make the rigid, fearful, insecure heterosexuals flip out and really get upset over the movement. In another sense it would be extra bad because most of those now active in the beginning phase of this sexual revolution do not hold these viewpoints on a conscious verbal level. The homosexual today hates himself too much to even seek his own improvement much less to actively fight to carry a new source of physical pleasure and emotional communication into the realm of "accepted" and approved human experience. However, as the years pass and new generations grow up after us they will not be so enchained by these self-deprecatory attitudes. More and more they will grow to hold these viewpoints and as the stigma on homosexual behavior disappears, not only will heterosexuals feel less threatened by it but actual participation will skyrocket. I do not mean that everyone will be homosexual. The exclusive homosexual will always be a minority with some sort of "peculiar status." However, the average heterosexual will take homosexual activity as just a good source of sexual outlet (physical) even if it never gets any real emotional overtones in his mind. Well, I don't want to pursue this farther in written form or I will be getting in general outlines of my own personal philosophy which may or may not leave you gasping. It frequently startles even homosexuals themselves because they lack an objective concept of homosexuality and because of social attitudes they have absorbed from the dominant culture feel "this should not be encouraged." . . .

NEVER NEVER NEVER NEVER NEVER NEVER!!!!
Send anything to my home address at 170 East 2nd Street addressed HOMOSEXUAL LEAGUE OF NEW YORK!! God damn, you people must have mental lapses at times! All the neighbors press around the mailman as he slips the mail in the box and how do you think they would react seeing that going into my mailbox. I have a snoopy landlady as it is who is known to be a meddling nut. I do not want to be known in my building as the queer on the fourth floor and have my apartment raided every time I have a party for over four people!!!! Good God! Use good sense. Send only mail to Charlie Hayden to 170———Randolfe Wicker mail and HLNY stuff ALWAYS, ALWAYS, ALWAYS goes to Box 318 N.Y.C. 9 N.Y. (Be sure to put in the 9 or otherwise it won't ever get to me.)

Again must go . . . give them hell in Washington. Write soon. See you soon.

As always,
Charlie

P.S. Peter just pointed out to me that I did not answer your obvious misunderstanding of my tearoom position. I'm absolutely opposed to tearoom cruising and say that such activity must be curtailed by the police. The public deserves this much etiquette; the non-tearoom cruising homosexual masses should be protected from the unsightly and invalid impression made by public contact with tearoom cruising. I have said that I would have police clean up tearooms the way they cleaned up the meat rack at Washington Square . . . just by going in, clearing their throats and saying "All Right! What's going on in here! Let's break it up." Few visits by a cop like that (without arrests) would make the tearoom off-limits so to speak. Yet no one would really be hurt.

Kameny to Randy Wicker (Charles Hayden Jr.)

In his reply to Wicker, Kameny refers to a convention held by the East Coast Homophile Organizations (ECHO) in Philadelphia on Labor Day weekend of 1963. Kameny was a founding member of the umbrella group, which included MSW, MSNY, the Daughters of Bilitis of New York, and the Janus Society of Philadelphia. The conference was titled "Homosexuality—Time for Reappraisal," and Kameny spoke on "The Homosexual and the U.S. Government." According to Ken Travis, a reporter for Confidential *magazine, "Respectability was the keynote. Everyone was conservatively dressed, the men mostly in Ivy League fashion, the women in dresses or suits. No bottled-in-blond men, limp wrists or lisping here, thank you."[26]*

SEPTEMBER 25, 1963

Dear Charlie,

Thanks for your recent letter—full of "meat" as usual. I'll go over it in the order in which you brought up points, as I usually do. . . .

. . . For us, education is not really what we are seeking to do. As the Negro found out, simple presentation of truth does not eliminate prejudice. It never has. That is what education is. We are seeking to eliminate prejudice. If a certain selection has to be exercised in the facts we present, then we must do so. We are NOT an educational organization; we are a civil liberties organization. What we are engaged in never was education, per se, and is, as I said last time, rapidly becoming politics.

We too have been critical of our fellow homophiles and homophile organizations. We certainly were so, by implication, when we set our own course of evolution toward the civil liberties direction, and away from New York's and San Francisco's education and research direction.

Utopianism is fine, depending upon exactly what you mean by it. As long as you remember that you are, and *always* will be, dealing with very, VERY non-utopian people and situations, both inside and outside the homophile movement, and both inside and outside the homosexual community, and don't try to foist upon them solutions to problems which solutions demand utopian people, you will be all right. Educating people non-selectively, in an attempt to eliminate discrimination and prejudice, is utopian, and won't work. . . .

You commence a paragraph by saying that you are "OUT of the movement for good." You then proceed to discuss activities which indicate that you are neither out of it for the present, nor for good. Which are you?

I can see where you might be temporarily discouraged. No one—or few—wants to fight city hall. However, oft-times city hall needs to be fought; it MUST be done, and this is such a case. The simple fact that you have to plead for the right to give legitimate publicity to something legitimate is reason enough for continuing to fight until you no longer have to plead.

You say, "I have come to feel rather strongly that homosexuality is not a problem in itself. It is just one flaw in the defective fabric of a defective society." . . . If by your second sentence you mean that society's attitudes toward homosexuality constitute a flaw—then I agree with you fully.

You have seen our publication on Discrimination Against the Employment of Homosexuals, and have seen one of our premises there—that homosexuality is not a disease, sickness, ailment, defect, neurosis, psychosis, etc. I stand by that in the fullest possible sense. If you mean not that homosexuality is a flaw, but that society's attitudes toward it are—that, of course, is just what we are fighting about and for.

Some of us in the homophile (not homosexual) movement may put up with the "insipidness of professional men like Berger and Ellis"—I certainly don't. . . .

I think that the major thing wrong is that the professional people tend to make their judgments upon samples limited to those who come to their offices for assistance, and thus in the statistical sense, are sampling extremely poorly, and come out with results based on an atypical group. This is especially true of the homosexual group.

There are other faults too, of course, and one of the primary ones is a seeming inability, on the part of many of the professional people, to pull themselves away from the value judgments of the society around them, with the tie-in of those judgments to classical religion, convention, mores, etc.; and to look upon the ideal as conformity to the purely statistical "norm" rather than as an "adjusted" conformity to one's own self and one's own individuality, as one who is, with the limited assumption that anyone who is not like everyone else is abnormal (in the non-statistical, defective, emotion-laden sense). There is also a tendency to accept certain widespread phenomena (e.g., heterosexuality) as being so "natural" that they do not need exploration or research, that their origins do not need explaining, and that departures from them are automatically pathological. . . .

Your ideas in regard to homosexuality (e.g., that homosexuality is a legitimate and rewarding erotic endeavor—whether for simple pleasure or for communication—etc.) are neither so shocking, so revolutionary nor so unusual as you seem to think. The same things have been said, over and over, and over again, about sex (with the usual implication, I grant, of heterosexuality) for years. That "the homosexual today hates himself too much"—is unfortunately true of a number of homosexuals. It is VERY far from true of a VERY large number of homosexuals. You move in the wrong circles.

Your own personal philosophy on this, as indicated by your remarks, not only doesn't "leave me gasping"—it seems quite ordinary, common-sense, and largely self-evident. As for "this should not be encouraged"—I feel, as I said to Congress, that *any* private sexual acts on the part of adults should be permitted—that this is a matter of personal taste and preference. I feel that pleasure is a perfectly legitimate goal in its own right, as long as it does not involve inflicting displeasure upon others, against their will. As for the "private" and the "adult" part of the above, I have never accepted our society's dictum that sex is something which should be reserved to the state of adulthood—even to the extent of mere knowledge about it. In regard to heterosexual activity, I have long felt that (using a conventional analogy) children should be brought up, from earliest infancy, so that they will no more have sexual relations without using a contraceptive (unless children are specifically wanted) than they would go out of doors without clothes on—then set free to indulge in sex as they choose. As for privacy, this is a slowly changing attitude of society which is insufficiently important, for the present, for me to worry about. Beyond all of that (and most of this page has been on a very minor and unimportant point) I quite agree with you.

When you say, however, that "the average heterosexual will take homosexual activity as just a good source of sexual outlet (physical)"—you get into some interesting questions. I alluded to this in a question which I asked at the Convention. If "pure" physical outlet is desired, masturbation is still the best and easiest method of attainment of it. The moment this becomes something less than fully satisfactory (and that is usually the case) the satisfaction is becoming something more than merely physical—emotional and psychological factors have crept in (and, of course, this is what is usually beyond any seeking for sexual activity outside autoeroticism) and the average heterosexual will NOT take homosexual activity as just a good source of sexual outlet (physical)—any more than the homosexual will take to heterosexual activity. The question still to be answered is why is, and what is the nature of the drive for, satisfaction of the sexual desire in partnership with another person?

Jack Nichols was asking about you this evening.

I guess that's about all for the present. Give my greetings and regards to Peter. Keep in touch.

Frank

Jack Nichols had been collecting studies and opinions challenging American psychiatry's diagnosis of homosexuality as a disease, and in October 1963, at Kameny's urging, Nichols pitched the MSW executive board to make a formal statement declaring that homosexuality was not a sickness:

The mental attitude of our own people toward themselves that they are not well—that they are not whole, that they are LESS THAN COMPLETELY HEALTHY—is responsible for UNTOLD NUMBERS OF PERSONAL TRAGEDIES AND WARPED LIVES. By failing to take a definite stand, a strong stand . . . I believe that you will not only weaken the movement ten-fold, but that you will fail in your duty to homosexuals who need more than anything else to see themselves in a better light.[27]

The board did not immediately follow Nichols's counsel, and so he, Kameny, and MSW member Lilli Vincenz set about lobbying other MSW members, asking them to approve a resolution declaring that homosexuality was not a disease.

The end of 1963 also saw the FBI engaged in an internal discussion, directed by Hoover, about whether CSC was still excluding homosexuals from employment with the federal government. On December 19 an FBI agent drafted a memo indicating that "nothing has come to the Bureau's attention reflecting that the Civil Service has changed its policies with respect to homosexuals."[28] Hoover read the memorandum and directed the FBI's Liaison Section to check on the matter directly with CSC. A day later, Liaison filed a report stating that the MSW had been pressuring CSC in recent months but that CSC "has not changed its basic policy excluding all homosexuals from Government service." Hoover underlined this point when reading the memorandum and handwrote the following notation at the bottom: "They should stick to it—H."[29]

Kameny to Army Secretary Stephen Ailes

Rather than surrendering after his unsuccessful meeting with Lieutenant General Hershey, the head of Selective Service, Kameny simply shifted his efforts into a higher gear by taking his campaign to Stephen Ailes, the Secretary of the Army. Most striking in the following letter is Kameny's statement that he and MSW "are not, at this time, requesting a change in Army policy and practice in regard to homosexuals." In effect, the statement indicates that Kameny was willing at this point to focus on extracting minor victories for homosexuals without challenging the entire system that discriminated against them.

MAY 27, 1964

Dear Mr. Secretary:

We are writing to you on a matter which is of some concern to us, and upon which we have not been able to obtain satisfactory action, or even discussion. The problem is one involving the drafting of homosexuals.

At present, a potential draftee is required to fill out Public Health Service Form 89, which asks him whether or not he has homosexual tendencies. The information supplied on this form, while not available to private persons, is open to various official federal and state government agencies and individuals.

Many homosexual draft-eligibles come to us asking for advice in regard to the answering of this question. We cannot, of course, properly advise them to perjure themselves, and so we have advised those who feel that they can do so, to give a truthful reply, and escape the draft. At the same time, however, citizens cannot be expected to divulge information which is open to those who would do them harm, and many will not do so.

As you are no doubt aware, very close to 100% of homosexual draft-eligibles at present do indeed perjure themselves by answering the question in the negative. They serve well, and receive honorable discharges. However, a significant number of homosexual draftees receive the less-than-fully-honorable discharges which present Army policy unfortunately prescribes. These people should never have been drafted in the first place, and would not have been, had the Army not made it difficult or impossible for them to give a truthful answer to the question of homosexuality asked of them.

We wish to make it clear that we are not, at this time, requesting a change in Army policy and practice in regard to homosexuals, as indicated in AR 635-89 and elsewhere. What we seek is a change in procedure, so that homosexual draft-eligibles can comply with those policies by disqualifying themselves before induction. As long as the information on Public Health Form 89 is open to anyone at all, anywhere in the government, outside those in the Army immediately and directly connected with it, truthful answers to this question cannot and will not be given.

We have discussed this matter, personally and at some length, with General Hershey of the Selective Service System. He referred us to the office of the Surgeon General of the Army. After some dealings with them, we have been referred back to the Selective Service System. No constructive solution to the basic problem has been forthcoming.

If it is necessary to do so, we will take under serious consideration advising people to refuse, totally, to answer the question, upon the grounds that the information is available to improper persons (we consider the FBI, the US Civil Service Commission, and, in fact, anyone else at all, outside a minimal number of Army personnel, as improper, in this context).

This, to us, and to the homosexual community, is a serious question, which involves a large number of American citizens, and which needs serious attention. We do not feel that it deserves to be shrugged off, as it has been, simply because it is a difficult and somewhat delicate one.

We therefore request your assistance in effecting the necessary changes in Army regulations and procedure, to ensure *complete* confidentiality of information on their homosexuality supplied by homosexual draft-eligibles, in order that your present regulations excluding them from the Service may most effectively be implemented.

We will be pleased to meet with you or with any other members of the Department of the Army, in order to discuss this problem.

We look forward to your early reply.

Thank you.

Sincerely yours,
Franklin E. Kameny

The Secretary of the Army did not assist Kameny on this matter.

Charles Hayden Jr. (Randy Wicker) to Kameny

Wicker indicates that he and Kameny had been discussing picketing for homosexual rights, and that the MSW president had suggested picketing the Army headquarters in New York City to target the policy of releasing information about an inductee's homosexuality to employers outside the Army. Wicker also refers to Jefferson Poland of the League for Sexual Freedom in New York City. Founded in 1963 by Poland and Leo Koch, the league focused its efforts on waging campaigns for free love, public nudism, and the repeal of repressive laws regarding human sexuality.

NO DATE (1964)

Frank—

The boy who is in charge of the League for Sexual Freedom called today and he wants to picket. I suggested we picket the Army as you suggested. Right now, we have tentatively scheduled it for sometime in September with his group and the HLNY co-sponsoring the line.

Now WHAT I NEED IS a full statement of fact. (1) A copy of the presidential order (or at least number) (2) procedures we have from the thing you sent me . . . but can use U.S. Army as well (3) we are planning to protest discharge procedures, rather than 'exclusion' since 'exclusion' is actually an advantage for the homosexual.

PLEASE SEND ME ALL THIS INFORMATION . . . SUCCINCTLY STATED AND WELL DOCUMENTED. You might even send a page or (legal page length) statement which we could mimeograph for distribution to the press, etc. when picket line is in session.

I now have a job . . . and this is being typed hurriedly at home. I hope you will respond quickly and adequately so we can crystallize our plans and get them underway.

As always,

Charlie

Hayden followed through on his note, and on September 19, 1964, he and Poland led a small group of picketers in front of the Whitehall Street Induction Center in New York City. Their purpose, stated in flyers they handed out to pedestrians, was to protest the Army's policy of releasing records indicating a draftee's homosexuality. The picketers attracted no media attention, but their pioneering action left them excited about similar possibilities in the future.[30]

MSW to the FBI

One of MSW's early ventures was the publication of its own newsletter—the Gazette. *Kameny and his MSW colleagues decided to mail their newsletter not only to their own members and other interested parties but also to the president, the attorney general, Supreme Court justices, members of Congress and the president's cabinet, and J. Edgar Hoover. On July 20, 1964, FBI Agent DeLoach wrote an internal memorandum protesting Hoover's name on the mailing list:*

The above Society has apparently added the Director to its mailing list to receive its "Gazette," a newsletter for homosexuals.

This Society attempts to legalize the activities of homosexuals and carries on an active campaign to have these persons admitted to employment in the United States Government and elsewhere.

This material is disgusting and offensive and it is believed a vigorous objection to the addition of the Director to its mailing list should be made.

DeLoach concluded his memorandum with a recommendation that two FBI agents "contact the president of this group to advise him in strong terms that Mr. Hoover objects to receiving this material and his name should immediately be removed from their mailing list." Hoover did indeed object and made a handwritten notation at the end of the memorandum: "Right—H."

The FBI contacted Kameny on August 6, and on the following afternoon Kameny and *Gazette* editor Robert King met with two agents at the Bureau's headquarters in downtown Washington. The agents promptly informed Kameny and King "that the presence of Mr. Hoover's name on their mailing list is considered offensive" and then requested that the director's name be deleted from the MSW list. Kameny and King replied by saying "that their purpose in sending such material to governmental officials such as the Director was to attempt to influence these officials to become more understanding of the aims of their group." Kameny added that MSW members had a "great interest in seeing that their civil rights are protected, stating that they have a right to communicate with government officials in an attempt to gain sympathy for their cause." Nevertheless, Kameny and King did not outright deny the agents' request but rather agreed to take it back to the MSW executive board and to follow the board's decision. The meeting lasted less than ten minutes but not before King invited Hoover (through the agents) to attend a homophile convention to be held in Washington. "This invitation was emphatically and immediately declined," according to an FBI memorandum.[31]

In its meeting about the FBI request, the MSW executive board decided to remove Hoover's name from the mailing list if the director personally assured MSW, in writing, that the FBI had destroyed all files about the MSW. Gail Johnson, the secretary of MSW, communicated this decision in an October 1 letter to the Bureau.

In an internal memorandum on Johnson's letter, FBI Agent M. A. Jones wrote: "This letter is a blatant attempt to open a controversy with the Bureau. Any further contact with them will be exploited to the Bureau's

*disadvantage. It is apparent they are attempting to involve government offi-
cials in their program for recognition and any further contact by the Bureau
will only serve their ulterior motives."*[32] *Jones recommended that the FBI not
acknowledge Johnson's letter, and his recommendation was approved and
followed. The FBI did not reply to Johnson, and Hoover continued to receive
the* Gazette.

Kameny to the Editors of the *Washington Daily News*

*On October 7, 1964, two officials with the Morals Division of the Wash-
ington Metropolitan Police Department arrested Walter Jenkins, special
assistant to President Johnson, on charges of disorderly conduct—"indecent
gestures," as the police report described it.*[33] *The police officers had witnessed
Jenkins in a homosexual encounter at the YMCA located just a few blocks
from the White House, and Jenkins resigned as special assistant not long
after news of his arrest landed on the front pages of a national newspaper.
Charged by Johnson with filing a report on the incident, J. Edgar Hoover
reported that the FBI investigation had uncovered no information that Jenkins had "compromised the security or interests of the United States in any
manner." Hoover's report also noted that during the FBI's interview with
Jenkins, the presidential assistant insisted that "he would lay down his life
before he would disclose any information that would damage the best interests of the United States."*[34]

OCTOBER 25, 1964

Gentlemen:

The FBI has given Walter Jenkins a "clean bill of health" on security
matters. If there is anyone in this country who is now totally invulnerable
to threats of blackmail and other improper coercion, and who obviously
fully deserves a security clearance at the highest level, it is Walter Jenkins.
No one has questioned whether the quality of Mr. Jenkins' performance
of his duties in this White House position was of the very highest. His
unfortunate lapse of good judgment (in properly logical evaluation, it was
no more than just a lapse of good judgment, and, of itself, caused hurt or
harm to no one) occurred on his own time, in the course of his private
life. It is thus clear that there was and is no valid reason for Walter Jenkins

to have left his White House post, and very good reason for him to have remained.

Therefore, it seems absolutely plain that for the good of all concerned—nation, government, President, and Jenkins—the only proper course of action which can be taken by President Johnson is for him to re-appoint Walter Jenkins to the same post as that from which he has just resigned, and to do so promptly.

By so doing, President Johnson will have, thereby, indicated clearly his ability to take action which is based upon reason, in the best American tradition, and upon the public good, and not based upon mob-type emotionalism, or upon folklore and prejudice.

Sincerely yours,

Franklin E. Kameny

On the same day he wrote the aforementioned letter, Kameny also fired off a missive to Carl Shipley, chairman of the District of Columbia Republican Committee. Shipley had recently squared off in a debate over the Jenkins case at a meeting of the district chapter of the Federal Bar Association. In the heated debate, Shipley referred to Jenkins as a "sex pervert" and, wondering aloud how many more perverts held positions in the White House, depicted homosexuals as snakes, saying "where there is one there is a nest of them."[35] *After reading the news report of the debate, Kameny wrote Shipley a damning letter, excerpted here:*

> *Your characterization of Mr. Jenkins as a pervert is malicious. Your characterizations of homosexuals as "nests of perverts," etc., are gratuitous insults to the many tens of thousands of respectable, responsible, reputable, loyal, moral homosexual citizens of the District of Columbia, and to the 15,000,000 homosexual citizens of the United States. . . .*
>
> *You have presented no slightest indication of any reason for not retaining Walter Jenkins at his post—he was a dedicated public servant who did his job exceedingly well; logically, what else is important, after all? His "crime," in and of itself, caused neither hurt nor harm to anyone, and it can be disputed whether it was an act of immorality, and whether it ought to have been a crime at all. . . .*
>
> *Past government approaches to this matter have, traditionally, been of a viciously destructive and repressive nature. The homosexual community, for*

whom I am a spokesman, is rapidly losing patience with such approaches, and—with increasing support from important voices in the community-at-large—is demanding a constructive approach, consistent with basic American principles—including Mr. Goldwater's principles—of individual personal freedom, and the individual dignity of EVERY citizen, including the homosexual citizen.[36]

Four days after Kameny sent the aforementioned letter, the FBI's Washington field office sent Hoover a copy of a pamphlet that Kameny had authored and distributed—"How to Handle Federal Interrogations." According to the accompanying memorandum sent to Hoover, the pamphlet "had been obtained by an undercover investigator of one of the Armed Forces acting under the instructions of his supervisors."[37]

Kameny's document detailed the type of advice he was giving to the many homosexuals who sought his counsel after being denied or fired from federal employment. If interrogated about their homosexuality, Kameny counseled, admit nothing and instead say: "These are matters which are of no proper concern to the federal government of the United States under any circumstances whatever."[38] *Or, as he summarized this advice in a later letter, "Say Nothing; Sing Nothing; Get Counsel; Fight Back."*[39]

Kameny took his federal interrogation pamphlet, as well as one titled "What to Do If You Are Arrested," and placed them in holders marked "Take One!" all over the State Department and the Pentagon.[40]

Kameny to OEO Director Sargent Shriver

On November 20, 1964, Lewis Eiger, a director in the job corps program of the Office of Economic Opportunity (OEO), announced that the OEO would ban boys with homosexual tendencies from admission into job corps camps established as part of the government's anti-poverty campaign.[41] *Kameny responded to this announcement by writing an inflamed letter to OEO director Sargent Shriver, one of the most liberal members of the Johnson administration.*

NOVEMBER 28, 1964

Dear Mr. Shriver:

I write as a homosexual American citizen—with equal emphasis upon all three words.

I have just learned . . . that boys with homosexual tendencies will be excluded from youth camps planned by the Office of Economic Opportunity in the federal anti-poverty program.

As a taxpayer, I wish to place upon the record the strongest possible protest, and my sense of outrage against this discriminatory administration of the proceeds of the taxes which I and 15,000,000 other homosexual American citizens help pay. I question the legality of such discrimination.

Have you decided to read us completely out of American society? Have you decided to reduce us to a status of no-class citizenship? Is President Johnson's Great Society to be restricted to the favored few? Just what is going on here?

We have heard much, in the past four years, about the elimination of prejudice and discrimination against our nation's minorities, and about the "fact" that we do not have second-class citizenship in this country. Yet you are reducing the members of the nation's largest minority group after the Negro to a clearly second-class status.

I placed my life in jeopardy, in front-line combat, under enemy fire, in World War II. I did not do so in order that the government for which I fought could label me and my kind as unworthy of equality with all other citizens, and as worthy only of unrelieved poverty and of being ignored and written off as worthless.

Genocide is an ugly word, but when you systematically exclude all relevant members of a large class of the citizenry from a chance to raise themselves from a starvation level, genocide is the word that must be used.

I note, in addition, in the *Times* article, that we are placed in a class with criminals, narcotics addicts, and other such. I am a Physicist, with a Ph.D. in Astronomy from Harvard University. I am contributing to the society in which I live. I am a responsible, reputable, respectable citizen. As a homosexual American citizen, I and my fellow homosexual American citizens resent being placed in the company in which your Dr. Lewis D. Eiger has placed us.

I think that you and others in the Government had better start coming to grips with this question in a constructive fashion. Such an approach, rather than the traditional destructive, repressive, "look the other way," ostrich-like "sweep the matter under the rug" approach embodied in your policies in this instance, is long overdue.

If I and my fellow homosexual American citizens, because of our homosexuality, are not going to receive benefits from our taxes equal to those received by all other citizens, perhaps we should cease paying our full taxes.

I am not politically naïve, and I recognize that this is a difficult and delicate political question, but to allow political expediency to result in systematically denying to some needy citizens that succor which their fellow needy citizens are receiving, is barbaric. We are not prepared to be "sold down the river" in this fashion.

A large number of citizens are irate about this. I have no wish to threaten, but I feel that you should realize that a major public issue is in the making unless a suitable solution for this matter is arrived at. We do not desire to create difficulties for the administration and for the anti-poverty program—very much the contrary—but this sort of discrimination cannot be tolerated.

I will be pleased to discuss this matter personally with you.

Your early reply is requested and expected.

Thank you.

> Sincerely yours.
>
> Franklin E. Kameny

Unlike many other government officials, Shriver sent Kameny a reply:

The set of medical examination standards used by the Job Corps is a modified version of the induction standards applicable to candidates for the U.S. Armed Forces. Such instances where Job Corps standards are less restrictive than those of the Army are based on practical consideration, for instance, the Job Corps need not exclude persons of unusual height, weight, or body build, because the Job Corps does not need to fit its trainees in uniforms or place them in situations where unusual height or weight would be a danger to them.

But the living situation in the Job Corps and the Armed Forces have important attributes in common. Our panel of medical consultants, assembled from each of the Armed Forces, the U.S. Public Health Service, and other

agencies, has chosen not to recommend any variance from Armed Forces stan-
dards concerning homosexuality. We have no reason to doubt that this is the
best advice available.[42]

The end of 1964 saw a battle for the presidency of the MSW, with
Kameny pitted against Robert Belanger. Part of the issue fueling Belanger's
candidacy was Kameny's heavy-handed and abrasive leadership style; some
within MSW found him to be dictatorial rather than democratic. Kameny
waged his campaign with support from key MSW members, but Belanger
won the race and became MSW president for the 1965 term. Although
he lost the presidency, Kameny continued to play an activist role within
MSW—and to act with his characteristically abrasive style.

The MSW founder could indeed be harsh in his judgments of people,
and this became clearly evident as he and Jack Nichols grew apart in the
following year. Feeling Nichols was making a grab for power that would
undermine him within MSW and the wider movement, Kameny wrote an
especially negative assessment of Nichols (Warren Adkins):

> *Warren, I feel, does not measure up to "snuff" whether in stability, in intellect,*
> *or reasoning power. Virtually all of his ideas have come from me, and there*
> *is not an important letter that he writes, if it deals with ideas, which he does*
> *not submit to me over the phone first. He does not think things through, and*
> *doesn't see the interrelationships between things, nor does he, himself, have a*
> *good feeling for strategy at the philosophical level . . . He has poor judgment in*
> *many matters where judgment is important. He occasionally comes through*
> *with excellence, but only occasionally. His lack of college education shows*
> *through in many ways.*[43]

3

"We Have Outgrown the 'Closet-Queen' Type of Approach"

1965

Kameny to U.S. Senate Chaplain Frederick Brown Harris

Kameny takes issue with a commentary penned by U.S. Senate Chaplain Frederick Brown Harris. Harris argued that the church and wider society had been emphasizing "causes and enterprises and social crusades" to the neglect of individual spirituality and morality. "The keynote seems to be, not regeneration, but acceptation," he wrote.

> *This attempt to disregard the YOU . . . is illustrated in the present propaganda, even over television and radio, to stop even in decent society what is called discrimination of sex deviates and perverts who are addicted to disgusting practices which are not only degrading to those guilty, but whose abnormal debaucheries so often blight the lives of youth.*[1]

MARCH 13, 1965

Dear Dr. Harris:

. . . I write as a *moral* person. That my morality may, perhaps, be not quite the same as yours is not relevant. Men of good will may differ on matters of morality, as upon all other matters.

I resent, strongly, the implication of your statements that I am not a decent person, nor fit to be accepted in decent society. I AM a decent person, acceptable in any society in which you are acceptable, including that of your fellow clergymen—and acceptable AS a homosexual.

You seem to take exception to our call for an end to discrimination. Can you truly justify the denial of jobs, of livelihood, of opportunity, of a chance to contribute to the society around him to a man simply because he chooses to love one of his own sex rather than one of the opposite sex? I have starved (that is meant literally, and not merely as a figure of speech) because of the discrimination brought to bear by society against homosexuals. Can you, as an alleged Christian, truly defend this?

Can you truly defend the directing of contempt, derision, ridicule, and scorn against *any* human being? Can you truly defend placing a human being in second-class status, simply because he chooses to love in a manner other than that in which you do? I truly believe that Christ would not have defended your doing so. . . .

I do not find our sexual practices disgusting, degrading, degenerate, nor nauseating—no more so than *yours* are. If you find our practices not to your liking, you are free to abstain from them, as we do from yours, but you are *not* free, in propriety, to condemn these practices, or us. . . .

I resent being called a moral leper. I have a carefully devised moral code, to which I adhere closely. It is quite as good a code as is yours. One of the precepts of that code states that an act is not immoral if it does not cause hurt or harm to others, or interfere with them against their will; and that, given the preceding, an act is moral, in a positive and real sense, if it also brings happiness, pleasure, satisfaction, fulfillment, love, affection, to those participating in it. Under this, I must classify homosexuality, and private consenting homosexual acts—for those choosing voluntarily to engage in them—as being moral, NOT immoral, and as being good, and right, and desirable.

I feel that "what is inside" DOES matter, and that what is inside me and my fellow homosexuals is as good and as fine, and as noble as that which is inside you and your fellow heterosexuals. . . .

Without in any way intending to be disrespectful to religion, or blasphemous, or sacrilegious, I must say that I feel that Jesus would not agree with your statements. I feel that he would approve of a love between two men as he would of a love between a man and a woman—and I mean, in both cases, a love involving physical sexual acts as an important part of its expression.

I feel that you have chosen to follow the spirit of the harsh, un-loving, austere, intolerant, neurotic, near-psychotic Paul, rather than the spirit of the gentle, tolerant, loving Jesus.

I feel that in the most basic senses of the terms, you are a profoundly immoral, deeply un-Christian, and basically un-American person.

I suggest that you give some careful re-consideration to these questions, keeping in mind that there is, indeed, another side to the matter; that we are not evil, vile monsters interested in naught but the satisfaction of our own lust, but fellow human beings of yours, entitled to find our own way as human beings; to make the best lives for ourselves as best we may—true to our own selves—and to contribute as best we may, and are allowed to do, to making the best, happiest, and most contented lives for our fellow human beings, as for ourselves.

One of the prime Christian virtues is charity; another is compassion. I strongly suggest that you use them both to temper your viewpoint toward this question and to us. . . .

> Most sincerely yours,
> Franklin E. Kameny

Kameny to the Editors of *Science News Letter*

In his 1962 book on homosexuality, New York psychoanalyst Irving Bieber stated that "all psychoanalytic theories assume that homosexuality is psychopathologic."[2] The unqualified claim was erroneous, but it did accurately reflect Bieber's fundamental disagreement with Sigmund Freud's belief that environmental and constitutional factors accounted for the presence of homosexuality in adults. For Bieber, homosexuality was the result not of one's biological constitution but of "exposure to highly pathologic parent-child relationships and early life situations."[3] He also held that all homosexuals are "latent heterosexuals," and that psychiatric treatment could help heterosexuality to reemerge in the stunted psychosexual lives of homosexuals.[4]

Kameny refers below to both Bieber and Philadelphia psychiatrist Samuel Hadden, who had recently derided homosexual groups that "resent every suggestion that homosexuals are sick" and "foster an education program designed to make homosexuality a socially acceptable pattern of behavior." After sounding this warning to his fellow psychotherapists, Hadden also spoke of "a growing body of evidence that the homosexual pattern of sexual adjustment is but a symptom and is associated with other neurotic and characterological disorders in a high percentage of cases."[5]

In stating his disagreement with Bieber and Haddon, Kameny refers to Evelyn Hooker, whose 1957 study of homosexuals who were not already in therapy concluded that there was no necessary correlation between homosexuals and mental disorders. Some homosexuals are "severely disturbed," Hooker argued, while others "may be very ordinary individuals, indistinguishable from ordinary individuals who are heterosexual." And still others are "quite superior individuals not only devoid of pathology . . . but also functioning at a superior level."[6]

Kameny's argument below follows closely on the heels of MSW's decision on March 4, 1965, to adopt the following policy statement that Kameny, along with fellow MSW leaders Jack Nichols and Lilli Vincenz, had drafted and lobbied for:

> *The Mattachine Society of Washington takes the position that in the absence of valid evidence to the contrary, homosexuality is not a sickness, disturbance, or other pathology in any sense, but is merely a preference, orientation, or propensity, on par with, and not different in kind from, heterosexuality.[7]*

MARCH 13, 1965

Gentlemen:

I write in response to the article entitled "Homosexuals Need Help," which appeared in your issue of February 13, 1965, on page 102.

I write as (1) a homosexual; (2) one of the leaders of the homophile movement, so strongly condemned by Dr. Hadden; and (3) a scientist by profession (B.S. in physics; M.A. and Ph.D. in astronomy).

Dr. Hadden, like many of his professional colleagues, makes a number of unproven statements about homosexuals and the nature of homosexuality. I have read widely in the "scientific" literature on homosexuality. I have seen only theories and mere assertions—unverified, undemonstrated, unsubstantiated—that homosexuality is a sickness or disturbance. I have seen no scientifically acceptable evidence, anywhere, that homosexuality is a disturbance, sickness, disorder, neurosis, or other pathology of any sort.

What we find, instead, is (1) conclusions drawn from clearly biased and non-representative samplings—i.e., the patients who come to a psychiatrist's office, and who would not be there did they not have problems in regard to their homosexuality, and, hence, are no more representative of homosexuals generally; and (2) the drawing from studies of "conclusions" which were inserted as assumptions. One of the most flagrant examples of this—but quite representative of what is done over and over again—occurs in the widely publicized study by Dr. Hadden's colleague, Dr. Bieber. Dr. Bieber states, near the outset of his book, that (emphasis supplied here): All psychoanalytic theories ASSUME that adult homosexuality is—pathological." Obviously, if one assumes that homosexuality is pathological, then one will discover that homosexuals are sick. . . .

To my knowledge, there has been only one published professional investigation in which the homosexuals studied were explicitly those who had NOT—ever—come under psychotherapy of any sort. This study (by Dr. Evelyn Hooker) showed no difference, outside their homosexuality itself, . . . between the homosexuals studied and a comparable group of heterosexuals.

Dr. Hadden and others make much of alleged "cures" for homosexuality—"change" or "conversion" might be a better word. However, from neither him nor his colleagues do we see any meaningful evidence of systematic follow-up. When we are presented with instances of allegedly permanent changes, we are told nothing of whether the individual was typical of the homosexual community, or whether, as is much more likely, he was bisexual or otherwise atypical, and confused at the outset.

Much more important—are these "changed" people truly happier, more productive, and more useful to self and to society as heterosexuals than as homosexuals? Was the change—even if successful—worth the trouble? Or did it merely provide income for Dr. Hadden and his associates? Has the changed individual really accomplished anything more than merely to achieve submission to the demands of a rigidly conformist society? Dr. Hadden and his colleagues do not address themselves to questions such as these.

To say, as your headline does, "Homosexuals Can be Cured" is like saying "Jews Can be Converted." Left unanswered are the basic questions involved in the right of a human being not to be forced to be like everyone else, and to be free of pressures to conform just for the sake of conformity. If they are not sick—and clearly they are not—why should they change or be changed?

As a scientist, I find much of the work published by Dr. Hadden and his colleagues to be appallingly bad science—shabby, shoddy, slipshod, slovenly, with complete disregard for basic scientific logic and method. . . .

Sincerely yours,

Franklin Kameny

By the end of the year, Kameny was telling Dick Leitsch of MSNY that "IF society calls homosexuality a sickness (and it does) then the entire validity of our entire position, of our demands for equality, of everything for which we stand rests upon our responding to that sickness allegation with a denial. . . . I do repeat: A position denying that homosexuality is a sickness, disturbance, pathology, etc., etc. is the single MOST important position which can be taken, at the present time, by the homophile movement and its individual member organizations."[8]

Kameny to Edward Sagarin

In the early spring of 1965, the Mattachine Society of New York (MSNY) saw the emergence of young militants—namely, Julian Hodges and Dick Leitsch—pushing for direct-action campaigns designed to win civil rights for homosexuals. Opposing these militants was an older guard of MSNY leaders who preferred the method of "helping the individual homosexual adjust to society."[9] Edward Sagarin, author of The Homosexual in America, *was a key leader of the older guard. Kameny had found Sagarin's book pioneering in its approach, but by the time he wrote the letter below, the MSW leader had begun expressing frustration with Sagarin's more recent claims that homosexuality was a sickness and that homosexual militants like Kameny were ignoring credible scientific studies.*

APRIL 7, 1965

Dear Ed:

I am writing because I was very disturbed to learn that you and others boycotted the fundraising dinner of the Mattachine Society of New York, and not only boycotted it yourselves, but induced others to do so, as well. I, along with many others, with whom I've discussed this, find your action deeply offensive.

I realize that there are differences—some of them rather great and intensely felt—between you and those presently in control of the Society. I realize, too, that the present leadership of the Society are by no means paragons of total virtue, utterly without fault—nor would one expect any human leadership so to be.

Nevertheless, it seems obvious that the Society itself must come first, and that reasonable men will work within the existing framework, rather than to seek to destroy or to disable it, as you seem to be trying to do.

I feel that this boycott was a profoundly immoral act, which clearly indicates that those participating in it have anything but the best interests of the homophile movement at heart.

You do not advance the homophile movement by seeking to destroy or to impede the efforts of a hardworking, reputable homophile organization, simply because you do not agree with its leadership and emphases. Surely I ought not to have to tell you that!

You have justly earned the title of "The Father of the Homophile Movement." I know that you are not without pride in the appellation, and properly so. What you have done in the past is enormously to your credit; we *are* deeply indebted to you. You *can* contribute a great deal more.

However, I have watched, increasingly unhappily as—over the past several years—you have fallen by the waysides; as you have, in the eyes of very many in the movement, lost most of your effectiveness, by falling out of tune with the movement—it being the movement, and not you, which has kept up with the times; as the movement—having, now, a strong life of its own—has moved past you, leaving you behind, as your attitudes and approaches—so well-suited to the early days of the movement—have not kept up with a movement changing so rapidly, internally, in response to external changes which, in significant measure were precipitated by that movement (and by you) that even those in the forefront—as you, by your own actions and positions, no longer are—sometimes cannot keep up; as you have left the mainstream for the backwaters; as you have gotten yourself associated with bad company; . . . until now, you have become no longer the vigorous Father of the Homophile Movement, to be revered, respected, and listened to, but the senile Grandfather of the Homophile Movement, to be humored and tolerated, at best; to be ignored and disregarded, usually; and to be ridiculed, at worst.

This need not have happened; it is not irreparable. But the repair must come—or at least start—from you. You have indeed become alienated from the movement which you fathered; most of us feel that the alienation is, essentially, of your doing. I find that alienation deplorable.

There is SO much that you can do FOR us. At present, whatever you may consider it to be, you are only working against us.

This boycott, while in itself, only a minor act, is indicative of, and fully consistent with, the directions and approaches—obstructionist, destructive, above all, unprogressive—which you have adopted, of late.

I am writing this without animosity, hostility, or antagonism, and in a feeling of personal friendship—and with great sorrow that events should have taken the turn which they have. However, the clock cannot be turned back; either you keep up with the movement, or you will be dropped by the wayside—as is indeed now in the process of happening.

Please, for the sake of the movement which you have done so much to start, reconsider the issues involved in your position and approaches on some of the vital questions affecting a vitally alive movement.

Most sincerely,

Frank

In the MSNY election in May 1965, the young militants—Julian Hodges (candidate for president) and Dick Leitsch (candidate for vice president)—captured the vote, precipitating the quick exit of Sagarin and other old-guard members. As Kameny recounted the results in a letter to Barbara Gittings, "The vote seemed to represent a clear mandate for our views, and a clear defeat for the conservatives, the 'closet queens,' and Cory's sickniks."[10] The latter phrase referred to Sagarin's (pseudonym, Donald Webster Cory) insistence that homosexuality was not psychologically healthy. In the same election, Kameny was elected to the MSNY board, testifying to his influence beyond Washington, DC.

Kameny to Barbara Gittings

Kameny had long been talking with MSW and MSNY members about the possibility of public demonstrations for homosexual rights, and on April 16, 1965, just three days before he wrote the aforementioned letter, he had received calls from Randy Wicker (Charles Hayden Jr.) of the Homosexual League and MSW member Jack Nichols about staging picket lines in New York and Washington. Recent news coverage on Fidel Castro's plans to put homosexuals into labor camps precipitated the calls.[11]

Kameny was "dubious" about picketing in Washington. "There's no Cuban embassy," he thought, and "it seemed to stretch logic to picket the White House of the US government to protest an action taken by the Cuban government." But Nichols and his lover, Lige Clarke, were insistent, and Kameny eventually relented, saying he would support picketing the White House "if the Cuban issue and our own grievances could be suitably combined." Kameny then called MSNY members and "told them to picket at the Cuban mission to the UN."[12]

Kameny immediately began crafting the pickets' message to target discrimination against homosexuals in both Cuba and the United States, and Nichols and Clarke began stenciling the pickets and rounding up activists to march at the White House the following day.

On April 17, 1965, ten well-dressed picketers, carrying carefully stenciled pickets, demonstrated on the sidewalk in front of the White House to protest the persecution of homosexuals in Cuba and especially the United States. The neatly lettered placards included the following messages: "15 Million U.S. Homosexuals Protest Federal Treatment"; "Governor Wallace Met with Negroes, Our Government Won't Meet With Us"; "Cuba's Government Persecutes Homosexuals, U.S. Government Beat Them to It"; We Want: Federal Employment, Honorable Discharges, Security Clearances"; "U.S., Cuba, Russia, United to Persecute Homosexuals"; and "U.S. Claims No Second Class Citizens: What About Homosexuals?"[13]

Dear Barbara:

. . .

NEWS NEWS NEWS NEWS NEWS NEWS NEWS NEWS
NEWS NEWS

HISTORY IN THE MAKING ** HISTORY IN THE MAKING **
HISTORY IN THE MAKING

I'm writing this, very very wearily, and very very contentedly, after returning from home following a ten-person picketing—officially by the Mattachine Society of Washington—of the White House. There were 7 men and 3 women.

While, on two instances (by the same lone person, about a year apart) the White House has been picketed, in our cause, by one person alone, this is the first time that there has been any kind of mass picketing, and the first time by a homophile organization.[14] . . .

Because there were several tens of thousands of students in Washington today to picket against the Vietnam War, we had to schedule our demonstration after they were out of the way. As it came off, it ran from 4:20 to 5:20 PM. We were given a choice spot, directly in front of the White House. The police—both White House police and Metropolitan police—were courteous and helpful. The police had been informed in advance. The newspapers had also been informed in advance. . . .

Fondly,

Frank

While the demonstration attracted the attention of hundreds of tourists, some of whom took pictures, the only press to cover the event (other than MSW and MSNY publications) was the Washington Afro-American. *Despite the lack of national media attention, however, the event was historic. As the* Eastern Mattachine Magazine, *a joint publication of MSNY and MSW, described it: "It was the first demonstration in the nation's capital by a homophile organization for the rights and liberties of homosexual citizens."*[15]

The following day, Easter Sunday, twenty-nine picketers from MSNY, the Demophile Center of Boston, the Homosexual League of New York, and the League for Sexual Freedom marched from the MSNY offices on Broadway, up Fifth Avenue (where the Easter parade was in full bloom), and across town to the United Nations. Targeting Castro's policy, the picketers' signs included the following messages: "15,000,000 U.S. Homosexual Citizens Protest Cuba's Actions"; "Labor Camps Today—Ovens Tomorrow?"; and "Individual Freedom—Si! Persecution—No!" The demonstrators marched for two hours, also handing out flyers protesting the Cuban government's treatment of homosexuals. A passerby wearing a mink stole and an Easter bonnet remarked: "You know, when you're as disliked as homosexuals, it takes a lot of guts to stand up for your rights."[16]

Kameny was not satisfied with the publicity given to the White House demonstration. He recalled, "We wanted another crack at it, with publicity, so we started planning right away for another picket in six weeks."[17] Kameny began to chair MSW's new Committee on Picketing and Other Lawful Demonstrations, drafting guidelines and rules for the pickets, and writing press releases for the next White House march. And on May 29, thirteen protestors picketed the White House once again, their placards targeting discriminatory policies in the U.S. government ("Government Should Combat Prejudice, Not Submit to It and Promote It").[18] This time, the national press paid attention, and wire stories by AP and UPI appeared in newspapers across the country, including the New York Times, *the* Washington Star, *and the* Chicago Sun-Times.

New York activist Craig Rodwell was at the second march and suggested the protesters keep the momentum going by marching every Fourth of July in front of Independence Hall in Philadelphia. "We can call it the Annual Reminder—the reminder that a group of Americans still don't have their basic rights to life, liberty, and the pursuit of happiness," Rodwell stated.[19] Kameny, Nichols, and the other marchers readily agreed and started plans for the first Annual Reminder in July 1966.

A couple of weeks after the second White House protest, Kameny referred to himself as "the prime moving force in these demonstrations," while at the same time noting that the "actual spark" had come from others (namely, Wicker in New York and Clarke and Nichols in Washington).[20]

Kameny to the Editors of the *Christian Century*

In 1964, Ted McIlvenna, a Methodist minister and director of the denomination's Young Adult Project in San Francisco, became concerned about the divide he sensed between Christian churches and the young gays and lesbians he met during the course of his work—not only those on the street but also those who were leaders in budding homophile organizations, like the Daughters of Bilitis, the Mattachine Society, the League for Civic Education, and the Tavern Guild.

McIlvenna decided to do something about the yawning gap, and after consulting with his denomination's national offices, he and local leaders of the Daughters of Bilitis (Del Martin and Phyllis Lyon) helped organize a consultation that included representatives from homophile organizations, mainstream churches in San Francisco (Methodist, Lutheran, Episcopalian, and the United Church of Christ), and even national bodies like the National Council of Churches. The result was a meeting of twenty-nine men and women—lesbian, gay, and straight—at a retreat center outside of San Francisco from May 31 to June 2, 1964, with the intention of strategizing about ways to deepen the churches' understanding of homosexuality and strengthen the relationship between churches and homosexuals.[21] The group decided to give permanence to their efforts by forming the Council on Religion and the Homosexual.

In reporting on this development, the Christian Century, *the voice of mainstream Protestantism in the United States, offered the following assessment: "When homosexuality proves to be an incurable aberration, the victim needs the concern of the church as he seeks to accommodate himself to a society which considers him alien. And in those cases where the homosexual can be helped to develop a normal sexuality, the church should be for him both a guide and a strength."[22]*

APRIL 18, 1965

Gentlemen:

I saw, recently, a copy of the article "Clergy Shatter Another Taboo," which appeared on Page 1581 of the December 23, 1964 issue of the *Christian Century*. I write as a homosexual, active in similar work with the clergy here in Washington.

I agree fully with your article except for the final phrase ("those homosexuals who can be restored to a sexual life of the kind approved by the Christian church"). I feel—we feel—that it is the basic disapproval of a homosexual way of life by the Christian church which needs re-examination—by the Christian churches.

It seems to me that, except in a rigid, inflexible, fundamentalist, formalistic, traditionalistic sense, there is nothing un-Christian or incompatible with Christianity in a sexual life which is homosexual. Homosexuality carries with it the same expression of love and affection which heterosexuality does. Surely, in the most essential meaning of Christianity, as a way of life, there can be nothing un-Christian in a love between two men or two women, manifested sexually, as in other ways, just as there is nothing un-Christian in such a love between a man and a woman.

I enclose a news release reporting the first of a series of conferences taking place here in Washington between representatives of the homosexual community and representatives of the clergy of all three major faiths.

It should be pointed out that the approach by the homosexuals was *not* in terms of "rehabilitation" or change from homosexuality to heterosexuality, but in terms of the moral right of the consenting homosexuals to be homosexuals and to practice their homosexuality—and to do so as full, participating members of society, of the community at large, and of the religious communities, bodies, and congregations.

Constant pressure upon the homosexual to convert to heterosexuality is as much resented—and properly so—by the homosexual, as is pressure to convert to Christianity resented by the Jew. Each has the moral right to pursue his own way of life as long as he does not cause hurt or harm to others—and the homosexual does not—nor seek to impose his way of life upon others unwilling to accept it—and the homosexual does not. The homosexual human being does not wish to—and is not going to—enter the churches as the object of a campaign to convert him to a heterosexual way of life which, for him, is alien. . . .

The homosexual community feels strongly the position of outcasts into which they have been placed by organized religion, but we insist that we have the moral right to expect to be accepted by organized religion *as homosexuals*, as first-class human beings on equal status with other human beings, entitled to full respect for our dignity and for the integrity of our individual personalities, of which our homosexuality is an integral part.

Heartening progress is being made on this problem here in Washington.

Sincerely yours,

Franklin E. Kameny

Kameny to the Daughters of Bilitis

Not all homophile groups were pleased with the picketing in Washington and New York, and after a majority of ECHO delegates voted in favor of picketing for civil liberties, two disappointed members of the Daughters of Bilitis (DOB) in New York, Meredith Grey and Shirley Willer, sought counsel from the DOB national board. The board instructed Grey and Willer that picketing was a violation of DOB policy, and the two women asked ECHO to support a resolution to not form policies that were contrary to those of particular organizations within ECHO. After the motion failed on June 6, Grey and Willer took steps to cut formal ties between ECHO and DOB. Two days later, Kameny writes the following retort to DOB's president and governing board.

JUNE 8, 1965

Ladies:

I write this letter in NO official capacity, but merely as an active member of the homophile movement, who sees taking place things which sadden me, and which I am trying to bring to the attention of those with whom the remedy lies, in the hope that something constructive will be done. In any formal sense, I speak for myself alone; informally, my views are those of a number of others, including some DOB members.

I am writing in regard to two closely related matters having to do with the Daughters of Bilitis in ECHO.

First, the narrower and more specific issue—picketing. As you know by now, our picketing of the White House on May 29 was one of the most successful and important ventures our movement has undertaken.

We had nationwide—and worldwide—publicity—*in every favorable sense*. It was shown on TV in New York, Chicago, San Francisco, Miami,

Indiana, Texas, Seattle, that we know of so far. Articles appeared in the *New York Times, New York News, Washington Star, Chicago Sun-Times, Orlando* (Florida) *Sentinel*—all factual or sympathetic reports. It was reported by Associated Press, United Press International, Reuters, French News Agency, and others, including the White House Press Corps.

The picketing was well and properly done. The 10 men and 3 women participating were well-groomed, and well-dressed—suits, white shirts, and ties, for men; dresses for women were mandatory. We were told that ours was an impressive-looking picket line indeed.

I enclose a copy of our proposed picketing regulations. These are actually in force now, but are labeled "proposed" because our Committee and Board have not yet formally adopted them. They may be altered in a few non-essentials.

The entire enterprise was carried out with order and with dignity.

In the view of all of us, the adoption of picketing, on a regular basis, and properly done, is one of the most important advances in the homophile movement in recent years. In every good sense these demonstrations are gaining us attention and respect. . . .

At the ECHO delegates' meeting in New York on Saturday, June 5, we were informed that such demonstrations are considered to be against the policies and welfare of DOB, and that if ECHO supported them, DOB would have to leave ECHO.

In addition, we were informed that DOB would picket only when the action was backed by the larger community.

First, this is arrant nonsense! When one has reached the stage where picketing is backed by the larger community, such picketing is no longer necessary. The entire force and thrust of picketing is a protest on issues not yet supported or backed by the larger community, in order to bring issues to the fore, and to help elicit that support.

Second, this is in keeping with a mentality which has pervaded this movement from its beginning—homosexuals must never do anything for themselves; they must never come out into the open. They must work through and behind others. They must never present their own case— let others do so for them. We have outgrown this "closet-queen" type of approach, and it is well that we have.

ECHO, by formal vote, IS sponsoring the June 26 and July 4 demonstrations (the others are still too far ahead for formal action).

As Chairman of the Mattachine Society of Washington's Committee on Picketing and Other Lawful Demonstrations, I ask you: Will you join in the ECHO sponsorship of these demonstrations? Do you want yourselves listed as supporters?

According to Shirley and Marion, the motion mentioned above means that DOB is now withdrawing from ECHO.

I moved—and the motion was passed—that it be resolved that it is the sense of the delegates that DOB be exhorted to remain in ECHO. It is at my own volition, and in implementation of that motion, in part, that I am writing. . . .

I feel that there are certain important things to be kept in mind here. In any movement, such as ours, which is part of, and immersed in a rapidly changing situation, you either keep up, or you get left behind, get left out, and become totally ignored and insignificant. I have seen this happen, of late, to a man who was one of the more important figures in this movement.[23]

There are still organizations and people in the homophile movement whose minds are operating in the framework of 1955, not 1965. In 1955, reasonable emphases—aside from mere existence, which then, was an accomplishment in itself—were, among others, research, social services. These *still* have their places, but those places are not of the primary importance that they were then. If DOB wishes to remain a meaningful and effective organization, it must realize this.

I realize that you are very conservative in outlook. Since I am writing as an individual, I can say that I feel that this is unfortunate. But if it be so, so be it. I do not ask or expect that you will be the leaders, taking an avant-garde position, or that you will re-do and remake yourselves over in the image of other groups. But can you not even allow the ECHO affiliation, WITH YOU AS A MEMBER, to sponsor a demonstration?

The homophile movement is becoming increasingly activist. "Uncle Tomism" in our movement is on its way toward becoming as discredited as it is in the Negro movement. Surely you can find a compromise position which will not rule you out of the most important activities, and—in their way (think about it a bit) history-making ones (when have homosexuals, in mass action, ever before gotten up before the public, in the same fashion as other groups, to ask for their rights!?!).

With the kindest of feelings toward you, I will say that if you do not keep up with the movement, I predict that DOB will go "down the drain" as a meaningful organization—not by overt act of anyone else in the movement, but because that's just the way movements evolve.

We were told that perhaps at your biennial convention, in 1966, some of these matters would come up for membership consideration. The world moves too fast for a two-year wait between your conventions! One must seize opportunities when they arise, and then the situation makes them suitable. Surely you have the machinery for some sort of interim decision-making between biennial meetings! Remember that you can support these demonstrations without organizationally participating—although I think that as an organization you will be losing by not participating.

In summary, on this point, I will say, simply, that if you withdraw from ECHO at this time, you will be removing yourselves from participation in some of the most important activities ever to affect the American homosexual, and the loss will be primarily DOB's—and permanently so. . . .

Most sincerely,
Franklin E. Kameny

Kameny to Sir Cyril Osborne

Kameny did not protest merely to U.S. policy- and opinion-makers; he also took his case abroad shortly after the Labor Government in Britain decided, on May 12, 1965, to open debate in Parliament on a bill designed to decriminalize private homosexual acts between consenting adults.[24] The bill had its roots in a famous report published by the Wolfenden Committee. Headed by Sir John Wolfenden, the committee had recommended in 1957 that the government decriminalize consensual homosexual sex between adults. By the time Kameny wrote the following letter to Sir Cyril Osborne, a member of Parliament from Louth, the House of Commons had already twice rejected the Wolfenden Committee's recommendation.

JUNE 20, 1965

Dear Sir Cyril:

I write as a homosexual American citizen—or, more important, in this context, as a homosexual human being. I recently had the displeasure of reading . . . your oration in the House of Commons on May 26, 1965, against the homosexual law reform bill—a bill which no civilized, enlightened, intelligent, informed person could possibly oppose in principle.

You state that you regard this as a moral issue—and you are quite correct, but not for the reasons you give. The issue is whether or not a free society has a moral right to enforce upon its individual members conformity to those particulars and aspects of a moral code and a code of behavior, departures from which cause hurt or harm to no one, interfere with no one, are private, and are clearly the business of those directly concerned, and of them alone. I say that society clearly has NO such moral right; that the present laws on homosexual conduct are therefore patently immoral; and that those who oppose change in those laws are guilty, beyond question, of immoral conduct. . . .

I do not intend to get into a philosophical discussion here . . .

Suffice it to say, simply, that anyone finding sodomy or other homosexual acts distasteful or repellant is free not to engage in them. As long as the acts are done in private, with consenting adults, it would matter not that the two who were involved be the ONLY two in the entire world who do not find their own acts revolting—they have a moral right to engage in them if they wish, without interference and without penalty.

These are acts which cause hurt and harm to no one, and which interfere with no one. Therefore, they should be outside the purview of the law. Public opinion is totally irrelevant.

It is not the function of the law to enforce morality, or even to prescribe it. Morality is a matter of personal opinion and individual religious belief—matters for each man to decide for himself.

For myself, I consider private homosexual acts on the part of consenting adults not only to be NOT immoral but to be moral, in a positive and real sense, and to be good and right and desirable for these individuals who wish so to engage. . . .

I feel that in opposing this bill, thereby ensuring that millions of British citizens, engaging in harmless practices which you, personally, happen to dislike, shall continue to be imprisoned, threatened, and harshly penalized, you have shown yourself to be a profoundly immoral, fundamentally evil, and callously viciously cruel person. Homosexuals are human beings, too!! We are not monsters!

Once the threat of personal destruction (and what less can one call the harsh penalties of English law, in this instance) is considered to be an accepted means of inducing social and personal conformity in matters which do not directly interfere with the rights of others not directly involved (and homosexual acts do not), there is but a short step from prison sentences for homosexuals to gas ovens for Jews, and amazingly little difference between Osborne and Hitler. . . .

Sincerely yours,

Franklin E. Kameny

On July 4, 1967, the House of Commons voted 99–14 to approve the bill to decriminalize homosexual acts between consenting adults. Rear Admiral Morgan Giles, a Conservative member, declared that the results of the new legislation would be "catastrophic." "In a world too ready to criticize us," he added, "this bill will be looked on as further evidence of Britain's degeneracy."[25]

Kameny to Hendrik Ruitenbeck and Richard McConchie

On June 26, 1965, ECHO and MSW sponsored a demonstration at the U.S. Civil Service Commission. Kameny had sought meetings between CSC and MSW since 1962, and during the run-up to the protest, he sent a letter to CSC Chairman John Macy Jr., offering to call off the picketers if Macy "agreed to confer with spokesmen for the homosexual citizenry."[26] *The chairman declined, and on June 26 twenty-three picketers targeted the CSC, protesting the commission's barring of homosexuals from federal employment and its refusal to meet with leaders of the homophile movement. Kameny refers to this demonstration in the following letter.*

He also refers to the July 4 Annual Reminder demonstration at Independence Hall in Philadelphia. Thirty-nine picketers from MSW, MSNY, and other homophile groups had protested "the denial to the American homosexual citizen of benefits inherent to all citizens in the philosophy of the Declaration of Independence." The protest saw a young woman standing in the middle of the circle of picketers hurling "venomous verbal invective until led away by a plainclothes policewoman."[27]

As chairman of MSW's Committee on Picketing and Other Lawful Demonstrations, Kameny had drafted rules specifying the type of attire required of picketers—men were to wear suits, and women were to wear dresses; these rules were also approved by ECHO. Kameny's rationale for a strict dress code was simply that the picketers should look like decent, respectable, and employable American citizens. In the following letter, he refers to a controversial decision to prevent an MSNY member from picketing at the July 4 demonstration because he was not wearing a suit, white shirt, and tie.

JULY 7, 1965

Dear Hendrick and Dick:

I am writing to express my genuine regret over the unfortunate incident, last Sunday, when Dick could not picket because his clothing did not conform to rules. I am writing to both of you, because Dick indicated that Hendrick, too, was upset.

I realize fully the sense of frustration and infuriation which he must have felt. I would have felt the same.

By way of exculpation, let me say, first, that the enclosed set of precepts and regulations for picketing were sent to—and received by—the NY Mattachine office in May. They have been in effect for all three demonstrations thus far held in Washington. They were referred to at least once in every telephone conversation which I had with NY Mattachine (not less than two per week; six per week as the demonstration approached). In each instance, the NY people were asked whether their picketers knew the rules on dress; in each instance, I was told that they did. . . .

These rules have now been formally adopted—in even more rigorous form—by our Committee on Picketing and Other Lawful Demonstrations.

Strict adherence to these regulations has paid off well. A mere 13-person demonstration before the picket-weary White House was called "impressive" by several; a 23-person demonstration before the US Civil

Service Commission building was called "formidable." Virtually every newspaper account—including one of the July 4 demonstration—referred to us as "neatly dressed" or "well dressed." One passerby at the White House said (approximately): "Anyone who looks as presentable as they do can't be so bad"—precisely what we were trying to get across. . . .

The basis for an interesting psychological study might exist in an exploration of the differences between the rampant, unruly, undisciplined, anti-discipline, self-assertive, anti-conformity, non-conformity-for-the-sake-of-non-conformity attitudes of so many of the New York group, versus the willingness of the Washington people to submerge their individuality (no less strongly felt, let it be said) to the requirements of an effective group action. . . .

I hope that now that the stresses of the moment have passed, the ill-feelings have passed with them. In any case, I offer my sincere apologies for an unfortunate incident, caused largely by an apparent breakdown in proper communication. I will trust that no lasting ill-will will result.

Most sincerely,

Franklin E. Kameny

Three weeks after writing this letter, on July 31, Kameny and fifteen other activists picketed the Pentagon to protest the treatment of homosexuals by the armed services—more particularly, the issuance of "less than fully honorable discharges" to homosexuals in the armed services, the barring of homosexuals from entering the military, "offensively worded" regulations on homosexuality, and the military's refusal to meet with representatives of the homosexual community.[28] A local CBS affiliate in Washington aired footage of the protest in its evening news segment.

Kameny to Richard Inman

Kameny followed up his recent picketing with yet another letter to CSC chairman John Macy Jr.:

> As you know, our people picketed the U.S. Civil Service Commission recently. They are getting deeply and justifiably impatient with the refusal by our government and various of its agencies such as the Civil Service Commission even to

meet with us as American citizens, to discuss with us, with open minds, a resolution to our problems. This is a situation which we find profoundly immoral, in terms of the accepted standards of morality governing the conduct of our American government in its dealings with its citizens. It is one which is deeply offensive to all citizens having any conception at all of the basic principles upon which our country is founded. It is a situation which we correctly find intolerable.[29]

In the following letter to Richard Inman, president of the Mattachine Society of Florida, Kameny shares confidential news about a positive effect of MSW's demonstrations. He also sketches his early thoughts on the need to form a national homophile group similar to the NAACP or the ACLU—a group stronger than ECHO.

SEPTEMBER 2, 1965

Dear Richard,

I've been "threatening" to write you a letter for quite some time now, and now that picketing is over for a bit, I'm finally catching up on things, so here goes.

First, some news of the utmost importance—and (for the moment) UTMOST confidentiality. I'm telling you this because you have, from time to time, told me things which you also considered confidential. This is not a matter of OUR considering it confidential, but of the other party asking that (for the present) it be "kept between them and us" and not given publicity.

On August 28—three years to the day since we first requested a meeting, the U.S. Civil Service Commission agreed to meet with us. . . . [T]his was in direct consequence of our picketing, and was in reply to a follow-up letter from us to the Commission, after our picketing of them.

The meeting will take place next week. Five of us will go. We will have a briefing and policymaking session beforehand. We consider this as one of the most important breakthroughs we have had to date.

We recognize that this may well be just a gesture to get us out of their hair (if they give us 6 or 8 man hours now, they may feel that they'll save 57 stenographer hours in the next year answering our letters). However, all of our recent letters have asked for "meaningful," "constructive," "productive," etc., meetings to seek solutions to the problems involved and redress for grievances, and we will do our best to see to it that this meeting and any later ones are indeed so (They have indicated, in preparatory telephone conversations, that if we don't get everything done in the first meeting, we can arrange later ones).

I'll keep you posted on developments, and on the outcome of this first meeting. The meeting, incidentally, is NOT with Macy, but with two of his most important subordinates. They have been cordial in telephone conversations, and have indicated a great willingness to accommodate us—even to scheduling the meeting in the evening, because most of us are working people.

I have no idea, at this point, how broad or narrow the significance of this may be. I don't know . . . whether it has broader political and governmental significance in terms of fundamental policy, or what. All of this remains to be seen. In any case, life with the homophile movement continues to be exciting and stimulating and infinitely interesting and rewarding. . . .

Warren tells me that, despite your feelings, as expressed in some of your letters, for unity in the movement, you are opposed to any sort of centralized structured organization, as an outgrowth of ECHO. This seems to be an almost-about-face from what I interpret your position to be in your letters of July. Why the change?

I would like to see formed a single organization, similar to the ACLU, in which there is a headquarters, and regional affiliates or groups, with a good deal of autonomy, but with some sort of broad, overall policymaking procedures set up. (The ACLU has provision both for national ACLU policy and for affiliate policy.) I feel that this would provide for coordination of activities, all the benefits of unity, support of the weaker organizations by the stronger, the prestige of a large (Eastern, if national is too ambitious for the present, as it may well be) group speaking for many. . . .

If we are going to have a movement, and not just a collection of little, independent organizations—and I think that the time is riper than ever for our having such a movement—then let us go ahead and form it.

I assure you that the NAACP would have never gotten where it has had it been NOT the NAACP but the AACP of Washington and the AACP of New York and the AACP of Florida, etc.

Our problems are not THAT different, one place from another; our goals are all fundamentally the same; there is no good reason for not uniting.

The thirteen original colonies had some of the same problems of limiting individual sovereignty to some degree—and exceedingly strong objections to doing so—when this country was formed. The thirteen colonies wouldn't have lasted long, nor gotten anything accomplished, had they not united under a central government . . .

Well, so much for that for the present. Your thoughts will be much appreciated.

> Sincerely,
>
> Frank

On September 8, 1965, Kameny and four other MSW members met with two high-ranking CSC officials—the general counsel and the director of personnel investigations. It was the first time that CSC engaged in official dialogue with a homophile group about the commission's policy on the federal employment of homosexuals. The meeting lasted ninety minutes, and the most significant result was a promise by CSC officials to reply to a formal statement that the MSW would later provide in writing.

Another significant event within the federal government had occurred a few weeks earlier—Secretary of State Dean Rusk had publicly commented on MSW's picketing of the department. "I understand that we are being picketed by a group of homosexuals," Rusk stated. "The policy of the department is that we do not employ homosexuals knowingly, and that if we discover homosexuals in our department, we discharge them." The reason for the policy "has to do with problems of blackmail and problems of personal instability, and all sorts of things," he added, "so that I don't think we can give any comfort to those who might be tempted to picket us."[30]

Kameny and other picketers also faced criticism from within the homophile movement. The lesbian publication the Ladder *reported on one critic calling the pickets "ridiculous—if not utter insanity," another saying that "it's best to work quietly on an individual basis," and yet another declaring that the pickets were ill-timed, too soon for a budding movement.[31]*

Kameny to William Mauldin

In a brief report on the fad of long hair, Time *quoted fifteen-year-old David Mauldin as saying, "My father thinks it makes me look like a faggot."*[32] *His father was Bill Mauldin, a Pulitzer Prize–winning cartoonist whose most famous characters, GIs Willie and Joe, had lightened the hearts of millions during World War II.*

SEPTEMBER 29, 1965

Dear Mr. Mauldin:

In *Time* magazine (October 1, 1965), page 54, your son David is quoted as using the word "faggot" to refer to a homosexual, and as attributing the usage to you, as well. Writing as a homosexual, I wish to take issue on two counts.

First—I am sure that you did not bring up your son to use words such as "nigger," "kike," "wop," etc., in referring to Negroes, Jews, Italians, etc. Words such as "faggot," "queer" and the like are in the same class, and are equally offensive to our homosexual citizens.

You are expressing, here, against a very large group of people, a prejudice in the same class with that held by the rapid segregationist Southerner, by the anti-Semite and the Nazi, by the "White Anglo-Saxon Protestant" in the worst sense, and by others of similar ilk.

I write as a *homosexual American citizen*—proud of all three words. I fought in the front lines of the same war in which you fought and which you depicted so well. The comment attributed to your son and to you is not very consistent with the ideas expressed so ably and so admirably by you in other places at other times.

Second—Your son states that you claimed that he "looks like a faggot." Exactly what does a "faggot" look like? I should hardly need to point out to you that homosexuals are as totally heterogeneous a group (aside from their sexual preferences, in the narrowest sense) as are Negroes and Jews (aside from their skin color and their religious beliefs, in the narrowest sense). Generalizations and stereotypes of the sort implied in your statement are the stuff out of which prejudice and discrimination are fashioned.

In our country, as I certainly hardly need to point out to you, we have individual Negro people, Jewish, Catholic people—and homosexual people. We are *all* entitled to our dignity and to our respect; to our place as first-class citizens and first-class human beings; to our right to be different, one from another, without thereby being the recipients of prejudice, discrimination, contempt and ridicule.

This is what you and I both fought a war for. . . .

In closing, I should point out that statements such as yours are part of what some of us refer to as "the liberal syndrome"—liberals will stand up for the rights of all minorities, stand up for any underdog, vigorously protest discrimination and prejudice wherever they occur, stand up for the inherent dignity of all people—but let the question of homosexuals and homosexuality arise and—"Well, somehow that's a different question."

It isn't a different question at all!

I would appreciate your response and comments.

Thank you.

> Sincerely yours,
> Franklin E. Kameny

Mauldin replied that Time *was quoting "my young son reading my mind, which is a pretty far-out quote, even for Time," and that he did not "recall using words like 'faggot' in front of my children."* [33]

Kameny to President Lyndon B. Johnson

The following letter, penned by Kameny and excerpted subsequently, was hand delivered at the White House gate on October 23, while two dozen picketers demonstrated for their civil rights on the sidewalk in front of the White House. FBI agents were present for the demonstration—the agency tracked all homophile picketing—and so were two teenage males walking an "anti-picket line," as an FBI memorandum put it. The young men were carrying placards reading "Are You Kidding?" and "Get Serious." [34]

Although the turnout was decent, it was not as high as Kameny had hoped; in an earlier call to the Washington Police Department, he had stated that approximately 100 picketers would be present at the White House demonstration. [35] *Indeed, Kameny and other activists were beginning to feel that the tactic of picketing in Washington had run its course. The pickets had attracted national publicity and resulted in a high-level meeting at CSC, "but the walls didn't come tumbling down."*[36] *Discrimination against homosexuals continued to be enshrined in federal policy.*

OCTOBER 23, 1965

Dear Mr. President:

A group of homosexual American citizens, and those supporting their cause, is picketing the White House, today, in lawful, dignified, and orderly protest—in the best American tradition—against the treatment being meted out to fifteen million homosexual American citizens by their government—treatment which consistently makes of them second-class citizens, at best.

Our grievances fall into two classes: Specific and General.

I. *Specific:*

(a) *Exclusion from Federal Employment . . .*

(b) *Discriminatory, Exclusionary, and Harshly Punitive Treatment by the Armed Services . . .*

(c) *Denial of Security Clearances to Homosexuals as a Group or Class*

II. *General:*

(a) There can be no justification for the continuing refusal, through two administrations, and for more than three years, of our presidents and their staffs—as well as many government agencies and departments—to accord to spokesmen for the homosexual community even the common courtesy and decency of acknowledgements—much less meaningful responses—to serious and proper letters written to them in search of their assistance in the solution of serious problems affecting large numbers of citizens.

(b) Equally, there can be no justification for the continuing refusal of most agencies and departments of our government—including the staff of the White House—to meet with representatives of the homosexual community (our nation's largest minority after the Negro) constructively to discuss solutions to the problems besetting them—problems in significant measure created by and reinforced by our government and by its attitudes, policies, and practices.

(c) We find offensive the continuing attitude of hostility, enmity, and animosity—amounting to a state of war—directed by our government toward its homosexual citizens. No group of *our* citizenry should have to tolerate an attitude of this sort upon the part of their government.

Our government chooses to note that homosexual American citizens are homosexuals, but conveniently chooses to disregard that they are also Americans and citizens.

In short, Mr. President, the homosexual citizens of America are being treated as second-class citizens—in a country which claims that it has no second-class citizens. The advantages claimed by our country for all of its citizens—equality, opportunity, fair treatment—are not only denied to our homosexual citizens by society at large, they are denied at the active instigation and with the active cooperation of our government. This is not as it should be.

The right of its citizens to be different and not to conform, without being placed thereby in a status of inferiority or disadvantage, has always been the glory of our country. This right should apply to the homosexual American citizen as well. At present it does not.

You have proposed, and are indeed working vigorously and successfully toward what you have felicitously termed "The Great Society." Mr. President—NO society can be truly great which excludes from full participation and contribution, or relegates to a secondary role, ANY minority of its citizenry. The homosexual citizen, totally without cause, is presently systematically excluded from your Great Society.

We ask, Mr. President, for what all American citizens—singly and collectively—have a right to ask: That our problems be given the fair, unbiased consideration by our government due the problems of all the citizenry—consideration in which we, ourselves, are allowed to participate actively and are invited to do so, as citizens in our country have a right to expect to do.

We ask for a reconsideration of ancient, outmoded approaches to, and policies toward homosexuals and homosexuality—approaches and policies which are unseemly for a country claiming to support the principles and the way of life for which our country stands—approaches and policies which should long ago have been discarded. We ask that on these questions, our President and his government accept and shoulder actively the role properly attributed to them by The Report of the President's Commission on National Goals (1960): "One role of government is to stimulate changes of attitude."

. . .

Sincerely yours,
Franklin E. Kameny

Kameny to John Sweeterman

Kameny registers a loud protest with the publisher of the Washington Post *about the following advertisement he wanted to place in the newspaper:*

H O M O S E X U A L S
are an oppressed minority. They are:

1. Excluded from governmental employment and also systematically excluded from private employment, without regard to competence or merit.

2. Excluded from military service, and given less-than-fully honorable discharges when the Services successfully ferret them out.

3. Denied security clearances for both governmental and private employment, even when obviously not vulnerable to blackmail.

4. Subjected to a variety of official and private harassments, discriminations, and indignities, forcing them into the status of second-class citizens and second-class human beings.

For additional information, or for suggestions as to what you can do so that homosexual American citizens can attain the first-class citizenship claimed for all other American citizens, write to:

The Mattachine Society of Washington [37]

DECEMBER 14, 1965

Dear Mr. Sweeterman:

I write in my personal capacity as a regular reader of, and subscriber to, the *Washington Post* for many years.

I note that in the December 13, 1965 issue of the *Post*, you ran a full-page advertisement by the John Birch Society.

I note that you refuse to accept any advertisements from the Mattachine Society of Washington.

As a homosexual American citizen, I resent this; in fact, I take it as a personal slap in the face, as do many other respectable, responsible homosexual citizens, who have indicated to me that they find infuriating your acceptance of a John Birch advertisement, after your rejection of one from the Mattachine Society of Washington.

The John Birch Society stands in opposition to much for which the *Post* stands. You have attacked it in your editorial columns. But you accept its advertising.

The Mattachine Society of Washington stands for the kind of human freedom and dignity which you support—ostensibly—and the support for which has given you your reputation as a liberal newspaper. But you refuse its advertising. Apparently your support of the liberal ideal is just so much lip service.

I enclose a brochure recently published by the Mattachine Society of Washington. Read it. Look, in particular, at Page 1. Ask yourself whether, were the words Negro or Jew substituted for homosexual, the *Post* would not wholeheartedly support the principles expressed and the work undertaken by the Mattachine Society of Washington.

However, the Mattachine Society of Washington works in an area involving—horrors!—sex!! Apparently you can stomach the John Birch Society's political viewpoints sufficiently to be bought by them, but you are still sufficiently frightened of sex so that when it enters the picture, you are willing to allow your beautiful principles to be compromised, and to go down the drain.

I am not objecting, of course, to your acceptance of the Birch advertisement, per se—I am sufficiently imbued with the spirit of the First Amendment and with an appreciation of the obligation which it imposes upon news media, to realize that such objection would put me into an inconsistent and untenable position. Apparently, however, the *Washington Post* has not yet really absorbed the spirit of the First Amendment, and does not yet really appreciate the obligation which that Amendment and the concept of freedom of the press imposes upon it.

The John Birch Society, Nazis, Caribbean dictators—the pages of the *Washington Post* are open to advertisements from all of these—but not to the Mattachine Society of Washington—a group of unpopular American citizens, trying lawfully to improve their situation and to eliminate the prejudice directed against them. For an avowedly liberal newspaper, the *Post* has made a strange selection, indeed, as to who shall be within the pale and who shall be beyond it!

I would suggest that the *Washington Post* do some careful rethinking and soul-searching, in regard to its advertising policies; that it begin to realize that the Victorian era is most of a century behind us; and that it realize that, along with their fellow citizens, homosexuals are citizens, people, and members of the Washington community and the national one, which the *Washington Post* serves.

Your reply would be appreciated.

Thank you.

> Sincerely yours,
>
> Franklin E. Kameny

Sweeterman replied a week later, saying his advertising staff members had been in touch with MSW and that they "will continue to discuss any advertising copy that is submitted by either the Mattachine Society or any other advertiser or organizer."[38]

Kameny to *ONE* Magazine

In the November 1965 issue of ONE, editor Richard Conger called for the emergence of creative and dependable leadership in the homophile movement. Doing so he also directly criticized those in the movement who "feel that the path of success is found where there is the most noise"—in marches, pickets, and media appearances.[39] *Kameny took this as criticism of his own leadership style, and in the following letter he defends his actions to ONE's staff.*

DECEMBER 22, 1965

Gentlemen:

. . . We find Mr. Conger criticizing frequent radio and TV appearances. Does he object to our presenting our case to the public? If so, I think his position needs some careful justification. If not, how better would he do so than through radio and TV—and other public appearances? Or is it Mr. Conger's position that if we hide ourselves sufficiently well, everyone will think that we have gone away, forget about us, and that this, somehow, will get for us our rights and our equality? I will grant that some radio and TV appearances, including some very recent ones, have been deplorably poor. But this is not the issue raised by Mr. Conger.

Mr. Conger is under a not uncommon misapprehension if he believes that the primary purpose of our picketing demonstrations has been to call attention to ourselves.

To call very much needed public attention to *our cause*, and to the abuses meted out to our minority, is a very valid SECONDARY purpose of these demonstrations, and they have succeeded admirably in this, with no "disaster," "damage," or "setback"—in fact, very much to the contrary.

We are not seeking attention, per se, but *the right kind of attention.* Our demonstrations and our public appearances have gotten it for us! We are seeking shock, in a way, but in order to take fully proper and carefully calculated advantage of the novelty created by a firm public request for rights, by a group which has hitherto consistently been disregarded because no one expected them to put their protests in a form worth listening to, or nothing—or, in fact, in an "audible" form at all. . . .

Our demonstrations have been sober, serious, dignified, orderly, highly disciplined, fully lawful ones, by conservatively dressed (suits, white shirts, ties for men; dresses for women), well-groomed men and women. (When we picketed to protest federal employment policies, for example, we saw to it that we looked employable—by employers' standards, which is what is relevant here.) The signs carried, the press releases and leaflets distributed, etc., have presented our case, our philosophy, our position, in carefully worded, non-sensational terms.

However, our primary purpose, in picketing, apparently totally missed by Mr. Conger, was to attempt to correct the abuses against which we picketed. Our purposes in picketing at the Civil Service Commission building was to bring an end to the federal government's disqualification of homosexuals; at the Pentagon, to change the policies of the armed services toward the homosexual citizen and the homosexual serviceman; etc. We have very good reason to believe that we were not totally without success in this.

I feel that these demonstrations represent creative, dependable, responsible leadership at its best.

It should be pointed out that almost every demonstration was preceded by at least two months of correspondence (up to three years, in several cases) in which our grievances were spelled out, conferences and meetings were requested, advance notice of the demonstration was given, with the clearly made statement that "we prefer negotiation and discussion to demonstration"; but it takes two to negotiate and discuss; we are always ready.

Surely Mr. Conger does not expect me, having tried *every* door, and having traversed *every* other avenue of recourse, to accept the second-class status, the total dismissal of us as citizens, and as worthwhile human beings, and the implied contempt—to accept these with no response other than to crawl away, silently. Homosexuals have been doing far too much of this for far too many years.

We feel that, all other possible avenues for redress of grievance being exhausted, we have the *same right, in propriety, as have all other citizens and human beings,* to make public protest in this fashion—and that such protest is fully in order and tactically advisable. . . .

We have not undertaken picketing lightly or casually, either in consideration of the principles and possible consequences involved, or in formation of the details of the actual performance. Reactions have been good, whether from the public, from the news media, from the police, from members of other non-homophile organizations (such as the ACLU) or elsewhere.

For too long, too much of the efforts of the homophile movement have been devoted to homosexuals talking with and to homosexuals about homosexuality—or heterosexuals talking with and to homosexuals about homosexuality. It is about time that homosexuals talked to heterosexuals about homosexuality—and "talking" includes radio and TV appearances and picketing.

Now, for what Mr. Conger does not say—nowhere does he offer us as much as one constructive suggestion at all, as to what form alternative "responsible," "creative" action might take. . . .

Does Mr. Conger still believe, as some yet do, that homosexuals themselves should never work openly for their cause, but should always find heterosexuals—preferably "influential" or "prestigious" ones, or so-called "authorities"—to front for them? I believe that while assistance from such sources certainly should not be refused, we have advanced beyond reliance upon it, and are not at the point of presenting our own case for ourselves.

Let us have some positive and constructive alternatives to replace the destructive negativism of Mr. Conger's editorial—but let those positive alternatives consist of more than just continuing to talk to ourselves. I, for one, am more than merely open and receptive to such alternatives and suggestions.

In conclusion, I point to Mr. Conger's comment on the 15-year age of the modern homophile movement, and his statement that "today different standards must be used." Different methods must also be used. We are using them. Mr. Conger would have us remain with the methods and standards of a decade-and-a-half ago.

I will be pleased to continue this discussion, if Mr. Conger wishes, and to provide any additional information which he may desire.

Sincerely yours,
Franklin E. Kameny

4

"The Lunatic Fringe"

1966

Kameny to Richard Inman

Kameny begins the new year by criticizing the president of the Matta-chine Society of Florida for threatening not to attend what will become the National Planning Conference of Homophile Organizations in Kansas City in February 1966. The conference, initially conceived during a strategy ses-sion at the 1964 ECHO conference in Philadelphia, was designed to establish and deepen collaborative efforts of approximately fifteen homophile groups. Kameny's letter here offers a revealing look into his strategy for winning civil liberties, including tactics involving difficult personalities within the movement.

JANUARY 5, 1966

Dear Richard:

. . . I am going to speak firmly.

Among the things—the people—that I dislike most are those who act like "bulls in china shops"—people who take hasty, precipitate action which has all kinds of ramifications, but who give no heed to those ramifi-cations and thereby end up acting in a purely destructive manner, whether they intend to do so or not.

Regardless of what it looks like just at the moment, the Kansas City meeting is one of the most important events in the homophile movement in many years—potentially. Do you realize what your public announce-ment of non-attendance, and your reasons, can do? It can scuttle the entire meeting, by leading a stampede from it, leaving no one attending at all . . .

If you are so easily discouraged by not having things planned just exactly as you would like them to be that you'll withdraw—all right, do so—quite frankly, it doesn't do you credit—but don't destroy the entire conference as you do so. . . .

Your decision is not only self-defeating, in the worst possible sense, but it's also destructive of the progress of the movement for a long time to come.

It's also emotional, childish and immature—"They won't do things MY way, so I won't go." . . .

If you feel that there's apathy, etc., then DO something about it. Don't sulk in a corner. If you want to be considered a leader in the movement, act like one. Sitting home and destroying meetings isn't constructive leadership. It is "bull in the china shop" acts like your refusal to attend KC, and announcing it, which tear our movement apart.

You may not be TRYING to wreck the meeting, but you may well be doing so anyway. The bull in the china shop usually hasn't any slightest idea of the china he's breaking or what it may be worth.

Now, I strongly suggest that you reverse your decision. And don't let irrational emotions such as pride (one of mankind's most destructive emotions) . . . deter you.

Don't sit back and let the whole world prove you wrong—be in there proving yourself wrong!! . . .

I did not intend my remarks to be personally harsh. . . .

Most sincerely,
Frank

Kameny to Ann Landers

Kameny attempts to persuade the famous advice columnist Ann Landers that her beliefs about homosexuality are based on faulty data.[1]

JANUARY 6, 1966

Dear Miss Landers:

. . . You say that "I have heard from thousands of homosexuals these past ten years and most of them are unhappy, frightened and lonely. They long to lead normal lives—."[2] You are making the same error that innumerable psychiatrists, clergymen, and others do who consider themselves knowledgeable about homosexuals but who really are not so—you are seeing a biased, slanted, grossly atypical sample, and are generalizing from it—falsely so.

With a few exceptions, ONLY the unhappy, frightened and lonely homosexuals write to you for advice. Why would the others do so? Why would the very many happy, confident, socially active and gregarious homosexuals have occasion to write to you? Most homosexuals are not as you describe them, and have NO desire to change to heterosexuality.

Similarly, only the disturbed or otherwise maladjusted homosexuals go to psychiatrists and clergymen, etc. As a result, entire books have been written about these maladjusted people as if they were typical of *all* homosexuals. They are not.

This can well be illustrated by the apocryphal story . . . about two psychiatrists: First Psychiatrist—"But all my homosexual patients are seriously disturbed." Second Psychiatrist—"Yes, but then all my *hetero*sexual patients are seriously disturbed, too."

Naturally so, or they wouldn't be patients.

What percentage of the *total* number of people writing to you are unhappy, frightened, and lonely?—rather high, I should think. Do you really think that this is a representative sampling of everybody? Hardly.

Finally, have you considered that the reasons for the unhappiness, fright, and loneliness of many of these people lies, in major measure, with the prejudiced and discriminatory attitudes of the society around them, in which they live?

Suggesting that the cure for their unhappiness, fright and loneliness might be change to heterosexuality is like suggesting that the cure for the misfortunes that beset the Negro and the Jew, as a result of segregation, white supremacy, and anti-Semitism would best be cured by bleaching the Negro and converting the Jew to Christianity.

There are organizations working hard to solve the problems of the homosexual from the viewpoint from which those problems would be approached—as problems (basically, and primarily) in civil liberties, social rights, prejudice and discrimination; and (secondarily) as you correctly indicate, in adjustment of the individual homosexual to himself and to acceptance of himself and his homosexuality. These organizations deserve your support. I enclose a brochure of the more important of them. . . .

Sincerely yours,
Franklin E. Kameny

Landers replied to Kameny on January 13, referring to his letter as "extremely interesting and certainly one of the most realistic and intelligent I have ever read on the subject of homosexuality." She added that she had "passed your letter around to every member of my staff since I felt that the points you make will certainly add to their understanding."[3]

Kameny to Larry Littlejohn

In this letter to Larry Litlejohn of the Society for Individual Rights (SIR) in San Francisco, Kameny argues that homophile groups move far beyond their purview when they act like social clubs. A respected member of the homophile movement, SIR offered its members a wide variety of social events (e.g., dinners, softball games, and dances).

JANUARY 8, 1966

Dear Larry:

. . . I quite agree that there is a place in the movement for pin-ups and parties. Namely: The movement has the function of fighting, vigorously and unrelentingly, for the right of those publishing, purveying, and purchasing such literature so to do; and for the right of those giving and attending such parties so to do. But NOT so to publish and so to give by the movement itself.

As a case in point: When I was interviewed, not long ago, for the forthcoming article in Time (January 24), the interviewer said: "Of course your organization doesn't engage in any social activities." I can assure you that our status, and that of the entire movement, would have gone down badly had my answer been "yes." . . .

I think that SIR will make a great mistake if it does not limit itself to matters having to do with the homosexual, for two major reasons, if not three.

First, don't place yourself in direct competition with the ACLU. They're taking care of general matters of individual rights, and doing moderately well at it—better than you will do.

Second, it is almost always bad policy to mix causes. You end up diluting everything and doing nothing well. Each of these causes is different. Each demands its own careful attention to strategy and tactics—and the strategy and tactics are different for each. The images which different people have of each of these are sufficiently different, so that you will find yourself in conflict.

I made a remark at ECHO, which is appropriate here—It will be unfortunate if the homophile movement becomes the "conformophile" movement. It will become quite ineffective.

Third, one of the fastest ways to become totally ineffective is to become relegated to the "lunatic fringe." We always walk a line close enough to that as it is, which is why our public image is so important. When you start to come out against a whole variety of things—when you start taking up the cudgels for a large number of not merely unpopular, but emotion-laden causes, you will immediately be relegated to that fringe, and from then onward, you will NEVER be taken seriously in anything you do.

It has taken us years until the government would start to deal with us, and then only because of the way we have worked, the way we have presented our material, the level at which we have operated, the organizations with which we are associated (the Christian of the local ACLU has just joined MSW—that's confidential), etc. . . .

As always,
Frank

Kameny to Robert Walker

In this pointed letter to the treasurer of the Council on Religion and the Homosexual (CRH) in California, Kameny draws a sharp distinction between fighting for the civil rights of homosexuals and ministering to the individual needs of homosexuals. Doing so, he claims that the value of MSW's work will be far more enduring than the benefits of CRH's spiritual ministry to individual homosexuals.

FEBRUARY 10, 1966

Dear Mr. Walker:

... We are interested in the long-range approach, not in the immediate, short-range one. We are interested far less in the solution of short-range, immediate (often individual and personal) problems than in the underlying, long-range (usually impersonal, more communitywide) problems, so that the short-range, superficial ones will cease to occur, since it is the long range problems which cause the short-range ones (i.e., change the law, and we stop ministering to homosexuals who have gotten arrested, etc., etc., etc.).

By analogy: One can (by one approach) take care of the problems of poverty by giving food and money to the poor. And one will do it for this generation, and for the next generation, and for endless generations, and for never-ceasing lines of poor, thereafter. But until one tackles the causes of poverty—the lack of education and the reasons for it; the lack of jobs and the reasons for it, etc., etc., etc.—one will never accomplish ANY lasting good.

Similarly, one can attend to the individual needs of homosexuals at present—their social needs; their entertainment needs; their spiritual problems, etc., etc., on an immediate basis. But until one solves the underlying problems—the problems of prejudice and discrimination directed against the homosexual by the heterosexual—which are (or are the ONLY source of) the ONLY problems really faced by the homosexual—one will accomplish no *lasting* good, either....

We are not yet a mass movement—perhaps we will be some day.

I agree with you 100% that communication between the organizations is inadequate. A start at remedying this, hopefully, will be made at Kansas City....

I feel that the image of a professional, HIGH level (in the eyes of the onlooker) civil liberties organization is critically important to maintain. This is why MSW has, in its constitution, a flat prohibition against ANY kind of social events whatever—and we abide by the prohibition.

Functioning in this fashion is what has led the Washington ACLU to look upon the MSW as a fellow civil liberties organization, to be dealt with in that fashion, as an equal. This is what has led the chairman of the local ACLU to apply for full membership in MSW, and to be pleased that we have accepted him.

This is what has led us to be able to get meetings and conferences with high government officials.

This is what has led us to be able to use one of the area's more important and fashionable churches as our monthly meeting place, on a continuing basis. The church looked over our publications first. They wouldn't have approached us with a ten-foot pole if we'd had physique photographs.

We are not about to let all of this go down the drain by entering the entertainment field and/or publishing physique photographs.

There is plenty of opportunity to publish, for those who want to entertain, for those who want to socialize and to organize their entertainment and their socialization. These activities are at a much lower level than civil liberties ones. These are activities which meet merely immediate needs, and not long-range ones.

While I feel that many of these questions of our approaches and our tactics should certainly be discussed, fully, they should certainly NOT be discussed publicly, or in publications going out to the public at large. We should present, insofar as at all possible, a united, monolithic front to the world at large (by "we," I mean the homophile movement). We should adopt our "party line" by means of PRIVATE discussions, and our publications should reflect this party line, and this alone. I see very little proper place for controversy in those publications of the homophile movement which are seen outside the movement.

Kameny to Dick Leitsch

In May 1965, Warren Scarberry, an activist based in Washington, DC, published a periodical in which he claimed he had picketed the White House on April 3, 1965—more than a week before the MSW did in response to the story about Cuba's plans to send homosexuals to prison camps. Here is Scarberry's own account:

> *April 3rd the White House was picketed by Warren Scarberry in regards to Government discrimination of Homosexuals; the sign read: "Stop*

Discrimination Against Homosexuals." He picketed for one hour. The only response was when a policeman from the Third Precinct asked Scarberry if he was a homosexual. Scarberry asked the policeman if he was.

The Mattachine Society picketed the White House two weeks after Warren Scarberry broke the ice. They picketed in regard to Government discrimination and military policies. . . . It's about time the Mattachine Society of Washington came out from behind the rocks and took their protest to the public instead of running around to who knows who.[4]

Scarberry left out a key detail in his report—that he had informed the Washington Metropolitan Police Department about his plan to picket. The DC police then contacted the FBI, and a memorandum about Scarberry's picket landed on the desk of J. Edgar Hoover, who then passed along the information to Attorney General Nicholas Katzenbach. Interestingly, Scarberry's name, unlike the names of other homophile activists in FBI memoranda, is deleted in the unclassified FBI documents; this may suggest that Scarberry acted as an informant for the agency. Indeed, as the following letter to Dick Leitsch of the MSNY suggests, Kameny clearly distrusted Scarberry and imagined him as an FBI informant.[5]

FEBRUARY 14, 1966

Dear Dick:

I've just had a letter from Ronald Brass, mentioning that you may be visited by a person called Warren Scarberry.

I advise you, strongly, not to be taken in by him. He's much more of a "nut" and a "crackpot" than will at first seem apparent. I always have strong suspicions of his motivations—Warren rarely engages in anything out of which he does not expect to make a financial profit.

Don't trust him; don't gossip about, or otherwise discuss the internal affairs of MSNY, MSW, or any other organization, or any of the people involved (you will find that he knows many of the MSW people down here in Washington, including me). Don't be taken in by his pleasant manner and personable appearance.

This was the man who turned Ronald Brass into the FBI, and lost him his job.[6] Whatever you may think of Ronald Brass is irrelevant. I think that that act characterizes Warren Scarberry.

He's not well-educated (which isn't necessarily a drawback, of course); he's also not as bright as he might be, (which IS a drawback, when you're telephoning high government officials, as he does). For the sake of MSNY, I suggest that you don't involve yourself or the organization with him. Shunt him off, nicely but definitely.

I don't know what his connections are—it would not surprise me if he were acting as some sort of informer for the FBI or others (although that may well be doing the man an injustice). In any case I—and we—don't trust him, and I think with good reason. This is not my view alone—you will find that others in MSW concur.

I can discuss these matters with you further when I see you in Kansas City.

I would appreciate your NOT mentioning this letter to others and, particularly, not to Scarberry, of course.

> Sincerely,
> Frank

John Macy Jr. to the Mattachine Society of Washington

CSC Chairman John Macy sends his official reply (heavily excerpted in the following letter) to MSW's plea for a change in the way the commission understands and treats homosexuals.

FEBRUARY 25, 1966

Gentlemen:

Pursuant to your request of August 15, 1965, Commission representatives met with representatives of the Society on September 8, 1965, to enable the Society to present its views regarding the Government policy on the suitability for Federal employment, of persons who are shown to have engaged in homosexual acts.

The Society was extended 30 days to submit a written memorandum in support of the positions set forth at these discussions to ensure that full consideration could be given to its contentions and supporting data by the Commissioners. . . .

The core of the Society's position and its recommendations is that private, consensual, out-of-working hours homosexual conduct on the part of adults, ceases to be a bar to Federal employment. In the alternative it is asked that the Commission activate continuing discussions with representatives of the Society to take a "progressive, idealistic, humane, forward-looking, courageous role" to elicit the holding of objective hearings leading to the adoption of the Society's recommendation.[7]

The Commission's policy for determining suitability is stated as follows:

> Persons about whom there is evidence that they have engaged in or solicited others to engage in homosexual or sexually perverted acts with them, without evidence of rehabilitation, are not suitable for Federal employment. In acting on such cases the Commission will consider arrest records, court records, or records of conviction for some form of homosexual conduct or sexual perversion; or medical evidence, admissions, or other credible information that the individual has engaged in or solicited others to engage in such acts with him. Evidence showing that a person has homosexual tendencies, standing alone, is insufficient to support a rating of unsuitability on the ground of immoral conduct.

We have carefully weighed the contentions and recommendations of the Society, and perceive a fundamental misconception by the society of our policy stemming from a basic cleavage in the perspective by which this subject is viewed. We do not subscribe to the view, which indeed is the rock upon which the Mattachine Society is founded, that "homosexual" is a proper metonym for an individual. Rather we consider the term "homosexual" to be properly used as an adjective to describe the nature of overt sexual relations or conduct. Consistent with this usage pertinent considerations encompass the types of deviate sexual behavior engaged in, whether isolated, intermittent, or continuing acts, the age of the particular participants, the extent of promiscuity, the aggressive or passive character of the individual's participation, the recency of the incidents, the presence of physical, mental, emotional, or nervous causes, the influence of drugs, alcohol or other contributing factors, the public or private character of the acts, the incidence of arrests, convictions, or of public offense, nuisance or breach of the peace related to the acts, the notoriety, if any, of the participants, the extent or effect of rehabilitative efforts, if any, and the admitted acceptance of, or preference for homosexual relations. Suitability determinations also comprehend the total impact of the applicant upon the job. Pertinent considerations here are the revulsion of other employees by homosexual conduct and the consequent disruption of service efficiency, the apprehension caused other employees of homosexual advances, solicitations or assaults, the unavoidable subjection of the sexual deviate to erotic stimulation through on-the-job use of common toilet, shower, and living facilities, the offense to members of the public who are required to deal with a known or admitted sexual deviate to transact Government business, the hazard that the prestige and authority of a Government position will be used to foster homosexual activity, particularly among the youth, and the use of Government funds and authority in furtherance of conduct offensive both to the mores and the law of our society.

In the light of these pervading requirements it is upon overt conduct that the Commission's policy operates, not upon spurious classification of individuals. The Society apparently represents an effort by certain individuals to classify themselves as "homosexuals" and thence on the basis of asserted discrimination to seek, with the help of others, either complete social acceptance of aberrant sexual conduct or advance absolvent of any consequences for homosexual acts which come to the attention of the public authority. Homosexual conduct, including that between consenting adults in private, is a crime in every jurisdiction, except under specified conditions, in Illinois. Such conduct is also considered immoral under the prevailing mores of our society. . . .

We reject categorically the assertion that the Commission pries into the private sex life of those seeking Federal employment, or that it discriminates in ferreting out homosexual conduct. The standard against criminal, infamous, dishonest, immoral, or notoriously disgraceful conduct is uniformly applied and suitability investigations underlying its observance are objectively pursued. . . .

We can neither, consistent with our obligations under the law, absolve individuals of the consequences of their conduct, nor do we propose by attribution of sexual preferences based on such conduct, to create an insidious classification of individuals. We see no third sex, no oppressed minority or secret society, but only individuals; and we judge their suitability for

Federal employment in the light of their overt conduct. We must attribute to overt acts whether homosexual or heterosexual, the character ascribed by the laws and mores of our society. Our authority and our duty permit no other course.

By direction of the Commission:
John W. Macy Jr.

Kameny to Rae Kameny

In early 1966, not long after Kameny had come out to his mother, the two of them corresponded about his homosexuality. Initially, Rae Kameny did not react positively to news about her son's sexuality. "Now that I can no longer hope that my guesses are wrong," she wrote, "I am weighed down with an awful sense of guilt—guilt as being in some way responsible in the first place and guilt for not having had the courage to bring it up long ago, when perhaps something could have been done." But she also added that had the two of them talked about his homosexuality earlier, she could have offered practical help on ways to cope in an unwelcoming world. "When you took that job in Ireland," she wrote, "you did not discuss it . . . and I know you were terribly disappointed when it didn't work out. When you took the job in Georgetown U. it was the same. I might have pointed out that the climate in Washington was much worse than in N.Y., that you would be better off in a non-religious institution, or, if in one, to at least be careful about airing your views. Then, knowing your situation, someone might have pointed out the risks of taking a job with the Government." Clearly, Kameny's mother was pained by his lack of openness about his personal life. "You say that in your field virtually all jobs require a security clearance," she penned. "How did you lose it in the first place?"[8]

MARCH 2, 1966

Dear Mother,

. . . Yes, I DO actually believe that the direction of my life is NOT a problem—not one whit more than your religion is a problem, or a Negro's skin color is a problem.

I did NOT say that it's something that I do not wish to discuss with you . . . and I suggest you cease drawing such conclusions.

I think that if we are going to attempt dialog on these matters, you had better understand—CLEARLY—what my position is.

I do NOT look upon homosexuality as a sickness, disorder, disturbance, affliction, ailment, or something which, in ANY sense at all, is wrong or awry. It is simply a minority state, FULLY on par with the majority heterosexuality.

You say that you wish that I had discussed this with you earlier, when something might have been done. This overlooks two important facts.

1. Nothing could have been done at ANY time—regardless of the misguided information which might have been given to you by some psychiatrist.

2. You completely omit consideration of whether *I* would have wanted "something to be done." I assure you that in company with the vast majority of the 15 million fellow homosexuals in this country, I would NOT have wanted "something to be done" and would not have allowed it, or cooperated with you—at ANY age.

I will continue to draw analogies with various minority groups—I consider them to be FULLY valid analogies. You would not have cooperated in any attempts to "do something" about your Judaism at any age—and you would have been quite correct. The same applies to me. . . .

Now this is NOT the tragedy which folklore makes of it, and which folklore you have accepted, hook, line, and sinker. My life, through this, has been fascinating, exciting, varied, stimulating, interesting, full (in every good sense) in a way that it would and could never otherwise have been. It is a life right in human and personal values. It has been termed, by heterosexuals who know me, as one of the most colorful lives, and I as one of the most colorful persons they know.

I have good and close friends everywhere, in greater number than I think you can imagine. I would not change for all the money in the world.

You need have no sense of guilt. I don't think that you made me as I am in this context. I see nothing to blame you about if you did—you also made me a human and sensitive person; one with a brilliant and trained mind; one with an extraordinary personality (in every good sense), and many other things. . . .

If some of these characterizations of myself seem to you not to be the Franklin you know—remember, also, that I have been telling you, for almost 30 years, that you have never seen the real me.

Again, you need feel neither guilt nor grief. If you DID make me as I am—I thank you for it. . . .

With much love,

Franklin

Kameny to Don Slater

Kameny warns Don Slater, the former editor of ONE *and now chairman of the Tangent Group, a homophile organization based in Los Angeles, about the dangers of identifying the homophile movement with the anti-Vietnam War movement. Kameny refers to a series of pickets to be held across the country, from Philadelphia to Los Angeles, on Armed Forces Day—May 21, 1966.*

APRIL 3, 1966

Dear Don:

    . . . In your more recent leaflet, dated March 18, you ask whether people would take part in a

PRO Vietnam demonstration

ANTI Vietnam

The Vietnam question is one which we must keep TOTALLY *out* of— pro, con, or neutral!!! It just is not OUR question.

We simply cannot allow ourselves to become in *any* way involved in that matter. It has no logical or other relationship to us whatever, and involvement in it, in *any slightest* way, can only do us—and the entire movement—harm—very great, and very lasting harm.

All that your two questions are accomplishing is the taking of a poll among some homosexuals, on their personal support of, or opposition to the Vietnam War. This is not related, in any way, to the purposes of our demonstration. This has no relationship, *whatever*, to homosexuality and to the problem of the homosexual.

We are not taking up this matter of the homosexual and the draft in relationship to the Vietnam conflict—ours is a much deeper issue, of much longer standing. Similarly (since some people are raising this issue, too), we are not taking up, in any way, the merits of the draft itself. The validity of conscription *per se* is not our issue.

All that we are doing is to ask for a cessation of special, different, discriminatory treatment for the homosexual citizen. We are not—in the context of the homophile movement—attempting to enter into questions of foreign policy, international relations, or general internal public policy where it does not affect or relate to the homosexual *per se*, and in a manner different from the heterosexual.

I feel exceedingly strongly that we must divorce ourselves *totally* from the Vietnam issue—to the extent, very possibly, if it seems appropriate—of specifically (by formal statement) disavowing any connection between our efforts and the Vietnam War. The separation must be *complete*!!!!

While I can speak only for myself, at this point, I will say that if there seems to be any connection or involvement *whatever*, positive or negative, between our May 21 undertaking and the Vietnam conflict, or the merits of the draft *per se*, or any other extraneous issue, I shall completely dissociate myself from the whole thing.

As I see it, we are asking for three things. In simplified form, these are: (1) Equal treatment of homosexuals or heterosexuals by the Armed Services; (2) Elimination of less-than-fully-honorable discharges for homosexuals found in the Armed Services; (3) Elimination of insulting-worded and phrased military regulations relating to homosexuals and homosexuality. That is all!!!

Let's keep it to that! . . .

Cordially,
Frank

The Right Reverend Michael Francis Itkin, chairman of the Christian League for Sexual Freedom and one of the pioneers in the gay church movement, disagreed with Kameny's stance on the proper relationship between the peace and homophile movements. In a highly critical letter about Kameny's plans to picket the Pentagon in 1966, Itkin wrote: "It is our contention that while you may be quite correct that the law is unequal in refusing to draft homosexuals, this is indeed a blessed inequality that allows at least 1/6 of the population to opt out of the murder." Itkin held that the campaign for sexual freedom and civil liberties for homosexuals must take a backseat to the campaign to end the war in Vietnam.[9]

Kameny to Theodore Winston

Theodore Winston, a homophile activist from Los Angeles, had written Kameny about forming a small group of intellectuals, including Foster Gunnison Jr., founder of the Institute for Social Ethics, who would strategize about the homophile movement. Kameny subsequently refers to earlier letters in which Winston had asked Gunnison about the causes of homosexuality.

MAY 1, 1966

Dear Mr. Winston:

. . . Over the past number of years, in the course of public appearances, I have encountered just about every question on these matters that the public has to ask. I have formulated my answers to all of them, and have never really been stopped by any question. You raise—in one of your letters to Foster—the question of what answer should be given when asked about *cause.* This question comes up repeatedly—it is one of the most frequent to arise. While the answer has to be pitched to the particular audience and to the particular context in which the question arose, and so the answer varies considerably in its formation from case to case, my answer is:

> You are asking the wrong question. The much more fundamental question—the one which is never asked by anyone—is "What is the cause of *hetero*sexuality?" Or perhaps even more fundamentally, what are the causes and nature of sexuality in general? If you think about it a bit, you will realize that the most convenient method of satisfaction of the simple physical sexual drive is obviously masturbation. This is clearly unsatisfactory, for purely emotional reasons. Why? Given that a partner is desired for emotional satisfaction, why a choice of a type of partner? And what determines the choice? Why do most men choose women; most women, men—and, usually, particular types of men and women? All of these questions are quite unanswered and largely unasked.

I feel that the answer to the question as to the cause of homosexuality will never be found as long as we seek just that. When we ask and find an answer to the question as to the causes of *hetero*sexuality, the causes of homosexuality will drop out as an incidental byproduct.

> For the present, all that we can say is that homosexuality seems to be the result of subtle and as yet unknown environmental factors, occurring in very early infancy—factors of the same type as, and occurring at the same time as, those producing heterosexuality in the heterosexual.

> However, basically, I find the question quite unimportant, and of little concern to me. I do not see the Negro rights movement concerned with questions of which gene on which chromosome produces a black skin, nor do I see them subsidizing research into skin pigmentation. The Negro, the Jew—and the homosexual—ask for acceptance, equality, rights, dignity—as Negros, as Jews, and as homosexuals. It doesn't much matter how any of us got that way. . . .

> Sincerely yours,
> Franklin E. Kameny

Kameny to Richard Inman

A month before Kameny sent this letter, Inman appeared on "The Homosexual," an episode of FYI, a television news program produced by WTVJ in Miami, Florida. Seeming uncomfortable before the camera, Inman briefly explained his work for civil rights for homosexuals. When asked whether he was homosexual, Inman stated that he had given up homosexuality four years earlier. "It's not my cup of tea," he stated.[10]

Inman was unemployed and spent the majority of his time leading the Mattachine Society of Florida. The letter following offers rare evidence that Kameny offered financial help to gay pioneers in dire straits.

JUNE 25, 1966

Dear Dick:

I was sorry, indeed, to learn of your employment problem. As one who has been through this kind of thing on several occasions (I was unemployed for 20 months the first time, and lived on 20 cents worth of food a day for the last 8 months of that), I know, very much firsthand, how you feel, and I can sympathize. My most recent siege of unemployment lasted a year (to the day) and others have lasted 2 months, 4 months, and 7 months. It IS possible to survive.

The free time can be put to good use. I got an enormous amount done during my most recent period as a "gentleman of leisure"—I sometimes yearn for those days, when I see my desk piling up with unanswered letters and unwritten articles.

I enclose a small check, which you may consider as a gift—not a loan. Because I am still over $3000 in debt to kindhearted friends (and landlord) as a result of my last period of unemployment, and must pay this money back at a rapid rate, as a matter of conscience and honor, I cannot, for the present, send more—much as I would like to—nor to promise anything on a regular basis. I will do what I can.

In the meantime, if there is anything else that I can do, please let me know; if you need any hints on how to live on no income, and how to fend off your creditors, let me know—I am *very* experienced.

Lots of luck, and keep me closely posted on developments.

Sincerely,

Frank

Kameny to Evelyn Hooker

Facing discrimination from the government, gay men and lesbians visited and phoned Kameny at all hours of the day for consolation, encouragement, and especially legal remedies. Kameny had no formal training as a lawyer, but after his firing in 1957, he educated himself in the nuts and bolts of anti-homosexual policy and practice in the federal government. In turn, he offered legal counsel to numerous homosexuals facing discrimination by the government, often charging them for his services.

While acting as personal counsel, Kameny met with individuals at his home in Washington and frequently accompanied them to their interrogations and hearings at federal agencies. During this pre-court stage of the cases, he often offered written evidence suggesting that his client posed no security threat or any other sort of harm to the federal government. This is the type of evidence that Kameny seeks in this letter to Evelyn Hooker.

SEPTEMBER 17, 1966

Dear Dr. Hooker:

You probably do not remember me—we met in Philadelphia, in September 1963, when you were attending a meeting of the American Psychological Association, and I was attending the ECHO (East Coast Homophile Organization) conference. I was then President of the Mattachine Society of Washington.

I am writing to ask for your assistance in the matter in which I believe that it can properly be given, and would be of the greatest value.

I am currently assisting someone in a security clearance case. One of the several "rationales" brought by the government to justify its blanket denial of security clearances to all homosexuals, is that homosexuality, *per se*, is an indication of either emotional or psychological instability, such that a homosexual cannot safely be entrusted with classified information. I think that you would probably agree that such a generalization is invalid.

By homosexuals and homosexuality, here, I refer to individuals whose tendencies and preferences are for sexual and emotional involvement with those of their own gender, and who, in consequence, engage in sexual relations with those of their own gender in significant or major degree.

One of the bases upon which this case is being handled is that citizens should be considered, by their government, as individuals. Those who are, indeed, unstable, may well properly be denied clearances; those who are not unstable, judged as individuals, should be granted clearance, insofar as this context is concerned.

What I need—rather promptly—is a letter . . . to the effect that in your professional judgment, there is no correlation—or insufficient one-to-one correlation—between homosexuality . . . and psychological and emotional instability, adequate to justify automatic denial to all homosexuals, *per se*, of security clearances. To the extent, of course, that you see fit to go beyond this, and make your statement a stronger one, it will be quite welcome.

What is being asked is that you affirm that, in your professional judgment, it is indeed possible for a homosexual—including, specifically, those engaging in a continuing pattern of homosexual acts, making up most of all of their sexual outlet—to be sufficiently emotionally stable to present no danger when entrusted with secret information (by "no danger" is meant no greater danger, through instability, than for the average, "normal" heterosexual.")—and (if you see fit to emphasize your statement to any degree) that not merely is it possible that he is so, but that there is significant probability that such stability exists, or, in fact, that it is likely. . . .

I would be most appreciative of a very prompt response, since a hearing in this case will be scheduled shortly, and we would like to have your letter in advance of it, to have on hand if it should prove necessary.

Please be assured that your letter (while it will, in high likelihood, go into the federal record of the case) will be considered confidential by us, and will not be publicized by us in any way, without your explicit permission. . . .

Thank you very much for your assistance and cooperation.

Sincerely yours,

Franklin E. Kameny

Kameny to Harry Morgan

Kameny lobbies Harry Morgan of CBS News about a documentary in production. Titled The Homosexuals, *the controversial documentary would be anchored by Mike Wallace and aired on March 7, 1967. During the production stages, Wallace interviewed several gay men, including MSW's Jack Nichols.*

NOVEMBER 25, 1966

Dear Mr. Morgan:

. . . Mr. Nichols indicated that you will have someone to discuss the "homosexual Mafia" in the arts.

I feel that this is a bit of sensationalism which can only degrade your presentation. Those who are knowledgeable will find it ridiculous and ludicrous. Those who are not knowledgeable will only be misled, to the unnecessary detriment (based upon a non-existent situation) of the homosexual.

That there are homosexuals in the arts is, of course, true. For a variety of somewhat obscure historical reasons, there has been less prejudice there; any group of people who are generally discriminated against will tend to move into areas of endeavor where—for whatever the reasons—discrimination is less. The process will tend, to a degree, to "snowball" (look at industries, professions, occupations, and the like, dominated by Jews, Irish, Catholics, or other groups, for very similar reasons). The process will continue as long as the prejudice continues, and will go when the prejudice goes.

But the idea of a "mafia" implies conspiracy, organization, coordination of activity, direction, goals. Certainly there is not the slightest indication that these are present in any degree whatever.

Actually, those who make these allegations just don't like to see homosexuals *any*where, and really object to our having any kind of jobs at all, or to our playing any kind of a role at all in society—or at least anything more than a menial or marginal role.

I am sure that you see the similarity between the charges of a "homosexual mafia" and the charges of a "Jewish conspiracy," which one hears endlessly from anti-Semitic sources. Both charges are a discredit only to those making them and to those believing them.

Sincerely yours,
Franklin E. Kameny

5

"We Are People; We Are Not Specimens or Inanimate Objects"

1967

Kameny to Randy Wicker (Charles Hayden Jr.)

Randy Wicker had attracted the attention of major media outlets since first appearing on WBAI in New York in 1962. Reporters and producers identified him as a major spokesman of the homophile movement and often turned to him for interviews and advice. In early 1967, The David Susskind Show, a nationally syndicated talk show known for its cutting-edge topics, had asked Wicker to appear in a discussion between him, Susskind, and Irving Bieber (a psychoanalyst who had written of homosexuals as mentally disordered). After learning this, Kameny felt compelled to send Wicker some unsolicited, and heavy-handed, advice. In the following letter he refers to his good friend Barbara Gittings, who had founded the New York chapter of the Daughters of Bilitis, recruited Kameny to write for the organization's newsletter (The Ladder), and also picketed with him in 1965. The letter offers insight into Kameny's hard-driving personality.

JANUARY 21, 1967

Dear Charlie:

Barbara Gittings tells me that you're going to be on the David Susskind show with Bieber. Congratulations and good luck!

I'm writing to express my concern that you properly prepare yourself, and to URGE that you do so.

If you handle this successfully, it can set us VERY far ahead. But if you mess it up, or don't show Bieber up, it will not merely be a chance lost—it'll be a very real and very tragic setback which we will take years to overcome. . . .

You MUST have your arguments and responses marshaled.

Do you know the faults of Bieber's study, from a scientific viewpoint, and the answers to his counter-answers, and can you present them so that they come across? Do you know of Schofield's study, and what it sows in contradiction to Bieber, and of the critical importance of this work?[1]

Do you know a teleological argument when you hear one, and which of Bieber's arguments are teleological, and why such arguments are bad science, and how to respond to them?

The question of the cause of HETEROsexuality MUST be asked—and pressed hard—and put in a way so that people will realize that it, indeed, IS a legitimate question. When you ask it you will get very good-sounding and very plausible-sounding answers. They won't really be good or plausible, but will just be evasions. Are you prepared to see through them? They must be responded to properly and fully.

There are many, many more such matters which you MUST have instantly and fully at your mental "finger tips," in the manner best suited to provide the most effective response to the way in which the matter is brought up.

There are a number of things which you must avoid as you would avoid the plague.

If you go into the subject of gender role-playing, you have lost the debate.

If you even breathe a word of your ideas that homosexuality results from the behavior and personality of women in our culture, or let any slightest amount of your hostility toward women come through, you might as well hand the program to Bieber on a silver platter. He'll have won, hands down. And he'll be smart enough to see it the instant you slip.

There are many, many other such points. You ought to be spending your full time from now until taping-time on getting these things down pat.

This is not the time for a "personality-kid," "likable-guy" kind of approach.

Further—Bieber (by a narrow margin) is not a complete villain, by any means. He can be used, if you know how. He recently sent a letter of support (at my request) for our side in a security clearance case for which I am counsel, and which is currently occupying every instant of my spare time. Given what seems to be his attitudes on those matters, it is possible that with careful tactics and careful "playing by ear"—perhaps—the program might be parlayed into something which will be enormously helpful to us in our battle with the government.[2]

You're assuming a VERY weighty mantle of the utmost importance. See that you live up to the responsibility that you're assuming!!! This program is not a "lark." We're not likely to have another such opportunity for a very long time.

I—and a lot of others that I know—will never forgive you if you "muff" this one. . . .

As always,
Frank

Irving Bieber refused to appear on the show with a member of the Mattachine Society. As for Kameny, he and Jack Nichols made their own television appearance on WOOK in Washington, DC, on February 7. According to Nichols's later report, Dennis Richards, the host of WOOK's "Controversy," screamed at Kameny and Nichols during the taping. "Get off my stage, out of my studio, you vicious, perverted, lecherous people!" he shouted. The host also screamed, "You make me want to vomit!" But according to Nichols, he and Kameny answered every question "coolly" and "effectively."[3]

Kameny to Robert Martin Jr.

Kameny often exchanged personal information in his correspondence with Columbia University student Robert Martin Jr. (later know as Stephen Donaldson). On January 7, 1967, for example, Kameny had written: "Was interested in the details of your exploits in Philadelphia, beyond what you'd told me by phone. Two at once! How? Explicit details please. What is the Stonewall, at which you danced?"[4] And back in February 1966 Kameny had written that he would like to take Martin up on his offer to see nude photos of him. "It's a pity there are none with an erection," he added. In the same letter, Kameny inquired about Martin's "reactions and sensations" when assuming the passive role in anal sex, sharing that he had recently had sex with a college student. Commenting on the young man, Kameny wrote: "Pleasant, but somewhat overweight, which I don't like."⁵

In another earlier letter, Kameny reported that he and Barbara Gittings had recently appeared as co-counsels at a hearing for a homosexual employee of the Defense Department.⁶ One of the so-called experts called by defense was Charles Socarides, a New York–based psychiatrist who held that homosexuality was pathological, the result of stunted growth in the preoedipal stage of psychosexual development. Kameny and Gittings later sent out a memorandum about the hearing to homophile organizations and activists, taking special care to emphasize the defense counsel's statement that the department did not automatically deny security clearances to individuals known to be homosexual. The more colorful part of the memo, however, centered on Socarides:

> *Following an hour's direct examination, by Department Counsel, during which Dr. Socarides' extreme, bizarre, and quite incredible views of homosexuals and homosexuality were brought out, we subjected him to almost three hours of intensive cross-examination.*
>
> *Our first question to him (and subsequent questions, by way of confirmation) asked where he had seen the homosexuals from whom he was drawing his broad generalizations about all homosexuals.*
>
> *His reply (and subsequent replies) indicated that they were ALL patients or seen in similar clinical, therapeutic circumstances; that he had never meaningfully seen or examined a homosexual who had not been a patient in a therapeutic manner.*
>
> *He was apparently quite unable to perceive the catastrophic consequences to his theories, of basing them upon an obviously atypical, non-representative sampling of this sort, although we pointed this out to him repeatedly.*
>
> *Thus this man, who publicly claims sufficient knowledge to call all homosexuals sick; to term homosexuality pathological; to say that there can be no happy homosexuals, has never seen a typical homosexual.*
>
> *He has no valid scientific or logical basis for adjusting the nature of homosexuality, and has absolutely no way of knowing whether or not there are or can be happy homosexuals, since happy people do not go into psychotherapy.*

This is characteristic of the "reasoning" engaged in by so many psychia-trists and psychoanalysts, and is clear basis for refutation of their claims.[7]

This brief background helps explain Kameny's subsequent reply. Martin had told him about a counselor's comments on homosexuality, and Kameny responds with some of his own counseling, encouraging the student to stay positive about his gay sexuality.

MAY 11, 1967

Dear Bob:

Just a comment in regard to Mitchell (or whatever his name is, in the counseling service, or whatever), who wrote the scathing letter about pros-elytizing, etc.

1. "Latent" homosexuals will discover their homosexuality sooner or later. It is far better that it be sooner than later—tragedies result from later discovery (after marriage and children, etc.)

2. Homosexuals who wish to change have been brainwashed. They are in a class with the Negroes who have been so thoroughly psychologically imbued with ideas of white superiority and Negro inferiority that they use hair-straightening devices and skin-whitening creams.

3. —and most important. Don't be on the defensive on these matters. Mitchell's entire comment is predicated on the assumption that homosex-uality is inferior to and less desirable than heterosexuality. But it is—and MUST be—our position that homosexuality is not inferior to or less desir-able than heterosexuality, but is precisely equal to it.

. . . Don't be stopped by the argument that society considers homo-sexuality inferior and less desirable, and therefore—. Obviously, in that case, it is society that is in error and is immoral and has immoral mores, not the homosexual, and society must be changed which is why homo-phile organizations exist. . . .

Have you considered setting up your own counseling service for homosexuals, until the university gets a competent one, which includes homosexuals on its staff? . . .

As always,

Frank

Kameny to Carl Rowan

During the Kennedy administration, Carl Rowan had served as both dep-
uty assistant secretary of the State Department and the U.S. delegate to the
United Nations. His government service continued when President Johnson
appointed him as director of the United States Information Agency. After
leaving government in 1966, Rowan became a columnist for the Chicago
Sun-Times.

MAY 17, 1967

Dear Mr. Rowan:

I write as a homosexual American citizen, and as a homosexual
human being, with equal emphasis on all three words in both phrases.

In your column . . . which appeared in the *Washington Evening Star* on
Wednesday, May 17, you referred to (my emphasis added): "a weird collection of *queers*, oddballs, no-goodniks and publicity hounds."

I do not think that you would use terms such as *nigger, kike, wop*, or
others, in referring to Negro, Jewish, Italian, or other American citizens
and human beings. No sensitive, civilized person would.

Homosexuals consider the term "queer" to be an epithet in the same
class, and we find it quite as offensive. It is totally as uncalled for. No sensitive, civilized person would use it either.

Your use of it indicates that—to your discredit—you do not yet consider homosexuals and others as being quite human.

As homosexuals, we have quite as much claim to our human dignity
and self-respect, and to freedom from irrational contempt, as do all other
citizens and persons. Attempts to dehumanize us, depersonalize us, and
degrade us are as unwarranted as are such attempts visited upon others of
our American minority groups.

I feel that you owe a public apology to our homosexual citizenry for
both your use of the term *queer*, itself, and for the derogatory and con-
temptuous tone of your allusion.

I strongly suggest that you do some careful re-thinking and make a
careful re-assessment of your own prejudices, which—seemingly—you
have accepted much too casually.

I will be pleased to discuss these matters personally with you.
I look forward to your early reply.
Thank you.

Sincerely yours,
Franklin E. Kameny

In his May 22 reply, Rowan wrote that his column was "further proof that people tend to be prejudiced toward things they don't know. My first-hand knowledge of homosexuals being nil, perhaps I have erroneously embraced the popular notion that they are 'queer.'" Rowan concluded by offering his "sincere apology."[8]

Kameny to Nevin Richardson

The Kameny Papers include more than a few letters in which Kameny fends off creditors, some of them his good friends. The following is typical of the correspondence he sent to individuals who had loaned him money. In this letter to a client, Kameny also justifies his recent purchase of a car.

AUGUST 30, 1967

Dear Nevin:

I also, in the past, have ALWAYS cleared up my debts as soon as money commenced coming in—to the extent that I did not wear decent clothes for considerable periods of time until all debts were paid off. However, you must keep in mind something else. We are not immortal. There are times when one realizes that life is passing by and feels that if one is EVER to enjoy any of the goods of the world he must make some compromises. So, after having literally not a possession to my name for a very long time, with, during each period of opulence, ALL of my money going into the repayment of debts, I decided, just once, to indulge myself somewhat, and use SOME (not all) of my spare income to get some things for myself—the remainder to go into the payment of debts.

In terms of the larger society—not any one individual such as you, but people collectively—I feel that I have earned some such self-indulgence—at least a little. Virtually all of my spare time, outside of working hours, is devoted to assisting others. Whether it is a momentary thing like going down to the Bethesda jail, last Thursday night, midst the downpour, to advise someone through the bars of a jail cell; or a much longer-range project, like the many test cases I'm involved in (and I have NOT overlooked yours), or the homophile movement generally, I have given of myself far more than most people that you know.

Not only do I feel that I have earned a little in the way of comfort and convenience (I get very little in the way of pleasure; I haven't had time for a social life, or even for a concert or movie in years), but some of these things are necessary. Without a car (my old one was falling apart) I would not be able to go down to the jail to assist people or to bail them out. One of the reasons why your letter to Mr. Macy hasn't been drafted was that in the absence of expenditures for desk, file cabinets, and office furniture, I had become SO inefficient that I was using up more than half my time in trying to find things which should have been filed and set out systematically . . . One doesn't get much done when most of one's time has to be spent in looking for books, documents and papers because of a lack of drawers . . . Instead of taking a pleasant three days off this coming Labor Day weekend, I intend to spend the entire 50 waking hours of the weekend filing, sorting and systematizing, so that I can—hopefully—be up to date by the end of September and then keep myself up to date with a growing work load.

I am not as wealthy as you think. The homophile movement takes a considerable amount of money—in telephone expenses and travel expenses, etc. These are not for pleasure. This is not being spent on myself, and represents a deep sense of responsibility.

As of Sunday, just 5 days ago, my bank account was down to $22.34. It is now back up again, but the point is that I have to budget my expenses—including repayment of debts—in terms not only of amount but of *time* of payment. I paid my August 1 rent this morning.

I realize that you are under severe pressure and—as you only too well know—I know exactly how you feel, from more than one first-hand experience. I am doing all that I can, and will, of course, continue to do so. Keep in mind, again, that my debts are to many more people than just to you—with some of the debts being rather larger than the one to you—and my responsibilities are to many, many people the country over.

I am doing the best that I can as one, fallible human being.

I am indeed sorry that this sort of bitterness has developed. I hope that it will pass.

How IS your job situation? Do you have any possibilities? Please keep me informed, because I do worry about you.

Most sincerely,

Franklin E. Kameny

Kameny to the Editors of the *Washington Post*

Kameny criticizes his new archnemesis—Charles Socarides—and calls for him to undergo psychotherapy. The New York psychiatrist, who also taught at the Albert Einstein College of Medicine, had stated in a recent speech at the National Institutes of Mental Health in Washington that homosexuality was a "tragic human condition" caused by a "crushing," "domineering," and "tyrannical" mother who does not allow her child to individuate. Homosexuality, he added, is a "condition of certainly epidemiological proportions," one that required the establishment of a national center that would study and rehabilitate homosexuals.[9]

OCTOBER 9, 1967

Gentlemen:

I write in response to Jean M. White's report . . . of Dr. Charles W. Socarides' recent lecture on homosexuality, given at the National Institutes of Mental Health. . . .

In short, we have been *defined* into sickness by the use of subjective and personal, moral and social value judgments, cloaked in the language of science.

As a scientist by training and profession, I can say that the treatment of the subject by Dr. Socarides and his colleagues is shabby, shoddy, slipshod, just-plain-bad science.

Their position on this matter represents the largest body of fuzzy-minded non-"reasoning" in a supposedly scientific discipline, of which I am aware. Perhaps a little psychotherapy, to help them to overcome their resistance to new ideas, would be useful.

More important than all this is the reaction of the individual homosexual. Dr. Socarides speaks of those who appeal for help. Most of those whom he sees are, naturally, trying to get help to change to heterosexuality, or are persuaded to do so by Dr. Socarides. Theses homosexuals are people who have been "brainwashed" into a belief in the inferiority and undesirability of their condition, like the Negro who tried to lighten his skin or straighten his hair.

A realistic approach *must* take into account the fact that when most homosexuals seek help, it is to alleviate the overt manifestations of prejudice and discrimination directed against them. They seek acceptance, an end to rejection, equality of opportunity to contribute to the society in which they live—AS HOMOSEXUALS. They do not desire change, and they very properly reject it. The very concept of "rehabilitation" does not apply. There is nothing to be rehabilitated from.

Most homosexuals do not need help at all. They live very happy, productive, well-adjusted lives, even with the continuing stresses induced by the prejudice directed against them.

Those few that do need help most often need help with *employment* problems, not *emotional* problems. But Dr. Socarides is not equipped to supply that kind of help. If Dr. Socarides really wants to help us, let him commence using his psychoanalysis to overcome prejudice and discrimination upon the part of employers and others. He might well start with that bastion of entrenched anti-homosexual prejudice, the federal government.

There is an unfortunate tendency to consider psychiatrists as *the* authorities and experts on homosexuality. They are not. Homosexuality is a psychological condition (as any preference is), not a psychiatric problem. It is a *sociological* problem—in prejudice and discrimination against a minority group. That no one publicly questions whether homosexuality is a matter for the NIMH at all lies at the heart of the problem. . . .

A few concluding remarks:

1. Unless Dr. Socarides is suggesting forced treatment, he will find his proposed treatment centers sparsely attended by homosexuals.

2. If a center is set up for the *study* of homosexuality, it is to be hoped that it is staffed—at least in major part—by others than Dr. Socarides and those of his like, and that the staff includes at least a sizable number of those who are most knowledgeable, most concerned, and least consulted about homosexuality—homosexuals themselves.

There is far too much tendency for others to pontificate about homosexuals and their homosexuality—usually on the basis of appallingly inadequate information—without ever actually dealing with us at first hand. We are people; we are not specimens or inanimate objects.

3. The National Institutes of Mental Health are to be severely faulted for presenting and publicizing as extreme and unrelievedly one-sided a view of this controversial subject (as Dr. Socarides), under circumstances which give at least the appearance of bearing the stamp of government agreement and approval.

4. I am informed by reliable NIMH authority . . . that Dr. Socarides's views and proposals definitely do NOT bear the official stamp of NIMH approval or scholarship.

Sincerely yours,

Franklin E. Kameny

Kameny to Drew Pearson

Syndicated news columnist Drew Pearson charged on October 30 that Governor Ronald Reagan of California had failed to act quickly after learning of a "homo ring" in the governor's office. Pearson added that evidence included a tape recording of eight men involved in a "sex orgy, which had taken place at a cabin near Lake Tahoe, leased by two members of Reagan's staff."[10] According to Pearson, Reagan waited six months after first learning of this alleged orgy before he fired the two staff members. In response to Pearson's column, Reagan denied all charges.[11]

NOVEMBER 5, 1967

Dear Mr. Pearson:

I recently read reports of your allegations that Governor Reagan of California, employed homosexuals on his staff. Apparently you consider this somehow objectionable and as something to be held against him.

I write as a *homosexual American citizen* (with as much emphasis upon the last two words of that phrase as upon the first) to ask why Governor Reagan should not have homosexual California citizens on his staff.

Homosexual citizens pay their taxes, vote, and are in all other ways first-class citizens (Our country claims that it does not have second-class citizens). Why should any position, public or private, be closed to them?

There is little difference between the attitude attributed to you on this matter, and that of the Southern racist who would look askance at a Negro on his Governor's staff, or the anti-Semite who would look askance at a Jew in a similar position.

Since 10% of California's population (as of the Nation's population) is homosexual, at least 10% of its Governor's staff should be homosexual.

We do not have apartheid in this country—at least theoretically.

If a man performs his job competently, his sex life is irrelevant. It is his own affair, and should not be considered in regard to any job or position at all.

Since homosexuals *are* citizens, like all citizens, entitled by *right* to all of the same rights, privileges, prerogatives and opportunities as are all other citizens, I feel that, if anything, you should have taken Governor Reagan to task for firing or otherwise excluding homosexuals from his staff, just as you would have if you were to learn that he excluded Negros or Jews from his staff.

I can assure you that were I a citizen of California, I would now be considering bringing suit against Governor Reagan for insidious discrimination and for denial of equality of opportunity. I and other homosexual American citizens have brought and are bringing suits on essentially this kind of basis, against the Federal government in increasing numbers.

I would appreciate your reply.

Sincerely yours,
Franklin E. Kameny

6

"Gay Is Good"

1968

Kameny to the Editors of the *Washington Post*

Depicting the type of image that Hoover frowned upon, the Washington
Post *reported that the FBI director had once said: "I certainly would not
want any of the beatniks with sideburns and beards as employees of the
Bureau. . . . No member of the Mattachine Society or anyone who is a sex
deviate will ever be appointed to the FBI."*[1]

FEBRUARY 25, 1968

Gentlemen:

Mr. J. Edgar Hoover's comment . . . that "no member of the Mattachine Society will ever be appointed to the FBI" is revealing.

The Mattachine Society of Washington is an organization working by
lawful and orderly means to better the lot of the homosexual citizens in
our society and nation. Its membership includes men and women, heterosexuals as well as homosexuals. (The Society has had heterosexual officers.)

Surely no valid objection can be raised to lawful attempts (and those
who engage in them) at the betterment of the situation of any group of
citizens in our country, no matter how controversial they may be.

For Mr. Hoover to make employment by his agency contingent upon
working only for the good of "acceptable" people, but not for the good of
"unacceptable" or unpopular, or controversial people, indicates only how
shallow is Mr. Hoover's grasp of the basic meaning of Americanism.

Mr. Hoover states, in addition, that homosexuals are not employable by the FBI. This, of course, is merely another manifestation of the

150

American version of apartheid, practiced quite as fanatically by our government, as is the South African version by theirs, but with a different group of people as its victims.

Unfortunately, since Mr. Hoover's agency is responsible for clearances of individuals for jobs in many other places, the pernicious effects of his prejudices extend far beyond more harm to his own agency.

It is obvious both that private, consensual adult sexual conduct bears no rational relationship to eligibility for employment by the FBI or by anyone else; and that, of course, like all government agencies without exception, the FBI is not without its share of homosexual employees.

I might point out that a few years ago, Mr. Hoover asked to be removed from the Washington Mattachine Society's mailing list (upon which he had been placed, at the Society's initiative, along with many other government officials obviously needing education on homosexuality). Apparently he was rather more afraid of appearing upon the Mattachine Society's lists than the Society is of appearing on Mr. Hoover's lists.

When Mr. Hoover refused to comply with—or even to have the common courtesy to reply to—the Society's counter-condition (written assurance that all reference to the Society had, in turn, been removed from the FBI's files and would remain so), Mr. Hoover's request was turned down. If his remark, quoted in the *Post*, is any indication, he apparently did not profit by the Society's literature, which he continued to receive. Like the ignorance to which it is so closely related, entrenched prejudice is often invincible.

Sincerely yours,
Franklin E. Kameny

Kameny to Robert Martin Jr.

Kameny comments on the 1960s in general and, more particularly, events at Columbia University and Northwestern University. Militant students at Columbia had occupied five campus buildings in late April to force university officials to meet a series of demands, including halting plans to build a gymnasium in a nearby neighborhood, cutting ties to an institute that allegedly studied riot control, and forming a student-faculty process for addressing disciplinary matters. Early May also saw over one hundred

African-American students at Northwestern occupying the school's finance building to win increased scholarship funding, separate living quarters, and black studies courses approved by students. In the following letter, Kameny expresses irritation with these events and with the "all you need is love" philosophy he detected in Martin and others in the younger generation.[2]

MAY 8, 1968

Dear Bob:

. . . As I observe our society and culture today, I become more and more convinced that this decade will go down in history as the Mindless Sixties—as a decade of loose-minded, fuzzy-edged, slovenly, superficial thinking and slipshod reasoning, without any pretense at intellectual rigor. More than anything else, that is what seems to characterize the social and intellectual ferment of our times (which is not to say that I do not sympathize with a great deal of it . . . ; I still place myself, intellectually, on the younger side of the "generation gap," although with a certain leavening through age). From the hippie movement, with its emotionally appealing but completely, impossibly impractical philosophy (to the extent that it had one at all; and a lack of carefully constructed philosophies when they are needed is endemic these days) to the Negro movement, which, having made enormous progress in eliminating segregation with all of its evils, is not busily bringing it back again (see Northwestern University) with brand new evils which will become evident soon enough, to various other phenomena of our society, we see, persistently, a dominance of emotion and demagoguery over reason and reality—and that is what is happening at Columbia. Love is all very fine and wonderful, and I do NOT down-rate it in any way. But love does NOT keep the stomach full, and someone does have to do the just-plain-unpleasant work of raising the crops, and love does NOT cure the ills of the flesh (unless one believes in Christian Science) and it takes some thoroughly disciplined and unloving training and some rigorous thinking, and lots of tedious, unloving labor to create the intellectual and psychical wherewithal to eliminate disease. THIS is what your universities are for. And those who would prevent that are the ones who are betraying you, not those who seek to keep alive and to pass on traditions of sound thinking. . . .

To the dismay of many with whom I have discussed these matters, I have spoken in empathy with the Negro rioters (although continuing to deplore violence, destruction, and flagrant violations of the rights of others). I have used those riots as illustrative of our own feelings of frustration and infuriation with an obdurate government and an intransigent society. BUT—the Negro has truly explored and exhausted well-nigh, if not actually *all*, other avenues, and has gotten to the firm, unyielding stone wall of prejudice which blocks them. WE have run into this, but have not yet reached the end of all avenues. So we are continuing to use orderly—if sometimes radical and unorthodox—procedures.

You (pl.) at Columbia have exhausted few if any avenues of recourse—you hadn't even explored them! . . .

Keep in touch.

As *ALWAYS*,
Frank

Kameny to Robert Martin Jr.

Kameny continues his rant against the "Mindless Sixties," especially its calls for racial separatism from black militants and attempts at participatory democracy in such organizations as the Students for Democratic Society. He sometimes stated, jokingly, that one of the worst decisions he ever made was to create the MSW as a democratic organization.

MAY 18, 1968

Dear Bob:

. . . I must express my bitter opposition to the misguided efforts by Negro militants to reinstitute segregation and separatism. This is indeed another demonstration of the Mindless Sixties.

Racism is racism and segregation is segregation, and they are illogical, irrational, harmful, wrong and evil, whether imposed by whites upon Negroes, whites upon whites, Negroes upon Negroes, or Negroes upon whites.

They make of the color of a person's skin—a characteristic not merely of small importance, but of NO importance—the entire basis for classifying him. This is degrading to and destructive of EVERY meaningful human value. It relegates to zero importance EVERYthing that makes a human being a human being.

Further, this is directly antithetical to what, to me, has been one of the finest aspects of the American system—its ability to assimilate diverse groups. I am strongly opposed to approaches which contribute to fragmentation and separatism in our society—particularly based upon as superficial and meaningless a criterion as skin color.

The Negroes' feeling of alienation is part of the maiming of his personality caused by his minority condition—as with the homosexual.

That may make it understandable, but not acceptable or to be condoned.

Requests for segregated dormitories in colleges should be rejected firmly. Requests for courses in Negro culture should be turned down as should requests for courses in Irish culture by the Irish, Israeli culture by Jews, Italian culture by Italians, or Mexican culture by Mexican-Americans.

Efforts to create a separate Negro community and to maintain a ghetto should be discouraged by every means possible.

That the Negro may—in many instances—want this is irrelevant. He has been badly misled. Most people are sheep, and the Negro is neither more nor less so. A few vociferous leaders, also beautifully representative of the Mindless Sixties, have, unfortunately, not been offset by some equally vociferous leaders of more thoughtful and long-range view.

I am indeed sorry to note indications (perhaps wrong) that you have "bought" some of the facile arguments and approaches of the many Negro militants who are only doing harm to their own community and to the nation.

I judge that you approve of "participatory democracy." I suppose that one must go through that stage. The United States did from colonial days until 1787, when it adopted representative democracy, although the New England town meeting continued on into the 19th century, I believe, but soon became clearly impractical. But at least that was conducted under rules of procedure and firm discipline.

Unfortunately, the Mindless Sixties don't believe in rules of procedure, or in any sort of discipline. And they believe ONLY in total consensus, not in any kind of majority rule. That is why your meetings go on for hours. That is also why they never accomplish anything truly meaningful.

As pointed out in *Newsweek*, they believe in action without ideology. But meaningful action is impossible without ideology. And so the so-called "new left" . . . has accomplished absolutely nothing, and won't.

I don't think that they've realized that the only way they will ever get the unanimity that they insist upon is either to rule by force . . . or fragment into smaller and smaller groups, and form new groupings and alliances whenever a new question arises.

Their deadly fear of any kind of delegated authority results in an endless change of chairmen, vanishing short terms, when they formalize their structure at all, instability, inability to create or to carry out long-range plans, and total non-accomplishment.

Participatory democracy is a nice-sounding idea. It doesn't work. . . .

Keep in close touch. My greetings to all who know me at Columbia.

Affectionately,

Frank

Kameny to the Editors of the *Washington Post*

JUNE 3, 1968

Gentlemen:

I note that the State Department has just gone through its annual American "fertility rite" by announcing the firing of a certain number of homosexuals in the preceding year. . . .

The ancient Aztecs or Mayas used to sacrifice virgins, annually, to propitiate the gods and to gain favors from them. The State Department sacrifices homosexuals, annually, to propitiate the House Appropriations Committee, and to gain money from them. There is little difference.

Sincerely yours,

Franklin E. Kameny

Kameny to Dick Leitsch

In this historic letter to MSNY leader Dick Leitsch, Kameny lays out his "Gay Is Good" philosophy, noting its parallels with the "Black is Beautiful" slogan found in the modern civil rights movement. He also argues that transsexuality is "not our problem," and that bisexuality is sociologically rare.

In addition, Kameny refers to a fissure in his relationship with the MSNY leader. Kameny had been a major source of Leitsch's earlier turn to militancy—Leitsch was inspired by a 1964 speech in which Kameny had called MSNY to focus on direct action campaigns designed to secure civil liberties—but the two had since grown apart. Kameny was especially irritated by his sense that Leitsch had failed to cooperate with efforts to build a national homophile movement, and that he had not wholly embraced the premise that gay was always a good to be affirmed without qualification.

JUNE 19, 1968

Dear Dick:

I am writing with care here. I trust that you will read this with equal care.

I write sincerely, and with no intent at sarcasm, when I say that I was pleased to receive your letter of June 14 . . . *Pleased* because it represents the first letter which I have received from you in a very long time which attempts reasoned communication and exchange of ideas instead of tirade, polemic, recrimination, casting of aspersions, expression of baseless suspicion, attribution of discreditable motive, noncooperation, and the like. . . .

One of the points which I have made, with increasing intensity, over the past few years . . . is the pervasively negative attitude toward homosexuality with which the homosexual is surrounded, and with which society is imbued. You will find a little of that in my 1964 speech. My attitude has solidified since then.

I always commence my "standard speech" by pointing this out, and stating that I intend to take a positive, affirmative attitude.

Within the movement, I point out that many of the people in our own movement are often the unwitting purveyors of the same attitude. Read Hal Call's remarks some time, as an extreme case.[3]

I have been dismayed and distressed to see increasing amounts of that coming out in you of late.

Now, I take credit for a good many of the worthwhile ideas floating around in this movement, and for the phrasing of them. One which was not initially mine came from several sources, but I subscribe to it fully. It came from SIR, for one, and from the Negro movement, for another. I had thought that it might have come from you, too, but perhaps I am wrong. The sources of good ideas don't concern me nearly as much as the ideas themselves.

This is the point: that we must instill in the homosexual community a sense of the worth of the individual homosexual. A sense of high self-esteem. We must counteract the inferiority which ALL of society inculcates into him in regard to his homosexuality.

SIR overdoes it with its homosexual ghettos, to which I do NOT subscribe. The Negro militants overdo it, with their renewed separatism. But the basic idea is there.

The other day, on television, I saw Stokely Carmichael, before a group of Negroes almost chanting "Black is Beautiful." To a Negro, living in a society in which "white," "snow," "purity," and "good" are all equated together; and "black," "evil," "darkness," "dirt," and "ugliness" are all equated together, Carmichael's tactic is understandable—and necessary, and desirable.

Within our somewhat different framework, we need the same kind of thing.

Again—please don't get me wrong—I'm not preaching homosexual superiority, or any of that stupidity. But I do not grant one single whit of inferiority.

Our people need to have their self-esteem bolstered—singly and as a community.

The very idea of changing to heterosexuality (I will come to "free choice" below) is a tacit acknowledgement of inferiority.

When you say, publicly, that were you advising 9-year olds, you would try to have them grow up as heterosexuals, there comes across a sense of the inferiority of homosexuality. . . .

People who are TRULY equal, and TRULY not inferior, do NOT seriously consider acquiescing to the majority and changing themselves. Ask a Protestant in Southern Ireland, or a Catholic in Northern Ireland, or a Jew in Russia whether he would change his religion, even though it would make his life far easier, or whether he ought not to advise his youngsters to become Catholics, or Protestants, or atheists (as the case may be), and see the response.

To submit to the pressures of immoral societal prejudice is immoral. Self-respecting people do not so submit. Self-respect is what *I* am trying to inculcate into my people, even if you are not.

When you acquiesce to "therapy" and "change" in the manner in which you do, you simply confirm (on a "gut" basis) to all of the feelings of inferiority, wrongness, and self-contempt with which society has inculcated the individual homosexual. You harm the homosexual, and you harm the movement.

The very word "therapy" (whatever the particular, individual circumstances) confirms the image of sickness.

I would be most surprised if the Negro militants would not roundly condemn the Negroes who use the complexion-lightening drugs of which *Esquire* speaks. And they would consider your reaction to reverse-acting drugs as being insufferably patronizing.

Why?

Because, in *our* society, now, the choice is *NOT* a free one, based upon rational considerations.

To change from Negritude to whiteness for esthetic considerations represents a free choice. To change because (your words) "they find being a Negro debilitating" is NOT a truly free choice. It is submission to the immoral demands of an immoral society and will simply support and reinforce the immorality.

If people can choose hair color on esthetic or some generally similar basis, then they are making a free choice. If they choose hair color because one color might subject them to severe disadvantage, then they are not making a free choice.

How do we know whether the choice is free or not? One can examine the motives of each individual, of course. Another, more general way of judging is very simple. Is the traffic two-way? When I see significant numbers of whites using negritude drugs, then I will feel that society has relaxed its pressures and the choice has become a free one. This is not a "foolproof" criterion, of course, nor a rigorous one.

When I see heterosexuals going into "therapy" for change to homo-sexuality, then I will feel that the choice is a free one.

Until this occurs, negritude and homosexuality ARE (in fact) badges of inferiority in our society, and the Negro and the Homosexual needs to be reinforced in his own self-image, not to have it subtly torn down even further by his own "leaders."

You bring up the question of gender-change. You may note that I have never discussed that in any of my writings, and have never spoken against it. My main reason was that transsexuality is not our problem, and I don't believe in mixing causes, as you well know.

However, I've recognized that that was a superficial reason, and have never tried to verbalize other feelings.

Your comments have caused me to formulate my attitudes, and for that I thank you. The answer, of course, is contained in the above.

Within the framework of this discussion, and in terms of the kind of prejudice we're discussing, society accepts men and women as equals. The operation change is a matter of personal choice, and not a flight from a condition of societally induced "inferiority."

Therefore, while such a change is one which I would never make, and which, in fact, "rubs me VERY much the wrong way" emotionally, my reaction has always been that if the individual will be happier that way, let him go ahead.

The ONLY people in this entire country—in the entire world—that I know of, who are standing up and telling the homosexual person that he IS equal, and that this homosexuality is NOT a badge of inferiority, etc., and who are doing it without reservation, without excuse, not as a "crumb of pity from the table, for those psychologically maimed people who can't help themselves," who is saying NOT grudgingly, "homosexuality is a valid way of life for some people, but, in parallel to Carmichael, "homo-sexuality is GOOD—positively and without reservation—the ONLY peo-ple in all the world who are doing this are the pitifully small handful of us in the homophile movement. And our people are very sensitive to any squeamishness and half-heartedness on our part.

There are times when leadership requires the taking of total positions. Give this some thought.

In regard to your comments about bisexuality . . .

In any case, my definition of homosexuality—which I always state, is not and never has been a matter of exclusivity.

I have always said that it is a matter of dominant preference. That—for whatever the reasons—we find that almost everyone has a dominant preference either for affectional and sexual relationships with persons of the opposite gender, or for such relationships with persons of the same gender. That there are relatively few with an equal or near-equal preference.

Put differently, the average male, walking down the street, with the "erotic eye" which is characteristic of the male species (regardless of orientation), either notes the attractive women passing by OR the attractive men passing by. Rather few notice both and even fewer notice neither. There you have, in a nutshell, all of humanity—the heterosexuals, the homosexuals, the bisexuals, and the asexuals.

Tell it the way it is, man. THAT'S the way it is. They ain't no bisexuals (or damned few of them).

But exclusivity is NOT MY criterion. NOR is actual activity. It's a matter of *dominant preference.*

And so I will agree with you—when the choice is *truly* free (which means that it is made upon bases relevant to the choice, and not in flight from society's prejudices) AND when the methods for making the choice have been devised (the whole discussion is academic anyway, because changes don't occur—at ANY age), then I will support encouraging those who wish to change to do so.

But we're a VERY long way from that yet. We will get there a lot faster if we encourage our own people to hold up their heads, look the world in the eye and say *"Gay is Good"*—without ANY reservations—and . . . face the world with solidarity and self-confidence.

I must close this now. I hope that it's provided you with some food for thought.

I hope, too, that it will mark the beginning of something much more like the old cooperative relationship between us, which you have slowly destroyed over the past two years. . . .

Cordially,

Frank

Kameny to the Mattachine Society of New York

Kameny was a member of the Committee to Fight Exclusion of Homosexuals from the Armed Forces, and in the following excerpted letter he argues that the homophile movement should not encourage homosexuals to seek an exemption from the draft for the Vietnam War or any other war. In a section of the letter not included, Kameny wrote that Pentagon officials had told him that "the Mothers of America would never tolerate a change in this policy [of excluding homosexuals from the armed forces], which would then permit their sons to be thrown into contact with 'perverts.'"

JULY 10, 1968

Gentlemen:

. . . I feel that opinions and feelings on this draft and upon war—any war or all wars—should be studiously avoided by the homophile movement.

If we are asking for equality in terms of rights, benefits, privileges, freedoms, opportunities, etc.—the "good things"—we must be explicitly prepared to ask for equality in terms of duties, obligations, and responsibilities—the "bad things."

If, *as citizens*, we wish to see and to work for a change in the duties, obligations, and responsibilities borne by ALL citizens, this is certainly in order and very proper. But *as homosexuals*, and *as homophile organizations*, we have to work both sides of the equality coin. We cannot expect to be able to have our cake and eat it too.

Fundamentally, and on philosophical and ideological principle, discrimination is wrong, and we must work for an elimination of ALL of it, not just for those parts, elimination of which would benefit us—and we must work for the elimination of both aspects of it all the time. Any other course of action is shortsighted and intellectually dishonest.

An approach which says "Let's get the benefits first, and then we'll assume the obligations" is, to me, completely morally and ethically untenable. It will be taken by others for exactly what it is—a selfish attempt to get what's nice and good and pleasant and convenient, and to continue to avoid what's bad and unpleasant and inconvenient.

Much more important, such an approach can also be used, very easily, as a basis for continued denial of rights, on the argument that everything balances out if we are also excused from responsibilities and duties. Thus arises second-class citizenship.

In any battle for rights and for first-class citizenship, one is always on much stronger ground if one can argue from a position of already doing MORE than one's share, and of demanding proper recompense. . . .

Sincerely yours,
Franklin E. Kameny

Kameny to William Scanlon

In this letter to the director of the Defense Department's industrial security clearance program, Kameny offers a patriotic defense of his request for a security clearance. The letter's language of civil disobedience mirrors the rhetoric of the peace and modern civil rights movements.

JULY 27, 1968

Dear Mr. Scanlon:

I thank you for your willingness to invest a sizable amount of your time in our conversation last Thursday, even though, from my viewpoint, it was not as productive as I might have hoped. I do think that someday, if we can discuss some of these things in other than an adversary context, we might really be able to do something constructive about our security program—it certainly needs it.

In pursuance of that discussion, I wish to quote three items which, along with some others, will probably go into the preface of my soon-to-be-submitted statement:

There is a limit to the legitimate interference of collective opinion with individual independence; and to find that limit, and maintain it against encroachment, is as indispensable to a good condition of human affairs as protection against political despotism.[4]

John Stuart Mill, "On Liberty"

I don't think any man ever has the right to break the law; but I do think that upon occasion, every man has the duty to break the law—when the law begins to dominate rather than serve man.[5]

The Reverend William Sloane Coffin

Chaplain of Yale University

If I had been a Negro living in Birmingham or Little Rock or Plaquemines Parish, Louisiana, I hope I would have disobeyed the state law that said I might not enter the public waiting room reserved for "whites."

I hope I would have insisted upon going into the parks and swimming pools and schools which state or city law reserved for "whites."

I hope I would have had the courage to disobey, although the segregation ordinances were presumably law until they were declared unconstitutional.[6]

The Honorable Abe Fortas

Associate Justice of the

Supreme of the United States

If I were to tell you, Mr. Scanlon, that during my travels in the South in the early 1950's, I purposely and intentionally violated state statutes by sitting in the back of busses, and defied the orders of bus drivers to move forward; and used Negro drinking fountains and rest rooms, would you add that, too, to the allegations and supporting facts against me?

If I were to tell you that about 1960, in knowing violation of D.C. statute forbidding any kind of alteration of a D.C. driver's license, I erased the racial designation (a "W") from my driver's license (because I don't believe in the existence of any race other than the human race), informed the director of motor vehicles, and effectively dared him to impose the fine and license-revocation prescribed by law (he didn't; the next year the District changed its drivers licenses, so as to eliminate the racial designation; I take a great deal of personal pride in having been one of the very few who were directly, personally, individually responsible for the change).

If I were to tell you these things, would you add them, too, to the "criminal conduct" allegations against me?

What you have totally missed, Mr. Scanlon, is that personal principles are of infinitely more relevance to this context of reliability, responsibility, trustworthiness, and ability to safeguard information, than your silly laws. That is the entire thrust of the quotations above, from people of credentials far more impeccable than mine, and that is the thrust of the actions of my own mentioned here.

If you are going to conduct your security program in an ethical and moral fashion, with *proper, reasonable* attention to justice and fairness, you have a *duty* and an *obligation* to look into the applicant's *principles* and his adherence to them, not merely into his attention to or inattention to your trivial laws. Anything less is irresponsibility on your part, in its most virulent form.

MY principles—as enunciated and as lived, for the 30 years of my adult life, will stand up to inspection—ANY inspection—however close and minute and exacting. And the principles, *as practices*, will be found to be identical with the principles *as preached*. EVERYone who knows me knows that. How many of your clearance-holders can say that?

And by MY principles, my word is my bond. And if I say that I will (or will not) do something, EVERYone who has ever dealt with me for over 30 years KNOWS that I will (or will not) do it—including not disclosing the large amounts of confidential personal information entrusted to me by my associates and others, without qualms or hesitation. My obedience to your immoral laws is irrelevant. I will stand upon my record and my reputation—things which you and your criteria ignore totally.

I think that you had better begin to realize that it is just this kind of ritualistic imposition of unexamined immoral laws—this ritualistic, ceremonial adherence to the word of the law, with total disregard for justice, morality, and human values—which is leading to so much of the gradual disintegration of the fabric of our society, which we see around us every day, and which is destroying this country. You are seeing it all around you—you are a part of it—and yet you persist. If ever the prayer "forgive them for they know not what they do" applies to anyone, it applies to you and your colleagues, as you pull this country, and all that it stands for, down around your—and my ears. . . .

Well, Mr. Scanlon, I believe in what this country *really* stands for. I put my life in jeopardy fighting for those things. And I intend to continue to. And what I fought for—and am still fighting for—are justice, morality, ethics, equality, opportunity, and freedom for *all* citizens—ALL, Mr. Scanlon—not just the popular ones. I am not fighting for and I was not fighting for the killing of humanity and human values by the ritualistic imposition of the dead hand of outmoded customs and ideas, entombed in archaic laws. I am fighting for principles and for justice, not for dogmatic laws and public officials who play politics with human lives.

That is why I should have my clearance. And I *will*. . . .

Sincerely yours,

Franklin E. Kameny

Kameny to Randy Wicker and Peter Ogren

In the following letter to Wicker (Charles Hayden Jr.) and his companion Peter Ogren, who together operated a successful political button business in New York, Kameny sends important news about the slogan "Gay Is Good," though he fails to mention that he was responsible for coining the slogan.

AUGUST 23, 1968

Dear Randy and Peter:

Just a short note relating to buttons and the like.

I've just returned from Chicago, where we had our annual National Conference of the Homophile Movement.

Among the actions taken was the adoption, by the Conference, as a slogan or motto for the Movement, of: GAY IS GOOD in obvious parallel to the Negroes' "Black is Beautiful."

The purpose is to try to provide a strong positive approach to homosexuality, to offset the pervasive negativism which we find everywhere, both as psychological sustenance to the homosexual with his impaired self-image and damaged self-esteem, and as an affirmative approach to the heterosexual community.

We want to get this published as widely as possible, and are hoping to have it made into buttons, stickers, etc., etc. Anything that you care to do would be appreciated. At least one of your competitors on the West Coast is going to be making up *Gay Is Good* buttons and stickers.

Things proceed busily here. . . .

Unfortunately, for the present, I am once more out of work, with my creditors howling. I am looking around somewhat more broadly this time than in the past, however, because by virtue of lots of prodding and goading of the Pentagon, I've gotten the processing of my own security clearance (the major obstacle to a stable job situation) beyond the point where that terminates when my job terminates, so I can continue to work to clear up the situation once and for all.

That's all for now. Keep in touch. Let me know . . . about our slogan.

GAY IS GOOD!

Cordially,

Frank

Wicker reacted negatively to the slogan in his October 2 reply:

The "Gay is Good" slogan is not nearly as good as "Black is Beautiful" simply because it soft sells rather than puts the idea over with a punch. We even have an "It's Great to be Straight" button . . . why didn't they at least decide "Gay is Great" . . . in any event, it's so wishy washy, I'm afraid I'll let my competitor on the West Coast distribute it. If you want to have it printed, I will give you the buttons at absolute cost—which is ½ the listed price. A thousand would then cost you around $25.00. But I just can't see putting $25 of my money into a slogan that is so absolutely colorless.[7]

Kameny to the Editors of the *Washington Daily News*

The Soviet Union, along with four of its allies in the Warsaw Pact, invaded Czechoslovakia on August 21, 1968, suppressing the liberal politics of Alexander Dubcek and his progressive colleagues in government. Less than two weeks later, fifty-three members of the Association of Washington Priests signed a statement declaring that married couples may use birth control "according to their conscience."[8] The statement provoked Patrick Cardinal O'Boyle to announce that unless the priests retracted their statement, they would face stiff canonical penalties. Kameny connects these two seemingly unrelated events, writing that "intellectual fascism" is present in both communism and Catholicism.

SEPTEMBER 4, 1968

Gentlemen:

The parallel between what is currently taking place in Czechoslovakia and what is currently occurring in the Archdiocese of Washington and elsewhere in the Catholic Church (Cardinal O'Boyle's disciplining of priests dissenting from the Pope's recent birth-control encyclical) is remarkably close and precise. Even the vocabulary of the headlines is the same: Dissent, warnings, ultimatums, repression, etc.

In both cases, an authoritarian, intellectually totalitarian establishment, intolerant of dissent and incapable of comprehending it, convinced that it, alone, is the possessor of revealed truth, is acting brutally and shamelessly to suppress freedom of thought and expression on the part of those under it—and is acting in manners which are remarkably similar, point by point.

Communism and Catholicism are traditional enemies. I would suggest that recent events show that they are close brothers under the skin, and would do well (from their viewpoints, at least) to join forces. They are actually both religions, and might be able to teach each other how better to suppress "heresy."

They are both expert at destroying mankind's supreme and unique glory—the free and untrammeled exercise, of all manners, of his God-given intellect. By denying him his individuality, his freedom of thought, and his freedom of choice, which are part of the human dignity which defines and characterizes man, they are trying to convert human beings into mindless robots.

Intellectual fascism is repugnant and offensive, wherever it originates—whether from the Kremlin or from the Vatican—or from the Archdiocese of Washington.

Sincerely yours,
Franklin E. Kameny

1. Soldier: Kameny fought in the Battle of the Bulge in World War II and often cited his Army years when writing to politicians and military leaders. Unknown photographer, Kameny Papers, Library of Congress.

2. Astronomer: Kameny studied astronomy at Harvard University and, before the federal government fired him from his position at the Army Map Service, dreamed of working in the U.S. space program. Unknown photographer, Kameny Papers, Library of Congress.

IN THE

Supreme Court of the United States

OCTOBER TERM, 1960

No. 676

FRANKLIN EDWARD KAMENY, *Petitioner*

v.

WILBER M. BRUCKER, Secretary of the Army, et al.,
Respondents

**PETITION FOR A WRIT OF CERTIORARI
TO THE UNITED STATES COURT OF APPEALS
FOR THE DISTRICT OF COLUMBIA CIRCUIT**

FRANKLIN E. KAMENY
2435 18th Street, N. W.
Washington 9, D. C.

Pro Se

PRESS OF BYRON S. ADAMS, WASHINGTON, D. C.

3. Writ: In his petition to the U.S. Supreme Court, Kameny advanced the radical argument that homosexuals were an oppressed minority. Kameny Papers, Library of Congress.

JUN 2 2 1961

Dr. Franklin E. Kameny
2435 Eighteenth Street, N.W.
Washington 9, D. C.

Dear Dr. Kameny:

The Civil Service Regulations include the following as a disqualification for employment in the Federal service: "Criminal, infamous, dishonest, immoral, or notoriously disgraceful conduct."

The Commission's policy, based on impartial consideration of many cases involving all aspects of human behavior, is that homosexuals or sexual perverts are not suitable for Federal employment.

On considering the representations in your letter of June 5, 1961, I find no basis for changing this policy.

Sincerely yours,

John W. Macy
John W. Macy, Jr.
Chairman

4. Macy: This letter helps explain the reason that John Macy, chairman of the U.S. Civil Service Commission, was Kameny's archnemesis at this point. Kameny Papers, Library of Congress.

5. Nichols: Jack Nichols and Kameny first met at a party in Washington, DC, in 1961, and bonded over their appreciation for Donald Webster Cory's pioneering book on homosexuality. Nichols and Kameny soon laid plans for organizing what would become the Mattachine Society of Washington (MSW). Also pictured is lesbian rights pioneer Barbara Gittings. Photo by Kay Tobin © Manuscripts and Archives Division, The New York Public Library.

6. Independence Hall: Initially hesitant when he heard of Nichols's plan to march on the White House on April 17, 1965, Kameny crafted the event to his liking and later participated in this march at Independence Hall in Philadelphia on July 4, 1965. Photo by Kay Tobin © Manuscripts and Archives Division, The New York Public Library.

7. White House Letter: Delivering a gay rights letter to the White House on October 23, 1965, Kameny would gain access to the White House only after the election of Jimmy Carter. Photo by Kay Tobin © Manuscripts and Archives Division, The New York Public Library.

8. Prisoner: Part of Kameny's activism included offering counsel to gays imprisoned during police raids of gay bars and other spaces, public and private, known
as gathering places for gays. Photo by Kay Tobin © Manuscripts and Archives
Division, The New York Public Library.

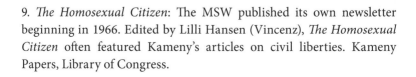

THE HOMOSEXUAL CITIZEN

50¢

JANUARY 1967

● NEWS OF CIVIL LIBERTIES
● AND SOCIAL RIGHTS
● FOR HOMOSEXUALS

FEATURE

If You Are Arrested

9. *The Homosexual Citizen*: The MSW published its own newsletter beginning in 1966. Edited by Lilli Hansen (Vincenz), *The Homosexual Citizen* often featured Kameny's articles on civil liberties. Kameny Papers, Library of Congress.

10. Gay Is Good: Kameny coined the phrase "gay is good" in 1968, and here he carries a placard with the message in the Christopher Street Gay Liberation Day March, June 28, 1970, New York City. Photo by Kay Tobin © Manuscripts and Archives Division, The New York Public Library.

11. Capitol: In 1971 Kameny became the first openly gay candidate for the U.S. Congress when he campaigned for the District of Columbia's nonvoting delegate seat. After his defeat, the campaign committee formed the Gay Activist Alliance of Washington, DC. Photo by Kay Tobin © Manuscripts and Archives Division, The New York Public Library.

12. "Gay, Proud, and Healthy": Lesbian rights pioneer Barbara Gittings and Kameny staff an educational exhibit ("Gay, Proud, and Healthy: The Homosexual Community Speaks") at the annual meeting of the American Psychiatric Association, Dallas, Texas, May 1–4, 1972. Photo by Kay Tobin © Manuscripts and Archives Division, The New York Public Library.

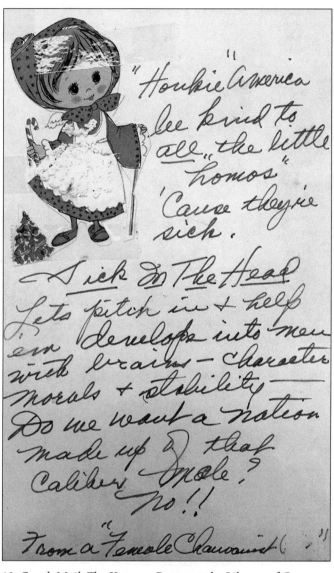

13. Crank Mail: The Kameny Papers at the Library of Congress indicate that the gay rights pioneer had more than a handful of critics through the years. Kameny Papers, Library of Congress.

14. Kameny at the Smithsonian: Kameny donated his papers to the Library of Congress, and the protest signs he and others carried in the early marches are among the Smithsonian's vast holdings. Once the target of government surveillance, Kameny is now celebrated for his contributions to U.S. history. *Washington Blade* photo by Henry Linser.

Sincerely yours,

Franklin E. Kameny

Franklin E. Kameny, Ph.D.

15. Signature. Kameny Papers, Library of Congress.

7

"Without Our Demonstrations . . . Stonewall Would Not Have Happened"

1969

Kameny to the Editors of the *Washington Star*

In its January 10 editorial on prostitution, the Washington Star *argued there was "a great deal to be said" for "schemes to license and control 'the oldest profession.'" Illegal prostitution, after all, had led to increases in cases of venereal disease and police corruption. "Licensing and control would certainly reduce both these evils," the editors wrote.*[1]

JANUARY 14, 1969

Gentlemen:

I was pleased to note the enlightened position taken by the *Star* . . . on the legalization of prostitution.

While the "sexual revolution" may reduce the incidence of female prostitution and alter some of its superficial aspects, it is quite unlikely to eliminate it; the "revolution" will probably serve to increase male prostitution (already estimated, by some, to exceed the incidence of female prostitution).

Basically, of course, prostitution is simply a private, consensual, contractual, business matter between two people. The prostitute is supplying a useful public service for which there is an obvious demand, or she (or he) would not remain in business. Since one of the purposes—if not the primary purpose—of having a society at all is the satisfaction of the needs and desires of its members, and since the prostitute satisfies demonstrably persistent needs and desires of some members of society, totally without demonstrable harm to those not involved, or to the structure of society itself, it is obvious that prostitution, if not actually encouraged, should, at the very least, not be discouraged.

There is no real, conceptual difference between the woman who rents out the use of her genitalia for sexual purposes and the woman who rents out the use of her hands for stenographic purposes—or the man who rents out the use of his muscle and strength for laboring purposes or the person who rents out the use of his or her brain and the knowledge, skills, and training contained therein for any of a large variety of purposes or, in fact, anyone who takes a job or supplies a service for which he or she is paid. These are all matters of private agreement between a buyer with a need or requirement and a seller able to fulfill the need or requirement. They are properly subject, perhaps, to certain superficial legal and societal controls and safeguards (labor laws, public order, force, exploitation, etc.) but otherwise are not matters in which law or society has a proper basic interest, nor into which they should intrude. Those who disapprove of prostitution are free to abstain, but they do not have the right—even if they be in the majority—to impose their own, personal, subjective value judgments upon others. . . .

Sincerely yours,
Franklin E. Kameny

Kameny to Barbara Grier (Gene Damon)

Barbara Grier (pseudonym, Gene Damon), the editor of the Ladder *since 1968, had initially opposed Kameny's decision to picket federal buildings. So Kameny was surprised when he read the following section of her review of Martin Hoffman's* The Gay World.[2]

> *His concluding recommendation is that which the homophile organizations have been talking about for years. Homosexuals must be treated as a minority, given full minority status, and must work toward overcoming altogether all forms of minority status prejudice. He likens this to going from our present state (social outcasts, totally) to the black stage (he refers to this as the "talk about giving 'civil rights' to others") and then, finally, to full rights and*

social privileges such as the relative lack today of prejudice against the Roman Catholics.

He admits that he doesn't even know if it is possible for society to do this, but there may be some militants made by this book, particularly when he offers evidence that a person can be driven insane by social forces. Superficially, this is an obvious truism, but looked at in the form of a case history or two, you come up wondering why only black people march on Washington.[3]

FEBRUARY 5, 1969

Dear Miss Damon:

I noted with some interest—and wry, but not malicious amusement— your comment in . . . that "you come up wondering why only black people march on Washington."

As you may remember, precisely such marches (*in,* if perhaps not *on*) Washington and Philadelphia, by homosexuals, were the subject of lengthy and mildly heated discussion and correspondence between us in 1966. At that time you were quite unequivocal in your disapproval and condemnation of such activities and of those who participated in them.

Am I to assume, from the remark quoted, that you have reversed your position, and that we may welcome you into the ranks of militant homophile activists? I sincerely hope so.

Cordially,
Franklin E. Kameny

Grier replied on February 14, 1969:

What is with this "Dear Miss Damon"? People I have snarled at in my own front room are usually less formal—I never bite people I don't know. . . .

I still feel as I did about the well-dressed demonstrations. I still feel that the people who run the world are not impressed with any kind of demonstration (except negatively). I still believe that each issue of The Ladder *and comparable . . . does more to aid our cause than any and all of the marches. . . . Actually, just such a statement as mine in that review is meant to be a militant statement. I live the propaganda life constantly, and am directing the magazine in that way. I simply believe that education is the only way to get anything. I also believe that pens work better than swords. Don't worry—everyone agrees more with you than me. There are far more people eager to march than to simply sit down and work. (I am not including you, I know how hard you work. We have no direct contact, but I hear of you constantly.)*[4]

Kameny to Barbara Gittings

Kameny's short letter offers a humorous look at the wide gap between him and Edward Sagarain (Donald Webster Cory), who had authored the book that inspired Kameny to fight for civil rights for homosexuals.

MARCH 10, 1969

Barbara:

A little gem from a letter received today from Ed Sagarin. I'd sent him a copy of the Gay Is Good resolution and a button, and had mentioned my article in *Playboy*:[5]

> Alas, I do not think gay is good, and I do not think the slogan is good, and I do not think it is good for gay people to have such a slogan, and I do not think it is good for a society to say that gay is good, although it is bad for a society to say that gay is bad, and it is good for a society that people have the courage and fight to say that gay is good even though gay is not good. Whew! Don't quote that—I might want to refine it a bit!

Frank

Kameny to Barbara Grier

In this continuation of correspondence with Grier, Kameny argues, though without characteristic details, that a positive effect of picketing was the U.S. Court of Appeals ruling in Scott v. Macy *(1968).[6] After the federal court's 1965 ruling that the Civil Service Commission had not provided sufficient reason for disqualifying Bruce Scott from federal employment, the commission sought to bolster its case against him. But on September 11, 1968, the U.S. Court of Appeals found the CSC's additional arguments to be "unavailing," and once again ruled in favor of Scott.[7]*

Note Kameny's comment on the relationship between feminism and homosexual issues. After assuming editorial control of the Ladder, *Grier made sure to draw close connections between the campaign for lesbian rights and the burgeoning U.S. feminist movement.*

MARCH 26, 1969

Dear Barbara:

. . . There is little point in getting into a long discussion, via letter, on demonstrations. I think that current events prove the effectiveness of demonstrations, after other methods have failed. Our demonstrations have been effective, and went a long way, just recently . . . in getting us an important decision from the courts in *Scott v. Macy.*

I would be delighted to write an article for *The Ladder* . . . Do you have any specific ideas for a subject? Once we've worked that out, I'll be glad to get to work on it. There should be no problem with its being applicable to female as well as to male homosexuals, since I (like Barbara) do not recognize any difference at all in the basic interests and concerns of the two groups (I am deeply distressed at the increasing tendency to inject feminism and women's rights into DOB and *The Ladder*—these are commendable causes in their own right, and I'm wholeheartedly a supporter of them—but I don't believe in mixing causes). . . .

Sincerely,
Frank

Kameny to Barbara Grier

Kameny begins to detail his controversial position on the relationship between lesbianism and feminism—a stance at radical odds with Grier's.

APRIL 25, 1969

Dear Barbara:

. . . Now with regard to your note of April 8—

You say (first paragraph): "It was a good article but it isn't anything special for women." But DOB is for *lesbians*, not women. Lesbians are homosexuals, first, and women only incidentally. Women's rights organizations are a dime a dozen; lesbian organizations are unique. Don't degrade yourselves (and that carries with it NO implications as to a lower valuation of women or women's rights).

While you may feel strongly about the matter of women's equality, I feel, to put it bluntly, that you make yourself more than a bit ridiculous when you say that "women in general are still 9th class citizens (homosexuals are only 2nd rate, really)." It just is NOT so. The homosexual—male or female—has very, very, very, very much farther to go before he or she is even in the place of the woman of 50 years ago. Come, come now—a little proper perspective and sense of proportion are in order.

Obviously, if anti-homosexual discrimination died out overnight, Lesbians would still have the "woman" issue to cope with. And if the "woman" issue dies out overnight, they would still have the homosexuality issue. And if the Negro issue dies out overnight, the black homosexual would still have the homosexual issue to cope with; and if the homosexual issue dies out overnight, he would still have the Negro issue to deal with. And if anti-Semitism died out overnight, the Jewish homosexual would still have the homosexual issue to cope with; and if the homosexual issue died out overnight, he would still have the Jewish issue to deal with—ad infinitum.

All that that says is that many people (the lesbian among them) have more than one problem to cope with in their lives. These remain—in EVERY case cited above, including the lesbian one—TOTALLY and UTTERLY *separate* problems, which only interact to the detriment of both if mixed.

The fact that a news item or a story deals with homosexuals and homosexuality—generally—does not mean that it's dealing with the male side or evaluating the female side. It's dealing with homosexuality—not with women, with Negroes, Jews, with Catholics, or with any other minority group. And homosexuality is the proper—and ONLY—business of DOB.

The article I'm enclosing happens to deal with a pair of WACs. There is hardly a detail in the story which would have had to be changed, had it dealt with a pair of male soldiers. And the lessons to be gained from it, the techniques applied, the policies at issue, vary not a whit from men to women. Nor would I have handled the case differently in any slightest respect (except only bringing a woman to accompany me at the meeting with Army Intelligence) had the principals been male soldiers instead of female ones—because the issue was *homosexual soldiers* not *women soldiers* or *women*.

Point made. 'Nuff said.

Cordially,
Frank

Kameny to the Editors of *Medical World News*

In this heavily excerpted letter, Kameny addresses the issue of aversion therapy in response to an article titled "The Homosexual Patient." The article cited Richard Socarides and Irving Bieber, Kameny's archnemeses, as experts on the treatment of homosexuals. "Dr. Socarides and others," the article stated, "voice a growing optimism that sexual redirection is possible for many homosexuals."

> *Leaders in the field report that from one-third to one-half of their patients are successfully converting to heterosexuality. Some therapists are treating with psychoanalysis. Some are using group therapy, alone or with individual psychotherapy. Some are using hypnosis. Others are using conditioning—aversion therapy—with electroshock or nauseating drugs and photographs of nude men.*[8]

With a clear bias toward Socarides and Bieber, the article also reported that "twelve troublesome homosexual inmates at New Jersey State Hospital, who were so overtly aggressive that they were placed in the maximum security building, were given 50 mg to 200 mg of the drug [thioridazine] three times daily. Within a week, attendants and nurses were commenting on the improvement."[9]

APRIL 28, 1969

Gentlemen:

Your article . . . illustrates how far medicine and its related disciplines (psychiatry, psychoanalysis, etc.) have yet to go before they move out of the realm of spells, incantations and witchcraft, cease being pseudo-religious, and become the sciences that they should be. . . .

You refer to aversion therapy. So intent are you people upon your monomania of conversion to heterosexuality that you do not perceive the utter barbarism of these methods. They are horrifying. Descriptions of aversion therapy remind one of a page out of a tome on medieval torture, a discussion of the techniques of the Spanish Inquisition, or a text on modern Russian brainwashing. The techniques involved are an offense to any civilized human being. Pavlovian techniques are best confined to the dogs upon which they were developed. There had better be a truly compelling reason to apply them to human beings. Without such compelling reason, the human victims of those techniques are being degraded to the level of dogs. Something as trivial and innocuous as homosexuality is NEVER reason for such human degradation by our self-appointed "saviors." . . .

I repeat that what we have here is sloppy, slovenly, slipshod, non-objective, just-plain-bad science. Basically, we have been *defined* into sickness by moral, cultural, social, and theological value judgments, cloaked and camouflaged in the language of science. . . .

Sincerely yours,
Franklin E. Kameny

Kameny to Louis Crompton

In this letter to a noted scholar of Bernard Shaw and British literature, Kameny sketches his answer to the question of whether homosexuality is genetically determined—and offers some encouragement along the way.

MAY 29, 1969

Dear Lou:

. . . I am surprised and a little dismayed that you take the position that homosexuality is innate—if I interpret you correctly. It has been my position—consistently and strongly—that sexual preference—homosexual and heterosexual both—is environmentally determined, in the earliest stages of life, by factors, the nature and details of which we are, as yet, totally ignorant. There is no evidence whatever that stands up to inspection in support of an innate, inborn, or genetic origin. . . .

Don't get discouraged at slow progress . . . I learned long ago that things move with excruciating slowness. When I founded the Mattachine Society of Washington 7½ years ago, I felt sure that now that we had an organization, all we had to do was to approach the government, and the "walls of Jericho" would come tumbling down at once. It's almost a decade later, and they're still standing, if somewhat weakened.

> Cordially,
> Frank

Kameny to Hobart Bissell

In the following letter to Hobart Bissell of Virginia, Kameny comments on the sociological makeup of the homophile movement, expressing frustration that "the people of highest caliber" rarely become active members.

MAY 30, 1969

Dear Mr. Bissell:

. . . One of the problems faced by the movement dealing with a group of oppressed people who do not have an intrinsic, inescapable "invisibility" is the fact that with rare exceptions the people of highest caliber feel that they have too much to lose by association with the movement, and steer clear of it. We have long ago become resigned to the fact that wealthy, professionally established, prominent homosexuals, for example, will give us no support whatever. . . .

> Sincerely yours,
> Franklin E. Kameny

Kameny to Arthur Warner

Kameny sends a direct-action plan for attacking sodomy laws to Arthur Warner, a specialist in sodomy legislation and the leader of MSNY's legal campaigns.

MAY 31, 1969

Dear Arthur:

I simply want to present to you . . . my ideas on a "stated" act of sodomy as a test case. I do not intend to make a continuing issue of this, nor to commence "grinding an ax." I will have done my duty by presenting the idea, and you can do what you wish from then on.

Given the problems in real, practical life in getting a good, pure, "uncluttered" test case, I would think that it would be desirable to create one.

The jurisdiction should be chosen with great care, in terms of prosecutors, courts, the actual wording of the applicable laws, etc., etc.

The act should be simple, uncomplicated, consensual adult sodomy. It should be announced beforehand.

I feel that no prosecutor could refuse to arrest and prosecute a felony committed in his jurisdiction, if the matter were suitably publicized in advance, so that he were faced with no choice but "to do his duty."

The pre-publicity and pre-announcements would have to be handled with some care in order that the act not be aborted by an arrest, before the fact, for conspiracy, but I think that that could be managed with some ingenuity.

The goal, of course, would be to elicit an arrest *in flagrante delicto*.

Done properly, I think that you could create an absolutely perfect test case. . . .

Sincerely yours,
Franklin E. Kameny

Kameny to the Editors of the *Washington Star*

In a May 6 editorial, the Washington Star *expressed support for President Nixon's plan to restrict "the growing volume of smut mailings."*[10] *Nixon's proposal called for prohibiting the postal service from delivering any material deemed obscene and pornographic.*

JUNE 1, 1969

Gentlemen:

I read with total disagreement your editorial "Nixon on Smut."

First, I feel that those in any position, from newspaper editors up to Supreme Court justices and presidents, who use words such as "smut," "dirt," "filth," etc., in regard to sex and sexual matters, could profit from a little time spent in therapy with a good psychiatrist.

Second (and without entering into semantic squabbles as to the meaning of fundamentally meaningless terms such as "*pornography*" and "*obscenity*"), as one who happens to look upon pornography as good, clean, harmless fun (*fun* obviously having "redeeming social value"—an arrogant phrase)—and feeling thus in agreement with a very, very large number of my fellow citizens who are, perhaps, somewhat less willing than I am to admit it publicly—I deeply resent efforts by my president to make us feel guilty about our reading it and enjoying it. He is entitled to his choice of reading matter, but so are we without disparagement from him. He is president of the pornography-reading citizens, too. He has overstepped himself rather presumptuously.

Third, I have searched the Constitution in vain for any slightest indication that in the First Amendment's "no law abridging freedom of speech or of the press," that phrase "no law" *really* means "no law except in matters of sex" or "no law except in matters involving prurient interest" or "no law except in matters violating community standards" (the First Amendment was written to ensure the right to violate such standards; other materials do not need such protection) or "no law except for commercial advertisements." "No law"—two simple little monosyllables—means NO law, and that is what the Constitution says, the writings of the Supreme Court notwithstanding. The president has indicated that he is a "strict constructionist" in constitutional matters and has just chosen a new chief justice who has a reputation as such a strict constructionist. The president had better realize that his proposals are totally inconsistent with a strict construction of the First Amendment. "No law" means NO law. There is just no way around that.

Fourth, if I have the right to enjoy these materials—and even the president's proposals do not attempt to deny me that right—then, of course, I have the right to purchase or otherwise obtain them. If I have the right to purchase them, then, of course, I have the right to expect that those who wish to sell them to me will not be prohibited from exercising their right to do so. And having the right to purchase them, I have, of course, the right to know what is available to be purchased and to receive advertising materials informing me of what is available. Those who object to such advertising materials can dispose of them as I do of advertising materials for which I do not care. But I find offensive the efforts of an overly paternalistic Victorian government to "protect" me against that from which I not only wish no "protection" but which is clearly not harmful and to which I affirmatively desire exposure.

Finally, I hope that if these ill-conceived legislative proposals proceed, some of our more intelligent, more enlightened, more sensible, more emancipated young people will picket the White House under the heading: "Youth for Pornography." That should shake up some of our puritans a bit and perhaps lead them to some badly needed second thoughts!

Sincerely yours,

Franklin E. Kameny

By the end of the month, some of the young people in New York City's Greenwich Village were undertaking even bolder action than the type Kameny describes in the previous letter.

On June 28, 1969, New York City police officers raided a gay bar on Christopher Street in Greenwich Village. Controlled by the Mafia and operating without a liquor license, the Stonewall Inn served watered-down drinks at high prices. But it was also one of the few places where young gays—many of them quite unlike the "wealthy, professionally established, prominent homosexuals" Kameny wrote about in his May 30 letter to Hobart Bissell—felt free to socialize and dance with one another.

The Stonewall Inn had been raided before, and each time the gay patrons had followed police instructions without offering any sustained or significant resistance. This time, however, some of the patrons had had enough, and as the police released them into the street, expecting them to disappear into the night, they stayed close by the bar, fueling their long-simmering discontent with police harassment and the payoffs the police allegedly received from the Mafia. "As one Stonewall patron put it, "Everybody was like, 'Why the fuck are we doing all this for? Why should we be chastised? Why do we have to pay the Mafia all this kind of money to drink in a lousy fuckin' bar? And still be harassed by the police."[11]

As the tensions increased, the growing crowd began to throw coins at the officers, mocking the payoffs that would most likely follow the arrest. Rocks began to fly, soon followed by airborne bottles, loud shouts and jeers, even slashed tires on the paddy wagon. The embattled police inside Stonewall called for backup, and as the reinforcements began to attack the mob, the rioters fought back, refusing to disperse quietly. The riots continued the following two nights, with shouts of "gay power" thundering from the angry crowd.

Less than a week later, on July 4, Kameny traveled to Philadelphia for the Annual Reminder March at Independence Hall. The orderly demonstration, with picketers dressed in suits and dresses, resulted in no arrests. But the event was tainted by a flare-up between Kameny and New York activist Craig Rodwell after Kameny separated two lesbian picketers who had begun to hold hands. Rodwell, no longer tolerant of Kameny's insistence on appearing respectable to heterosexual America, protested the break-up and proceeded to tell the media that the Stonewall riots had sparked a new militancy in the movement and that the old-guard leaders did not represent the new wave.[12] Following this, Rodwell and some other New York picketers marched in pairs and held hands, disobeying the carefully defined rules initially formulated by Kameny and approved by the Eastern Regional Conference of Homophile Organizations (ERCHO). Kameny recounted the disagreement in a later letter to Rodwell:

> "Love-ins"—homosexual and/or heterosexual, both—have their place, so do picketing demonstrations. Neither is likely to be effective, and both are more likely to be ineffective, if they are mixed.
>
> As the elected chairman of ERCHO, it was my duty and obligation to administer the demonstration in keeping with the spirit of ERCHO . . . That spirit has always been in the direction of a somewhat conservative, image-conscious, conventionally dignified demonstration, designed to get a message across by avoidance of needless abrasion of the sensibilities and sensitivities of the large mass of people.[13]

Rodwell was unconvinced and decided to push ahead with an idea he had formulated in conversation with other New York activists on the train ride home from the Philadelphia march—that the movement should begin to hold an annual march in New York City, this one with no dress regulations, to mark the anniversary of the Stonewall riots.[14] Rodwell conceived the anniversary event "not as a silent plea for rights but as an overt demand for them." He also "thought of a name right then and there: Christopher Street Liberation Day."[15]

Rodwell's idea later gained traction within the budding gay liberation movement, and the 1969 march in Philadelphia marked the end of the conservative, quiet, and respectable marches that Kameny had organized and implemented since 1965. In the following years, Kameny would often *maintain that the 1965–1969 marches had given birth to Stonewall and ensuing developments within the gay liberation movement. "Without our demonstrations starting in '65," he stated, "Stonewall would not have happened because what they did was to create the mindset for gay people, who had never ever before done this, to demonstrate publicly, to dissent publicly, to do things out in the open. . . . The '69 Fourth of July demonstration was already being advertized in Greenwich Village at the time that Stonewall happened. . . . So the idea of gay people demonstrating publicly was in the air."*[16]

Kameny to Dick Michaels

In the following letter to Los Angeles Advocate *cofounder Dick Michaels (his real name was Richard Mitch), Kameny responds to an article suggesting that members of the North American Conference of Homophile Organizations (NACHO) disagreed about the proper functions of the homophile movement.* Advocate *reporter Dal McIntyre wrote that a major point of controversy was "the view, most predominant in the East, that we ought to have two exclusive concerns: changing the law and giving homosexuals a respectable image. This view disapproves all social activity, all individual counseling or assistance, and all educational activity not aimed at the general public."*[17]

JULY 20, 1969

Dear Mr. Michaels:

. . . The basic starting point, as I see it, for the whole homophile movement is:

> The problems of the homosexual, in their entirety, either are—or stem directly from—problems of prejudice and discrimination directed against the homosexual minority by the heterosexual majority around them.
>
> It has been well and accurately said that there is no Negro problem; there is a white problem. We can say, equally well and accurately, that there is no homosexual problem; there is a heterosexual problem.

That tells us where our primary *emphasis* should lie. One can deal with the effects of poverty by setting up "soup kitchens" to feed the poor—the equivalent of counseling—but one gets nowhere, from a *long-range* viewpoint, until one gets at the roots of poverty—its causes. Counseling is "repairing broken china." Broken china, mended, is never as good as the unbroken original. Society—the intolerant heterosexual majority— is doing the breaking. Therefore where limited organizational resources have to be allocated, and where priorities have to be set up, long-range prevention rather than counseling homosexuals is in order. Certainly there is nothing inherent or intrinsic in homosexuals or homosexuality which causes a greater need for counseling homosexuals than for counseling heterosexuals. Emphasis on counseling represents dominance of the short-range over the long-range viewpoint. There is, of course, a very real place in the movement for organizations doing counseling primarily; there are homosexuals in very real and immediate need of aid. But . . . one can counsel the needy of this generation forever, and the next generation of homosexuals will have just as many problems. Change attitudes, laws, etc., and the problems of the next generation will be infinitely fewer.

A beautiful example of this occurred in New York a few years ago. For years, the Mattachine Society of New York counseled and assisted countless homosexuals caught by police entrapment (and, I am sure, many more were caught than ever came to MSNY), referred them to lawyers, etc.— "mended the broken china"—and, if possible, helped them to get jobs if they were fired after an arrest, and otherwise "to pick up the pieces." For years I urged them to stop the breakage by stopping the entrapment. Ultimately, they diverted some of their efforts—temporarily—from counseling those caught and started pulling political strings, meeting with officials, conferring with the mayor, forcing the issue. They succeeded in stopping ALL entrapment. Now there is no more breakage: all the community is helped on a permanent basis (not just that small minority of entrapees who formerly appealed to Mattachine for help). That is why I down-rate emphases upon counseling and social service and up-rate civil liberties.

Similarly, there is no *inherent* reason why homosexuals need more education than heterosexuals. Our plight is NOT our fault. Those who insistently claim that the only way we are going to improve our situation is by "education" of our own community have been more brainwashed with a sense of inferiority than they realize. We will be doing a lot more for the next generation—and the generation after them—of homosexuals by getting *good* sex education courses in the schools than by all the education of our own community in the world. . . .

The preceding is not at all to rule out education of our own community in a psychologically self-supportive fashion, to free them of societally induced preconceptions about themselves . . . "Gay is Good" is part of that. . . .

Cordially,

Franklin E. Kameny

Kameny to Rona Barrett

Kameny criticizes Hollywood gossip reporter Rona Barrett for having commented negatively on the recent presence of homosexuals in films. In 1969, homosexuality was prominently depicted in Midnight Cowboy, Staircase, *and* The Damned, *among other films.*

JULY 25, 1969

Dear Miss Barrett:

On a recent television broadcast, soon on WTTG-Channel 5, Washington, you deplored the current appearance of a number of films on homosexuality, with words to the general effect that, while we know that these things exist, must we show them on the screen? . . .

Your comments are remarkably similar to those heard in the South in past (and present?) years—"We all know that Negroes and whites marry, but must we see them on the screen?" In fact, except for portrayals of them in the most menial of roles, Negroes did not appear on the American screen at all until recently (nor on television). Negroes objected, of course, and properly so, and so do we.

I placed my life in jeopardy for this country, in front line combat under enemy fire in World War II. I did not do so in order that I and my fellow homosexuals should simply be "swept under the rug" and kept out of sight.

If you do not like us, leave the theater—it will be your loss, not ours. If you find us distasteful, the fault is yours, not ours. The Ku Klux Klan finds Negroes distasteful; the American Nazis find Jews distasteful. That is the company in which you place yourself, although I am sure that you have not considered it in quite that way.

I will grant that the current flood of pictures on homosexuality shows us in a distorted and most unfavorable light. We have our love and affection, our tender moments, our joys and happinesses, our lasting and meaningful relationships, in no smaller number than you and your heterosexuals do. And, in due time, when the sensational phase and the novelty have passed, these, too, will be shown. . . .

In parallel with the Negro slogan "Black is Beautiful," we have adopted "Gay is Good." It is. Whether you like it or not, we are here to stay, we are part of American life and society, and you will be seeing a lot more of us, both on and off the screen.

Sincerely yours,

Franklin E. Kameny

Kameny to Foster Gunnison Jr.

In this letter to good friend Foster Gunnison Jr., Kameny sketches the evolution of his tactics and philosophy. His insight here is a response to people who support civil liberties for homosexuals even as they are opposed to homosexuality and homosexual practices.

AUGUST 1, 1969

Dear Foster:

. . . Over the years, one's own ideology becomes altered and, more particularly, sharpened up. Similarly, in a movement having to do with changing public attitudes, one's ideology has to keep up with subtle changes in those attitudes.

I have become increasingly impressed over the past year or two with the need to make explicit and distinct the TWO closely related but separate aspects of our demand for equality. This arises, in part, as indicated, from a sharpening up of my own approaches, but it also arises from the responses of the larger society.

Our demand for treatment as whole, full citizens and human beings is so completely compelling to most even moderately enlightened and civilized people that it is accepted with little qualm or quibble. I was first impressed with that when I formed our Washington Area Council on Religion and the Homosexual some years ago. Whatever misgivings the assembled clergy may have had about our homosexuality, they were all with us on the civil rights and human equality side of things. BUT they had grave misgivings about the equality of homosexuality with heterosexuality.

And we find everywhere now that the pseudo-liberals (and many of the real liberals) have fallen back upon all kinds of bases for keeping us in second-rate condition NOT by assaulting our personal first-rateness, but by operating upon homosexuality as a second-rate condition.

Cory uses the analogy of blindness. "Of course the blind are full first class human beings and deserve all the consideration and dignity that goes with their first-class humanness" (figurative quote, not actual one), "BUT no one would compare blindness with sightedness." And he then goes on to compare homosexuality with blindness. Unfortunately, it is simply unrealistic to expect actual first-class status for homosexuals as long as their homosexuality is considered as a second-class condition.

Therefore, in summary, our fight for equality must operate upon two fronts:

Homosexuals are equal to heterosexuals;

Homosexuality is equal to heterosexuality. . . .

Cordially,

Frank

Kameny to Potential Draft Inductee

The following is an example of the detailed advice and counsel Kameny often gave to gay men facing the potential of being drafted into the U.S. military.

AUGUST 2, 1969

Dear Mr. ——:

We have here your two letters . . . requesting advice in regard to the draft.

First, I assume, from your letters, that you have had your pre-induction examination, and are expecting induction with its induction examination. Do you have any idea when?

Now, what to do. First, get to a psychiatrist and get a letter from him attesting to your homosexuality. This should be an accredited psychiatrist. The letter should be quite explicit about your being a homosexual—no vague terms such as "emotionally unsuited" or anything like that. . . .

Second: I enclose a draft copy of an affidavit. Retype it in five copies, with the three blanks which I've left properly filled in (your address *as it appears* on the draft board records—I assume that you've kept them up to date on address changes; your selective service registration number; and the number of years that you feel you have been actively homosexual, in the terms of the affidavit). Take all copies to a Notary Public and have them notarized. Remember that having something notarized is the equivalent to swearing to its truth.

Third: Send one copy of the affidavit and one copy (not the original) of the psychiatrist's letter to your draft board with a covering letter pointing out that under Army Regulation 635-89 you are not eligible for military service, and you wish your draft classification changed to 4-F.

This will probably NOT work. But it should be done anyhow as a necessary preliminary.

You will probably, in due time, be called in for your induction examination. At the outset, "check the box" (in answer to the question about "homosexual tendencies"). Take with you to the examination the original and one copy of the psychiatrist's letter and the original and one carbon of the affidavit.

Near the end of the physical examination, there will be someone who will check and evaluate the entire examination. *Take the initiative* to point out to him that you have checked the box—he will not expect this since very few people do check it. He will refer you to a psychiatrist there who will ask you questions about your homosexuality. Answer them. Submit the copies of your psychiatrist's letter and the affidavit.

DO NOT ALLOW YOURSELF TO BE INDUCTED. Since you are homosexual, the Army is acting illegally in inducting you. They might tell you differently, but they are still acting illegally in inducting you. You are a civilian until the time when you raise your right hand to take the oath and take a symbolic step forward. Do NOT do so. Remember that as long as you are a civilian, you outrank ANY military man, even a 5-star general;

and as long as you are a civilian, you outrank *any* public official. They have to treat you with dignity, politeness, and respect. You are at the top of the "totem pole." The moment you take that oath and that step forward, you have dropped to the bottom of the totem pole. Do not do it. Do not let them threaten you into doing it. They may tell you that they want to induct you, investigate, and then later discharge you. Do not go along with them. Simply refuse to be inducted. . . .

Sincerely yours,
Franklin E. Kameny

Kameny to Foster Gunnison Jr.

Gunnison had earlier commented on the style of Kameny's typed letters: "Got yours of July 27—easily spotted from stack of correspondence by profusion of crossed out words, dashed lines, truncated capitals, liberal underlining, strewn with parentheses, heavy on two-line paragraphs, and no farewell—all well familiar to me now."[18] Kameny responds to this and offers a comment about his sex life.

AUGUST 4, 1969

Dear Foster:

When I write to people I know well, I don't take any particular trouble with my typing accuracy; I don't pre-draft my letters, as I do with most; and I don't bother with amenities like addresses at top and farewells at bottom. There is just so much time in life, and it's not enough to be wasted on those things when they aren't—or shouldn't be—needed. My style is my own. As the Defense Department Screening Board noted, at our last hearing, in admonishing the stenographer with regard to it: Dr. Kameny uses very complicated sentences, but they're always complete and he never leaves one unfinished. . . .

Yes I've been to quite a number of orgies. They're usually fun. . . .

Frank

Kameny to Dick Leitsch

In this sharply worded letter to Dick Leitsch of the MSNY, Kameny refers to the recent picketing at Independence Hall in Philadelphia—an event Leitsch had decided not to support. Leitsch had explained his decision in an earlier letter to Barbara Gittings:

> *We cannot support a demonstration that pretends to reflect the feelings of all homosexuals while excluding many homosexuals from participating in the demonstration. Since our membership covers all the spectrum of gay life, we encompass drag queens, leather queens, and many, many groovy men and women whose wardrobe consists of bell-bottoms, vests, and miles of gilt chains. Rather than risk the embarrassment and insult of having some of our people rejected (as did happen a few years ago), we choose neither to participate nor support the demonstration and to make our reasons plain in our publication. . . .*
>
> *The Annual Reminder held out such promise at its inception, and I am sorry to see it become the personal property of a few who would set themselves up as an "establishment," no less bigoted and exclusionary than the real "Establishment" we're supposedly fighting.*[19]

SEPTEMBER 4, 1969

Dear Dick:

Some time ago, Barbara Gittings showed me a copy of your letter of June 24 to her in regard to the July 4th demonstration. I have several comments.

1.(a) You are misinterpreting our purpose if you say that "we are trying to reflect the feelings of *all* homosexuals" (my emphasis added). We are not. We are trying to achieve certain things for *all* homosexuals—rights, equality, acceptance, dignity, etc. . . .

2. The composition of your membership—or of anyone else's—is utterly irrelevant. Some of our organizations consist of men only; some of women only; some of both; some of homosexuals only; and some of both homosexuals and heterosexuals, etc., etc. Not only is there no effort to select a representative sampling—there is no need to.

The purpose of the demonstration is NOT to put homosexuals on display in their chosen finery; it is NOT a chance for homosexuals to "do their thing"; it is NOT an opportunity for homosexuals to have a day's outing in Philadelphia. It IS an effort to change the negative attitudes of the populace at large *by the most effective means.*

If we thought that we could best change attitudes on homosexuality by a picket line consisting of sexual eunuchs dressed in loincloths and riding unicycles, our picket line would consist *solely* of asexual, loin-clothed, unicycle-riding eunuchs. EVERYone else would be excluded.

3. The incident of a few years ago was 100% *your* fault, personally and individually. The dress regulations had been formally agreed upon by all participating organizations, including MSNY. At that time, I was in far more frequent telephone conversation with both you and Julian Hodges, and in the days and weeks before the demonstration, I asked, in the course of EVERY conversation, whether your participants were being informed of the dress regulations. In EVERY conversation, I was assured that they were so informed. The two who were turned away very explicitly indicated that they had NOT been informed—in fact, their jackets were on the bus (which had left the site and was inaccessible), and they would have worn them had they known.

What happened was that—with the duplicity which renders you so impossible to work with, because everyone has long ago learned that any relationship between what you say and actual fact is purely coincidental—you told me what you believed I wanted to hear, while not telling your picketers what you didn't want to tell them. And your lies caught up with you. Be man enough to take the blame for the consequences of your own misdeeds. . . .

. . . As I have pointed out before, if a "hippie" dressed as such, and a man in a suit, shirt, and tie get up before an average audience and present the same identical message, the suited man will be listened to and his message accepted by far more people than in the case of the hippie. That is NOT as it should be, but it is as it IS. If you are really genuinely interested in getting your message across, rather than in displaying yourself and exercising your vocal chords, your message bearers WILL wear suits. That this may exclude hippies as message bearers is unfortunate and is not right, but it is not bigotry, only practical, pragmatic sanity.

Finally, considering the little, self-perpetuating cabal who have taken over MSNY and run it, I hardly think that you have any valid comments to make about "establishments." You didn't even bother to send out ballots to all of your members this year.

6. I would write a response to your comment in the MSNY Newsletter (this letter is not for publication, of course) if I thought it would be printed, but given the controlled news policy of your newsletter (which compares well with that of the best and most effective dictatorships) under which, for example (to my recollection) there has not even been so much as a mention of NACHO, ERCHO, Gay is Good, most of the remainder of the Movement, etc., etc., it would probably be a waste of time, so I won't bother.

◀▶

Now, having said all of the preceding, let's call a spade a spade. I suspect that, being a basically sensible and intelligent person, you probably agree with most of the above, although you would never admit it. What *really* bothers you is that MSNY generally, and Dick Leitsch in particular, are not the ones running these demonstrations and heaven forbid that anything in the Movement should go on of which MSNY is not in control. That has been the unfortunate pattern of MSNY's relationships with other groups throughout the years; the leopard seems never to change its power-mad spots.

It's really a pity because you could contribute so much more and accomplish so much more, and put your evident abilities to so much more effective use if you worked in cooperation with others rather than in endless competition, conflict, and rivalry, all quite unnecessary.

Sincerely,

Frank

Kameny to Carolyn Hagner Shaw

In her column on "modern manners," Carolyn Hagner Shaw wrote of being "appalled" while watching everyday citizens say "Hi, Dick" when greeting President Nixon at a recent gathering. In response to such informal behavior, Hagner Shaw called for the use of formal titles (e.g., "Mr. President," "Mr. Secretary," and "Mr. Attorney General") when addressing "the men who hold high official positions in our government."[20] Kameny detested such advice, and in the following letter, although he does not mention his work in the homophile movement, he sketches the understanding of public authority that supported his efforts to transform the government's treatment of homosexuals.

Dear Mrs. Shaw:

I must say that I disagree quite completely. You have the shoe very much on the wrong foot.

Your sentiments strike me as a singularly outdated holdover from the not-unrelated court etiquette of the Middle Ages and the exaggerated respect accorded their royalty and nobility by the Victorians, both profoundly antithetical to the essence of basic democracy and to respect for the dignity of the individual human being and, therefore, fundamentally un-American.

In a democracy such as ours, public officials are public *servants*. I take the term literally, and apply it to *all* public servants, from the humblest clerk on up to presidents, congressmen, and Supreme Court justices. I should hardly have to give you instructions on the proper relationship between servants and those whom they serve. I do not give respect to my servants, public or private, by ceremonial gestures or otherwise; I expect them to show respect for me. Within their capacities as public servants they exist to serve me—hand and foot—not I them. I expect from my servants—public and private—humbleness, humility, civility, servility, politeness, respect, and obedience. I owe my servants—public and private—nothing except a decent wage and reasonable treatment as human beings, as long as they behave themselves properly and do their duty. That includes presidents, congressmen, and Supreme Court justices.

I give respect to no man because of title, rank, position, or high office. I give him my respect only when, in my personal view, he has earned respect—and such earning has nothing whatever to do with his rank or office. Remember, in a democracy, the private citizen outranks the president, the congressman, or the chief justice. It is an honor for *them* to shake *my* hand, not for me to shake theirs. I am willing to look down upon, or, upon occasion, directly across at these officials, but *never* up to them, even slightly (with rare, individual exceptions, having to do with individual accomplishment, not with the office held). That is always poor tactics in dealing with the servants. I expect the president to address me as Dr. Kameny until I give my assent to greater familiarity; I will address him as I choose from the outset; that is my prerogative. . . .

Let me say, in closing, that because the sentiments expressed in your column were so far on one side, I have responded rather more strongly to the other extreme than, in actual practice, I conduct myself. Proper attention to the ordinary amenities of civilized discourse is always in order; groveling before the servants—never. An American citizen deals with his public officials politely, courteously—and firmly—but never lets them forget that, in the last analysis, the citizen is in charge, and the public officials are merely "the servants" and that the whole structure, including the offices and positions themselves, was created explicitly to serve the individual citizen, and has no other *raison d'etre* whatever. . . .

Sincerely yours,

Franklin E. Kameny

Kameny to Louis Crompton

In the immediate wake of the Stonewall riots, Martha Shelley, president of the New York City Daughters of Bilitis, headed to MSNY offices proposing the DOB and MSNY join together to sponsor a march. Dick Leitsch did not seem especially pleased with the idea—he rarely appreciated coordinated efforts—but he did call for interested individuals to convene a march committee, partly to appease all the new activists in his MSNY office.

More than 500 demonstrators turned out for the July 2 march, which saw some protestors throwing bottles and setting trash cans on fire.[21] There was no dress code for the march.

After the protest, the march committee continued to meet, expressing a vision that tied gay liberation to other liberation movements, especially the one carried out by peasants in Vietnam (the National Liberation Front in North Vietnam). In one of these early meetings, Martha Shelley suggested that the group call itself the Gay Liberation Front (GLF). The GLF fashioned itself to the far left of MSNY, and it did not take long for the GLF to build alliances with other protest movements. As Shelley put it:

In Mattachine and DOB we couldn't openly state that we were against the Vietnam War because they believed that getting mixed up in other struggles was bad strategy. They thought that fighting for gay rights was difficult enough without having to take on all these other struggles. But those of us in GLF felt that the struggles should be united: the black civil rights movement, the struggle against the Vietnam war, the women's movement, feminist politics, socialist politics. And of course, the gay cause.[22]

Kameny attended some of the early GLF meetings with Barbara Gittings and her partner and fellow activist Kay Lahusen. Given their conservative appearance, the veterans of the early gay rights movement—altogether unknown to the young GLF leaders—seemed oddly out of place. And during one of the meetings, according to Gittings, "the gay liberation people called us on the carpet . . . and asked us to explain who we were and what we were doing at a GLF meeting . . . It was incredible. For once, I think even Frank was dumbfounded."[23]

OCTOBER 17, 1969

Dear Lou:

While I was in New York last weekend, and, again on Thursday night, I attended a meeting of the Gay Liberation Front and had some very long talks with some of the people involved. They're an interesting group. While I have some reservations about what they're doing and how they're doing it, by and large I liked what I saw. If they don't get taken over by some of the extreme-extreme radical groups (non-homophile) for their own ends, they should do well. Most importantly, they're a group of dedicated, enthusiastic, mostly youthful people who aren't afraid to come out in the open. They have a lot to learn and will almost certainly make some egregious errors, but I think that they will accomplish quite a bit of good.

At the moment, they're busy heckling Procaccino and Marchi in the NY mayoralty race—they go to campaign rallies and get up and ask pointed questions about the candidates' attitudes towards the problem of NY city's homosexuals—questions for which the candidates are totally unprepared.[24]

They recently picketed the *Village Voice* (which used to be *avant-garde*, but which has steadily moved over in the middle) to force them to accept ads using the words "gay" and "homosexual" and to modify their attitudes toward homosexuals and the activities of homophile groups. They were totally successful.

They're now trying to set up a community center. I referred them to SIR for advice on that (although they and SIR are very different as organizations—SIR being highly structured and GLF being resolutely unstructured). I've gotten them interested in the Clearinghouse, so they can "plug in" to the rest of the Movement.[25] Unfortunately, there's a conflict situation arising with MSNY (entirely by MSNY's choice). MSNY is resolutely non-cooperative. I urged Dick Leitsch to work *with* GLF instead of against them, with the feeling that each can contribute a great deal to the other— but he's not buying that.

Cordially,
Frank

Kameny to Barbara Grier

In the following two letters to the editor of the Ladder, *Kameny mounts his case that "gender is irrelevant" in the quest for civil liberties for homosexuals.*

OCTOBER 26, 1969

Dear Barbara:

. . . To say that male homosexuals and lesbians have less in common than almost any two groups is one of these statements which is just so far "out of this world," so utterly detached from reality, and so far "off the deep end" that I am quite unable either to take it seriously or to reply to it.[26]

I simply do not accept your statement that "Most lesbians do not agree to that (that male homosexuals and lesbians have a great deal in common) at all." I question seriously your definition and usage of the word "intelligent" in "Most intelligent lesbians seem to feel that male homosexuals and lesbians have less in common . . ."

I feel that you have unfortunately created for yourself (yourselves) a little, unreal, viciously anti-male world which can only do you and others a great deal of harm and accomplish no good whatever.

I spent yesterday afternoon and early evening with a group publishing our new community paper, *The Gay Blade*. It is being put out by an enthusiastic group consisting, in part, of MSW's Community Service Committee (chaired by Lili Vincenz). They have gone, as a group (or in sub-groups), to the various bars, clothing shops catering to homosexuals, etc., to get it carried openly for their patrons, etc. The group is just about half-and-half men and women—all homosexual. I assure you that your comments would be greeted with derision by these people who recognize that—within this context—THE battle is for THE homosexual and that gender is irrelevant.

Two weeks ago in New York I attended a meeting of the Gay Liberation Front and have subsequently talked at length with some of their people. Theirs, after the dust has settled, is the direction in which much of our movement activity is going to go, I predict (and I know that you will detest every bit of it judging from our discussions of picketing a few years ago). They have just started to put out a newspaper called *Come Out* (i.e., come out of the closet). They have gone completely "public." Women were very well represented at the meeting. They are welcome, and they are participating fully.

I feel that by your views you are backing yourself off into an unfortunate corner of total unreality and total irrelevancy to the real world of here and now.

You may be horrified, but I equate your statements with the anarchistic ones of SDS and others about "destroying the 'system'" and others of the mindless maunderings of which we hear so much these days.

I sincerely expected much better of you. I am deeply disappointed and hope that this was merely a momentary aberration to which we are all subject once in a while.

I know that I have written exceedingly strongly here and hope that it will not destroy or damage the good personal and working relationship which we have. But I was really quite incredulous at reading your remarks.

> Cordially (but somewhat dismayed
> and disappointed and startled),
> Frank

Kameny to Barbara Grier

OCTOBER 27, 1969

Dear Barbara:

In further response to your incredible remarks in your note of October 23:

To say that male homosexuals cannot speak for lesbians and to justify this by drawing analogies with whites not speaking for blacks or Jews not speaking for Catholics, etc., is utterly ridiculous.

Black *males* can and do speak for black *females* and vice versa—in terms of the problems of *blacks*, blacks are blacks are blacks, and their gender is irrelevant.

Catholic *females* can and do speak for Catholic *males* and vice versa; and Jewish males and Jewish females. In terms of the problems in our society of Jews and Catholics, Jews are Jews are Jews, and Catholics are Catholics are Catholics, and their gender is irrelevant.

Male homosexuals can and do speak for female homosexuals and vice versa. In terms of the problems in our society of *homosexuals* (NOT of women) homosexuals are homosexuals are homosexuals.

The fuzziness of the "reasoning" involved here on your part is incredible and disappointing.

The problems of the WACs whom I have defended are representative of what I am talking about. They are lesbians. Their problems, in the context in which I am dealing with them—and speaking for them—are absolutely indistinguishable from those of male homosexuals in the service. Their gender is utterly irrelevant to anything with which I am concerned. They are *homosexual people*, and that is the way I am handling their case, and that is all that is necessary to know.

The Nazis discriminated equally against Jewish men and Jewish women, and in any meaningful sense, the problems involved had to do with being Jewish, not with gender. The Protestants in Northern Ireland (where I lived for a year) discriminate against Catholics, irrespective of gender. And our society discriminates against homosexuals irrespective of gender.

In ALL of these contexts (and our American one as well), since the society in each instance is (was) ALSO male-dominated, the women in each instance—Jewish, Catholic, black, homosexual—had an *additional* problem. But that was a problem which is utterly irrelevant to the particular problem at hand.

Do you think that I, as a male, am any less capable of handling a military case, a civil service employment case, a security case, a case of blackmail (all of which and many more, I have gotten in regard to women) because the homosexual involved is female rather than male? Those whom I assist don't feel that I am any less capable.

Do you think that when the Gay Liberation Front in New York puts an advertisement into the *Village Voice* for a gay dance, for men and women, and the *Village Voice* refuses to allow the word GAY in their ad, and the GLF pickets, and the *Voice* revises their previous ban on the words "gay" and "homosexual" that there is any slightest difference or distinction in the interests of the male and female homosexuals involved in the dance, in the picket lines, in the negotiations, or referred to by the advertisement? Obviously not.

Now, you have harped on this matter endlessly, without ever stating the bases for your incredibly extreme statements. Please set out for me what you feel ARE the differences between male homosexuals and female homosexuals which you find to be of such incredible importance; and what you see as the problems besetting the female homosexual which are so different from those besetting the male homosexual and vice versa.

BUT be SURE that the differences which you set out, and the problems which you set out, are problems of HOMOSEXUALS, not of WOMEN.

I think that it's about time that you thoroughly disentangled the two causes.

I await your comments and replies—and retorts?—with eager anticipation.

> Cordially,
> Frank

By taking a legitimate grievance and cause—women's rights and equality—and combining it with another legitimate grievance and cause—the plight of the homosexual—you have created a mystique which has no relationship to reality, which will be deeply harmful to *both* causes and which, finally, make you (pl.) look more than a little ridiculous—and that last saddens me.

The following is an excerpt of Grier's October 31 reply:

I can no more separate being a Lesbian from being a woman than you can separate being a male homosexual from the fact you are a man. On your arguments . . . given your premises you are wholly correct. It is the same sort of thing that our mutual enemy Socarides does . . . he starts out convinced that homosexuals are sick . . . You are just as convinced that our battles are the same as I am they are not. The thing here though is that from your viewpoint as a member of the current "master race" it is logical, sensible and wholly right. From my viewpoint as a second class citizen . . . the handicaps are dual and not separable. Since yours is single and mine double you really do not know how you would feel or act in some circumstances.[27]

Anonymous to Kameny

Kameny received numerous crank letters. The following text appeared on a page with drawings of death symbols.

NO DATE (OCTOBER 1969)

Frankie, the Lust Crazed, Demon Possessed, Dirty Lust Vomit* or Puke*:

Please, please, please, fall on your dirty Lust Stained knees and truly repent of all your dirty Lust Crazed Sins, and let the BLOOD of the Murdered SON of GOD, wash away all your Dirty Lust Crazed Sins . . . Jesus Wants to save your dirty lust crazed Puke soul, I will not be satisfied to let Satan dump you into the Pits of Hot HORROR, HORROR, HORROR HELL to burn like a Hot Dog on a stick forever! Frankie . . . You are unclean!!! . . .

Puke or Vomit

Jesus the Murdered SON of GOD said, "I will spue (Puke* or Vomit*) you out of MY mouth into Hell!"

Kameny to the Editors of the *Washington Post*

In her article on the "homosexual revolution," Washington Post reporter Nancy Ross wrote about "the new militancy on the part of homosexuals," drawing attention to tactical differences within the movement. Her explanation cited Jack Nichols, the cofounder of MSW.

> As among black leaders, controversy has developed within the ranks of homosexuals as to the best method of achieving their ends. San Francisco's Leo Laurence, an avowed militant, revolutionary homosexual, has allied himself with organizations like the Black Panthers. Jack Nichols, managing editor of New

York's Screw *magazine, suggests, instead, peaceful protests such as a subway kiss-in and a dance-in to integrate straight nightclubs.*[28]

NOVEMBER 3, 1969

Gentlemen:

As the person who coined and originally publicized the slogan *Gay is Good*, I was gratified, indeed, to see it in the form of a photograph of one of our lapel buttons gracing the head of the generally excellent article by Nancy Ross on the new homosexual militancy.

For members of the homosexual minority, the slogan is intended to serve the same much-needed supportive and reparative function served by the parallel slogan *Black is Beautiful* for the black minority. *Good*, of course, is intended in *all* of its various senses, not excluding the psychological, the sociological, and, of course, the moral.

One cavil: The immediate present often tends to loom up too large and out of proper perspective, at the expense of the achievements of the past. The picketing by homosexuals of the White House, Civil Service Commission, State Department, and Pentagon, done by the Mattachine Society of Washington in 1965 and 1966, and continuingly at Independence Hall, Philadelphia, each July 4, and passed off so cavalierly and almost apologetically by Miss Ross, were, at that not far-distant time in the past, at least as novel, as pioneering, as militant, as "extreme" and as indicative of a "new openness" as the more recent demonstrations in New York and elsewhere, and, in fact, prepared the groundwork without which those more recent demonstrations would have been quite impossible and simply would not have occurred.

All of us working in the homophile movement, by various methods, tactics, and techniques, are very much determined to achieve full recognition and acceptance of two related but quite distinct points: (1) The equality of homosexuals with heterosexuals; and (2) The equality of homosexuality with heterosexuality, with all that goes with both of those in terms of civil rights, human rights, and basic human dignity for homosexuals *as homosexuals*. Gay *IS* good!

Sincerely yours,
Franklin E. Kameny

Kameny to Foster Gunnison Jr.

Ever since assuming a leading role in the homophile movement, Kameny attracted young men in need of a mentor. In the letter below, he reflects on the role he has played in so many of these young men's lives.

NOVEMBER 26, 1969

Dear Foster:

I have found, over the past ten or twelve years (and, in some ways, going back most of another decade before that), that a large number of people tend to place me in the role of their surrogate father. I can usually empathize with the people who come to me with problems (with occasional major failures) and can give advice and counsel which people find continuingly valid and valuable, with insights which seem to me completely obvious, but which (I find continually surprising) my advisees don't find at all obvious until I point out the way.

The result has been that over these years, a large number of people have adopted me, on an interim basis (and that phrase is the key to the relevance of all this), as a "father figure." Sometimes this was by mere implication, but often quite explicitly and statedly. Since this started in my early thirties, when it did not concord at all with my own self-image, I originally found it somewhat disturbing (very mildly—nothing that I got excited about), but no longer do.

However, being a father figure is "not my bag" for a very simple reason. Within the "father-son" relationship, the father must be somewhat more than a mere human being, and the son somewhat less than a whole human being—both virtually by definition. The father must be an authority figure. In personal relationships (as distinguished from organizational ones), both by personality and by choice, I do not play these roles. I have my faults, failings, weaknesses, and defects, as we all do. A father figure must conceal those, lest he become an idol with clay feet. I do not bother to do so. Much more important, I enter into all personal relationships on a basis of essential equality. This means that I don't refrain from criticizing and disagreeing—not in a high and mighty, paternal fashion, but in an equal-to-equal fashion—when those are in order, nor do I go to great lengths to "pat the good little child on the head" when praise is due (although I never knowingly withhold credit when that is due). I do not play the role of the "indulgent father," etc.

I expect the "son" to shoulder his full obligations as another person—whether, if he is living here, that means his full obligations in household matters or, much more important, in intellectual give-and-take. A father figure has to be an emotional and psychological crutch (a real father plays the same role to a real son, but then one substitutes the non-pejorative phrase "supportive role" for the word "crutch"—they're identical). I have no liking for being a crutch for anyone, and it grates upon my acceptance of people as basically equals.

The result has been over the years that I have tended to throw my self-chosen "sons" into roles of greater responsibility than they were psychologically bargaining for, have supplied less of the emotional support than they bargained for, have insisted (tacitly) upon more total self-reliance than they wanted. This has been interpreted (subconsciously) as rejection, and, in a number of cases, has resulted in a somewhat hostile departure from the scene of the "son."

Following this, however, an interesting thing has occurred in a gratifyingly large number of cases. In due time the individual seems to consider the relationship (by *relationship* I am not referring here to a sexual, lover-type relationship) of sufficient value, and there is a return, on a much more mature basis. The result is that some of my closest friends now, by their choices, are those who formerly used me as a father figure and have gone through this whole evolutionary process. . . .

Keep in touch.

Frank

By the end of 1969, the father figure was also experiencing additional discontent within the wider gay liberation movement. Militant leaders of the movement, with their calls for revolution, were at radical odds with Kameny's reformist approach to society. Kay Lahusen—a lesbian activist and partner of Barbara Gittings—distilled the opposition's sentiment in a November 9 letter to Kameny. "I believe the opposition will try to get ERCHO and NACHO to repudiate your and B's work against the federal gov't on grounds that it is irrelevant, and who wants a security clearance anyway and who wants to work for the government anyway. And 'burn the universities,' too. . . . I think the movement will just have to split, and you had best not waste your precious time trying to save it."[29]

Lahusen also expressed concern about Kameny's earlier claim that he might lose his redbrick house in Northwest DC. Kameny had rarely kept a lucrative job through the years, his bills piled up regularly, and he was not interested in everyday labor. Consequently, he often sought and relied on benefactors within the gay rights movement. Lahusen offered a bit of counsel:

> Frank, your big car and house really get people who live more simply on very nice incomes. Had you a modest apartment and were you less of a big spender on long distance calls, I believe, but cannot promise, that you would have more offers of help. Another thing bugging those who care most for you is that you have done so little to help yourself. Well, we have been over this ground too. I am only making a last try since I do certainly care very deeply about your welfare and want to see you get out of the hole you are in, and quickly so if that is in any way possible.

Lahusen's other practical advice was for Kameny to write a book about the movement, using his "fightin' prose—which is your best. When you are back to the wall, your prose gets much more incisive and great to read."[30]

At the same time he was experiencing conflict within the gay liberation movement, Kameny sent his friends and colleagues some exciting news in another area of his life:

> It is with a feeling of great pleasure and honor, and with a sense of deep personal satisfaction, gratification, and pride, that I am able to inform you that . . . I was just chosen, by a large majority, to membership on the Executive Board of the Washington, D.C. affiliate of the American Civil Liberties Union (the National Capital Area Civil Liberties Union).
>
> Second only to my devotion to the homophile movement and to work for the creation of better lives for homosexuals as homosexuals, and in no way conflicting with that (in fact, complementing and supplementing it), and of much longer standing in my personal life, is my devotion to the implementation and safeguarding of the precepts of certain basic American documents and the human ideals contained therein, including but certainly not limited to the Bill of Rights and its shining star, the First Amendment.[31]

8

"Psychiatry Is the Enemy Incarnate"

1970–1971

Kameny to Dick Leitsch

Leitsch had earlier accused Kameny of "foolish meddling" in the affairs of MSNY. The MSNY leader considered New York state to be "the exclusive territory of MSNY" and was angered by Kameny's recent visit to a gay organization in Buffalo, especially because he believed the MSW leader had advised the organization to operate an unlicensed club using the name "Mattachine Society." Leitsch also used his letter to reply to a piece of gossip he had heard:

> *I understand you've been spreading about some wish that I would become the NACHO/ERCHO delegate from MSNY because you can "deal" with me. That, I presume, is a compliment to me, but I cannot "deal" with you. You are a psychic cripple, and a menace to other organizations . . . I have a soft heart for cripples, and tend to give in to them. That's exactly why I don't deal with you. Psychic cripples are a menace to "do-gooders"; they need a strong hand to deal with them and prevent them from making a mess of everything. I cannot deal with you, and I am not equipped to handle people like you.[1]*

MARCH 16, 1970

Dear Dick:

 . . . I am curious as to the basis for your designation of me as a "psychic cripple." The term is an unusual one, and I am not at all clear as to what it implies. I do note that . . . I manage to work rather well and effectively with just about everyone in the movement and they with me. Virtually no one is able to work with you or you with them. . . .

216

My objections to MSNY have been essentially the same as those of people throughout the movement—your disdainful, haughty, "better than thou" attitude. I have ALWAYS given full credit to MSNY for its significant accomplishments and to you personally for yours. However, I always do that for all organizations and for all people in the movement. When I make public appearances, however, I discuss homosexuality and the movement. I do NOT . . . as you do . . . play up any one group. . . .

My personality is far from the smoothest or most unabrasive, but people know that what I say is the truth to the fullest extent of my abilities to convey my meaning accurately and unambiguously, and that any views I express are what I actually think, and are the actual bases for my actions. Therefore people are willing to work with me.

I have pleaded with you over the years to make certain modifications in your methods of operation. They would make life far pleasanter and provide for far more cooperation.

The third area which makes working with you impossible is your paranoid-type reaction to those around you, in which you assume that everyone is against you and against MSNY, is out to "get" you and out to "get" MSNY. This certainly was not true in the past; it certainly is not true in regard to me. Unfortunately, such an approach to the world tends to be self-fulfilling to a considerable degree, and so there is a good deal of quite unnecessary hostility toward both you and MSNY, engendered, in last analysis, entirely by your own *a priori* but false assumption that this existed to begin with.

Under all of these conditions, I hardly feel that you are the one to call anyone a "psychic cripple," whatever that is. . . .

Sincerely,

Frank

In spite of his longtime conflicts with Leitsch, Kameny believed the homophile movement enjoyed a degree of cooperation that other contemporaneous progressive movements lacked. He explained this in an earlier letter to Foster Gunnison:

We have done far better than—say—the Negro movement in the achievement of unity. The type of bickering, personality problems, mistrust and the like, are—I am rapidly realizing, as I never did before—universal. Look at the "new left"; then take another look at the homophile movement as a utopia of unity and cooperation.[2]

Kameny's life as a gay activist was becoming busier than ever, and he highlighted this in a letter to British gay rights activist Anthony Grey. The following excerpt of Kameny's letter refers to a Time *magazine article in which he was featured and to a chapter he drafted ("Gay Is Good") for an edited collection titled* The Same Sex.[3]

I've been frantically and increasingly busy in the past six to nine months. I was just beginning to get my affairs current, in the late summer, when a veritable tidal wave of paper proceeded to inundate me. As a result of the appearance of the Time *magazine article and the United Church book, I began to receive other publicity in the homophile movement press. I have had a few letters printed in Playboy magazine. As a result I have become a minor national figure, and I get phone calls and letters from the entire country—and abroad— seeking advice, assistance and counseling.*[4]

No doubt another reason Kameny was becoming a "minor national figure" was that his cause had attracted major national attention ever since the Stonewall riots. Kameny commented on this, too, in his letter to Grey:

As I mentioned, the homophile movement here is growing incredibly. People are increasingly coming out into the open. This was particularly spurred by the riot which occurred in Greenwich Village last June—the first homosexual riot in history as far as I know. Whatever judgment one may pass upon this form of activism, it has served to galvanize the homosexual community.[5]

Kameny to Johnny Carson

*In this letter to the famous talk show host, Kameny writes about the "grossly distorted" view of homosexuality that appeared in the bestselling book by David Reuben—*Everything You Always Wanted to Know about Sex but Were Afraid to Ask. *Reuben had depicted homosexuality in negative terms, even claiming that most homosexuals were obsessed with using vegetables for sexual pleasure:*

Most homosexuals find their man-to-man sex unfulfilling so they masturbate a lot. Much of their masturbation centers around the anus. The question, of course, is what to use for a penis. Carrots and cucumbers are pressed into service. Forced into the anus, lubricated with vegetable oil, they give some homosexuals what they seek. . . .

The homosexual who prefers to use his penis must find an anus. Many look in the refrigerator. The most common masturbatory object for this purpose is a melon. Cantaloupes are usual, but where it is available, papaya is popular.[6]

MAY 26, 1970

Dear Mr. Carson:

. . . Along with most other homosexuals I bitterly oppose Dr. Reuben's views on homosexuality and feel that the chapter in his book on the subject is a grossly distorted, totally inaccurate representation of homosexuality and homosexuals, which is doing us incalculable harm. There is a great deal of strong feeling on this matter in the homosexual community the country over, and a storm of protest has been aroused by the book. . . .

Keep in mind that Dr. Reuben, by his own admission, on your program, stated that the homosexuals whom he has seen are all his patients—clearly an atypical, non-representative sampling. These are obviously disturbed people, or they would not be patients, just as the heterosexuals whom he sees are disturbed people. People without emotional problems do not go to see psychiatrists, and so Dr. Reuben and his colleagues have never seen the innumerable healthy, happy, emotionally problem free homosexuals who make up the bulk of our community. . . .

We—most homosexuals and the homosexual community—do not consider psychiatrists and psychoanalysts as our keepers, as our spokesmen, or as authorities upon us and our condition. We never gave them authority to tell you about us. At the very best, their view is as distorted as that of the classical, well-intentioned "white liberal" in the 30s and 40s discoursing upon the Negro, his attitudes, his problems, and his community. In fact, increasingly, the homosexual community is growing to consider a discussion of homosexuality by a psychiatrist or a psychoanalyst as equivalent to a discussion of Negritude by a Ku Klux Klansman or of Judaism by a Nazi.

We do not consider homosexuality to be a psychiatric problem at all. It is a . . . *sociological* problem in prejudice and discrimination against an unpopular minority. Dr. Reuben and his book are one of the more sophisticated and insidious manifestations of that prejudice (calling people mentally ill, as he does us, is as "lethal" in our society as calling them criminals). . . .

Accordingly, because I (and many other homosexuals) feel that Dr. Reuben and, through him, your program, has presented a grossly distorted view of homosexuals, homosexuality, what we are, what we think, what we want—and what we are doing to achieve in society the rightful place of homosexuals as equal to heterosexuals and of homosexuality as equal to heterosexuality—and has done us severe injustice and major injury, I request *equal time* on your program to appear *as a homosexual*, to present *our* side of this controversial question, and to offset the damage done to us by Dr. Reuben, his book, and his appearance on your program.

There is a major movement afoot to change the status of homosexuals and homosexuality in our society and to achieve our rights, freedoms, equality, opportunity, and basic human dignity, as the homosexuals that we have a moral right, in our pluralistic society to become, to be, and to remain. It is time that this view had an airing in your program. I can present our position in an informed, interesting, articulate, and dignified fashion. . . .

Sincerely yours,
Franklin E. Kameny

Kameny did not receive an invitation to appear on The Tonight Show.

After Reuben's book was published in Great Britain, gay rights leader Martin Corbett arranged the delivery of a twelve-foot-long cucumber to the offices of Reuben's publisher.[7]

Kameny to Anthony Grey

On June 28, 1970—exactly one year after the Stonewall uprising—thousands of activists marched from Greenwich Village to Sheep Meadow in Central Park, New York City, for a "gay-in" to protest discrimination and celebrate the "new pride" found among them.[8] *Although he appeared nowhere in the front-page coverage of the event, Kameny was pleased not only to be present for the rally but especially to see and hear the slogan he had coined two years earlier—"gay is good." As he later recalled the event, "In that march up Sixth Avenue for the first Christopher Street Liberation Day, I was moved to a feeling of pride, exhilaration, and accomplishment, a feeling that this crowd of five thousand was a direct lineal descendent of our ten frightened people in front of the White House five years ago!"*[9]

In this positive and enthusiastic letter to Anthony Grey—who spearheaded the Homosexual Law Reform Society, which aimed to decriminalize homosexual sex between consenting adults in Great Britain, and who served as secretary of the Albany Trust, a philanthropic organization that played a pioneering role in offering counseling services for homosexuals in Britain—Kameny refers to just a few of the numerous gay and lesbian groups that had emerged since Stonewall. The group most in line with Kameny's philosophy and tactics was the Gay Activist Alliance (GAA). Founded in 1969 by activists dissatisfied with GLF's alliances with the Black Panthers and other militant organizations with various causes, the GAA fashioned itself as a single-issue group—singularly and militantly devoted to securing and advancing rights for gays.

JULY 3, 1970

Dear Tony:

The enclosed article from the *New York Times* of June 29 may interest you.

It was a great day!!! Some 2,000 of us marched over three miles up Sixth Avenue from Greenwich Village, in New York, to Central Park. It was the culmination of Gay Pride Week, and that—gay pride—was the theme of the march—be proud of your homosexuality; come out into the open; hold up your head in pride.

Two lanes of Sixth Avenue had been set aside for us. The police were out in force to stop traffic on the cross streets and to protect the line of march. Parking was prohibited at the assembly area and along the line of march.

The marchers carried signs with such slogans as: Gay Pride; Gay is Good; Lesbians United; and a variety of others. There were frequent chants—e.g., "2, 4, 6, 8, gay is just as good as straight."

There were also banners and signs representing the many organizations which participated (some 15 to 20 from all over the East coast), including the old-line Mattachines of Washington and New York, the conservative West Side Discussion Group, the militantly activist Gay Activist Alliance, the very radical Gay Liberation Front of New York, and the not-so-radical Gay Liberation Front of Philadelphia, the Student Homophile League of Columbia University and of Cornell University, Homosexuals Intransigent of City University of New York—and Gay Youth, a newly formed group of homosexuals under 21 (no lower age limit)—and others.

At Central Park we were joined by at least 2,000 more people, for a gay festival in the Park, attended by some 4,000 to 5,000 people, and including dancing, a kissing booth, couples making love in the ancient tradition of heterosexual couples in parks, etc., etc.

The mood was proud and happy from start to finish. There was not an incident to mar the occasion. The day was glorious—a bright, sunny, cloudless day, warm but not hot—absolutely perfect.

The week preceding had included a series of events—mostly but not all in New York—including public talks, seminars and workshops, dances, etc. The Gay Activist Alliance had a huge dance in a hall at New York University on Friday night; the Gay Liberation Front had one on Saturday night—both open to the public, of course.

Media coverage—radio, television, newspapers—was excellent. One of our people discussed it on television here in Washington a few days later.

Parallel demonstrations were held at the same time in Boston, Chicago, and Los Angeles. I've been told that the Chicago groups planned to burn several symbolic closets constructed for the purpose.

Plans are already under way for next year's demonstration—the planning committee will be meeting next weekend to start the ball rolling for June 1971.

The movement here is burgeoning at a rate beyond any expectations a year ago. There's still a long way to go, but the push is really on, in all areas—the political, the legal, the civil rights, the religious, and many others. . . .

Let me hear from you soon.

As always,
Frank

Kameny to Anonymous

Gays and lesbians were not the only ones to seek Kameny's advice, and in the following letter he offers counsel on a potential marriage between his heterosexual correspondent and her gay boyfriend. Of special interest is his commentary on effeminacy.

OCTOBER 20, 1970

Dear Miss ——:

I am writing in response to your letter of October 10 in regard to your homosexual friend and the relationship between you.

You ask a number of questions, and I will try to answer them in order.

1. No, it is very unlikely that a homosexual can change with or without will power. There is no reason why he should change. Homosexuality is as good as heterosexuality and it should be enjoyed. The homosexual should learn to live WITH his homosexuality, not AGAINST it, and to build for himself a satisfying, rewarding, fulfilling life AS A HOMOSEXUAL. . . .

2. Neither homosexuals NOR HETEROSEXUALS are born that way. . . .

3. Very large numbers of people—both homosexual and heterosexual—can "cross the line." The term "bisexual" is a vague one. Most people can function "on the other side of the fence" but do not find it as satisfying.

4. It is unlikely that a homosexual will really fall in love with a girl, straight or gay. If he is confused and is fighting himself and trying to talk himself into being straight when he is not, he might convince himself that he has fallen in love heterosexually, but any marriage coming out of this is very likely to be a disastrous mistake—although not always. Such an affair or marriage will NOT change him to heterosexuality.

5. There is unfortunately confusion in the minds of many people between homosexuality and effeminacy. A great deal of that confusion has crept back from the larger heterosexual community into the homosexual community, and many homosexuals—particularly younger ones just "coming out"—think that that is the way homosexuals should act and do so. For most, this is just a passing phase. For some it is not. This is a complicated subject which I have touched upon only superficially here. Most homosexuals correctly consider themselves as men who are

interested in men, with equal emphasis on both words "men" in that phrase. . . .

8. The gay bars are essentially the only resource or facility presently provided by society for homosexuals to congregate and socialize. Where else are they to go?

9. Obviously since a homosexual—by very definition—is interested in men, not women, he is going to tend to be warmer to more men than to women.

In general, I advise against marriage between homosexual men and straight women. They have a way of not working out. On the other hand, this is certainly not always true. I know of some very successful marriages of this kind. Provided that both parties go into the marriage with "all the cards on the table, face up," as seems to be the case with you, it might well be successful. If either side—or both—go into it in the hope of "reforming" the homosexual, it won't work.

I hope that this answers some of your questions and has been of some help.

Sincerely yours,
Franklin E. Kameny

Kameny to Admiral Elmo Zumwalt Jr.

In this letter to the navy's chief of naval operations, Kameny protests the "human scrap heap" created by the navy's policy prohibiting homosexuals from serving honorably. Unlike some of his early letters to the military, this one demands the full inclusion of homosexuals.

DECEMBER 23, 1970

Dear Admiral Zumwalt:

The North American Conference of Homophile Organizations is an affiliation of organizations working by lawful means to create better lives for our homosexual American citizens as homosexuals and to improve the status of the homosexual in this country. It is always noted that we are *homosexuals*, with distorted ideas which usually go with that term, but it is always conveniently overlooked that we are also *American citizens*, with all that should go with that term, and that this is *our* country, too, as homosexuals, quite as much as of the heterosexuals, and *our* government, and *our* Navy. We do not have second-class citizens in this country—or at least we claim that we do not.

. . . We are writing to suggest that the Navy's policies and practices with regard to homosexuals and homosexuality are also long overdue for a change. These policies hark back to the Middle Ages; they are a disgrace to any civilized country; they serve no useful purpose; they serve no valid interest of the Navy, of the government, of the country, or of society, and serve only to give aid and comfort to the enemies of this country; they are irrational; they are fundamentally un-American and are antithetical to the human rights, freedoms, and dignities which we subsume in the term "Americanism."

Homosexuals everywhere find SEGNAVINSTR 1900.9, with the entrenched bigotry articulated in its statement of policy, deeply offensive and insulting—particularly when, despite this regulation, 10% of our Navy (the same percentage as of the populace at large), at all ranks, officers and enlisted men both are homosexual and always have been, and serve well and honorably, contributing to the Navy and to our country, providing pragmatic demonstration of the lack of need for these policies and regulations.

Under SEGNAVINSTR 1900.9, large numbers of servicemen are cast out every year with less-than-fully-honorable discharges, which effectively consign them to the human scrap heap—to a lifetime of underemployment and underproductivity. I, personally, receive phone calls and requests for assistance from people who have received such discharges as long ago as the end of World War II and who, because of those discharges, have not been able to obtain a decent job since. Can this possibly be construed to serve *any* valid interest of the Navy or the country? . . .

Accordingly, we wish to suggest that you consider the following three points:

1. That the existing exclusion of homosexuals from the Navy be totally terminated.

2. That even short of the ideal goal enunciated in (1) just above, that if homosexuals are not wanted in the Navy, that homosexuals found in the Navy be given fully, unqualifiedly honorable discharges with all accrued rights and benefits. . . .

3. That all less-than-fully-and-unqualifiedly honorable discharges issued over the past two to three decades because of homosexuality be upgraded to fully honorable.

While the preceding is a necessarily simplified presentation of the situation and of our requests, we feel that what we ask is not unreasonable.

We will be pleased to meet with you and/or other appropriate Navy officials—and, in fact, are desirous of doing so—formally or informally, "on the record" or "off the record" (we recognize that this may be considered a sensitive issue) to engage in constructive and productive discussions directed toward remedying and rectifying a situation long overdue for rectification, to the mutual benefit of all concerned—the Navy, our country, and our homosexual American citizens.

We look forward to your early, favorable reply.

Sincerely yours,

Franklin E. Kameny

Captain G. H. Rood, U.S. Navy assistant chief for performance, sent Kameny the following reply on February 25, 1971:

> I appreciate your concern that no American be relegated to second-class citizenship and certainly none should be persecuted. Nevertheless I am convinced that the long-standing policy of the United States Navy of excluding homosexuals is in the best interest of the Navy.
>
> The directive to which you make specific reference, SECNAVINST 1900.9, has its origin in policy promulgated by the Secretary of the Navy in 1943. The current directive, and Articles 83 and 125 of the Uniform Code of Military Justice, have evolved as a result of experiences and in response to a genuine need. I realize that you do not agree with these regulations and strongly oppose this policy; however, I feel I must point out that the Navy is not the proper forum for any challenge to the legality or appropriateness of existing laws within the United States regarding homosexuality. The Navy is a statutory creation which functions under statutes, court decisions, and policies decreed under granted statutory powers. Should you counsel homosexuals to fraudulently enter the Navy, you place them in jeopardy of receiving a less than fully honorable discharge, and you would be doing the individual and the Navy a disservice.[10]

Kameny to Anthony Grey

In the following letter, Kameny refers to GLF "invasions" at a recent American Psychiatric Association meeting. For many years, Kameny had been willing to engage in public discussions with psychiatrists who understood homosexuality to be a mental disorder, but the younger gay militants adopted a fundamentally different tactic. As historian Ronald Bayer has described the shift: "Since discussions would impart a modicum of credibility to those with whom one spoke, they were politically unacceptable. Psychiatrists were war criminals, the enemy; they were to be defeated, not won over. It became a matter of principle for Gay Liberation to denounce discussions with psychiatrists as acts of 'collaboration.'"[11] In 1970, the denunciations came in the form of a loud disruption at the annual meeting of the American Psychiatric Association. In one session on aversion therapy, for example, gay activists screamed "torture" and demanded the right to conduct their own panel at the following annual convention in Washington, DC. A sympathetic APA member, Kent Robinson, agreed to chair the meeting and invited Kameny to moderate and speak at the upcoming panel. Kameny's verb selection in the letter is noteworthy.

JANUARY 12, 1971

Dear Tony:

 . . .

 We're finally penetrating the psychiatrists. I have an article coming out shortly in a journal called *Psychiatric Opinion*, and I've been asked to moderate a panel at the forthcoming meeting of the American Psychiatric Association in May. That resulted from the Gay Liberation Front invasions of their last two meetings. . . .

Cordially,
Frank

Kameny agreed to moderate and speak on a panel titled "Lifestyles of Non-Patient Homosexuals," but partly because he found the panel to be another insufficient response to the homosexual community, he also formed an alliance with the local GAA and GLF to stage a protest, a "zap," at the APA convention in Washington. On May 3, Kameny and his fellow protesters invaded the convention hall where the APA members had gathered, and the

*gay rights veteran seized a microphone. "Psychiatry is the enemy incarnate,"
Kameny announced. "Psychiatry has waged a relentless war of extermination
against us. You may take this as a declaration of war against you."*[12]

*After speaking on the panel, Kameny and Larry Littlejohn, a leader of
SIR in San Francisco, told Kent Robinson they wanted to appear before the
APA's Committee on Nomenclature with a formal request that the committee delete homosexuality from its list of mental disorders in* Diagnostic
Studies Manual*—II. Richard Bayer has captured the significance of that
request: "Though little came of that effort, it represented the first attempt
on the part of gay activists to enter into direct discussions with those within
the APA leadership who were responsible for the classification of psychiatric disorders. The process of turning general outrage into a specific political
demand had been set in motion."*[13]

Kameny to President Richard Nixon

*On February 3, 1971, Kameny announced that he was running as an Inde-
pendent to become the District of Columbia's delegate to the U.S. Congress.*

*His announcement had received an unexpected boost a day earlier
when the* Washington Post *published an editorial defending the right of
Otto Ulrich, an openly gay man who had been denied an industrial security
clearance, to federal employment. "The man cannot conceivably be considered more subject to blackmail than other men for the simple reason that he
has made no attempt to conceal his homosexuality," the* Post *wrote.*[14]

*In the prior month, the ACLU, with Kameny's encouragement, had filed
four separate lawsuits on behalf of four men whom Kameny had long counseled: Ulrich, Richard Gayer, Benning Wentworth, and George Grimm, all
of whom had lost top-secret positions with defense contractors because of
their homosexuality. In Ulrich's case, the ACLU argued that he had a right
not "to disclose matters of an intensely private and personal nature in the
absence of any demonstration of a legitimate government interest in such
matters," and that there was no "rational connection" between his homosexuality and his ability to keep secret classified information.*[15] *The landmark
filing of the lawsuits, as well as the substance of the arguments, directly
resulted from Kameny's longtime work with both homosexuals denied security clearances and the local branch of the ACLU.*

The conclusion of the Post's *editorial on Ulrich read partly like a tailor-made rationale for Kameny's lifelong work as well as his entrance into electoral politics:*

Persecution of homosexuals is as senseless as it is unjust. They may have valuable gifts and insights to bring to public service. If they are qualified for a job in terms of intelligence, experience and skill, if they conduct themselves, like other employees, with reasonable circumspection and decorum, their private sexual behavior is their own business so long as it does not affect their independence and reliability. Like anyone else, they have a right to privacy, a right to opportunity and a right to serve their country.[16]

Kameny could not agree more. Indeed, he had emphasized Ulrich's right to privacy in an amusing 1970 letter to Richard Farr, a Department of Defense examiner in cases of industrial security clearances:

We feel, in fairness to you that you should know that we consider these interrogatories to be one of the most obscenely offensive invasions of privacy by our government that we have seen—and our experience with obscenely offensive governmental invasions of privacy is extensive. Mr. Ulrich, personally, is outraged. He has stated to me that he intends, publicly and for the formal record, to offer to purchase for you and your colleagues in the Defense Department, dirty books, preferably with pictures, so that you can "get your rocks off" without having to resort to the details of his sexual life for your titillation and arousal.[17]

A year earlier Kameny had written an equally pointed letter about the discrimination Ulrich had faced in one of the proceedings against him.

Applicant was asked (approximately) whether he had ever engaged in public or non-private homosexual acts. We refused to respond upon grounds of irrelevancy and upon grounds of discriminatory questioning.

We point out that "lovers' lanes" are as American as apple pie. They are noted for the occurrence, therein, of heterosexual sexual acts, which occasionally result in arrests. Are all (or any) heterosexual clearance applicants queried about such public sexual activity upon their part? No!

We point out that numbers of our younger generation (and others) accurately refer to drive-in movie theaters as "passion pits." They are noted for the *occurrence of heterosexual sexual activity taking place in cars parked there ostensibly for the viewing, by the occupants, of moving pictures. Are all (or any) heterosexual applicants queried about such public sexual activity upon their part? No!*

When I was a student at Harvard University, I witnessed, upon many occasions, heterosexual sexual activity occurring at night on the long wide stretch of lawn along the Charles River bank, in front of the Harvard (student-residence) Houses. Such places and such activity occurring therein are common, universities over and the country over. Are all (or any) heterosexual former Harvard men-applicants (and appropriate others) queried about such public sexual activity upon their part? No![18]

Back to Kameny's campaign: When successfully filing the nominating petitions on February 22, Kameny became the first openly homosexual candidate for Congress.[19] In his pitch to gay voters, he stated: "I offer you beyond what the other candidates offer you, a special sensitivity to personal freedom, the right to live your life as you choose to live it."[20] But Kameny sought to appeal to the whole electorate, too, staking out positions on a wide variety of issues.[21]

After telling one local citizens association that the city's problems were "equally apparent to all decent men of goodwill," but that he would exercise "a special concern for what America stands for in terms of human rights" for minorities, including homosexuals, an audience member asked: "Are you serious?" Kameny replied without hesitation: "Yes, I certainly am."[22]

On March 20, Kameny and about fifty campaign supporters marched to the White House carrying placards and chanting "two, four, six, eight, gay is just as good as straight," and "three, five, seven, nine, lesbians are mighty fine." At the White House gate, Kameny handed a guard the following letter to the president. A photograph of the event appeared in the Post *on the following day.[23]*

MARCH 20, 1971

Dear Mr. President:

This letter is written to you as a letter has been written to each of your predecessors in the White House, since 1962, on matters of concern to 15,000,000 American citizens and 80,000 citizens of the District of

Columbia—homosexual American citizens and homosexual citizens of the District of Columbia.

But this time, this letter is being written not merely from an organization working for homosexuals, but by a candidate on the official ballot for Delegate to Congress from the District of Columbia—a candidate placed there by a homosexual community becoming increasingly impatient with the intransigence and recalcitrance of its government and its presidents—because you are OUR president, too.

I am running as a candidate emphasizing personal freedom and individual liberty—the very basis of this country, and the essence of what Americanism is all about. From our nation's birth certificate, the Declaration of Independence, with its guarantee of the inalienable right to the pursuit of happiness, to the pledge of allegiance to the flag, with its exaltation of this nation as one with liberty for all, we have exulted in the right to conduct our personal lives as we individually see fit, except only when our freedom directly limits that of someone else.

But our performance has been far inferior to our words. And our homosexual citizens, more, perhaps, than any other group, have borne the brunt of that discrepancy between performance and promise. Our homosexual citizens are our first disadvantaged minority group for whom nothing is being done and in whose behalf not a word is being raised. We are determined that that is going to change, and promptly so. We simply will no longer tolerate second class citizenship in a country which piously disavows the existence of second class citizens.

Among our grievances are four which come within your purview, in one way or another. These are:

1. The ban on Civil Service—executive branch—employment of homosexuals. This policy represents mere supine submission to bigotry. We want this eliminated totally and without a trace as unbefitting to a civilized, enlightened nation.

2. The exclusion of homosexuals from the armed services, and the issuance of less-than-fully honorable discharges to homosexuals found in the armed services, disabling them for life, to the benefit of neither society, nation, service, nor serviceman.

3. The group or class denial of security clearances to homosexuals. Any such group or class disqualification is fundamentally un-American.

4. Non-inclusion of homosexuals among those protected by equal opportunity and other civil rights laws preventing discrimination in private employment. Denial of employment to a citizen on the basis of his personal life is as offensive and unconscionable as such denial upon the basis of race, religion, sex, or national origin.

As American citizens, we insist upon remedy for these abuses.

Mr. President, you are president of ALL American citizens, including homosexual American citizens. As homosexual American citizens, these are OUR country, OUR society, OUR government, OUR Civil Service, OUR Armed Services, OUR government secrets. We insist on playing a full role in the mainstream of OUR society and OUR country. We insist on being allowed to contribute fully to our country and to enjoy its full benefits. We WILL do so.

In implementation of that legitimate and valid aim, and as a representative of the homosexual community—our largest minority after the Negro—I request an appointment with you at an early date to discuss our grievances and to seek remedies for them.

We look forward to an early, favorable reply.

Sincerely yours,

Franklin E. Kameny

On March 23, 1971, Democrat Walter Fauntroy defeated five opponents, including Kameny, to win the race for DC delegate to Congress. Kameny finished in fourth place, garnering 1.6 percent of the total vote.[24]

Kameny assessed his campaign not by the total number of votes but by its impact on the DC community—a point he explained in a letter to his brother-in-law Ira Lavey:

> *My campaign was seriously run, carefully calculated and, in terms of its real objectives—impact on the governmental-political structure, impact on the general community, and impact on my own community as a trailblazer toward politicization—was completely successful. We are still reaping a harvest from it, as (one of many possible examples) when we approached our City Council the other day*

in regard to some legislation we wanted, found them surprisingly receptive, and were told that their receptivity resulted completely from my campaign.[25]

Kameny also hoped that his campaign would inspire other gays to run for office, as he stated in another letter, this one to Ian Dunn of Scotland: "I do expect that this will be a trailblazer. I hope to see gay candidates running for office in the next two years in New York, San Francisco and Los Angeles, Chicago, and elsewhere."[26]

With leftover money in the campaign treasury, Paul Kuntzler and a few other campaign operatives traveled to New York, without having invited Kameny, and began discussions to begin a DC chapter of the Gay Activist Alliance. "There was an important decision that was made in New York," Kuntzler recalled.

The movement from '61 to '71 was dominated by Frank Kameny. Frank Kameny was the movement. The movement was Frank Kameny. We made the decision that the movement had to move beyond the identity of one individual and that we would not offer Frank Kameny an office in the new GAA. Frank Kameny complained to me about that. . . . He said to me, "I am not going to be put out to pasture."[27]

According to Kuntzler, Kameny eventually accepted his new role. "He sort of became unofficial chairman of the board," attending and participating in most meetings.[28] *The new branch, according to journalists Dudley Clendinen and Adam Nagourney, "would become the city's premier gay political group," displacing Kameny's longtime and largely uncontested dominance through the MSW.*[29]

Kameny to William Scanlon

Kameny replies with a blast of criticism to recent news from the Defense Department's director of industrial security clearance reviews.

AUGUST 5, 1971

Dear Mr. Scanlon:

I am in receipt of your letters of July 27 to me and my counsel, informing us of the denial of my security clearance.

The outcome was pre-ordained, of course, from the moment the word "homosexual" entered the picture in this irrational travesty and exercise in entrenched bigotry and political corruption which you misname a security clearance program. We could really have disposed of all of the hearings, with the fraudulent, sham appearance that they give of an actually non-existent due process, fairness, justice, and rational, considered action.

It is clearly you and your colleagues and boards and your contemptible security clearance program itself that are not consistent with the national interest and, in fact, are an affirmative menace to the safety and security of our nation. . . .

Sincerely yours,
Franklin E. Kameny

Kameny to the Editors of the *Advocate*

Kameny reflects on his campaign in the following letter, criticizing an Advocate *article written by Nancy Tucker as well as a letter penned by Dick Leitsch. In her article on Kameny's campaign, Tucker had reported that Kameny had dissenters within the local gay community and that these critics felt that since he had "no chance to win the election," he should have used "all of his campaign time to discuss homosexual issues."[30] And Dick Leitsch, in his letter to the* Advocate, *denied that he had any interest in assuming a leading role in electoral politics. "Those who are trying to involve homosexuals in the sad, grim—and very silly—game of politics might do well to stick with Kameny," Leitsch wrote. "He digs jockeying for power, slogan-spouting, and mouthing easy solutions to difficult problems. And he's not that much more boring than Richard Nixon or the garrulous Mr. Humphrey."[31]*

AUGUST 8, 1971

Gentlemen:

I can understand the pique felt by my former friend Dick Leitsch at being upstaged and outclassed by my recent congressional campaign, and the self-castigation which he must feel at having so woefully botched his personal and organizational relationships over the past half-decade that the total-gay-community draft which persuaded me to run and placed me on the ballot in Washington would have been utterly impossible for him in New York.

Nevertheless, I strongly question the editorial judgment exercised by the *Advocate* in printing factually unsubstantiated, purely subjective, personal attacks of the kind found in Leitsch's letter (*Advocate*, August 4–17).

Similarly, I must question the *Advocate's* editorial judgment in printing the sour, jaundiced, pitifully politically naïve and simplistic, virtual-minority-of-one view of the campaign expressed by Nancy Tucker in her article appearing in the *Advocate* last April. The universal reaction to the campaign has been one of enthusiastic praise from gays and straights both, including the other candidates and their staffs, and in the months since the campaign, I have felt mounting pressure upon me from the gay and straight communities both to run again.

When you print a single view of an important event (even when it is labeled as an individual view and not a news report), at least some effort should be made to see that the facts stated are correct and the view is representative of the general consensus (when one exists, as it does very strongly in this case). Tucker's article did neither; her "facts" were inaccurate, and almost literally no one shares her evaluation of the campaign and the manner in which it was conducted.

Sincerely yours,

Franklin E. Kameny

Editor Dick Michaels replied that the Advocate *was trying to show the various sides of the issue at hand. "But if you intend to remain in public life and you intend to personally answer every bit of criticism you receive," he added, "you are going to be busy indeed."*[32]

Although defeated at the polls, Kameny received a personal boost on September 13, 1971, when U.S. District Judge John H. Pratt ruled that federal security evaluators may not ask homosexuals "probing personal questions" about their sex lives. The judge also ruled that the government may not deny security clearances to individuals who refuse to answer such questions. Pratt based both of his rulings on an individual's First Amendment right to privacy. With this ruling, Pratt ordered the Department of Defense to restore security clearances to Otto Ulrich and Richard Gayer, both of them openly gay men whom Kameny had counseled to keep quiet when federal investigators inquired about their sex lives.[33] *The ruling represented Kameny's most significant victory to date on the issue of security clearances. The government went on to appeal Pratt's ruling.*

Kameny received even more good news in late September, when the APA's Kent Robinson approached him about serving on a panel and hosting a booth at the following year's annual meeting. Kameny passed along the exciting news to his colleague-in-arms Barbara Gittings, asking her to take part in both activities.[34]

9

"The Ground Rules Have Changed"

1972

Kameny to CSC Chairman Robert Hampton

In this sharply worded letter to the chairman of the United States Civil Service Commission (CSC), Kameny demands that the commission consult with him and MSW before issuing any changes to its policies on employing homosexuals.

MARCH 5, 1972

Dear Mr. Hampton:

. . . It has come to our attention that the commission is currently preparing to issue a new or revised policy on the federal employment of homosexuals. It is on that matter, and at the explicit suggestion of your general counsel, that we are writing. . . .

As the persons who have in the past been the victims, and will in the future, at the very least, be the objects of the policies in question, it is a matter of moral and legal *right* under *our* system, that we be consulted with *before* the issuance of policies concerning and affecting us. A refusal to consult is simply unacceptable, and we will not accept it. Please do not waste your time and ours with one of the bureaucratic "brush-offs" or evasions that you people are so expert at. Our request is simple and direct. We expect a simple and direct proposal from you for arrangements for your receipt of input from us. . . .

It must be remembered that we are *homosexual American citizens.* . . . Therefore, as homosexuals, this is OUR society, OUR country, OUR government, OUR Civil Service Commission, and OUR government jobs, just as much as they are those of heterosexual American citizens. As a matter of *right*, we *WILL* play a participatory role in the governance, administration, disposition, and dispensation of what is ours. Ours is an increasingly activist, increasingly militant, increasingly impatient community. We are getting tired of spending our lives and our resources fighting for rights (such as federal employment) which are ours from the outset and which we should have been enjoying all along. Further, we are no longer satisfied to be relegated to the non-participatory sidelines, to be talked *about*, decided *for*, acted *upon*, and disposed *of* by others. As a matter of principle, we are determined to be talked *with*, decided *with*, acted *with*, and to do our own disposing of our own fate. These are our rights in democracy.

Finally, we have had enough also, over the years, with dealing with your subordinates who, as an excuse for inaction and for "passing the buck," always fall back on the excuse that they do not set policy. We are told, invariably, that "the commissioners set policy." Very well: You are setting the policy; we are the objects and victims of that policy; this is a government not only *for* the people, but *of* and *by* the people; therefore we *insist* on meeting directly with *you* (the three commissioners) first-hand and face to face. That is what America is all about.

Accordingly, we expect your prompt response, providing information as to the manner in which you are going to consult with the homosexual community or its representatives and spokesmen prior to issuance of new or revised U.S. Civil Service Commission policies in regard to the employment of homosexuals. A preliminary working draft of your proposed new or revised policy would be helpful.

Your immediate reply is requested and expected.

Thank you.

Sincerely yours,
Franklin E. Kameny

Chairman Hampton replied that "the time is not yet ripe for meaningful discussion between you and your constituency on the one hand, and this Commission on the other." Such a meeting would be premature, he added, because he and his fellow commissioners first needed to consider a study on the issue that the CSC general counsel was in the midst of preparing. Hampton thus sent his regrets and asked Kameny to "continue to keep our General

Counsel informed, as I am told you have been doing, of the shifts in case law, statutes, lesser ordinances, and public attitudes so that the presentation he makes to the commission can be complete."[1]

Kameny to the Editors of the *Red and Black*

University of Georgia administrators were not receptive when a group of gay students sought to form the Committee on Gay Education in November 1971.[2] *The students eventually sought counsel from Kameny, and in the following letter to the student newspaper he addresses yet another issue that irked the governing authorities.*

MARCH 9, 1972

Gentlemen:

I write as one who is informally and unofficially advising the Gay Education Committee from afar and also as one of the growing number of national spokesmen for the gay community.

Dean O. Suthern Sims claims that he is banning a proposed gay dance because sodomy is illegal and "one may not abet or aid to condone the violation of a Georgia state law."

I point out:

(1) That under Section 26-2010 of the Georgia Criminal Code, *fornication* is a crime.

(2) That far more acts of fornication result from *hetero*sexual dances than acts of sodomy from homosexual dances.

(3) That because fornication can have serious and lasting consequences in terms of pregnancies and illegitimate births, while sodomy has no consequences, fornication is a far, far graver "crime" than sodomy.

Therefore, by Dean Sims's peculiar "reasoning" ("peculiar" because dancing is dancing is dancing; dancing is not sodomy or fornication), all *hetero*sexual dances on the University of Georgia campus must be banned because they, too, are "aiding, abetting, and condoning" a violation of Georgia state law.

One of the essentials of due process is equal administration of law and regulation to all who come under it. I am recommending to the Committee on Gay Liberation that they take the necessary legal steps to see to it that if Dean Sims's ban against their dance is not lifted, the ban and the "rationale" for it be compelled to be applied to *all*.

Either gays will dance on the University of Georgia campus or *no one* will dance on the University of Georgia campus.

Idiotic regulations enforced by idiotic administrators lead to idiotic results. . . .

Sincerely yours,

Franklin E. Kameny

Near the end of March 1972, Kameny lined up gay ex-Marines, one of whom had earned an award for combat gallantry during the Tet Offensive in 1968, to testify at a Marine Corps discharge hearing for Jeffrey Dunbar, an eighteen-year-old lance corporal charged with having committed homosexual acts. Kameny also offered testimony at the March 21 hearing, and other members of GAA-DC were also present. Seeing the gay activists, a gunnery sergeant announced: "I wish I had a grenade. I'd drop it right in the middle of them."[3] Kameny's efforts did not succeed, and the Marines granted Dunbar a dishonorable discharge. Kameny took the occasion to write a letter to Secretary of the Navy John Chaffee, calling for "elimination of policies excluding homosexuals from service in the Navy," and in the meantime, "the granting of honorable discharges to gays found in the Navy."[4]

Kameny to CSC Chairman Robert Hampton

Kameny sent a copy of this letter—a reply to Hampton's refusal to meet with him and MSW—to CSC General Counsel Anthony Mondello. "We have just about lost patience with that whole scruffy crew of yours over there," Kameny wrote Mondello. "While you people dither endlessly and quiver in fear at approaching this question like sensible adults, our people are continuing to have their lives and careers destroyed by your petty tyrants. . . . We are fed up!!"[5] Especially clear in the following letter is the increasingly belligerent and threatening tone of Kameny's words.

MAY 15, 1972

Dear Mr. Hampton:

. . . Now, Mr. Hampton, you do not seem to perceive yet that the ground rules have changed and that time has run out for you on this question. You are no longer solely calling the terms. We are taking no more of your nonsense. We are no longer granting you the privilege of disposing of us without interference. *We* will determine the disposition of our people.

We did not write to *ask* to meet with you. We wrote to *tell* you that we *will* meet with you, willy-nilly.

Such a meeting is not a privilege to be granted or denied by *you* at *your* choice; it is a *right* to be invoked by *us* at *our* choice. If you disagree with that, then once again you do not know what Americanism is all about. You are public servants, we are the public, and this is the way that the servants are dealt with when they persistently misbehave and will not reform or become rehabilitated. In short, we do not recognize your right to refuse us the meeting which we want. Therefore the meeting which we want IS going to be held, simply because we want it.

We have gotten nowhere playing by your rules, and we have gotten nowhere playing with kid gloves on, so henceforth we will play by our rules and with the kid gloves off. Sooner or later you are going to have to do things the American way. We will see to it that it is sooner—*very* soon.

In April 1965, almost exactly seven years ago, we were informed that the commission had recently reconsidered its policy in regard to homosexuality and had decided not to change it. In response, we pointed out that we were aware of no consultation with the homosexual community in the course of that reconsideration and asked for such consultation. When it was not forthcoming, we picketed you as mentioned above.

Apparently, in seven years, the commission has neither changed, learned, grown, nor been rehabilitated. It is as arrogant, as immoral, as fearful, as intransigent, as bigoted, and as un-American as it ever was. Here, in 1972, it is preparing to repeat exactly what it did in 1965.

While the commission may not have progressed, we have. And so have methods of expression of discontent with government. There *will* be consultation with *you, personally,* and with your two fellow commissioners. It will occur in your office (or some other place *mutually* acceptable) at a time *mutually* acceptable. If you will not enter into such a bilateral agreement, then the consultation *will* take place, *in your office* at a time of *our* choice. But it WILL occur.

And it will occur because we are right and you have been wrong. It is as simple as that.

We have had our fill of stupid bureaucratic games and have ceased playing them. For at least twenty years we have been complaining about your anti-homosexual policies and practices, and for at least ten years have been attempting to get them changed. We have been refused discussions and have been shuffled around among underlings who piously disclaim authority to take any constructive action—or any action at all—and who refuse to put us into contact with those who do have the authority to do so: *YOU*.

THEREFORE:

1. We have written this letter to *you*, Mr. Hampton. We expect a reply from *you* personally. No answer to this letter from anyone other than you will be accepted or considered. *We will return, unread, a reply from anyone else.* As first-class citizens representing the largest minority group in the country after the Blacks, with long-standing, deep-seated, festering grievances, we have a *right*, not merely to negotiate with our public officials but to negotiate with those at the *topmost levels*.

A reply from anyone at all below those topmost levels—from anyone at all below you, individually—will be considered insulting and demeaning and will be responded to accordingly.

2. We request a meeting with *you* personally *and* (not *or*) the two other Civil Service Commissioners. Others may be present, of course, as you may choose (except for Mr. Kimball Johnson, who is personally offensive to us, and whom we will not permit in the same room with us).

3. While we prefer to arrange and conduct such a meeting in a civil fashion at an early date, time, and place mutually acceptable and convenient to all, if you do not agree to such a meeting, it WILL occur anyhow in such manner as WE find appropriate.

It will occur in *your* office at a previously unannounced time of *our* choosing. The communications media will be suitably informed. If we have to sit-in and set up housekeeping in your office for an indefinite duration until you agree to confer with us and do confer, we will do so. If you choose to have us arrested, we will convert the arrest, and the court proceedings following it, into a "publicity circus," making of them a forum for the public presentation of our grievances and of your un-American intransigence, cowardice, and arrogance. You will not come off looking very good.

We do NOT wish to adopt these tactics. But you are dealing with a militant, activist community whose patience has been *totally* exhausted. . . . We have had quite enough of your relentless, irrational war against us. We did not start that war, and we do not want it, but if it goes on, it will be waged increasingly on OUR terms. No group of American citizens need tolerate a declaration of open hostility and warfare against them by their government; our tolerance for your antics has run out.

That is the way it IS going to be, Mr. Hampton. You have been informed.

Sincerely yours,

Franklin E. Kameny

Kameny to CSC Chairman Robert Hampton, CSC General Counsel Anthony Mondello, and CSC Personnel Investigations Director Kimball Johnson

On May 25, the DC city government signed a stipulation—a formal agreement with the ACLU arising from a lawsuit brought by four homosexuals against the city—stating that the DC sodomy law "does not apply and cannot be applied to private consensual acts involving adults." Kameny celebrated the ruling in an interview with the Washington Post, *noting that such sodomy laws had provided legal cover for discrimination against homosexuals in federal employment.[6] Three days after the stipulation was signed, Kameny wrote the following angry letter to top CSC officials.*

MAY 28, 1972

Attached is a copy of a stipulation for dismissal, invalidating the sodomy statute in the District of Columbia not only for the present and future, but, obviously, retroactively. . . .

If ever again you or any other person affiliated in any way with the U.S. Civil Service Commission, in your official capacity, refers to homosexual conduct on the part of D.C. residents or others coming within the purview of the attached stipulation, as criminal conduct, or in any way at all, by any verbiage at all, directly or indirectly, explicitly or by implication, refers to us as criminals, you will feel the full wrath and outrage of the homosexual community in no uncertain terms.

We expect—and hereby demand—that the Commission issue forthwith a letter of retraction and apology to every person whom you have accused of such criminal conduct in this regard over the past 25 years, and a public statement of apology to those people collectively.

The homosexual community is fed up with the contemptible, despicable antics of you and your crew. We have had just about enough. It is about time that you commenced acting morally and ethically, and consistently with basic principles of Americanism, instead of as craven, cringing, politically corrupt cowards. If you do not do so, you will be compelled to do so. . . .

Franklin E. Kameny

Kameny to Frank Caprio

The 1972 APA convention in Dallas marked a turning point in Kameny's approach to the psychiatric profession. Just a year earlier, he had stormed the APA's convention hall, seized the microphone, and bitterly denounced the treatment of homosexuality as a sickness. But in 1972 he and his fellow activists left behind the nonviolent direct action campaign and adopted a comparatively moderate stance. Driving this change of tactic was APA's willingness to make space for a gay-friendly booth at the convention and its inclusion of another panel on homosexuality. In the following letter to DC psychiatrist Frank Caprio, whose published work had depicted lesbians as neurotic and in need of psychiatric treatment, Kameny refers to a flier he penned and distributed at the booth. He also provides helpful details of his work with gay teenagers seeking his advice and counsel.

MAY 30, 1972

Dear Dr. Caprio:

At the May 1–5, 1972 meeting of the American Psychiatric Association in Dallas, some of us as members of the homosexual community had a display booth in the scientific exhibit area of the convention hall. The booth was entitled *Gay, Proud, and Healthy: The Homosexual Community Speaks*. I was also asked by the APA to help organize and to participate in a panel discussion on *Psychiatry: Friend or Foe of Homosexuals*. . . .

At both of these, we distributed a leaflet entitled *Gay, Proud, and Healthy*. We are now sending copies of that leaflet, from time to time, to psychiatrists who are working in connection with homosexuality or are "treating" homosexuals—particularly those whose approach is to change (or try to change) homosexuals to heterosexuality or who we feel are otherwise in opposition to or hostile to the spirit embodied in the leaflet. Accordingly, we enclose herewith a copy of our leaflet. We urge you to read it carefully. Additional copies are available if you wish.

We must point out that we feel that the handling of homosexuality by psychiatrists has moved out of the realm of a matter strictly between doctor and patient, into a matter of concern to our entire community—the homosexual community. We consider efforts to persuade, pressure, or compel unwilling patients into conversion to heterosexuality to be tantamount to genocide and to be a matter of our collective concern. We will take such counter measures as may, in our view, be appropriate to protect our people.

This is particularly true of "patients" brought to psychiatrists through legal channels and teenage "patients" brought by parents (I refer, in both cases, of course, only to cases involving homosexuality). In the latter case, particularly, it is the parents, almost invariably, who badly need the therapy to relieve their anxieties and their bigotries, not the teenagers who simply need assurances that they are all right (as they are, of course), a healthy, congenial homosexual social and sexual life, and a comfortable acceptance and enjoyment of their homosexuality.

Because our people like to date, dance, fall in love, and do all the other enjoyable things that heterosexuals like to do, we are trying, with growing success, to provide the resources and facilities for them to do those things. There are public gay dances at the University of Maryland and in the ballroom of the student center of the George Washington University. There is a weekly gay coffeehouse at the University of Maryland in the student union building. These events are open to off-campus as well as to on-campus people. We now have a large gay community center only a few blocks from your office. There are large public gay dances there every week. All of these events and activities are open to people of all ages and are regularly attended by a growing number of gay people of both sexes from about 13 years of age upward.

I receive many phone calls from gay teenagers—a rapidly growing number, from age 12 or 13 upward, mostly boys, but a growing percentage of girls. I instill them with comfortable assurance and pride in their homosexuality and in its rightness, goodness, and desirability, provide them with techniques and arguments for coping with and countering hostile parents and conversion-minded counselors and psychiatrists, and refer them to the growing number of social resources for homosexuals, of which a few have just been mentioned, so that they can commence to lead a healthy, happy, rewarding, satisfying, fulfilling, loving and affectionate, social and sexual life, on par with that led, as a matter of course, by their heterosexual peers.

All of this is directed, actively, effectively, and successfully, at removing homosexuality—for persons of all ages and in all circumstances—from the realm of the covert, furtive, secretive, and clandestine, and bringing it out into the realm of healthful, exuberant, open love, affection, and sex, precisely on par with what heterosexuality now is. We are succeeding well and are prepared vigorously to oppose those who, in implementation of sheer bigotry and archaic outmoded prejudice and Victorian morality, masquerading as science but without the substance of science, would persist in approaching homosexuality as something pathological, undesirable, and to be avoided, prevented, or changed.

We are instilling into these people of all ages a secure knowledge that *Gay Is Good*, and being good is just as good as heterosexuality; that as homosexuals they can and should hold up their heads in pride, confident that when they differ with society, family, psychiatry, and law, it is they who are right and society, family, psychiatry, and law who are wrong. And we are succeeding!!

In some cities—we hope, soon, in Washington and area—the younger homosexuals have organized themselves into groups called *Gay Youth*, with an upper age limit (not the traditional lower age limit) of 21, and no lower age limit, to provide younger gays with a good social life and with resources for dealing with parents, psychiatrists and counselors, schools, and other forms of constituted authority.

We are much concerned at reports that you are using hypnosis to convert people from homosexuality to heterosexuality. Not only must we raise grave ethical questions here—once again we consider such efforts as an assault upon our community, particularly when directed against younger people brought to you not at their own initiative, but by their parents—but we must question the validity of as superficial a technique as hypnosis in the redirection of drives as deep-seated as one's emotional, affectional, and sexual preferences. The use of hypnosis in cases of homosexuality can only lead to conflicts of the most pernicious kind. We object to having our people messed up in this way.

We must repeat that we are not willing to leave these matters to the doctor-patient relationship—particularly in the case of younger people who are not really patients at all but are the unwilling victims of parents who ought to be patients. As with racism and anti-Semitism, these are matters of concern to the entire community involved—the gay community in this case.

We will be pleased, indeed, to discuss these matters with you.

Gay is Good!!

Sincerely yours,

Franklin E. Kameny

Kameny to Congressman Walter Fauntroy

Encouraged by Kameny and members of GAA-DC, the Washington, DC, school board approved a policy of nondiscrimination against homosexuals in the area of employment. In commenting on the policy, board vice president Mattie Taylor stated: "We may be opening up the road to advocacy. This raises the question of whether a teacher has the right to stand up in front of a class wearing a button saying 'Gay 1972, Try it, You'll Like It.'" Four of her board colleagues, including board president Marion Barry, disagreed with Taylor, approving a statement that "sexual orientation, in and of itself, does not relate to ability in job performance or service."[7]

When asked for his response, DC Representative and Baptist minister Walter Fauntroy stated that he had recently delivered a "strong" sermon on homosexuality, telling his members that homosexuals, like all sinners, are welcome at his church as long as they do not try to recruit young people there. To those who lived out their gay sexuality, he said, "You can do better; get right with God."[8]

MAY 30, 1972

Dear Mr. Fauntroy:

I recently read your remarks, as quoted in the *Washington Afro-American*, in response to the passage of a resolution by the D.C. Board of Education on the employment of homosexuals.

On the assumption that you were accurately quoted and not meaningfully out of context (and I recognize the frequent failings of the newspapers on both those counts), I have a few brief comments.

You refer to homosexuals recruiting youth. This is a factually unsubstantiated—and impossible—accusation, endlessly directed against homosexuals. No one can be recruited into either homosexuality or heterosexuality. What is possible is self-discovery, and it is critically important that such self-discovery occur as soon in the life of the individual as possible, whichever way it goes.

Much more important, however, is that your admonition be taken *both* ways. You people endlessly try to recruit *our* youth into *hetero*sexuality. If you people will cease trying to recruit our youth into your heterosexuality, we will promise not to recruit your youth into our homosexuality. What is sauce for the goose is sauce for the gander!

You stated that homosexuals are welcome to your church, which is open to all sinners. We resent and reject the implications of your phrasing.

If you operate upon the common Christian precept that *all* PEOPLE are sinners, then homosexuals are sinners—but because they are people, NOT because of or in connection with their being homosexuals, which is NOT sinful. Whatever sins each of us may have, homosexuality is not part of the list because homosexuality is no more sinful than heterosexuality.

We may well take you up on your offer and appear at your church, on the clearly enunciated philosophy not only that *Gay is Good* but also that *Gay is Godly*.

Finally, you are quoted as saying "to the gay lifers themselves: You can do better; get right with God."

We see no slightest inconsistency whatever between a gay life and being right with God. There is no need to abandon the one for the other.

We are confident that as homosexuals, living our gay life style, we are as fully right with God, right now, as are you and your fellow heterosexuals, living your heterosexual life styles.

It is just this kid of negative comment, so similar to the more benign but equally vicious and poisonous aspects of racism to which you as a person would be sensitive, which you as a congressman representing *all* the people in the District should be taking particular pains to avoid, and which we, as homosexual persons, as homosexual citizens, and as homosexual Washingtonians, bitterly resent. . . .

Sincerely yours,
Franklin E. Kameny

Kameny to Rae Kameny

Kameny was delighted with the school board's commitment not to discriminate against homosexuals in employment as well as with the District's decision not to apply sodomy laws against adults engaged in consensual acts in private. His sense of accomplishment continued to build on May 26, when a federal court ruled, in the case of Benning Wentworth (a case that Kameny had long advocated), that the practice of homosexuality did not offer sufficient grounds for denying individuals a security clearance to work with classified defense information. More positive news followed five days later, when a DC Superior Court judge ruled as unconstitutional the District's law prohibiting "soliciting for lewd and immoral purposes." Judge Charles Halleck ruled that the law—which was usually used to arrest homosexual men soliciting other men—was an unconstitutional infringement on the right to privacy.[9] Kameny shares all this exciting news in the following letter to his mother and asks her to share the letter with his sister and brother-in-law, Edna and Ira Lavey.

JUNE 3, 1972

Dear Mother:

The past two weeks have been among the most gratifying I have experienced in a very long time, and I thought I'd share them with you. I assume that you will share this letter with Edna and Ira.

We had four major victories between May 23 and May 31.

The first, on which I sent you some material, was the passage, by our Board of Education, of our resolution banning discrimination against homosexuals in employment anywhere in the school system. A copy of the resolution and some related articles are enclosed.

Because this has been one of THE most sensitive areas of employment, on this question, it marks a major forward step, which, as far as we know, sets a precedent across the country.

Then, on Wednesday, May 24, the government agreed to a settlement of our case striking down the sodomy laws in the District of Columbia.[10] A copy of the stipulation is enclosed. These are the laws under which homosexuals are commonly considered criminal (although they apply to heterosexuals as well). They are used against us by the government and elsewhere. The case was conceived by me, in slightly different form, about 7 years ago and pushed hard for just over two years. I consider this a personal victory. . . .

It IS possible to change society by one's self; it IS possible to fight city hall successfully.

Then on Friday, May 25, we won the Wentworth security clearance case. This is one of my oldest security cases—going back to 1967. It went through five hearings, one of them lasting for three days, in New York, in August 1969. The clearance was ordered restored, the government's right to pry into the intimate details of personal life was restricted; the class disqualification of homosexuals was struck down.

Then, on May 31, a local Superior Court judge struck down the solicitation laws as unconstitutional. These are the major basis under which the police harass homosexuals.

We are truly elated. Our weekly dance tonight will be a victory celebration.

These things represent many years of work for me and many hundreds of thousands of typed words.

Some 32 years ago, I told you that if society and I differ on anything, I will give society a second chance to convince me. If it fails, then I am right and society is wrong, and if society gets in my way, it will be society which will change, not I.

That was so alien to your entire approach to life that you responded with disdain. It has been a guiding principle of my life.

Society was wrong. I am making society change. . . .

> With much love,
> Franklin

Kameny to *GAY* Magazine

The summer of 1972 saw Kameny appearing as a spokesman for the National Coalition of Gay Organizations before the platform committees of the Democratic National Committee and the Republican National Committee. Speaking to the Republicans, Kameny began with a leading question: "Why should the Republican Party include us and our concerns in its platform?"[11] One of the answers he provided—votes—reflected the emerging power of gay voters. The Republicans were unmoved, however, and included nothing about gay rights in their platform.

But Kameny's arguments, as well as those made by others, persuaded the Democrats to include subtly worded gay-friendly phrases in their platform. The platform never used the words "gay rights"—Democrats had killed a proposal using exact language—but it did defend an individual's right to be free from an "invasion of privacy" as well as the "right to be different, to maintain a cultural or ethnic heritage or lifestyle, without being forced into a compelled homogeneity."[12] Not all gays appreciated the inexact language of the platform, and in the following letter to the editors of GAY magazine, Kameny responds to these critics.[13]

SEPTEMBER 28, 1972

Gentlemen:

. . . I want to express my disagreement with those who are so vigorously attacking McGovern these days. Whatever one may think of "political expediency"—and there is much to be weighed on both sides—we ARE included in the Democratic Party platform. . . . McGovern *has* made a rather detailed statement in favor of gay rights, which he may not be trumpeting, but which you will obtain upon request from McGovern headquarters.[14] The Republicans and Nixon have provided us with nothing (and should be publicly confronted on the issue at every occasion).

As one of the few people who were involved in the formal gay effort at both Miami Beach conventions, I can testify that going to the Republican Convention after the Democratic one was like plunging into an icy-cold pool after basking in a warm bath. It was like going from day into night.

This presidential campaign represents the first real essay by gays into national politics. I am as impatient as anyone to see us get our rights NOW and am as tired as anyone of spending all my time and efforts on fighting to get what we should have and should be enjoying. Nevertheless, it must be recognized that most controversial goals are not achieved all at once, in one fell swoop, but take time. For a first effort, we have done satisfyingly well in our entrance into presidential politics.

I suggest that the kind of insistence on everything precisely to our prescription, all at once, upon penalty of condemnation, attack, and the throwing of tantrums, is unrealistic and more than a little childish.

Subject only to a highly unlikely pledge of support from Nixon for gay rights, it would seem to me that we would be well advised to forego the destructive, self-defeating attacks and do our best to turn out the McGovern vote. As the candidates, the platforms, the parties, and the campaigns stand at the writing of this letter, whether McGovern wins or loses the more votes he gets, the better off gays will be.

Sincerely yours,
Franklin E. Kameny

Kameny campaigned for McGovern and served as a delegate to the 1972 Democratic National Convention.

Kameny to Robert Saulsbury

Kameny explains an important part of his countercultural sexual ethics to an inquirer from suburban Philadelphia.

NOVEMBER 26, 1972

Dear Mr. Saulsbury:

. . . Might I suggest that you would do well to reexamine your attitude toward sex somewhat. I think that a reevaluation could go a long way toward resolving some of your social problems. You say: "any sexual act—is a good thing—if the participants have love in their hearts." I would say, simply: "Any sexual act is a good thing." The difference is important. Pure, physical sex, for its own sake, is good in its own right. Physical sex does not have to be "redeemed" by love. Sex *with* love is wonderful. Sex *without* love is also wonderful. Do not attempt to force-fit your relationships into the traditional heterosexual mold from which more and more heterosexuals are escaping.

Far more often than not, relationships have their inception in sex alone, and the love arises—or does not arise—later. If it does arise, good. If it does not arise, also good, if the sex itself was good and was not forced into a strait jacket of an as yet non-existent love relationship. . . .

Sincerely yours,

Franklin E. Kameny

Kameny to Charles Socarides

Three months before typing the following letter, Kameny described Socarides in another letter as "a fanatic who uses a cloak of pseudo-science to cover a rabidly fanatical anti-homosexual bigotry which he pursues zealously."[15]

DECEMBER 1972

Dear Dr. Socarides:

You are quoted in *Newsweek* . . . as saying (in regard to homosexuals and homosexual relationships): "You don't treat fetishists to enjoy their fetishes."[16]

I must ask: Why on earth not?

The great majority of fetishes are utterly harmless to the fetishists or to others. They are a source of potential and actual pleasure to the fetishists. Why should not the fetishist, who is, for some reason, not enjoying his fetish to the maximum, be assisted in so enjoying it? I can think of no reason other than desire upon the part of the psychotherapists such as you to force-fit all people into one arbitrary mold.

Apparently you are, as usual, trying to impose upon everyone your own narrow, fanatically rigid religious beliefs, camouflaged as "science." You would compulsively have all people conform to the single rigid mold which you and your co-religionists—that is, your fellow psychoanalysts— would set up as the *only* model for everyone. Fortunately for all of us, but unfortunately for you, the glory of humanity is its richness and diversity in all things. We are not stamped out of the same mold; we do not all come off the assembly line as alike as so many faceless robots. We are freed of the pre-programming which directs the activities of most other animals. We follow different courses of *equal* value leading to different goals of equal value—in sexual practices and psychosexual development as in all other areas of life.

Dr. George Weinberg, in his superb book, *Society and the Healthy Homosexual*, deals with the matter on page 59ff, referring to the treatment of a man who was sexually aroused by women's buttocks and bloomers and had been given aversion "therapy," he says. "He had sought help to procure more sexual fulfillment, not less. However, here the therapist ruthlessly set out to deprive the patient of his enjoyment, on the highly speculative theses that doing so would benefit him."[17]

His passion is a far more reasonable one than yours. . . .

As a scientist by training and background (as you are not), I am particularly offended by your persistent characterization of yourself as a scientist and your work as science and scientific. You do not know the meaning of science. Your dogmatic statements, unsupported by any showing of scientific investigation, and your clear, total lack of comprehension of the canons of scientific investigation put you into the class of a religious fanatic, not a scientist. Your rationales for terming homosexuality pathological can be termed a pseudo-scientific rephrasing in terms of sickness of the "natural law" philosophy, phrased in terms of sin, of St. Thomas Aquinas. But Aquinas lived in the 12th century, and this is the 20th century. "Natural law," so-called, is no longer considered a sound theological basis for an attribution of sin; a reformulation of it is certainly not a sound scientific basis for an attribution of pathology.

You are clearly using the attributions of science, scientist, and scientific to provide "legitimacy" for yourself, to bolster your low self-esteem, and to buttress a shaky and fragile ego. You are badly in need of therapy—and of a good course in science and the scientific method so that you can be brought to a realization of just how remote from science is everything you are doing.

Let me say finally that, as a scientist by training and background, I find it offensive that you designate yourself as a scientist and what you do as science. It is quite clear that like many of your professional colleagues, you do not have the faintest notion of what science is all about or of how good science is done.

Apparently you feel a need to bolster a shaky ego by "legitimizing" yourself by calling yourself a scientist and thus misusing that designation to support a dogmatic, authoritarianism which is intellectually offensive and arrogant, utterly boorish and uncouth, to a degree such that at least a few of your professional colleagues of the highest repute consider you highly disturbed at the very least.

I suggest that you would be much happier as a priest and an open moralist than as a psychiatrist and psychoanalyst. You would certainly do far less harm than you are now doing.

10

"VICTORY!!!! WE HAVE BEEN 'CURED'!"

1973

Kameny to the Washington Area Peace Action Coalition

Although he was initially opposed to efforts to build alliances between the gay rights and peace movements, Kameny evidently had second thoughts about speaking on the Vietnam War as a representative of the gay community. In the following letter to DC-based opponents of the war, he sketches a brief history of his position on the war and takes a nuanced stand on civil disobedience.

JANUARY 12, 1973

Gentlepeople:

I write to indicate my strong endorsement of mass, peaceful, lawful demonstrations on January 20, 1973 (or any other lawful measures at any other time and in any place) against the war in Southeast Asia.

I have opposed United States participation in this war, and its various guises and stages, for over twenty years, from the time when, as a student still young enough to be subject to re-drafting for what looked like active U.S. involvement on behalf of the French in Indo-China, I stated that I would not go, to the time of my congressional campaign in 1971, when opposition to U.S. involvement in the war was one of the major planks of my platform.

We should never have gotten into this war. Our participation in it has proven to be unmitigated disaster for everyone concerned (including the South Vietnamese whom we are supposedly assisting), the evil

256

consequences of which we will be reaping for many years to come. We should get out immediately, totally, and unconditionally. Any lawful steps of any kind which will hasten that withdrawal, even if only slightly, are not only justified but should be encouraged, and should be taken. At the rate we are going, not only will we have destroyed Southeast Asia, but there will be no United States (as we know it) left either. Our dishonor is already so deep and so vast that no peace terms can either mitigate it or exacerbate it, so there is no point in wasting time on further negotiations. Let us get out now!

Most sincerely,
Franklin E. Kameny

A massive march and rally against the war, sponsored in part by the National Peace Action Coalition, took place at the Lincoln Memorial and the Washington Monument on January 20, 1973—coinciding with Nixon's inaugural festivities. Kameny's comments on his appearance at the demonstration in a later letter to Democratic Representative Robert Drinan, of Massachusetts, clearly suggest that he was representing the gay community—the type of action he opposed in earlier years:

> My appearance at the January 20, 1973 rally was as a representative of the gay community. . . . We have systematically welcomed all opportunities to participate in all community events, in a calculated effort to bring ourselves into the participatory mainstream of public and national life.[1]

Kameny to Cade Ware

Gay activist and writer Cade Ware had sent Kameny a questionnaire seeking information and opinions that he planned to use for an article for the New Republic. *Kameny's reply, excerpted in the following letter, offers his historical perspective on the Stonewall riots, his evolving thoughts on the interrelations of cultural identities, his take on the GLF's attempts at participatory democracy, and his sense of the future of the gay rights movement. In the attached cover letter, Kameny wrote: "Your questions, taken together, could easily provide material for a book, so my answers are necessarily simplistic. The responses were composed at the typewriter, and so are not as polished as they might otherwise be, or as complete."[2]*

FEBRUARY 25, 1973

How do you describe the objectives of gay liberation? To what degree have they been achieved since Stonewall? Conversely, has the movement failed in certain respects, and if so, how?

In responding to this question and (whether explicitly stated below or not) to all others, I take the long-range view. Gay liberation and, more specifically, the gay liberation movement, did *NOT* start at Stonewall. (The phrase *Gay Liberation* originated then, that is all.) They started close to 20 years before, and there has been a movement *with unbroken continuity* since about 1951.[3] It has had various evolutionary phases (the third major one of which commenced at Stonewall . . .), but each built upon and succeeded the ones preceding and would not have been possible without them (e.g., Stonewall just would not have occurred if we had not picketed in Washington and Philadelphia in 1965 and commenced the whole process of group public action by gays, including psychologically preparing the community for what it did on Christopher Street in 1969).

The basic objective of gay liberation is the creation of better lives for homosexuals *as homosexuals*—the achievement of full equality of homosexuals, as people, with heterosexuals and (much more controversial and less acceptable to many, but equally uncompromisingly insisted upon) the full equality of homosexuality—as a condition, a state of being, a preference, a way of life or a lifestyle, an expression of love and affection, or whatever—with heterosexuality.

Differently and perhaps more broadly, the full freedom of the individual to determine and live his or her own lifestyle without societal interference or the imposition of penalty, disability, or disadvantage (as long as that lifestyle does not interfere with others against their will), can be considered a goal or objective of gay liberation.

Stonewall and the period following it provided an impetus and acceleration to processes long under way and the achievement of goals long worked toward. The movement became, for the first time, something of a mass, grassroots, popular movement, as it had not been (and long lamented as not being), and it became far better known publicly and in the gay community both.

Movements for social change and reform are (conceptually) self-limiting, self-terminating, and (in no undesirable sense) self-destructive, in that they hope to achieve goals which, when achieved, deprive the movement of its *raison d'etre* and lead to its disappearance (not always without some anguish—witness the peace movement now that peace is nominally here, more or less.)

That the gay liberation movement continues actively and adds new accomplishments to those already achieved means that the goals have not yet been achieved—nor were they realistically expected to have been. Progress is being made on many fronts—as it has been for 20 years—but all of the *ultimate* goals are still to be sought—although they are much more in sight than they were in past years.

In terse summary, the movement since Stonewall has moved far ahead in bringing the subject of homosexuality out into the open, in putting the opposition almost totally on the defensive, and in achieving many specific advances (a growing number of law changes, significant changes in attitude, growing freedom for the individual homosexual and alleviation of much negative societal pressure, etc., etc., etc.).

It has failed—if failure it be—only in that, as indicated, it has not yet achieved everything, and much remains yet to be done. . . .

What, to your mind, is the most significant recent development in the gay community? Why?

. . . I think there are two, not unrelated. One is the entrance of gays into active, first-hand politics (as distinguished from the second-hand involvement in politics which has been ongoing since about 1965). Here, I feel, is the wave of the future. This is THE way, par excellence (although, of course, far from the ONLY way) truly to make this OUR society, in a real, participatory fashion.

Second, different, but not unrelated (and much more related in the future) to the first, is the appearance on the scene (all at the municipal-ordinance level so far) of law-as-friend instead of merely the traditional law-as-foe—affirmative, supportive, civil rights-type law. . . .

Third (and, again, not unrelated) is the growing willingness of rapidly growing number of gays to come "out of the closet" and emerge fully into public view as gays. It is impossible for a hidden group to achieve goals of the type indicated in response to the first question—beyond certain limited gains. It is possible for some to work for the rights of many, but the achievement of those rights is an empty one unless the many are going to come forward and proceed to enjoy the rights achieved. . . .

What differences do you observe in the current evolution of the situation of the gay woman and the gay male? The gay black and the gay white?

I differentiate sharply between gay problems and other problems. Women *as women*—straight or gay—have problems. Blacks *as blacks*—straight or gay—have problems. Gays *as gays*—male or female, black or white—have problems. Those who belong to more than one of those groups have multiple sets of problems, but I think that those sets of problems—largely—MUST be considered separately.

Women, as women, have problems the men do not have, and so gay women, as women (but not as gays) have problems that gay men as men (but not as gays) do not have. Similarly with gay blacks. However, except for some subtleties, the basic problems of all gays—black and white, male and female—are identical.

Anyone in more than one of these minority groups must decide for him or herself where the priorities lie. Unfortunately, from my viewpoint, many gay women or blacks see their problems as being greater as blacks or women than as gays—or, for other reasons (including the fact that fighting racism or sexism is more easily done and is more "respectable") they choose to fight the racism or the sexism. Others choose to give their priorities to the gay rights battle.

One of the unfortunate legacies of the past few years . . . has been an exacerbation of the male-female, black-white differences (especially the former) within the movement, and the development of a divisiveness and separatism which was not there before, and which is quite unnecessary from the viewpoint of gay rights and the gay liberation movement.

On the other hand, there has been achieved a considerable measure of support for gay liberation from women's liberation.

Basically, however, in reiteration, the *gay* problems do not seem to be racially or gender related, and . . . I do not see any real or significant differences in the "current evolution" of the situation of gay women and men, blacks and whites.

What internal problem has the movement dealt with and solved? Not solved?

. . . The major real, continuing problem arose in 1969 and is gradually fading from the scene, although it really is not gone yet.

The past three years have seen a very great deal of intellectual ferment which provided much of value in the way of new insights, new perspectives on old problems, etc. It also provided an incredible amount of fuzzy-minded thinking, poor logic, utter impracticality, and just plain bad tactics and strategy which were counterproductive and self-destructive.

In particular, there appeared on the scene many people for whom the gay movement—or any movement—was merely one of the several ways which they were using to achieve "the revolution" or the end of capitalism, or otherwise to attack society. For them, the fight for gay rights was secondary. They insisted upon a rigid orthodoxy as oppressive and limiting as that imposed by the society which they condemn, and refused to recognize that the major enemy is straight society, not their fellow gays who chose different methods and different emphases and different ideologies to achieve the good of all gays. These people then directed their destructive energies at their fellow gays in the movement, rather than at straight society, and became deeply destructive and disruptive of the gay liberation movement. They insisted that things be done THEIR way or not at all. Unfortunately, their way also usually involved a resolute rejection of structure and a lip service to an exaggerated, town-meeting type of democracy which resulted in getting nothing at all done—their way or anyone else's.

With the passage of time and the beginning of the settling of the dust and the further evolution of the movement . . . some of the shoddy intellectualizing and the poor thinking has become evident, the disruptors have (1) begun to fade from the scene and (2) been kept from disrupting, and things are moving onward. . . .

Some gays are saying that gay power is dying or dead. Please comment. Does the movement have a future? . . .

The only gays who are saying that are those who think that the whole world—and certainly gay liberation—started in June 1969. It didn't, of course, and so like all living things, it is continuing its process of evolution . . . with changes in the form and implementation of protest, dissent, and work for change.

Basically, since 1969, the movement has gone through what might be epitomized, simplistically, as the GLF phase and the GAA phase. The latter MAY be drawing to a close now, to be succeeded by something else (hindsight is always better than foresight, so we will have to wait to see whether the GAA phase is really drawing to a close, and what does emerge).

The movement is still growing. New organizations are still forming at a rapid rate. Victories are still being won—and in the here and now, not in the distant future, as was the case for workers in the movement of years ago.

As long as gays are disadvantaged in any way—legally, societally, culturally, attitudinally, etc.—there will be a movement and it will have a future. Society can be changed—we have been doing it with some successes for over 20 years, and as long as that is so, and there are changes to be made, the movement has a future. . . .

Kameny to Kay Lahusen

On February 8, 1972, the APA's Committee on Nomenclature—charged with recommending revisions to DSM-II—held a closed-door meeting with a small group of activists who supported the deletion of homosexuality from DSM-II. The group included Ronald Gold and Jean O'Leary of GAA, Charles Silverstein and Bernice Goodman of the Institute for Human Identity, and psychologist Ray Prada.

Silverstein presented the group's critique of the traditional APA position, and his argument, coupled with prepared statements by Wardell Pomeroy and Alan Bell, both first-rate sex researchers, impressed committee members. Henry Brill, the chairman of the Committee on Nomenclature, told the New York Times *that he and other members were planning to draft a revised position on homosexuality for consideration at the APA annual meeting in May. "There is no doubt that this label [homosexuality] has been used in a discriminatory way," he stated. "We were all agreed on that."*[4]

Committee member Robert Spitzer had arranged for the February 8 meeting after experiencing a "zap" carried out by the New York GAA at an October meeting of the Association for the Advancement of Behavior Therapy. In conversation with Ronald Gold, Spitzer also agreed to sponsor a panel centered on deleting homosexuality from DSM-II at the 1973 APA convention in Honolulu. It is this panel Kameny refers to in the following letter to Kay Lahusen, one of the early founders of GAA and partner of Barbara Gittings.

MARCH 27, 1973

Dear Kay:

I'm getting ready to go to Honolulu, for the APA annual meeting, where they're discussing removing us from their Diagnostic Manual—curing us, *en masse*, by semantics, instead of individually, by therapy. I am chief discussant for the special half-day session, so our viewpoint will be well represented. Included on the panel are Bieber and Socarides. Also on are Marmor, Green, Stollar, and Ron Gold.[5] Should be fun. The gay community has come through with contributions to get me out there. I'll be on a plane for some 11 hours each way with 150 psychiatrists—ugh! . . .

Keep in touch.

As Always,

Frank

Kameny to Governor Marvin Mandel

The state legislature of Maryland had recently passed a bill prohibiting same-sex marriages, and in the following letter Kameny explains some of his views on the topic as he lobbies the governor to exercise his veto power.

APRIL 6, 1973

Dear Governor Mandel:

The Mattachine Society of Washington, Inc. is an eleven-year-old, well-established civil liberties organization, working to create better lives for homosexuals as homosexuals. . . .

We are writing to ask that you *veto* the Bill, just passed by legislature, banning homosexual (male-male, or female-female) marriages. . . .

It seems to us that the marriages forbidden by this bill interfere with no one, and cause no discernible harm, either to any other citizens or to society, while, at the same time, providing much good for the parties to the marriages and for society.

While homosexual marriages are, of course, non-procreative, procreation is no longer the sole *raison d'etre* for marriage, if it ever was. There are valid pragmatic factors relating to taxation, property, inheritance, etc., as well as equally valid human factors involving love and affection and the psychological support of meaningful human relationships. The sterile *heterosexual* couple, or the heterosexual couple voluntarily choosing to have no children, are conceptually in a situation no different in any slightest degree from the homosexual couple. If those heterosexual couples can marry legally—and, of course, they should—then there is no rational basis for denial of marriage to homosexual couples.

Homosexuals are persistently (and far from accurately) accused of instability in our relationships. Yet when we seek to stabilize our relationships through the use of a supportive legal formalization available to heterosexuals, we are denied it, making the accusation viciously and malevolently self-fulfilling.

It would seem to be clearly in the interests both of society—and therefore of the collective citizenry of Maryland—and of the individual homosexual Maryland citizens involved, to provide all possible assistance for the formation and maintenance of stable, lasting relationships. . . .

This bill seems to be a singularly vicious, backward, and benighted manifestation of archaic, outmoded prejudices and bigotries, demeaning and degrading to a state with the stature of Maryland. This bill provides no protection for any societal interest of any kind, nor for any interest of any individual citizen, and severely transgresses upon the rights of many citizens. There is no "balancing of interests" here, as there is so often in the formulation and passage of legislation. This bill harms one group without providing benefit for anyone at all, while its non-passage (or veto) harms no one and leaves no valid interests unprotected.

Our country's birth certificate, the Declaration of Independence, guarantees to *all* citizens, as an *inalienable right*, the pursuit of happiness, and declares *all* citizens to be equal before the law. For us, as homosexual

American citizens, this is *our* country and our Declaration of Independence, too, and our equality and our happiness and the pursuit thereof. This Bill would deny us all of that, in this context, and in doing so would be volatile of the most fundamental precepts of Americanism.

THEREFORE we urge, in fairness to a large minority of the citizenry of Maryland, and in the interest of enlightened, progressive governance, that you *veto* this unfortunate bill, which represents a step backward at a time when everyone else is stepping forward. . . .

Sincerely yours,

Franklin E. Kameny

After learning that Mandel signed the bill prohibiting same-sex marriages, Kameny typed another letter to the governor. "Your state has designated itself 'The Free State.' What a travesty of that motto you have made by your signing of this bill into law. For shame!!!"[6]

Kameny to John LaMonthe

Kameny writes a letter of protest to the chairman of the Prince Charming Pageant in New York—a gay affair celebrating male beauty and talent.

APRIL 23, 1973

Dear John:

Thank you for your leaflet in regard to the Prince Charming Pageant to be held at the Waaay Off Broadway Club on May 5.

As a homosexual who firmly believes that gay is good, and in gay pride, I must, however, raise some objections to your programming, under which "Toward the end of the evening a CINDERELLA will be chosen for Prince Charming on the basis of observations throughout the evening."

Don't we have enough, in everyday straight society, of having heterosexual-couple models thrown in our faces at every turn? Everywhere we go, we see male-female couples, never male-male or female-female ones. Everywhere we turn, the "desirable" goal is presented as a heterosexual coupling, and homosexual relationships are put forward as—at best— some kind of second best.

For you to schedule such a Cinderella–Prince Charming event is a slap in the face to every self-respecting homosexual. It creates and supports the self-hatred so common among minority groups including gays. It is insulting to the gay community.

We have enough heterosexual models thrown in our faces as something to which to aspire, without getting them from our own community. We need *support* of our homosexuality from our community, not a subtle but *very* clear message that: You should *really* be aspiring to heterosexuality; heterosexuality is *really* the *right* way.

Let us exult in our homosexuality and celebrate it, not put it down!

Why not choose a Groovy Guy (or something of the sort) for your Prince Charming? It would be *much* more appropriate.

Please don't misunderstand. I fully support the pageant, and the criticism contained in this letter is intended fully constructively. It is just that one single aspect of it to which I object.

Gay IS good. Let's keep things gay. Let's have people coming away from the Pageant feeling good about their gayness, not feeling that even their own community is labeling them as some kind of oddballs.

Cordially,
Frank

P.S. With regret, I will not be able to attend the Pageant. I will be in Honolulu on May 5, trying to convert the American Psychiatric Association.

Kameny attended the APA annual meeting in Honolulu from May 7 to 11. The following is a relatively comprehensive report he wrote about the panel on which he served, as well as the context leading up to it. Although the Committee on Nomenclature had planned to present a proposal on revision at this annual meeting, it did not, and the process of changing the diagnosis of homosexuality continued. Given the importance that Kameny ascribed to his work on this matter, the report is worth quoting in full.

> *For at least a decade, the homophile and gay liberation movements have been insisting that homosexuality is not a sickness, illness, neurosis, sign of immaturity, or other pathology, disorder, or dysfunction of any kind, but merely a preference, orientation or propensity, not different in kind from heterosexuality, and fully on par with it. Psychiatry, as the "authority" on these*

matters, has steadfastly characterized homosexuality as a disorder and an illness. Such characteristics, especially coming from psychiatry, where illness means mental illness, is devastating both to homosexuals themselves, and to their aspirations for acceptance and equality in society.

Thus a goal of the movement has been removal of homosexuality from the APA's Diagnostic and Statistical Manual of Mental Disorders, thereby "curing" us all, en masse, by semantics, instead of individually by therapy.

Because, in part, psychiatry refused to discuss the issue with the gay community, and because, on the other hand, the gay community insisted that on this matter we be talked with, not merely about, in 1970, the gay liberation movement commenced to invade APA meetings. At the meeting in Washington, in 1971, this writer personally mounted the platform, seized the microphone, and "laid down the law" to the assembled psychiatrists.

Our efforts first bore fruits at the 1972 meeting, in Dallas, when the program included an evening panel discussion entitled "Psychiatry: Friend or Foe of Homosexuals." Panelists included both psychiatrists and homosexuals, including this writer.

This year, a half-day special session was scheduled, entitled "Should Homosexuality Be Included in the APA's Nomenclature." Participants included psychiatrists of various views, and a homosexual. The moderator was a member of the Nomenclature Committee, which compiles the Diagnostic Manual. This reporter was chief discussant.

The session was the best-attended of any at the meeting. Drs. Judd Marmor (a vice-president of the APA), Richard Green and Robert Stoller argued, in different ways, and on differing grounds, for removal of homosexuality from the Diagnostic Manual, and from characterization as a sickness or disorder.

Drs. Charles W. Socarides and Irving Bieber argued for its retention, largely on the basis of ancient, outmoded psychoanalytic theory, and of their own highly questionable researches (like most psychiatric research on homosexuality, Bieber's and Socarides's violate all the canons of good scientific investigation: No control groups; poor sampling technique; non-separation of variables and multiple variables; inept use of statistics; no follow-up). Drs. Bieber and Socarides underwent what they must have found to be the unaccustomed, unexpected, and unpleasant experience of being jeered, booed, and laughed at by their professional colleagues.

Mr. Ronald Gold of the Gay Activists Alliance of New York made a fine presentation of the gay position and of the disastrous effects upon gays of classing homosexuality as a sickness and homosexuals as ill.

This writer summed up and commented upon the various presentations.

Among the viewpoints presented in the course of the discussion was that not homosexuality but homophobia (and racism, and other forms of prejudice and bigotry) should be considered as psychiatric and emotional disorders and listed in the Diagnostic Manual.

Later in the week, a less-formal discussion session entitled "Gay Liberation Meets Psychiatry" was held. There was also an informal meeting of the "Gay PA"—a large group of gay psychiatrists.

While no actual changes occurred at the Honolulu meeting, the net result was that the whole, massive, complex, "wheels within wheels" machinery of the APA has finally been set into motion on this matter, and it seems likely that a major change in the official APA approach to homosexuality will be occurring soon.

Specifically, a number of resolutions are in various stages of processing through one APA channel or another.

1. A resolution to remove homosexuality from the APA Nomenclature.

2. A resolution supporting civil rights for homosexuals (employment, etc.) and opposing criminal laws against homosexuality.

3. A resolution to indicate (to government agencies and the like) that it is misuse and abuse of the listing of homosexuality in the APA Diagnostic Manual to impose upon homosexuals a greater burden of stability, reliability, trustworthiness, etc., than upon heterosexuals.

Some of these may be acted upon within the next few months at meetings of the APA Board of Trustees, the Assembly of District Branches, and other subordinate arms and agencies of the APA; others may take longer.

Ultimately, these resolutions or ones like them will also have to be acted upon on an international basis, but it seems that one of the major sources of our oppression is about to be removed: the characterization of homosexuality as an illness.[7]

Kameny to ——

This letter, written to a young man from Pennsylvania, offers a look at the type of advice Kameny gave to gays facing family pressure to see a psychiatrist.

JUNE 10, 1973

Dear ——:

. . . Since you say that your father already knew that you are gay, why the strong reaction, now, that he saw you with your boyfriend? Insofar as seeing a psychiatrist is concerned, I would suggest, first, that you resist as strongly as you can. No useful purpose would be served, of course. Make it clear to him that you have no desire to change, and are not going to allow yourself to be changed, so there's no point in his wasting his money.

If he insists, and you have no choice, then go. At that point, you'll have to "play it by ear" depending on the psychiatrist. Some psychiatrists will explore the matter with you, and then take you at your own evaluation of your homosexuality. Others are not nearly as enlightened. So start out by making it clear to the psychiatrist that you are content with your homosexuality; that you have no desire to change; that you are proud to be gay and firmly believe that gay IS good. Insist that all discussions take place ONLY between you and the psychiatrist, WITHOUT the presence of your father or mother.

If the psychiatrist is one of the backward, benighted, unenlightened kind, who believes that homosexuality is some kind of sickness, or neurosis, or immaturity . . . then I am sure that you have some of the arguments to counter this. Insofar as you do not, let me know what is being told to you, and I will supply you with the counter arguments as you go along, argument by argument. On one occasion, someone here of about your age was sent to a psychiatrist by his parents. He would phone me after each session and I would undo all of the psychiatrist's arguments, in preparation for the next session. After a couple of months, the psychiatrist, who was somewhat elderly, retired to live in the Virgin Islands, and the parents did not follow the matter further. . . .

I guess that's all for the present. Let me hear from you when convenient. By the way—what's your last name?

Sincerely yours,

Franklin E. Kameny

Kameny to the Editors of the *Advocate*

Kameny expresses appreciation for a letter written to Ann Landers by Michigan physician Loren Burt in reply to the columnist's earlier characterization of homosexuality as unnatural. But Kameny also takes a swipe at Burt's willingness to defend the argument that homosexuality is natural.[8]

JULY 5, 1973

Gentlemen:

While Dr. Loren G. Burt's letter . . . to Ann Landers is excellent as far as it goes, it fails in that it takes the usual defensive line with regard to allegations of *unnaturalness* instead of confronting the issue squarely.

To consider an attribution of *unnaturalness* as being condemnatory or pejorative . . . is to accept the ground rules of our adversaries, instead of examining and discrediting those ground rules. There is no rational basis for equating *unnatural* with *bad* and *undesirable*, and *natural* with *good* and *desirable*.

Being unnatural is the very essence of being human; it is the very hallmark of our humanity.

Our distinguishing feature, as human beings, is our brain, which we properly use to convert all that is around us to purposes most satisfying and rewarding to us, and so we do little that cannot be considered unnatural. If we were truly and narrowly "natural," we would live naked in the woods, subsisting solely upon those few fruits and berries which seem to have evolved to have their seeds disseminated through the alimentary canals of animals.

Wearing clothes is unnatural, and the use of non-artificial fibers for any purpose other than keeping a sheep warm or disseminating cottonseed is obviously unnatural. Eating cooked or otherwise prepared food is unnatural. If we were natural, we would eat our meat raw, bloody, warm and quivering, on the hoof. In fact, we would not eat meat at all, since "obviously" the "natural" purpose of the muscle tissue of which most meat is composed is to mobilize animals, not to feed humans.

Similarly, sleeping on a bed; traveling other than on bare feet; living in warmed rooms in winter or cooled ones in summer; using wooden furniture ("obviously" the "natural" purpose of wood is to support shrubbery not humans) are all unnatural. One could go on; the list is endless.

In point of fact, we hardly do a natural thing in our lives, from the moment we are born and our umbilical cords are unnaturally cut with an unnatural knife, until the moment we die and afterward, when we are unnaturally buried in a very unnatural coffin (or, even more unnaturally, cremated). So why all the fuss about the so-called "unnaturalness of homosexuality"—or of anything else?

Being unnatural is the unique and special quality of being human.

So let us get off the defensive on this issue, and cease wasting our time on meaningless, silly discussion based upon an assumption that to be unnatural is to be bad or that unnaturalness is undesirable, and that therefore we must prove that homosexuality is natural. Let us stop wasting our time trying to justify ourselves through demonstrations that animals engage in homosexuality, therefore homosexuality is "natural" and "good." Animals do not wear clothes, eat prepared food, or fly airplanes, either, but no one that I know of finds it necessary to question the desirability of those practices by such comparisons, criteria, or arguments. Let us extract ourselves from an intellectual bind going back, at least in part, to St. Thomas Aquinas and his "natural law." Thomas was fine for the 13th century, but we are entering the 21st century. There is no need to prove that we are "natural" or not "unnatural" in order to demonstrate that we and our homosexuality are good, desirable, and acceptable.

Let us have more and better unnaturalness; it is what makes us uniquely human. Let us exult in our unnaturalness; we will be better humans for it. . . .

Sincerely yours,

Franklin E. Kameny

Kameny also commented on the morality of homosexuality in a July 31 letter he wrote to Johannes Werres, the editor of Gay News *in Germany. "In my view," Kameny wrote, "homosexuality is good, right, and desirable, and if it were a completely free choice made in adulthood, it would be no less right and good. I do not hide behind excuses and 'That's the way I am; I can't help it.' Even if it could be 'helped,' it would be no less right."*[9]

Kameny to Harold Titus Jr.

Kameny had asked Harold Titus Jr., U.S. attorney for the District of Columbia, to render an advisory opinion on the sodomy statute in the DC law code, and in the following letter he lays out a plan to solicit oral and/or anal sex from Titus.

SEPTEMBER 9, 1973

Dear Mr. Titus:

I write in response to your insolent, arrogant, insubordinate, and cowardly evasive reply . . . to my letter of July 19 regarding the sodomy statute in the District of Columbia and related matters, in which you state that your office does not render advisory options.

I.

Your response—actually your non-response—is unsatisfactory and unacceptable. While I recognize that there exists a long and solidly based tradition going back at least to the earliest days of our Republic (e.g., Thomas Jefferson and Chief Justice Jay, in 1793) of refusal by the *courts* to render advisory opinions (although I wonder if the time has not come for a searching re-evaluation of that tradition, and modification of it), that applies to the *judicial branch.*

You are the *executive branch.*

The executive branch exists, in significant part, to provide information, advice, guidance, counsel and other assistance to the citizenry, individually as well as collectively, as to the policies and practices of that branch in the administration and enforcement of the laws which they are given by the legislative branch to execute. The executive branch exists to do precisely what I asked you to do. . . .

Now, Mr. Titus, you apparently need to be reminded of the relationship—central to our American system—between citizen and government official. This is a relationship in which public officials are public servants. Never forget that word servant; I do not intend to let you forget it. I am a member of the public; in our official capacity, you are my servant in the fullest sense of that term.

I do not tolerate insolence, impertinence, arrogance, insubordination, or disobedience from the servants, public or private, nor need I. When, as a member of the public, I make an inquiry of you or of any other public servant, you have but one choice: to answer. If you disagree with this precept, you have forgotten what America and Americanism are all about. If you object to this precept, then you are temperamentally unsuited for service as an American public official; become a U.S.S.R. attorney—their system would suit you better. . . .

II.

All the preceding aside, I remain continuingly determined to get rid of our abominable sodomy statute. While I am exploring many avenues, both legislative and litigative, and exclude none, I continue to believe that for the District of Columbia, the litigative route is the most likely to succeed most rapidly—that, in fact, it has already succeeded through the as-yet-unvacated Schaefers Stipulation,[10] which is still in full effect for all purposes in the District of Columbia; that the sodomy law is patently unconstitutional on its face and just needs the proper case to establish its unconstitutionality for all jurisdictions everywhere. Accordingly, I am going to precipitate a litigative confrontation, as I attempted to do when I created the Schaefers case, and again in my letter of July 19.

Therefore, within a short time, letters from me, personally, will be sent to you, to Corporation Counsel Murphy, and to Chief of Police Wilson. The three letters will differ from one another in tone, somewhat, because of the contemptible, uncooperative arrogance of your response to earlier correspondence, contrasted with the admirable, cooperative response of Chief Wilson, but their basic thrust will be the same.

Each letter will carefully set out the competing legal theories on the present status of acts of sodomy in the District of Columbia, as I see them, and the legal rationale for the action being taken in that letter.

There will then follow a clear, unambiguously phrased solicitation and invitation to each of you, urging you to engage with me in an act of oral and/or anal sodomy of your choice in some private place in the District of Columbia.

I will demand that you prosecute me for the solicitation.

The letters will be made public.

In addition, the solicitation may be publicly extended to you by me in the course of radio and television appearances by me.

If you prosecute the case, it will be fought as a formal constitutional attack on the D.C. sodomy law—and, in fact, on all sodomy laws, the country over.

If you do not prosecute, I will make the most of the fact that the three top law enforcement officials in the District of Columbia (and, therefore, by clear implication, all law enforcement officials and agents, and therefore by further clear implication, all persons in the District of Columbia) can be solicited for sodomy with impunity. At the very least, you and your henchmen will become the objects of the local and national derision, ridicule—and contempt—which you so richly deserve for your medieval, fascistic attitudes in seeking to re-criminalize half-a-million residents of the District of Columbia. You will become national laughing stocks. . . .

It should be a "real fun" test case!! I am looking forward to the fray! The media will love it. I suspect that you won't.

I see no way for you to forestall it, short of agreeing to the full effect of the Schaefers Stipulation, or coming up with some other method of invalidating the sodomy law. (Chief Wilson's enlightened and admirable polity of non-enforcement, which is about as far as he can go—short of going back to court, as he should do, formally vacating the Schaefers Stipulation, thereby re-opening that case—is insufficient. It is not merely non-enforcement that we want; it is a new law).

Now, let me make it clear that I have no desire to create confrontation for the sake of confrontation, or embarrassment or other unpleasantness for the sake of embarrassment or other unpleasantness. I only harass my public officials for constructive purposes. I am interested *solely* in getting rid of the sodomy statute—as quickly and as totally as possible. Therefore I am quite willing to meet with you and (*and* but not *or*) your subordinates for constructive, productive discussion on these matters, at a time and place of our mutual convenience in the very near future. That is why I am "telegraphing my punches" through this letter before I actually make the solicitation discussed above. But let us have no more arrogance and cowardly evasions out of you! . . .

Sincerely yours,
Franklin E. Kameny

P.S. Since you profess to consider sodomy a felony, what would you do if I were to present you with an affidavit or other credible, uncontested evidence or testimony that I and some other named person, at some specified time and place(s) in the District of Columbia, had engaged in sodomy, and demanded that you go to the grand jury and seek an indictment? Would you perform your duty and do so? If not, why not? Your non-evasive answer, please.

Kameny to William Berzak

Kameny describes William Berzak, chairman of CSC's board of appeals and review, as a "legalistic pervert," even referring to him as "Pervert Berzak."

SEPTEMBER 13, 1973

Mr. Berzak:

I write in response to your obscene letter of August 6, 1973, responding to mine . . . regarding your continuing use of envelopes bearing the legend: *An Equal Opportunity Employer.* I find it appalling that you should take a hard-line position instead of showing contrition, remorse, and apology for your shameful, immoral conduct. . . .

I base my objection to the legend upon the *fact* that the commission is not an equal opportunity employer as long as it denies equal employment opportunity to homosexual American citizens by excluding them from federal employment. . . .

You and other bigots in the commission and elsewhere in the government have, from time to time, alluded to our conduct as *sexual perversion* and to us as *sexual perverts.* If that be so, well and good. Our "perversion," so called, is a source of pleasure and enjoyment to many, causing harm to no one at all. If that be perversion, let us have more and better perversion; we will all be the better for it.

However, we have recently defined the new concept of *legal perversion* as follows:

Legal Perversion: The misuse, abuse, and perversion of law, regulation, policy, criterion, order, and of government itself, to convert and pervert them from their proper function as servants and protectors of the citizenry, individually and collectively, into vehicles for the perpetration, perpetuation, support, reinforcement, advancement, and active implementation and furtherance of prejudice and bigotry, and of the discrimination which flows therefrom.

Those who engage in legalistic perversion are *legalistic perverts.* Among the perverted practices engaged in by legalistic perverts are: selective application to the victims of their bigotry, of laws, regulations, orders, and policies; ignoring of facts which they find inconvenient or which impede them in the implementation of their bigotry; the distortion of facts to suit their perverted purposes; the outright creation of non-facts, blandly presented as facts, in order to further discriminatory practices; selective invocation of court decisions . . . supine cringing, cowardly submission to corrupt political pressures and to the lowest elements of popular opinion; and a whole host of other equally insidious, immoral, intellectually dishonest, illegal, and un-American practices.

Unlike sexual perversion and sexual perverts, legalistic perversion hurts, harms, and destroys countless people; legalistic perverts are vicious, evil, immoral people, causing untold, unnecessary human misery and suffering; they are among the worst and most contemptible of human vermin; our government is thickly populated with legalistic perverts—as is the Civil Service Commission.

Clearly, your August 6 letter to me makes of you a *legalistic pervert.*

You closed your August 6 letter by stating: "The Board will continue to use the envelopes furnished by the Civil Service Commission." . . .

Very well, Pervert Berzak, if that is the way you want it, so be it. As long as (1) the commission continues to exclude homosexual American citizens from federal employment; and (2) your Board continues to use envelopes . . . falsely claiming that the commission is an equal opportunity employer, I shall address *my* envelopes to you . . . as: *Pervert William F. Berzak,* and shall so refer to you, by name, in my many public lectures, on radio and television appearances, and elsewhere.

If you are going to trample, roughshod and with hobnailed boots, upon our sensitivities, Pervert Berzak, we will do the same to your sensitivities. . . .

. . . What is sauce for the goose is sauce for the gander. See how you like that, Pervert Berzak!

With contempt,
Franklin E. Kameny

Kameny to Bill Gold

In this letter to Washington Post *columnist Bill Gold, Kameny addresses the question of whether there is or should be any relationship between a political candidate's sexuality and his or her eligibility for office.*

SEPTEMBER 14, 1973

Dear Mr. Gold:

I am writing in somewhat belated response to your column in the August 27, 1973 *Washington Post.*

In that column you say, in relevant part:

> What he has in mind is the difference between saying or writing that a candidate is a homosexual because you really believe the charge to be true, and saying or writing it when you know it is not true, or have no reason to believe it true.[11]

You miss the basic point which is . . . why should it matter whether it is true or not? What possible rational relationship is there between a candidate's homosexuality (or heterosexuality; or bisexuality; or asexuality, for that matter) and his eligibility for office—*any* office? There obviously is none.

Your use of the word "charge" is indicative of the unfortunately negative (or, perhaps, merely not-carefully-considered) approach which you are taking. An allegation of homosexuality—true or false—is no more a charge (that is, an accusation) than is an allegation of being blond, of being married, of being Jewish, or being 5'9" tall, or of weighing 165 pounds. It is simply a matter of a fact irrelevant to an election, or to anything else of concern to the public.

I ran for Congress, from the District of Columbia, early in 1971, as the first openly declared homosexual candidate for any public office anywhere.[12] Rapidly increasing numbers of people are following my lead, now, all over the country.

I ran as a qualified Washingtonian who happened to be a homosexual, just as, a decade earlier, John F. Kennedy had run as a qualified American who happened to be Catholic. In both instances, the collateral, irrelevant issue was raised in order that it be laid to rest, once and for all and forever.

John Kennedy succeeded, of course, in respect to religion generally, and to Catholicism specifically. I had no illusions as to the impact that my candidacy would have in any immediate sense, but, as intended, it has started the process moving. In due course, a candidate's personal life (Is he divorced? Does he have a mistress? Is he a homosexual? . . .) will be as irrelevant to a determination by the voters of his qualifications for office as his religion usually is considered to be, as his race is becoming, and as the color of his hair always has been.

But meanwhile, you should take care not to give tacit acceptance or approval, as you did in your column, to the view that it makes any difference at all whether he really is a homosexual or whether he is merely "accused" of being one. In so doing, you are sustaining and reinforcing unfortunate, long-established patterns of prejudice, bigotry, and discrimination. . . .

Sincerely yours,
Franklin E. Kameny

Kameny to ——

Kameny writes a young man with whom he had had a sexual encounter, expressing uncertainty about his correspondent's age. The age of consent in DC was sixteen.

Shortly before writing this letter, the APA's Council on Research and Development unanimously approved Robert Spitzer's recommendation that homosexuality be deleted from DSM-II. The decision did not mean the APA as an entire organization had approved of the deletion, but the council's approval marked a significant step in that direction.

OCTOBER 13, 1973

Dear ——:

Your letter arrived this morning, and I am responding promptly.

In advance: Happy Birthday!!! Is that your 16th or your 17th?—it's your 17th, I think, isn't it? . . .

Incidentally, if anyone tells you that homosexuality is a sickness, and that homosexuals are sick (or some other such word: ill, a disorder, a disturbance, a neurosis, etc., etc.), you can tell them that just two days ago—this past Thursday evening—the American Psychiatric Association decided that homosexuality is NOT a sickness, illness, disturbance, disorder, etc. etc. This won't be publicized until December at the earliest, but I'm giving you special, personal news about the decision. . . .

Sincerely,

Frank

Kameny to Chief of Police Jerry Wilson

Following up on his letter to Titus, Kameny solicits the Metropolitan DC chief of police to engage with him in an act of sodomy.

NOVEMBER 6, 1973

Dear Chief Wilson:

. . . I write in further pursuit of correspondence of the past three or four months in regard to the D.C. sodomy statute . . . in order to try to bring this matter to a climax and to an ultimate legal resolution. . . .

I consider our sodomy statute (and approximate equivalent in some 42 states) to be abominations and excrescences upon our legal landscape. They are legal garbage, left over from bygone and more backward and primitive eras. They are antithetical to everything for which this country was founded and for which it stands. They are un-Americanism embodied. They are unconstitutional on their face. . . .

If a private and consensual act of sodomy is criminal, a solicitation therefore is a crime. . . .

. . . The U.S. attorney and the D.C. Corporation Counsel and, through them, the D.C. Chief of Police, take the position that in the District of Columbia, private, consensual acts of sodomy involving adults are felonies. . . .

Having set out the opposing views . . . I now put the matter to a clear, unambiguous, unequivocal test, to resolve it once and for all.

I hereby invite, suggest and propose to, solicit, encourage, and urge you to engage with me in an act or acts of oral and/or anal sodomy of your choice, in the role or roles of your choice, in a mutually agreeable, indisputably private place in the District of Columbia, at an early time of our mutual convenience. Try it; you'll like it.

I demand that you take steps to institute and pursue prosecution of me for whatever—by your stated view of the law (but not mine)—is a crime, consummated by my delivery to you of the solicitation for sodomy set forth just above.

The case will be fought as a carefully constructed challenge to the constitutionality of the sodomy law upon which the solicitation law and prosecutions thereunder stand or fall. . . .

Very well, Chief Wilson, the deed is done hereby. I await notice that the prosecutorial machinery has been set into motion. It should be a "real fun" test case; I'm really looking forward to it.

I'll see you in court!

Sincerely yours,
Franklin E. Kameny

Chief of Police Jerry Wilson to Kameny

The police chief sends a wry reply to Kameny's invitation to engage in sodomy.

NOVEMBER 8, 1973

Dear Dr. Kameny:

This is in reply to your letter of November 6, 1973, soliciting me to engage with you in an act of sodomy and demanding that I institute prosecution against you for that solicitation.

It is my view that both acts of sodomy and solicitations of acts of sodomy are violations of the laws of the District of Columbia. As I have informed you earlier, simply as a matter of setting priorities for use of police resources, this department does not vigorously seek to ferret out and prosecute consensual acts of sodomy committed by adults in private. (Neither do we seek to ferret out and prosecute consensual acts of fornication or adultery by adults in private, which also are violations of District of Columbia statutes.)

For the same reason—allocation of resources according to existing priorities—we do not vigorously seek to ferret out and prosecute solicitations for those kinds of unlawful acts, except at locations where such solicitations lead to other community problems such as assault or robbery of participants or complaints of residents or businessmen.

Frankly, Dr. Kameny, even if I thought you were sincere in your solicitation, I would not view it as a sufficient police problem to assign police resources to your prosecution. And I certainly would not want to spend my own time in court on a single misdemeanor charge.

Further, I don't believe your invitation to be sincere. You make it in a context which clearly indicates that you do not really expect an affirmative response. I think the courts would take a dim view of my bringing before them a criminal case just for test purposes, especially when I do not believe that the element of criminal intent exists.

I am unable to test your intent, firstly, because I find the notion unappealing, secondly, because sodomy is against the law and, thirdly, because my wife would never allow it. But if either Frank or Harold undertakes to verify your sincerity, be sure to let me know and I will consider whether or not any police department action is warranted.[13]

Sincerely,

Jerry V. Wilson

Kameny to Contributors to Honolulu Trip

After the APA's Council on Research and Development approved Robert Spitzer's resolution to delete homosexuality from DSM-II, the association's Assembly of District Branches did the same in November. That same month saw passage of the Spitzer proposal at APA's Reference Committee, which included chairs of all APA councils and the association's president-elect. The next step for the proposal was a vote to be taken by the Board of Trustees, the top governing body of the APA. Kameny recounts the vote in a memorandum with a telling subject line: "VICTORY!!!! We have been 'cured'!"

DECEMBER 15, 1973

. . . Finally, the matter came before the APA's top-level body, the Board of Trustees, at their semi-annual meeting held in Washington on December 14–15. On the afternoon of December 14, our old enemies, Drs. Bieber and Socarides . . . made an impassioned special presentation to the Board of Trustees, in an effort to prevent passage of the Nomenclature resolution. The Board was unimpressed.

At approximately 8:30 A.M. on Saturday, December 15, by unanimous vote (with two abstentions) the APA Board of Trustees passed the nomenclature resolution, and by unanimous vote (one abstention) passed the civil rights resolution, making them final, and "curing" us all, instantaneously, *en masse*, in one fell swoop, by semantics and by vote, instead of by therapy. . . .

As a careful reading of the cautions and politically conscious wording of the nomenclature resolution shows, a homosexual who is satisfied with his or her homosexuality is not sick, ill, disturbed, disordered, neurotic, pathological, etc., and his or her homosexuality is not a sickness, illness, disturbance, etc. However, a homosexual wishing to change to heterosexuality *IS* sick, as the now-revised APA nomenclature and policy stand.

The net effect of this resolution is to remove *homosexuality* from the APA's nomenclature (its list of mental and emotional disorders) and from their *Diagnostic and Statistical Manual of Mental Disorders* (their "sickness" book), thus effecting the miraculous "cure" which I promised you almost a year ago when I solicited your support for my trip to Hawaii. . . .

This represents the happy and successful conclusion of a more-than-ten-year effort on my part, at the outset of which I had to persuade my own fellow gays, in and out of the movement, to join me, and which almost all of them opposed. In important matters, it has been my personal approach to the world that (in pseudo-psychiatric jargon), I have no intention of adjusting myself to society; I will adjust society to me. As these events indicate, this is indeed a possible and practical approach and was exactly what happened here. I commend the approach to you all. It is effective.

But this is certainly not my personal victory alone. Many, many others helped indispensably—particularly (but by no means only) Barbara Gittings and Ronald Gold from the gay movement, and Drs. Robert Spitzer and Kent Robinson from among the psychiatrists. More importantly, it is a major victory of vast importance not merely for me and us, but for all gay people everywhere. Its implications and its consequences for good are enormous, as the near future is bound to show. Its ramifications are almost without limit; it will have impact everywhere. . . .

So I thank you . . . Gay *IS* Good; we have all just made it a lot better.

Franklin E. Kameny

Here is the first resolution—approving the deletion of homosexuality from the list of mental disorders and adding a revised category—to which Kameny referred to in the previous letter:

This category is for individuals whose sexual interests are directed primarily towards people of the same sex and who are either disturbed by, in conflict with, or wish to change their sexual orientation. This diagnostic category is distinguished from homosexuality, which by itself does not necessarily constitute a psychiatric disorder.[14]

The second proposal, below, is often referred to as the "civil rights resolution":

Whereas homosexuality in and of itself implies no impairment in judgment, stability, reliability, or vocational capabilities, therefore, be it resolved, that the American Psychiatric Association deplores all public and private discrimination against homosexuals in such areas as employment, housing, public accommodation, and licensing, and declares that no burden of proof of such judgment, capacity, or reliability shall be placed upon homosexuals greater than that imposed on any other persons. Further, the APA supports and urges the enactment of civil rights legislation at local, state, and federal levels that would insure homosexual citizens the same protections now guaranteed to others. Further, the APA supports and urges the repeal of all legislation making criminal offenses of sexual acts performed by consenting adults in private.[15]

In a memorandum written a day after he sent out the one above, Kameny wrote about his involvement in drafting the resolution on homosexuality and civil rights: "I had major input in the drafting and formulation of this (I wrote the original draft). The verbiage was carefully chosen to apply to such contexts as the industrial security clearance program."[16]

Kameny to Rae Kameny

In this letter to his mother, Kameny reflects on the significance of the past year and expresses delight that his mother has made contact with a new organization—what would become Parents and Friends of Lesbians and Gays (PFLAG).

DECEMBER 23, 1973

Dear Mother:

Thank you for both your letters of about a week ago, with their enclosures. Thank you also for the shipment of oranges and grapefruit from Florida, which arrived during the week.

I'm still tremendously elated by the outcome of the APA effort. It's very pleasant to have a dozen-year effort of that kind work its way out so successfully. I started, in 1962, essentially alone, and had to persuade first my own organization, then my own community, and then the larger establishment. It confirms the correctness and the practicality of my personal approach to the world, of which I first told you over 30 years ago, that if the world and I have to adjust to each other, the world and society will do the changing, because I won't. They have.

You don't know how delighted I am that you were at the Firehouse. I've been mentioning it to a number of people. Is there a contact address for the gay parents' organization? I've had some inquiries from people who want to get in touch with it by mail. Please check.

Thank you for your good wishes in lieu of a card. Actually, 1973 was a pretty good year, all in all. Like any year, it wasn't perfect and could have been better, and its passing means that we're all a year older at a time when, for me, I'm beginning to be conscious of the limited number of years remaining but, whatever things like the energy crisis and Watergate and other national, international and societal issues may mean for the past, present or future, on a personal basis, it was a pretty good year, and there is hope for an equally good one in 1974. . . .

Love,

Franklin

The issue of gay families became prominent in Kameny's life in 1973 when he received calls from foster-child placement officials in Maryland and Virginia. They had turned to Kameny for assistance in seeking homes for gay teenagers. Kameny later recalled his personal contribution:

From time to time they found it necessary to place gay teenagers (or late pre-teens) in foster homes. Heterosexual foster parents were uniformly either unwilling or unable to accept the homosexuality, and the placement did not work out. What they wanted were volunteer gay foster parents—either singles or couples; male or female—with whom to place these children. After some discussions and approaches, I had an article run for some two or three issues of our local, monthly gay newsletter "The Gay Blade" asking for such volunteers to contact me. There were about 35 responses . . . Most were singles; some were couples. Most were men; some were women. . . .

. . . I do understand that there have been some satisfactory placements as a result of all this.[17]

Kameny to the National Gay Task Force Board of Directors and Staff

Kameny became a founding member of the National Gay Task Force (NGTF) near the end of 1973. Like other activists, he was hoping that the new organization would professionalize the movement in ways that GAA, with its participatory democracy, would never be able to accomplish, and also bring "gay liberation into the mainstream of the civil rights movement."[18] *However professional it wanted to be, NGTF got off to a rocky start. Kameny was not pleased, and in the following memorandum the veteran leader slams down the gavel, seeking to create order out of chaos.*

DECEMBER 25, 1973

Along with some others, I was dismayed and, in fact, appalled, at the December 2 meeting of the Board of Directors, by the display of utterly disorganized lack of systematic planning which unfolded, with no slightest indication of remedy, and no indication of any effort at leadership to pull us out of the morass in which we are wallowing—or even recognition that we are wallowing in anything. We spent our hours unproductively dithering about matters of internal structure and organization which should have been disposed of . . . at—or, in fact, before—the *first* meeting of the Board. . . .

We are drifting and getting nowhere. If we do not commence, *promptly*, to get the basic organizational structure built—and built *properly* and *systematically*—we are likely to get nowhere, and gradually disintegrate into dissension-ridden nothingness. . . .

At the end of the December 2 Board meeting, someone tried to dispose of the need for a detailed constitution, setting out internal structure, with a comment to the effect that "we all trust each other" or something of the sort. This is naïve and impractical; that way lies disaster. It doesn't work that way—at least not for long.

Every organization passes through a series of evolutionary stages. The first of these is an all-too-short-lived period of enthusiasm and good will, during which personal and ideological differences are subordinated or ignored totally, and everyone works together effectively, frictionlessly, and highly productively. This is the time to draft and to adopt constitutions and statements of purpose . . . and to select initial officers and staff . . . make an initial choice of projects . . . and get underway. It is an apolitical era with minimal necessity for ideological- and purpose-diluting compromises. The entire future of the organization may depend upon taking proper advantage of this almost-always-too-brief era. Signs of its end are already visible in NGTF. . . .

So let us get on with the organization of NGTF and get it over with. But let us do it in a *proper, logical, systematic, orderly*—and efficient—fashion so we can get it behind us and go on to more useful things. . . . So . . . let's stop merely *talking* about NGTF and start *forming* it; it doesn't *really* exist yet. . . .

Franklin Kameny

11

"So Much to Feel Satisfied, Content, Victorious, and Enthusiastic About"

1974

Kameny to Ann Landers

Kameny was an avid reader of Ann Landers, and was taken aback when he came across her reply to a homosexual who had asked why he and his lover could not be physically affectionate in public without earning society's disapproval. In her answer, published on January 9, 1973, Landers stated:

> *Why can't members of the same sex kiss publicly and dance together and proclaim their love as heterosexuals do? Because homosexuality is unnatural. It is, in spite of what some psychiatrists say, a sickness—a dysfunction. In our culture, in the year 1973, we are not conditioned to accept homosexuality as the normal human condition.*
>
> *For 18 years I have been pleading for compassion and understanding and equal rights for homosexuals, and I will continue to do so. But I do not believe homosexual activity is normal behavior.[1]*

JANUARY 3, 1974

Dear Ms. Landers:

Over many years I have written to you complimenting you on your approach to homosexuality. Our last such letter on that matter and in that tone was written on December 31, 1972, and responded to by you on January 8, 1973.

Commencing one day later, with your column of January 9, 1973, you have waged a vicious and irrational vendetta against homosexuals

287

. . . which has done incredible damage and harm to untold numbers of people, and which represents an abrupt, total, 180-degree about face from the position for which we complimented you since 1965.

In so doing, you have placed yourself in a class with racists and anti-Semites, with the Ku Klux Klan and the Nazis, and with the worst and most offensive elements of societal prejudice and bigotry. The psychic destruction which you have wrought upon countless homosexuals is not less than the physical destruction wrought upon blacks and Jews by the lynch mob's noose and the Nazi's gas oven. That the noose and the oven are deadly and lethal is balanced off by the fact that at least they are fast, while the kind of self-hatred and other internal psychic trauma which you either create or reinforce, and the kind of entrenched bigotry, prejudice, and discrimination which your ill-considered and ill-founded statements buttress, bolster, and support, produce an entire lifetime of misery, anguish, and harassment in and for their victims.

The suddenness of the appearance, and the virulent intensity of the tone, of your repeated diatribes, contrasting strongly in both tone and substance with your earlier commentary on the subject, has led to considerable speculation as to who had bought you out or paid you off, and for how much. Many of us continue to wonder.

We had intended to respond in rebuttal, in due course, point by point, to the faulty reasoning, shoddy logic, and inane commentary from your ludicrous stable of selected non-authorities on the subject, with which you attempted to bolster and support your homophobic bigotry and philosophy of social conformity at all costs. It is no longer necessary for us to do so.

As you are undoubtedly aware, the Board of Trustees of the American Psychiatric Association—the Association's highest and final administrative-legislative body, speaking in an official and formal sense for all psychiatrists (or, at least, for the psychiatric profession as such)—by *unanimous* vote, declared that homosexuality is NOT a sickness or illness. A copy of their resolution . . . is enclosed, along with another copy of their resolution on civil rights for homosexuals (the latter being a practical impossibility without the former, which is why your pious solicitude for our civil rights while terming us "sick" is so meaningless)—in real life, "mentally ill" people just do not enjoy civil rights. . . .

Under these circumstances, we feel that intellectual and moral integrity, and common decency, require and demand that you *publicly* reverse your previously stated position on homosexuality as a "sickness" *and that you do it in firm, clear, unambiguous, unequivocal, non-evasive language.* That would seem to be the only course through which you can achieve the redemption, rehabilitation, and atonement which you so badly need in respect to this issue, and express the apology to the homosexual community so much in order. . . .

> Sincerely yours,
> Franklin E. Kameny

Rather than issuing an apology, Ann Landers sent Kameny the following reply:

> Before I published the particular letter with which you take exception, I consulted with some of the most liberal of the American Psychiatric Association's most distinguished members. They all felt that the letter was an extremely good one, and congratulated me for having the courage to print it. I am terribly sorry that you felt that I did an injustice to your cause.[2]

Kameny to Ann Landers

In commenting on the APA's decision to delete homosexuality from its list of mental disorders, Landers wrote the following in her January 8 column: "In the past I have said that homosexuals are sick, in the sense homosexuality is a dysfunction, a form of aberrant behavior. My opinion has not changed."[3] And in her January 13 column, she offered her opinion on gay pride: "I have supported homosexuals in their fight for civil rights and will continue to do so, but Gay Pride is something else. I don't view deviant sexual behavior as something to be proud of."[4]

JANUARY 29, 1974

Dear Ms. Landers:

So now homosexuality is merely "aberrant" (your column of January 8, 1974). That seems to be the new code word for us, now that "deviation" and "perversion" and "sickness" have fallen somewhat into disfavor.

You people simply cannot bring yourselves to stop putting us down and just accept us, can you?

You do not seem to realize that for all of your patting of yourselves on the back for 18 years of pleading for compassion, understanding, and equal rights for homosexuals, you are making impossible, or at least incomparably more difficult, the achievement of that compassion (which we do not want; it is patronizing, condescending, and therefore demeaning, degrading, and dehumanizing) and of understanding and equal rights (which we not only want; we *demand*). As a matter of simple, hard realities, compassion, understanding, and equal rights just simply *will NOT* be given to "perverts," "deviants," "aberrant," the "abnormal," or the mentally ill (which is what your "sickness" label means, no matter what verbal gymnastics you may go through to say otherwise). . . .

I point out, in passing, that "abnormal" and "normal" as *properly* used, are *solely* statistical terms. Anything less than 50% is abnormal. Thus, in our country and society, it is *normal* to be: white, brunette, Christian and Protestant, female, and to have an IQ of about 100. It is *abnormal* and deviant to be: Black, blend; Jewish, Catholic, or atheistic; male; and to have a high IQ.[5]

On that basis, if homosexuality is abnormal, deviant, and aberrant, we are in good company. Let us have more and better abnormality, deviance, and aberration!

Then, in your January 13, 1974 column, you come back to "deviant" when, in response to an inquiry about *Gay pride*, you disparagingly and snidely comment: "I don't view deviant sexual behavior as something to be proud of."

Why not?

No one questions *Black pride* (deviant skin color)

No one challenges Jewish or Catholic pride (deviant religious behavior)

No one challenges pride in ancestral country (deviant ethnic origin)

To put it bluntly: What the hell is wrong with deviance and deviant behavior? All the term refers to is *variance* and *difference*. Ours is a pluralistic society; give some careful consideration to what that really means and where it leads. Variance—variety—choice—difference—are at the very heart and soul of our society's vigor and vitality, and that includes homosexuality along with other forms of personal variance, choice, and difference, and in equal measure. . . .

Franklin E. Kameny

Kameny to Edna Lavey

In this angry letter about a recent visit to see his family, Kameny claims that his sister and mother have failed to pay attention to his significant achievements and have instead focused on such "petty" matters as his financial insecurity and the civil-service job from which he was fired in 1957.

FEBRUARY 26, 1974

Dear Edna:

. . . As much of a disaster as 1973 may perhaps have been for the country and for the world, it was a truly memorably good year for the things of substance and meaning in which I have been involved. There had been enormous achievement, for much of which I felt I could take personal credit. Personal efforts going back 12 and 16 years had been crowned with success. . . . I had compelled the American Psychiatric Association to reverse itself, and had broken the back of the U.S. Civil Service Commission. I had been instrumental (though not alone) in achieving the enactment in Washington of the most advanced and sweeping civil rights legislation in the country, covering not only homosexuals but just about anyone and everyone else as well. I'm known and I and my work are respected all across the country—and very much in Washington, both in my own community and in the general community—by everyone, apparently, except by you.

In recent times, with the arrival of home rule upon the Washington scene, local politics—of which we have had virtually none in the past—have emerged actively. Based upon the almost universally highly favorable impression left by my campaign for Congress in 1971, many people—sometimes from surprising directions—are asking me whether I am going to get into politics in 1974, whether I am going to run for office, etc., and urging me to do so. There are pros and cons, based both upon political and demographic realities and upon personal factors, which I am considering carefully. I still have not at all decided.

And so I have been feeling very elated and very satisfied, since the latter part of 1973. I saw this past New Year's Eve as a celebration of a truly good year past, with the feeling that if 1974 is only half as good as 1973 was, it will be a good year indeed. The past few months have been ones of great contentment, of a sense of solid achievement and vindication, and of much work well and successfully completed.

Do you have any idea—any at all—as to how I spend my time? I've been telling you and Mother for years that I'm extremely busy. Have you ever expressed the slightest interest in knowing what actually occupies my time? What I am doing? What I am accomplishing and trying to accomplish, and how? Do you have any slightest idea or knowledge of what I'm doing aside from my public appearances? No, you have never expressed any such interest and have no such knowledge.

These and other things like them were the things that I wanted to share with you that evening. They are meaningful. I did not want to wallow around in the meaningless darkness and dreariness of economics, which I find repellant. Whatever may be the situation in the future, and whatever may have been the situation in parts of the past (and it was considerably bleaker than you seem to think it was—at least at times), for the moment my bills are all paid up to date (and some of them ahead) and I have enough money to get by on (even if not lavishly and only with careful, farsighted planning). So, as of that evening, there was no dire pressing financial urgency, or crisis.

I was so close to 100% certain that either you or Mother (or both) were going to raise these matters—you (pl.) almost always do—that I debated asking Mother, in the weeks preceding our meeting, not to do so, and to ask you not to do so. I'm sorry, now, that I didn't ask her.

In any case, there was so much of real substance and accomplishment and interest to discuss; so much to feel satisfied, content, victorious, and enthusiastic about; so much solid accomplishment to share, that I just did not, in this brief encounter, want to get into the things which you persisted in raising. That, of course, was my privilege. It was your privilege, of course, to raise an issue, initially, but the rules of ordinary, civil discourse would have required you to defer to my unwillingness at that particular time, to discuss the matters which you raised. And so, for example, when I did raise the matter of our success with the U.S. Civil Service Commission, after many, many years of effort, I raised it as a major accomplishment of national importance and of importance to vast numbers of people—a change in the policies and practices, after all, of the federal government itself. You immediately proceeded to make it petty and trivial by ignoring all the larger implications as if they did not exist, and reducing it to the long dead (13 years dead) issue of a civil service job; and when I disposed of your inquiry with a direct, full, factual answer, you used that, in turn, as a launching pad for a whole variety of other, equally petty matters.

I tried to make all that clear, but you and Mother, like two harpies, unsheathed your talons, sank them in, and just simply would not be persuaded to let go. I tried to indicate my feelings clearly, but nicely and civilly; and then clearly and firmly; and then clearly, bluntly, and adamantly. Nothing would swerve the two of you from your determination to leap the kill. Normal civilized discourse requires a sensitivity to signals provided by those discussions. I found your (pl.) performance incredible at the outset, more incredible as events progressed, and I find it is still more incredible in retrospect. . . .

As always,
Frank

Kameny to Barbara Gittings

A core of psychiatrists, with Charles Socarides and Irving Bieber leading the way, was angered by the APA board's decision to delete homosexuality from its list of mental disorders. In accord with APA bylaws, this dissident group successfully called for an association-wide referendum on the decision. In effect, the dissenters were hoping the decision on the mental status of homosexuality would be decided by the democratic principle of majority rule. It was an odd tactic for psychiatrists who had longed to be considered serious scientists rather than quacks with no hard data to back their diagnoses and treatments. But the referendum took place through mailed ballots, and Kameny reports on the results in the following letter.

APRIL 8, 1974

Dear Barbara:

I phoned today, as Kay probably told you, but you were out of town. The big news, of course, is the vote on the APA referendum. The results are as follows:

Of 17,905 APA members qualified to voted, 10,555 (58.4%) voted.[6] Almost all of those voted on "our" referendum. Of those, the vote was: 5854 (58.4%) to support the Board of Trustees; 3810 (37.8%) opposed; and 367 (3.8%) abstaining. . . .

So we are permanently healthy!!! . . .

As always,
Frank

Kameny sent similar news to the gay activist who was by his side at the founding of MSW—Jack Nichols.

> *As I'm sure you have heard, the APA Board of Trustees was upheld by referendum of the membership . . . so our health has now been permanently confirmed. That really concludes a 12-year battle which I started back in 1962 and which you and I waged well for many years. It's indeed pleasant to see some of these things really working out. Back when we started, I never really expected to see the psychiatrists really come around in a formal sense. The vote was announced on April 8, and is now final. The job is done.[7]*

Kameny to Robert Henle

In November 1973, the District of Columbia, at Kameny's urging, passed a law prohibiting discrimination against homosexuals in employment. Shortly after the law became effective, Kameny wrote to the DC chief of police, informing him that "D.C. Human Rights Law—Title 34 . . . prohibits (inter alia) discrimination against the employment of homosexuals by any employer in the District of Columbia, public as well as private."[8] Kameny now wields the new DC human rights law against the president of his former employer—Georgetown University.

APRIL 23, 1974

Dear Father Henle:

We read with interest the news reports . . . of the restoration to an accredited status of ROTC courses at Georgetown University.

We call to your explicit attention two highly relevant, interrelated, mutually exclusive facts:

1. In consistency with the formally enunciated discriminatory and un-American policies of our armed services, ROTC courses (to our knowledge) are closed to students known to be homosexual, just as the armed services themselves are closed to homosexual American citizens. Further, homosexual students who may successfully complete such courses undetected as homosexuals are not eligible to be commissioned as officers or otherwise to reap the benefits of their successful completion of the course, although their fellow heterosexual students are eligible for commissions and other such benefits.

2. The *D.C. Human Rights Law—Title 34*, signed into law on November 16, 1973, prohibits discrimination against homosexuals in *ANY* context in the District of Columbia. Title 34 applies specifically to educational institutions including Georgetown University and its course offerings.

It is our position that as long as fact 1 set forth above is true, Georgetown University may not lawfully offer ROTC courses at all, and certainly not for credit; such offerings place the University in violation of the law. If fact 1 remains in effect, and Georgetown University continues to offer ROTC courses (with or without credit), we shall see to it that through appropriate legal process Georgetown University is compelled to cease operation in the District of Columbia, and that you (personally and with other implicated Georgetown University officials) are sent to jail. . . .

It is as simple as that. That is the law. . . .

Thank you.

Sincerely yours,
Franklin E. Kameny

Kameny to Ethel Payne

Ethel Payne was an African-American commentator for the CBS radio news show Spectrum. *In her June 13 piece, she had commented negatively on Kameny's recent appearance on* The Advocates, *a PBS television program that typically presented both sides of a controversial social issue. In the episode that caught Payne's attention, Kameny had appeared with Elaine Noble—a lesbian activist on her way to becoming the first openly lesbian candidate to win a statewide political office (the Massachusetts House of Representatives)—to advocate for same-sex marriage. Payne had also offered a negative assessment of the largely gay-friendly audience who jeered, laughed, and catcalled during the comments by the advocate against same-sex marriages.*[9]

AUGUST 31, 1974

Dear Ms. Payne:

... Your primary criticism was directed against the audience, although I was also criticized for being "unnecessarily hostile and combative."

One way of understanding what took place is to translate the program into a racial context (or an anti-Semitic one). If the audience had been largely Black, and if the opposition had been espousing unvarnished, blatant racism, and if some of the opposition witnesses had been among the country's most vocal racists and were active members of the Ku Klux Klan (and correspondingly in an anti-Semitic context), neither you nor anyone else would have voiced a syllable of criticism at audience response identical to that which occurred on the program in question—nor would you have criticized a Black advocate for "hostility and combativeness." ...

The views of racists, sexists, and anti-Semites do not deserve respect. Neither do the views of homophobes. My witness, Ms. Elaine Noble, obviously did not respect the "straight" side of the issue because no one with any intelligence at all could. . . . Do you think that a Black, deeply involved in the black rights movement would—or should—for a moment have shown respect for an advocate openly expressing second-class status for Blacks . . . Then why should a gay show respect for someone openly espousing homophobia and second-class status for gays? . . .

You say: "It looks as if gays have come out of the closet thumbing their noses at the heterosexuals of the world."

What is sauce for the goose is sauce for the gander. One of the best ways to stop offensive behavior (the traditional behavior, over the centuries, of heterosexuals toward homosexual) is to give the offenders a "taste of their own medicine." . . . Heterosexuals have a very long and shameful record, quite unmitigated until recently, of rudeness, contemptuousness, and cruelty to homosexuals. Surely you cannot validly object if we visit upon our repressors just a little of what they have visited upon us since time immemorial. We are tired of being polite, civil, passive victims. . . .

I agree with you on the "overemphasis on sexual behavior." As soon as you heterosexuals (not you, personally) stop emphasizing our sexual (and affectional) behavior, we will be pleased to stop harping on it. As long as *you people* continue to make an issue of it by denying us our rights and equality, we *must* continue to make an issue of it, and we will. You will be hearing much more from and of us, until we have achieved our reasonable and proper goals of first-class citizenship and first-class personhood, as I set them out in the course of the Advocates program under discussion....

Sincerely yours,

Franklin E. Kameny

Kameny to William Safire

In his April 18 essay, New York Times *columnist William Safire defined homosexuals as "abnormal." "To be gay," he added, "is to be engaged in an activity that both moral absolutists and moral relativists would label 'immoral,' with both Scripture and sociological statistics on their side." Safire also claimed that homosexuality "should be discouraged," though without legal coercion. "The adult homosexual's right to be left alone must not be invaded by a majority seeking to make unlawful what it regards as sinful," he wrote.[10] In his reply to the column, Kameny clarifies the basic source of his libertarian ethics.*

NO DATE (APRIL 1974)

Dear Mr. Safire:

... The facts, of course, are completely against you. Many moral absolutists and most moral relativists do *not* label homosexuality and homosexual sexual activity as immoral. Quite to the contrary. This is especially so in light of the fact that homosexuality and homosexual sexual activity are as often expressions of or involved with love and affection as are heterosexuality and heterosexual sexual activity. In a world rife with hatred, one is hard put to rationalize labeling as *immoral* any form of love....

Ours is a pluralistic society. Our national-societal morality (given the church-state separation imposed by the First Amendment, which rules out Scripture and the like as a source of national-societal morality) comes from such sources as the Declaration of Independence, with its emphases upon individual freedom, and its highly relevant guarantee, as an *inalienable* right, of the pursuit of happiness. Therein lies the affirmative American morality of homosexuality. . . .

Finally, you make the incredible statement: "We can . . . counter their new proselytism with some missionary work of our own."

What do you think you people have been doing since time immemorial? For centuries, we homosexuals have been the objects (the victims) of one of the most intensive, extensive virulent, evangelistic, crusading missionary campaign of proselytization to convert us from our homosexuality to your heterosexuality, that the world has ever seen in any context. We run into it at every turn. It never lets up.

If you do not "get off our backs" and leave us alone, we really will start to reciprocate. . . .

Sincerely yours,
Franklin E. Kameny

Kameny to John Paul Hudson

In the following letter to a gay activist and writer who penned popular travel guides for the gay community, Kameny offers a partly negative assessment of the expansion of the gay rights movement in reference to bisexuals.

SEPTEMBER 10, 1974

Dear John Paul:

. . . I have mixed feelings in regard to bisexuality and in regard to the place that bisexuality and bisexuals should have in the gay movement. In the end, it boils down to the individual bisexual and the particular handling of bisexuality in a particular context.

For example (and I am making no effort at completeness in this letter), I object extremely strongly to the philosophy (it's more an ideology or rhetoric) which makes bisexuality superior to exclusive "choice- and relation-limiting" homosexuality (or heterosexuality). That is merely a "party line" which just dumps some more guilt upon gay people, and is just as offensively prescriptive as is society at large, even if the prescription is slightly different.

Similarly, for a significantly large number of people, a claim of bisexuality IS a copout. However, for others, it is not so at all.

For myself, I use the term "bisexual" hardly at all. . . . I use the term "bisexual" only for those who are very close to the 50-50 point—and there are, indeed, very few of those. While large numbers of people function both homosexually and heterosexually in their personal lives, almost all have their "druthers," and on the basis of those "druthers" I would classify them as either homosexual or heterosexual, but not bisexual. . . .

Cordially,

Frank

Kameny to President Gerald Ford

Just as he had written other sitting U.S. presidents, Kameny seeks to lobby President Ford on gay rights. For the first time, though, Kameny has a specific bill that he can point to as he seeks presidential support. The bill, highlighted in the following letter, was introduced by Democratic Representative Bella Abzug of New York.

SEPTEMBER 17, 1974

Dear Mr. President:

Shortly after taking office, in your address to a joint session of Congress, on August 12, 1974, you said: "I also intend to listen to the people themselves—*all* of the people." (Emphasis added).[11]

It is in pursuit of that thought that I write. . . .

We are approaching our nation's bicentennial, celebrating the 200th anniversary of the signing of our nation's birth certificate, the Declaration of Independence. That Declaration guarantees, as an *inalienable* right, to *all* citizens (homosexual citizens included, of course) the right to the *pursuit of happiness*. Fundamentally, what we are asking is your assistance in implementing that and other basic principles of Americanism for all of our citizens, including our homosexual citizens.

I have intentionally avoided specifics in this letter; it would take a book to treat them adequately. There are a number of explicit substantive issues and matters upon which you can be of assistance, in terms of executive branch policy and practice, and of congressional legislation to be proposed and/or supported (e.g., . . . the bill currently being introduced by Representative Bella Abzug, to extend the coverage of various of the existing civil rights laws to prohibit discrimination on the basis of both *sex* and *sexual orientation* [i.e., homosexuality]; your publicly expressed support would be enormously helpful).

I am writing, specifically, to ask for a meeting *between you personally* and representatives of the national gay community, at some early date, to discuss these matters. I would suggest that present from the homosexual community be myself and some reasonable number of other persons from the national gay community.

Such a meeting would be of enormous importance, not only in the direct, substantive furtherance of efforts and achievement of goals which are consistent with the best traditions of Americanism, but in terms of its symbolic significance for us.

We realize that this is a controversial, politically sensitive and delicate issue, and an emotionally charged one. We have no wish to embarrass for the sake of embarrassment. But we cannot allow emotion, controversy, and political caution to keep us consigned to second-class status in a country which claims that it has no second-class citizens . . .

If you really meant what you said, Mr. President—that you want to listen to *ALL* of the people, and that you want to be the president of *ALL* the people—then remember that we—your homosexual American citizens— are 10% of all of the people and of all of the voters—no small group. Will you listen to *us,* too? Will you work explicitly for *us,* too? Will you meet with *us,* too? . . .

Sincerely yours,
Franklin E. Kameny

Kameny did not win a meeting at the White House, until March 26, 1977, when he joined thirteen other members of the National Gay Task Force for a meeting with Carter White House staffer Margaret Costanza.[12]

Kameny to Monroe Neuman

Monroe Neuman, a psychiatrist based in Washington, DC, had written a letter to the Washington Post *after reading articles about individuals experiencing homosexual feelings while in heterosexual relationships. In commenting on the articles, Neuman wrote: "It would have been useful for the authors to point out that psychotherapy could help individuals with bisexual inclinations to become more heterosexual and less homosexual if they were so motivated to look at themselves. . . . The homosexual behavior is a symptom of other problems."[13]*

SEPTEMBER 17, 1974

Dear Dr. Neuman:

. . . I get many, many cases—the volume is growing rapidly—of heterosexually married individuals with homosexual urges. My advice and counsel vary, of course, with the circumstances and facts of each case, but in many cases where a homosexual drive is discovered by a long and satisfactorily married individual, I point out (if the facts warrant it . . .) that their homosexuality has in no way diminished or changed their heterosexuality; that they have found an additional option. Liking chocolate ice cream in no way diminishes or impairs one's enjoyment of vanilla . . .

Why do you not suggest the opposite alternative: To become more homosexual and less heterosexual? Or is that heresy?

Some day, we will have a society which will not pressure people into pursuing a heterosexuality which is not theirs, and in which people can non-judgmentally explore what is there within themselves, and then build their lives constructively around what they discover (homosexuality, heterosexuality, or some blend of the two) instead of fighting, destructively, against what they find. That is what I always suggest to people—particularly younger people—who seek guidance in deciding which way to go: Explore; try both; gather data; then decide. Your letter is typical of the psychiatric approach which leads us to urge people having problems or questions involving homosexuality to stay as far from psychiatry and psychiatrists as they possibly can, and to come to the gay movement for truly constructive, knowledgeable guidance. . . .

. . . I strongly urge that you reexamine and revise your ideas on homosexuality and homosexuals and how to deal with them. Meanwhile, we shall continue to steer the growing number of cases which come to us as far as possible away from you and your professional colleagues, except for a small (but growing) number of very carefully screened ones.

Psychiatrist, heal thyself. You need to, badly.

Sincerely yours,

Franklin E. Kameny

Kameny to WMAL-TV

Kameny writes to the programming department of WMAL-TV in Washington, DC, to protest the airing of a Marcus Welby, M.D. *episode about a science teacher who raped one of his male students.*

SEPTEMBER 26, 1974

Gentlemen:

As one of a number of organizations speaking and working on behalf of the local gay community, we are writing to protest your proposed showing of the Marcus Welby segment "The Outrage" dealing with a homosexual assault by a teacher upon a student.

The segment is offensive and defamatory to our community. It will have deeply deleterious consequences. It will reinforce strongly held and widely prevalent misconceptions. Its showing will degrade WMAL and everyone associated with the rhetoric and approaches of a generation ago. Even its handling of the medical aspects of the situation is inconsistent with fact and with reality . . .

Notwithstanding efforts by the producers at modification of the script, and the introduction of disclaimers (that "this is not homosexuality but pedophilia" or whatever), the program perpetuates and reinforces unfortunate, persistent, and deeply entrenched (and factually totally unsubstantiated) stereotypes of homosexuals as child molesters (pedophilia is a heterosexual problem, not a homosexual one). In its treatment of the victim of the assault, and in other ways, it falls prey to, and reinforces negative and inaccurate attitudes toward and misconceptions about homosexuals and homosexuality (no matter what term or phrase is used on the program).

We are sure that you would not, for an instant, seriously consider airing a segment which perpetuates and reinforces negative stereotypes of

Blacks, Jews, or other minority groups, and which defames them. You should not consider airing a program such as this, which perpetuates and reinforces negative stereotypes of homosexuals and which defames us.

WMAL-TV has taken an admirably progressive, enlightened, and supportive position on the question of homosexuality—well beyond any other television outlet in this area and in most places. It is sad indeed to see that cancelled out, undone, and thrown onto the trash heap by the showing of this outrageous "Outrage."

We strongly urge that you not air this offensive, ill-conceived program.

Sincerely yours.

Franklin E. Kameny

After learning that WMAL-TV decided to broadcast the program, though with a disclaimer, Kameny fires off another missive, this time to program director Irwin Starr.

We were unhappy to learn that unlike your more sensitive and perceptive colleagues in Boston, Philadelphia, and elsewhere, you have decided to air the Marcus Welby segment "The Outrage." We continue to hope that there may still be a last-minute reconsideration.

We note, however, that you are going to make one or two announcements stating that "homosexuals are no more likely to be involved in child molestation than heterosexuals."

THIS IS FACTUALLY UNTRUE!!

ALL studies quite uniformly show that homosexuals are much less likely to be involved in child molestation (even after the much smaller number of homosexuals has been accounted for; that is: for equal-sized samplings of homosexual men and of heterosexual men, the number of homosexual child molesters is significantly smaller). As we indicated in our last letter: Child molestation is a heterosexual problem, not a homosexual one.

Further, in such cases of homosexual child molestation as may occasionally occur, violence—rape, force, attacks such as provide the subject matter for "The Outrage"—virtually never takes place. It is heterosexuals trying to find a substitute (as in prisons) who are responsible for all but a small percentage of the homosexual rapes—whether of children or of adults—which occur.

Thus not only is the situation portrayed in "The Outrage" so atypical as to be almost non-existent, treated in a sensational and unrealistic fashion, but your grudging, factually inaccurate comment about it does not at all make clear how atypical, and where the vast bulk of the child molestation problem lies—with you heterosexuals.[14]

Kameny to Phyllis Schlafly

In 1972 Phyllis Schlafly founded and became president of the Eagle Forum, a conservative interest group focused on education and lobbying. A vocal opponent of the Equal Rights Amendment, she styled herself as a leader of the so-called pro-family movement of the early 1970s. In the following letter, Kameny refers to Schlafly's recent commentary on Spectrum.

NOVEMBER 2, 1974

Dear Ms. Schlafly:

. . . Like many of your fellow reactionaries on this issue of homosexuality, you make much of the spurious allegation that homosexuality is a threat to the family. I find that totally incomprehensible.

First, of course, persons—homosexual or heterosexual—have the right not to participate in the family system at all, if they wish not to do so. That is a valid option, open to anyone, without disadvantage.

Second, protecting the rights of homosexuals to work, to have housing of their choice, and to utilize public accommodations does not impair, impede, or obstruct, in any slightest way, the ability of any *het-ero*sexual to enter into the family system. (Do you wish to see homosexuals denied jobs, despite willingness to work and to contribute to society, forced onto welfare in order to survive—at *your* expense, as a taxpayer?—or are you just going to let us die of starvation, in the best Christian spirit?)

Third, I find it incomprehensible how you can, on the one hand, attack us for threatening the family system and then, on the other hand, propose to deny us the homosexual marriages which would allow us formal entrance into that family system. Extending or broadening the family system by broadening the definition of what constitutes marriage and the family, in no slightest way, detracts from what is already there. I challenge you to show otherwise.

Fourth, your remarks are singularly ill-taken, coming as they do from a person belonging to a religion in which a celibate clergy is the rule, and in which celibacy is exalted as a virtue. The example set by celibate priests and nuns, and by the institutionalization of celibacy and non-marriage, is a REAL threat to the family system, if anything is.

I, for one, am not going to allow you or anyone else—or EVERYone else, for that matter—to ram your damnable family system down my throat, as a condition for my enjoyment of the benefits of MY society. Nor do you have a right to do so; nor do I have to allow you to do so.

. . . I suggest that you give some thought to what this country really stands for, and to what it is all about—you haven't the faintest idea. Give some thought to what it is that is embodied in the bicentennial which we are about to celebrate. I suggest, also, that you re-think your ideas on morality. Your morality is one of the most immoral moralities that I know. And, also, reconsider your ideas on Christianity. You do not have a clue as to what Christianity means. Your views in regard to homosexuals are the direct antithesis of Christianity. There is no inconsistency whatever between being actively homosexual and being truly Christian.

I suggest that you ask yourself how it is possible to reconcile the real spirit of Christianity, as a religion of love, with your vicious, punitive, intolerant condemnation of anyone who chooses to make love differently from you, or of persons of whom you disapprove. You have made of Christianity a religion of hate. When Christianity is used to justify persecuting—or refusing to take constructive measures to relieve persecution— when Christianity is used to justify denial to people of jobs, and housing; when Christianity is used to justify consignment of people to the status of second-class citizenry and second-class personhood; when Christianity is used as a basis for making pariahs and outcasts of persons who have done nothing other than to love in a different way from yours—when Christianity is used for these purposes, then you have perverted Christianity beyond recognition. Christ must be wringing his hands in anguish at what you are doing in his name.

I am confident that if there is a hell, you will spend all of eternity burning there, because of the living hell to which you are so cavalierly consigning your fellow human beings—including homosexual human beings. . . .

Gay IS Good.

Sincerely yours,
Franklin E. Kameny

12

"I Have Brought the Very Government of the United States to Its Knees"

1975

Kameny to ——

Kameny's visible leadership in the movement attracted the attention of many men along the way, and in 1975 he received a graphic letter from a Tennessee man interested in a sexual liaison with the gay rights leader.

Kameny replied in equally graphic detail, describing his sexual preferences, his physical appearance, and his short-lived experimentation with smoking pot (it did nothing for him, he said). He also expressed his hope of getting together with his correspondent. "I think we'd have a very pleasant time," he wrote.[1]

Kameny's love life focused less on building long-term relationships than on seeking and enjoying short-term ones. In a book published in 1975, his good friend Kay Lahusen wrote a few sentences about this topic: "Frank has had two serious love relationships, but neither became permanent. He says candidly of himself, 'I have a somewhat acerbic and abrasive personality, and a rather strong one, and I'm not the easiest person to get along with, as anybody realizes who's around me any length of time.'"[2] Kameny addressed the same topic in a letter he had written two years earlier: "My love life is much more minimal than I'd like, and I keep resolving that I'll do something about it—'one of these days when my backlog has been brought down and I'm current'—but that never seems to arrive."[3]

Kameny to Greatest Is Love

A representative of a Christian organization named Greatest Is Love had written a letter asking Kameny to keep the group in mind should he "ever want a way out." The writer stated that while he had once been gay "for many years," he "couldn't handle it," and that he wanted to offer his help to "any gay you know that is seeking a way out." He had also enclosed literature in his letter. "To me," the writer concluded, "Jesus Christ, the living Son of God, is my deliverer."[4]

Kameny, just back from a trip to England, Ireland, and Amsterdam,[5] disagrees, referring especially to David Wilkerson, a popular Christian evangelist and writer. Wilkerson's most successful book, The Cross and the Switchblade, *had earned him an international reputation for his ministry to inner-city gangs.[6] In 1971 he published a popular booklet that roundly condemned homosexuals as sinners in need of a miracle wrought by God. "I have never met a truly happy homosexual," Wilkerson wrote. "The majority are sad, full of fear, shame, guilt, anxiety and torment. . . . Homosexuality is a life of self-torture."[7] Pointing to the personal testimonies of those he had counseled, Wilkerson added that homosexuality is neither inherited nor incurable. "You need a miracle that changes you from unnatural desires to natural ones," he wrote. "God's power can make you natural, clean and straight. . . . Quit crying in self-pity and begin to cry out in faith."[8]*

JANUARY 3, 1975

Dear Gentlepeople:

We have received some of your anti-gay literature, and totally reject your approach.

Homosexuality is no more something to get "out" of than heterosexuality is. If a person finds that his (or her) *heterosexual* relationships and lifestyle are not satisfactory, and do not lead to fulfillment, he rearranges the conduct of his heterosexuality; he does not even think of changing to homosexuality. Similarly, if the particular circumstances of one's homosexual life are unsatisfactory, one rearranges the particular circumstances, but does not attempt to change the homosexuality. Therefore, if someone came to us dissatisfied with his homosexuality, and asking for change, we would explore the reasons for the discontent, point out to him what a wonderful thing his homosexuality is, and lead him to satisfaction, enjoyment, and fulfillment as a *homosexual.*

We believe that homosexuality is affirmatively *good, right, desirable, moral, and Christian.* We feel that there is nothing whatever inconsistent about being a good Christian and a good gay, simultaneously, and nothing inconsistent in being a sexually and affectionally active homosexual and being a good Christian.

We look upon our homosexuality as a God-given blessing, for which we are thankful and grateful. We exult in our homosexuality. We feel that you are misinterpreting the Bible and distorting and perverting the meaning of Christianity, in condemning homosexuality, or in considering homosexuality to be inferior to heterosexuality, or in saying that homosexuality is in any slightest way un-Christian. . . .

I have been aware for many years of the vicious, poisonous, irrational, un-Christian diatribes sent out by David Wilkerson. He is a contemptible person who has tried to pervert Christianity from the warm religion of love established by Jesus into a vicious cult of hatred. I expect that he will spend all eternity burning in Hell.

I strongly urge that you contact the nearest affiliate of the Metropolitan Community Church, the gay Christian church established by the Reverend Troy Perry. You might learn what hogwash you have been fed about the supposed conflict between homosexuality and Christianity. There is no inconsistency.

Gay IS Good
Gay IS Godly
Gay IS Christian

> With best wishes for a good gay
> New Year,
> Franklin E. Kameny

Kameny to Jack Nichols

On February 22, 1975, Nichols sent Kameny news about the death of his longtime companion, Lige Clarke. "Some think that Lige was mowed down on a dark Mexican road near Vera Cruz," Nichols wrote, "that crazed bandits emptied an automatic round into his body as he traveled the open road.

Well, that's true. That happened."⁹ Kameny's reply here is significant partly because its beginning and end reveal his self-acknowledged difficulty with expressing emotions on an interpersonal level. The letter is also helpful for encountering Kameny's sense of the way his life had evolved from victim of unjust laws to executor of just laws.

In addition, Kameny also writes about a significant development in challenging discrimination against gays and lesbians in the military. In March 1974, Kameny received an anonymous call from a man claiming to be a technical sergeant in the U.S. Air Force. The caller had read that Kameny was looking for a test case to mount a legal challenge to the military's ban against homosexuals and suggested that he had a well-qualified friend who might be willing to bring suit. The so-called friend was in fact the caller himself—Technical Sergeant Leonard Matlovich.

Kameny was pleased when he later learned of Matlovich's stellar background in the military. The sergeant had no negative marks on his eleven-year record and had served with high honor in Vietnam, earning the Bronze Star, a Purple Heart, and other commendations. Matlovich had even taught a course in race relations, emphasizing the importance of equal opportunity within the Air Force.

Not long after the call, the two men met in Kameny's DC home, where the gay rights leader offered his own counsel and was impressed enough to contact David Addleston, the legal counsel at the Military Law Project of the ACLU, with a request that he meet with Matlovich for the purpose of setting up a test case. Addleston agreed to the meeting and set about plotting the case with Matlovich and Kameny. They decided to begin the process with a hand-delivered letter to Matlovich's superior.

In a letter dated March 6, 1975, and delivered to Captain Dennis Collins, Matlovich announced that

> *After some years of uncertainty, I have arrived at the conclusion that my sexual preferences are homosexual as opposed to heterosexual. I have also concluded that my sexual preferences will in no way interfere with my Air Force duties, as my preferences are now open. It is therefore requested that those provisions in AFM 39-12 relating to the discharge of homosexuals be waived in my case.¹⁰*

Before he finished reading the letter, Collins asked: "What does this mean?" Matlovich's reply drew from his teaching in the field of race relations: "This means Brown versus The Board of Education."[11]

APRIL 24, 1975

Dear Jack:

I'm writing, much too belatedly, in response to your xeroxed letter of February 22, written just after Lige's death and funeral.

As you know, there is absolutely nothing that can be said under circumstances such as these which is not trite, hackneyed, and been said ten thousand times over—and doesn't begin to convey one's true feelings. So I won't even try. You know that I grieve with you.

What are you doing now? Will you remain in Florida? Every now and then, I hear a rumor that you're in Washington, briefly, but I never hear from you or see you, so I never know whether the report is true or not.

Things here are excitingly busy. All the work that we did through the 60's, with faith and foresight that perhaps someday it might be productive—all that work is now paying off. Suddenly we find ourselves in the strange and unaccustomed position—but pleasantly and delightfully so—of being no longer a fringe group banging at the door to be let in, but right in the mainstream as a "respectable," accepted community group along with other groups—listened to, sought after and wooed by the politicians, etc. We're getting municipal budgetary funding for our gay community services by having all funding cut off for police plainclothes entrapment of gays.[12] We've moved in.

Symbolic of this was my appointment, by Mayor Washington,[13] at the end of March, to the D.C. Human Rights Commission. Now, as a commissioner of the District of Columbia, I have the full power of the law (our superb Human Rights Law—Title 34) at my command (having helped write the law and helped get it enacted) to bring an end to discrimination against gays—and others. I have always detested discrimination of all kinds and now, as a commissioner, along with my fellow commissioners, within this context, I AM the law, and no one is going to be discriminated against in the District of Columbia.

This will mean a certain rearrangement of my priorities, but that's not objectionable. I've been badly overextended for a very long time, and this will compel me to pull in a little, and to learn to say "no" to people—something which I've never done very well.

I'm still doing a good deal of public speaking—I'll be down in Georgia next week, and was out in Illinois last week—over 20 appearances (of which 2 were on television) this month alone.

Government cases still occupy a large amount of my time. We have a test case going against the Air Force, which has them all upset and paranoid. We're making an impact on the security people, although we have a way to go there. We've basically won the battle with the Civil Service Commission—they'll be announcing their changed regulations shortly.

Incidentally, I learned, a few months ago, that the State Department is still quivering in terror and panic at our picketing of them in August 1965. Those people are such idiots!

I guess that's all for now. I started this letter in response to yours and to unhappy events of February, and ended up making most of the letter about me. Please don't think, thereby, that I feel any the less deeply about the loss of Lige, for whom I always had the deepest of affection and regard. But I don't do well on condolences.

Keep in touch. The best of luck to you.

Fondly, as always,
Frank

Kameny to Herbert Kalin

On March 27, 1975, James Proferes, manager of a movie theater in Washington, DC, was convicted on fifty-five misdemeanor counts related to the showing of an uncut version of Deep Throat, *a pornographic movie starring Linda Lovelace.*[14] *Kameny protests the verdict in the following letter to Herbert Kalin, a DC probation officer.*

APRIL 24, 1975

Dear Mr. Kalin:

I write as a long-time resident, citizen, and voter in the District of Columbia. Because of my demonstrated and well-known concern for consideration of personal freedom and civil liberties, I was recently appointed by Mayor Washington to be a member of the D.C. Commission on Human Rights, although I do not write here in that or in any other official capacity, but solely in my capacity as a private citizen.

I am writing to you in respect to the forthcoming sentencing proceeding for Mr. James John Proferes, in the matter of his having shown the film *Deep Throat* at his theater, and in which I understand you must make recommendations. I have known Mr. Proferes personally for several years, and am familiar with various of his business enterprises. In my view and in that of many other citizens of the District of Columbia, he and his enterprises are contributing materially to the welfare of the District and its residents, and to the detriment of no one or of any community interest.

Unlike many people convicted of crimes, the acts of which Mr. Proferes was convicted cause no demonstrable harm to even one individual citizen, nor to any collective societal or community interest. Quite to the contrary, he brought pleasure, enjoyment, and harmless entertainment to large numbers of people, with no interference with the rights of anyone. There was not one single *victim* of any of Mr. Proferes' acts.

That he was able to show *Deep Throat* as a profitable business venture indicates that he was supplying a commodity or service desired by a sizeable number of citizens. Those citizens not desiring it, or offended by it, were free to stay away; it was not being forced upon them. That is what our American freedoms are all about.

Deep Throat, itself, is a delightful comedy, with a wry sense of humor. Unfortunately, some people in positions of authority in our government are quite incapable of thinking of sex and humor at the same time (except by degrading sex to the level of "dirty" jokes) and insist upon imposing their narrow, dour, joyless outlook upon everyone. I would be willing to venture a guess that were the facts of this case submitted to a vote of the citizens of the District of Columbia *NOT* (as it was to the jury) on the basis of the technical provisions of U.S. Supreme Court decisions or as an exercise in name-calling ("obscene"), but on the basis, simply and directly and pointedly, of whether or not the film should continue to be shown so that those wishing to see it could, and those not wishing to see it could stay away, the vote would be overwhelmingly in favor of showing it. . . .

The matter is wrapped up very nicely by noting that we are currently preparing to celebrate the Bicentennial of our country's birth certificate, the Declaration of Independence, which guarantees, as an *inalienable right* (not merely as a capriciously enjoyed privilege) the pursuit of happiness. That clearly means the *pursuit of the happiness* chosen by each citizen for himself (including the showing and viewing of *Deep Throat*), as long as those happinesses do not interfere with the pursuit by other citizens of their happinesses (and certainly the showing of *Deep Throat* interferes with *NO* one's pursuit of his happinesses). Thus the injection of a little bit of basic Americanism will resolve this whole matter in a way most favorable to Mr. Proferes (and thereby, to the entire District of Columbia).

In summary . . . I urge, along with many, many other District of Columbia citizens, that in view of the lack of demonstrable harm to anyone, individually or collectively, incident upon Mr. Proferes' actions, and in view of the fact that those actions provided many citizens with clearly demonstrable benefit (entertainment, enjoyment, pleasure, just-plain-fun), he can be given the absolute minimum penalty possible under law. We will all profit thereby, and no one will be harmed.

Sincerely yours,

Franklin E. Kameny

Kameny to Joseph Oglesby

On July 3, 1975, the U.S. Civil Service Commission announced new rules dictating that homosexuals may not be barred or fired from federal employment because of their sexuality. The change of rules did not apply to the FBI, the Foreign Service, or the CIA, all of which enjoyed separate employment systems, but they did hold for the rest of the federal government. As a long-time archenemy of the CSC, Kameny was delighted with the news, telling the Washington Post *that the change in rules marked "the successful conclusion of an 18 year battle on my part, which should never have commenced had the Civil Service Commission observed basic American practices from the beginning." The same* Post *article included quotations from two CSC spokesmen—Joseph Oglesby and Bacil Warren—and in the following letter*

Kameny ridicules and criticizes the quoted remarks. Warren had expressed doubt that the change in rules would result in a sudden influx of homosexuals into CSC jobs. "I think it will be gradual," he said.[15]

JULY 5, 1975

Dear Mr. Oglesby:

I write in response to your amazing and incredible remark . . . with respect to homosexuals employed in the federal civil service: "There's no question in anyone's mind that a few of them got through the door and a few of them are in service. I don't know who they are or where they are, but in a force as large as ours, there must be some."

I don't know whether that represents a truly astounding degree of naivete and ignorance of the facts on your part, or simply whether it is a propagandistic "window dressing" gesture, representing a continuation of the immoral, notoriously disgraceful, corrupt political expediency which has been the commission's primary motivation for some quarter-century for its squalid, un-American policy (now happily ended, seemingly) of excluding homosexual American citizens from participating in *OUR* government and in *OUR* civil service.

Whichever it may be, the facts are, of course, that the commission's (and, in fact, the entire government's) screening and detection processes are and always have been inherently ineffective. Some 10% of our population, men and women both, are homosexual; some 10% of our federal civil service employees (and of our security clearance holders and of our military personnel)—some quarter-million civil service employees—are and always have been homosexual, and always will be.

If a quarter-million is "a few of them," then you and I do not differ on this point. . . .

Your remark was very much the subject of humorous discussion, gibes, ridicule, and jocularity in the gay bars which I attended on the evening of July 4; there was hardly a person who had read the *Post* article who did not mention your absurd comment derisively. One person summarized the actual factual situation nicely when he said that if every homosexual presently employed by the federal civil service were to choose to stay home on the same workday, the entire government would grind to a halt. I tend to think that his remark was more likely to be factual than figurative. There ARE *lots* of us in civil service!

In any case, the matter is now moot. Mr. Warren's quoted remarks to the contrary . . . "great numbers" of homosexuals long ago entered the civil service, and will remain there, with the full protection of the newly issued regulations.

The commission's performance on this question of homosexuality over the past 25 years will redound to their permanent discredit and dishonor. One would think that instead of proclaiming, as you and Mr. Warren do, that the number of us in the federal service is small, and worrying lest it not remain so, your proper concern should be to try to make amends, and to try to diminish the stain and the blight upon the commission's reputation through the initiation of an effective affirmative action hiring quota program, to *raise* the percentage of homosexuals employed in the federal service to the level in the general population as quickly as possible if it is not already at that level, and to ensure that it remains there. That you do not do so is consistent with the commission's persistently low level of moral consciousness and of basic Americanism.

By right, we should be asking for reparations from the commission for 25 years of needless, immoral, infamous, notoriously disgraceful destruction of lives and careers, for the creation of untold amounts of human misery and suffering and untold numbers of human tragedies, for denying to our country the services of countless citizens capable of contributing much—all on the basis of supine and cowardly submission to bigotry (both internal and external to the commission), to public hysteria, and to corrupt political expediency. Certainly the consequences of the commission's anti-homosexual policies over the past quarter-century have been an unmitigated source of "aid and comfort" to the enemies of our country, in the truest sense of the definition of treason found in Section 3 of Article III of the Constitution. You people have a great deal for which to beg forgiveness; the hesitant, queasy, frightened statements of the kind quoted, by you and Mr. Warren, hardly seem to be the way to go about it.

In conclusion, it will do no harm, I think, to reiterate to you my publicly made remarks . . . that we *will* be as fully open about our homosexuality as heterosexual employees are about their heterosexuality. Those of us who may wish to do so *will* "shout our homosexuality from the rooftops" (as innumerable heterosexual employees, over the years, have done, figuratively, in respect to their heterosexuality) in the expectation of no adverse action whatever. That *other* people may consider our homosexuality and our homosexual conduct as "shameful in nature" and may "talk of it in a scornful manner" and that there may be "public censure" is *their* problem, and will *remain* THEIR problem.[16] We will not allow this commission to make it *our* problem. *WE* do not intend to suffer because *they* are narrow-minded or are bigots (or both); that was what was responsible for the past 25 years. Be warned that that is where the battleground lies, if you people are foolish enough to make it so.

We are proud of our homosexuality and of our homosexual conduct; it is not shameful, no matter who or how many may term it so. What is shameful is the bigotry of the homophobic bigots who consider homosexuality shameful. What is shameful and notoriously disgraceful is the past policy of the commission in submitting supinely to bigotry and excluding us, and any future efforts to exclude us. That is "where it's at" and that is where it's going to stay!

Gay *IS* Good! . . .

Sincerely yours,
Franklin E. Kameny

Kameny to Barbara Gittings

Just four weeks after the CSC announced its rule change, Kameny learned that the Department of Defense had decided not to continue its appeal in the security clearance case of Otis Tabler Jr., a gay man formerly employed as a computer scientist in a private industry holding U.S. Air Force contracts. In 1974, Kameny had forced the Department of Defense's Industrial Security Clearance Review Office to conduct Tabler's hearing in public, marking the first publicly open security-clearance hearing in the department's history. That hearing also resulted in a landmark ruling when field-board examiner Richard Farr granted Tabler a secret-level industrial security clearance. Farr wrote that "the applicant's sexual activities are not likely to subject him to coercion, influence or pressure which may cause him to take action contrary to the national interest." Farr also concluded that "the applicant successfully has rebutted any inference that his variant sexual practices tend to show that he is not reliable or trustworthy."[17]

Once again, Kameny also refers to the brewing case of Leonard Matlovich. On May 20, 1975, Matlovich received notice that the Air Force was taking steps to discharge him and that proceedings against him would soon begin. Matlovich's commander at Langley Air Force Base was recommending a general discharge—which was less favorable than an honorable discharge. In consultation with Kameny, Addleston, and military lawyer Captain Jon Larson Jaenicke, Matlovich requested a hearing before a board of officers. This dramatic challenge to the military's ban went public when the New York Times *published an article on Matlovich on May 26, 1975.*[18] *By the time Kameny wrote the following letter, anti-gay thugs had shot at Matlovich's home.*

JULY 31, 1975

Dear Barbara:

Enclosed, as you requested, are a number of copies of the CSC news release, announcing the change in their regulations.

Enclosed, also, is a copy of the changed regulations themselves, and a copy of the guidelines, issued at the same time.

Other news: This morning the Pentagon phoned and surrendered on the security clearance issue. They withdrew their pending administrative appeal in the Tabler case (the much-publicized California case, which we won at the examiner level last winter, after a hearing last summer), thus providing for issuance of the clearance. That will also mean a sizable chunk of back pay for Tabler.

They have also instituted a *de facto* change in their policies with respect to issuance of clearances to gays, so there would be very few such cases (if any) hereafter. There will be no formal, physically issued change in regulation or policy, as with the Civil Service Commission.

Thus the war which I started informally about 1959, and which you and I fought together in its more formal stages starting about 1965, has now ended with victory. I feel very contented. I hope you do; you deserve to.

As always, there is "dust to settle"—pending cases to resolve and close out, etc., which will take a little time. And the bounds and outer limits of the policy change will have to be ascertained over a period of time. But, apparently, the basic victory is ours.

That means that two of the three federal government battles going on since time almost immemorial are now won. The one remaining is of the armed services.

For me personally, that means that, once the few remaining cases are closed out, I will, at last, be able to turn my attention to other things. The endless, relentless procession of civil service and security cases over the years has consumed a vast bulk of my time, at expense of almost everything else. That would now seem to be over—or rapidly ending—and I will have to start to redirect my energies and efforts.

That's all for the present. Will be in touch with you soon. My best to Kay.

Frank

Kameny sent similar news to his mother but emphasized his bitter disappointment that rather than congratulating him on his work, she ignored it and focused on what she took to be his neglect of her during her recent hospitalization.

Another victory. On Thursday morning the Pentagon phoned me and surrendered. They have withdrawn their appeal in the major security clearance case which I have been fighting for years (the one which took me to California just a year ago) and are issuing the clearance, totally on OUR terms; AND they are reversing their traditional policy of denial of security clearance to gays. . . .

During the past month, I've been receiving a torrent of congratulations and applause from one end of the country to the other—phone calls, letters, personal comments—for my victory over the Civil Service Commission.

I have brought the very government of the United States to its knees, after a long and difficult fight. I sent you news of it in early July. I have not had a single word even of acknowledgement from you.

What did I get? A squalid little family squabble based upon . . . a compulsive need of yours to feel rejected, whether or not the facts warrant it.[19]

Kameny to Sergeant Leonard Matlovich

Kameny refers here to a New York Times Magazine *article penned by historian Martin Duberman of the City University of New York. By the time the article appeared, a three-member panel of the Air Force Administrative Discharge Board had recommended that Matlovich receive a general discharge from the Air Force.[20] In a last-ditch effort, Matlovich appealed the decision to Air Force Secretary John McLucas. The secretary denied the appeal, and Matlovich received a general discharge by the end of October.[21]*

NOVEMBER 9, 1975

Dear Lenny:

As you may have seen, Marty Duberman's article on your hearing appeared in the magazine Section of today's *New York Times*. Although I don't think the article was as good as it might have been . . . the article raises another matter of considerable direct importance (I predict) to you—a matter which I raised with you once before.

You are once again quoted as taking the position that "he admits that had he the choice—he would rather be straight."[22]

Now, you are obviously free to take whatever position you wish on that matter. I would not presume to dictate your feelings to you, even had I the power to do so. I do point out certain things, however.

If that IS, in fact, your view, then prepare yourself to defend it. I guarantee you that you WILL be attacked for holding that view by gays and gay groups wherever you go, as deeply and harmfully undercutting the gay movement. Further, you will find that it will place you at a severe disadvantage in making logical, compelling, persuasive pro-gay and pro-gay-rights arguments with *non*-gay audiences.

So IF that IS your position, you should be doing some VERY careful thinking as to the best way to present it and to defend it.

On the other hand: If it is NOT your view, then I urge—STRONGLY—an IMMEDIATE letter-to-the-editors . . . disavowing that as your position. The letter should be phrased firmly, and absolutely unequivocally and unambiguously, with an absolute minimum of words, phrases and clauses of modification and reservation which could conceivably be interpreted (i.e., misinterpreted) as evasion or "weasel words," because gays everywhere will be reading, intensely critically, what you say in this respect.

If you wish, I'll be more than pleased to discuss this with you at some early date of our mutual convenience.

While I'm writing, I'd like, just briefly, to follow up on some items raised in our conversation of yesterday. . . .

Your issue is a narrow and very specific one. Effective pursuit of the issues and causes raised by that issue—gays and the military—requires funding. So do you, individually. Fundraising is always more effective when narrowed to specifics, rather than when broadened with generalities. You have specificity; make the most of it. . . .

Incidentally, as a side comment, I would suggest that you don't make your endeavors too crassly commercial. . . . The measure of your success is your ability to persuade the public of the justness and the rightness of your (our) causes. Obviously certain purely practical considerations must be considered. We discussed those to some extent on the phone yesterday. Certainly your out-of-pocket expenses should ALWAYS be reimbursed to you (unless, in particular instances you choose to make an exception). Certainly the flow of funds into the support of the cause, as finally formulated, should always be kept in mind. But there is a difference between a commercial, in-it-for-the-profit performer, and someone fighting for a cause. Don't lose sight of those differences.

Keep in mind the very harsh reality that fame is fleeting. You are riding high—and properly should be—on the crest of a wave of publicity created by the immediacy of your case, plus the fortunate publicity which it received in *The NY Times* and in *Time*, plus your own personal charisma. But those WILL fade—and with a quickness which you may find traumatic. I would suggest that you make the maximum possible use of the fame, and of the time it persists, to grind your own particular axe, both in terms of pleading the cause and raising the finds. Naturally, that will rub off onto support for the general gay cause, and that is all to the good, but—I feel—your major effort should remain somewhat narrowed. . . .

Cordially,
Frank

Matlovich did not accept Kameny's advice about following up with a letter to the editor.

Kameny to Robert Spitzer

Kameny lights into his former ally Robert Spitzer after reading the psychiatrist's apparent admission that he considered homosexuality a condition representing "less than optimal functioning."[23]

NOVEMBER 18, 1975

Dear Bob:

In your letter printed in the *Psychiatric News* in the October 15, 1975 issue, you state your belief that homosexuality represents "less than optimal functioning."

I challenge you to provide even a shred of scientifically meaningful or scientifically valid support for the statement. I defy you to do so. I am convinced that neither you nor anyone else can. Your statement is a mere subjective value judgment, with no scientific or objective merit whatever. Frankly, I even defy you to justify your belief on a totally *non*-scientific, *subjective* basis of *any* kind.

Now that we are no longer pathological, we are merely "non-optimal," still defined, as before, not by science, but by moral, cultural, societal, and theological value judgments, cloaked and camouflaged in the language of science, but with none of the substance of science. You people are compulsively obsessed with the need to keep us—at any and all costs, and by any ruse or device that you can devise—in second-class status. I strongly urge that those sharing in your belief that homosexuality represents non-optimal functioning get the psychotherapy—and take the courses in logic and rigorous thinking—that you obviously so badly need. Certainly the thinking processes involved in the formulation of this belief are very far from optimal.

This illustrates, once again, the confused, non-optimal thinking which afflicts so much of psychiatry.

Sincerely,
Franklin E. Kameny

In 2003 Robert Spitzer authored a study suggesting reparative therapy could work for individuals highly motivated to change. He based his conclusions on interviews he conducted with individuals from centers performing reparative therapy. Critics slammed Spitzer's study for, among other things, relying so heavily on the (potentially faulty) memories of participants and the use of individuals who were politically active in the ex-gay movement. Nine years later, Spitzer offered a public apology to the gay community, stating that his conclusions about reparative therapy were not based on solid data.[24]

Kameny to the Editors of the *Catholic Standard*

DC City Councilman Arrington Dixon had recently introduced a bill designed to legalize same-sex marriage, and at the end of October Kameny began to organize a lobbying campaign in support of the bill.[25] *The Catholic Diocese of Washington was not pleased, and an editorial in its newsletter characterized the legislative attempt as an "abomination" and a "scandal." Public officials "are intelligent people; they must know better," the editorial stated. "It is equally scandalous that they have to be reminded to do their duty in a matter so sacred to the people they are called to serve."*[26]

DECEMBER 4, 1975

Gentlemen:

. . . Your intemperate diatribe, masquerading as a reasoned editorial, does not improve the situation; it presents not one single argument in logic or in reason. It is simply an anti-homosexual polemic, intended to keep us and our relationships in a second-class status which we have no intention of accepting. . . .

Your only effort at formulation of any kind of rationale at all for your opposition was an appeal to tradition. That is no argument. Anything which has existed long enough to have become traditional has existed long enough to have become at least potentially outmoded and obsolete and archaic, and is automatically suspect on that account alone. That is certainly true of the narrow, restrictive concept of marriage which you invoke.

Marriage is a close, stable, lasting, loving relationship between *two people*, based upon deep mutual affection. It is, by nature, the union of *two persons.* It need not involve procreation or the possibility of procreation (middle-aged, heterosexual couples, beyond child-bearing age, enter into completely valid, uncontroversial, recognized, legally and religiously formalized marriages). Homosexual marriages meet *every* criterion of a marriage. No reasonable person can do other than to equate homosexual and heterosexual marriages. A homosexual marriage is no more—or less—*artificial* a legal entity than a heterosexual marriage; they are precisely on par.

. . . We do not seek such marriages out of any sense of, or need for compassion. We neither need nor want your patronizing, demeaning, degrading compassion. We consider our homosexuality a blessing, not a misfortune; we look upon our relationships as fully on par with yours: and we consider *you* unfortunate in not being able to enter into our form of marriage. . . .

Our love is just as important to us as yours is to you, and our relationships are just as important and as sacred to us as yours are to you. Our marriages are just as sacred to us as yours are to you. . . . *WE* are fully competent to decide *for ourselves* how we will be best served by *our* public officials, and what interests are sacred to us whom they serve. *WE* (not you) will tell them how we will be best served, and as voters with full voting rights and full first-class citizenship, we will be listened to, on precise equality with all other citizens and community viewpoints, and as a segment of the community fully on par with other segments. . . .

. . . We will not allow OUR city to relegate us and our relationships to second-class status to "the back of the bus."

. . . You are converting Christianity from a warm religion of love into a vicious cult of hatred, for which I am sure that you will be punished in due course and through all eternity. I suggest that you give some careful thought to what Christianity is all about. If we judge from your editorial, you have not the faintest idea.

Your editorial is a disgrace to Christianity; it is a disgrace to the Church; it is a disgrace to our country and to everything for which our country and Americanism stand; it is a disgrace to our city; it is a disgrace to humanity and humankind. It is immorality embodied.

It is your editorial which is the true scandal!!

I recommend that in light of the true love and affection attendant upon homosexual marriages, you read John 14:34—"A new commandment I give unto you, that ye love one another; as I have loved you, that ye also love one another." That is all that is needed to validate *any* marriage.

I suggest, as well, that you note the clear applicability, by analogy, of Romans 14:1—"I know, and am persuaded by the Lord Jesus, that there is nothing unclean of itself; but to him that esteemeth anything to be unclean, to him it is unclean."

And Titus 1:15—"Unto the pure all things are pure; but unto them that are defiled and unbelieving is nothing pure." Under which it is you, defiled and with unclean minds, who are at fault, not we, who are clean and pure love (fully as clean and fully as pure as your heterosexual love; sexual activity itself, of course, whether homosexual or heterosexual, is neither unclean nor impure). . . .

Gay IS Good!!

Sincerely yours,
Franklin E. Kameny. Ph.D.

Conclusion

Jefferson, Lincoln, King—and Kameny

Franklin Kameny continued to type gay rights letters after 1975, of course. Just around the corner lay Anita Bryant's anti-gay rights campaign in Florida, the rise of the Moral Majority, the eruption of the AIDS crisis, and so many more threats demanding his attention and action. His old enemies continued to raise their heads after 1975, too—Charles Socarides and his negative diagnosis of homosexuality, the U.S. military and its discrimination against gay men and lesbians, and the "loony left" in the gay rights movement.[1] True to form, Kameny felt the need to respond to all of them. Here are a few excerpts from the many letters in his ongoing battle for first-class citizenship after 1975.

To the editor of *Newsweek*, October 24, 1976:

> To quote Socarides on homosexuality and homosexuals . . . is like quoting Hitler on Jews or the Grand Dragon of the Ku Klux Klan on Blacks.[2]

To conservative columnist George Will, no date (May 1977):

> Whether or not composed by you, the headline of your article as printed says: "How Far Out of the Closet?" I tell you, flatly and totally unequivocally, that that answer is: ALL the way out!![3]

On Anita Bryant and her campaign against a gay rights ordinance in Dade County, Florida, May 22, 1977:

> Anita Bryant and her crew of bigots are no different from the Ku Klux Klan, the Nazis, or any other hate group.

She has perverted Christianity from the warm religion of love created by Jesus, into a vicious cult of hatred; she will burn in hell throughout all eternity for that, and for what she is doing in Dade County. . . .

Gay is Good; Gay is Godly. Anita Bryant is neither.

Gay is moral; Gay is decent. Anita Bryant is neither.

Gay is Christian; Gay is American. Anita Bryant is neither.[4]

To Barbara Gittings on the new language used to characterize gays and the gay rights movement, March 7, 1981:

Gay/lesbian or lesbian/gay is as bad as lesbian and gay. It has the same elements of conceptual redundancy and slovenness and of political divisiveness as does gay and lesbian.[5]

To the Conservative Caucus, a lobbying organization founded by Howard Phillips, June 16, 1981:

I was under the impression that a central tenet of the classical conservative position was the reduction of the impact of government upon the life of the individual citizen, and reduction of governmental interference with the citizen in the conduct of his or her life—"best government is least government" and "get government off the backs of the people."

Yet in your full-page advertisement in the *Washington Post* for Tuesday, June 16, you take the position that the American Bar Association's 1973 urging of the legislatures of the several states to repeal all laws which classify as criminal conduct any form of non-commercial sexual conduct between consenting adults in private, saving only those portions which protect minors or public decorum, is not a conservative position.

Apparently you are suggesting that governmental surveillance of and intrusion into the very bedrooms of the citizenry, and the imposition of criminal penalties for nonconformity to YOUR moral code, is the conservative position.

Your carefully adjusted mask has just slipped, revealing the naked totalitarian, repressive fascism which is your real approach!![6]

To the editor of *Newsweek*, November 16, 1981, in response to a column penned by Reverend Jerry Falwell of the Moral Majority:

Falwell believes in fascism; he should have the intellectual honesty to say so.[7]

To William Casey, director of the Central Intelligence Agency, March 27, 1983:

> I am informed by one of my confidential intelligence sources that not long ago (probably in December 1982) at an intelligence meeting, you were overheard to make an informal remark to the effect that: "We (the CIA) are under strong and increasing pressure to admit homosexuals. It'll never happen. . . ."
>
> Mr. Casey—Why are you so adamant on this issue? It does neither you nor the Agency any credit, but redounds to your everlasting discredit, dishonor, disgrace, and shame. And certainly it serves only to damage our intelligence effort and our country.[8]

To Admiral James Watkins, chairman of the Presidential Commission on the Human Immune Deficiency Epidemic, April 8, 1988:

> The medical research establishment is taking a leisurely, "business-as-usual" approach. They need to be blasted out of their rut. This IS an emergency, and emergency tactics need to be utilized.
>
> FDA Commissioner Young is quoted as saying that he expects approvals of release of ten experimental AIDS drugs "in the next couple of years."[9] ONLY ten in the next couple of years!! There should be 100 in the next couple of months! What the hell is wrong here? Yet again, this is just simply obscene. . . .
>
> In summary: The solution to the AIDS epidemic lies ONLY in therapeutic prevention and cure (or, perhaps, effective insulin/diabetes-type control): vaccines and drugs. Therefore some form of a centralized 'Manhattan Project' type structure, involving a carefully crafted coordination of public and private investigation, backed up by appropriate statutory empowerment and, where necessary, legal 'teeth'—and generously funded—MUST be established, on a "crash basis," to function thereafter on a crash basis.[10]

To Elizabeth Rindskopf, general counsel of the Central Intelligence Agency, June 14, 1990:

> While NSA's handling of gay-related cases has been far from perfect, at least it has been possible to deal with that agency, on a rational basis, with issuance and retention of clearances and qualification for employment for gay people.

On the other hand, I have repeatedly referred to the CIA as the NSA's "redneck country cousin." Over the years, the CIA has become justifiably infamous as one of the last "holdout" agencies (unfortunately, not quite the only one) in the entire federal government, with respect to security clearances for gay people (and, collaterally, with respect to employment).

In numerous public utterances . . . I have characterized the CIA as "nutty" on this issue. The facts clearly bear me out. The CIA IS nutty on this issue.[11]

To the Executive Committee and the Platform Committee of the March on Washington, June 3, 1992:

My reaction as a gay person, on reading the platform/action statement put forward in connection with the forthcoming gay march on Washington, is that: Our march has been successfully hijacked by the "loony left." Our march has ceased to be a march for gay rights and liberation, and has become a March for a National Utopia, or a March for a Perfect Society, or a March Against All Oppression—or a Cure for Everything March. It has ceased to be a gay-related march at all. It is an Inchoate Hodge-Podge March.

It is all very nice to oppose all forms of discrimination, as set out in detail in the final clause of the introduction to the platform, but it is not for that that I, for one, am marching.[12] . . .

I am astonished that the environment was left out. How did that happen? And what about the animal rights nuts? They're not there either. Amazing! Everyone else got in!! . . .

I long ago learned that: If you try to do everything, you end up doing nothing well.[13]

To columnist David Hackworth, June 23, 1993:

I write in response to your article in the June 28, 1993 issue of *Newsweek* magazine, in which you say: "I'm so personally opposed to having gays openly serve in the military that I wrote Clinton and told him that if it happens he should be impeached."[14]

It is not President Clinton who should be impeached if the ban is lifted, it is you and people like you who support the ban who should be indicted, tried, convicted, and hanged for treason for giving aid and comfort to our enemies by attempting to degrade the quality of our armed services from excellent to mediocre, through the exclusion of gays, who, collectively, have a proven record of superior military performance and service.[15]

To journalist Tom Brokaw after the publication of his book titled *Boom! Voices of the Sixties*, November 26, 2007:[16]

Mr. Brokaw, you have "de-gayed" the entire decade. "Voices of the Sixties"??? One does not hear even one single gay voice in your book. The silence is complete and deafening. . . .

The whole thing is deeply insulting. . . . For shame, for shame, for shame. You owe an abject public apology to the entire gay community. I demand it; we expect it.

Gay is Good. You are not.[17]

Kameny also enjoyed the sweetness of victory in the years following 1975, and perhaps no occasion was sweeter than August 4, 1995, when President Clinton signed an executive order prohibiting the federal government from denying security clearances to homosexuals on the sole basis of their sexual orientation. "What this represents is the next step," Kameny stated at the time. "The Government has gone beyond simply ceasing to be a hostile and vicious adversary and has now become an ally."[18] Almost three years later, President Clinton also signed an executive order prohibiting discrimination on grounds of sexual orientation in the competitive service of the federal civilian workforce.

Now an ally, the government began to acknowledge and celebrate Kameny as one of the founding fathers of the U.S. gay rights movement. In 2005 it asked him for permission to display some of the pickets he and others had carried in their 1965 protests at the White House and other federal buildings. Kameny obliged, writing about the delivery of the pickets in an e-mail to his good friends Barbara Gittings and Kay Lahusen. (Yes, he had made the transition from a manual typewriter to an electronic typewriter to e-mail.)

I am not often at a loss for words, but as today sinks in, I find myself approaching that.

This afternoon, Charles Francis and I went to the Smithsonian Institution's American History Museum, on the Mall, to effect formal delivery to them of 13 of our 1960's picketing signs, selected from those visible in photographs of those demonstrations.

A small group of the very top brass of the Smithsonian was there.

The signs are now part of a large collection of American historical relics, presently in storage as the museum undergoes extensive renovation before being re-opened to the public in 2008.

That collection includes . . . the small portable desk which Thomas Jefferson used for writing the first drafts of the Declaration of Independence, and the inkwells used by President Lincoln in the writing of the Emancipation Proclamation, and memorabilia from Martin Luther King's 1963 march on Washington (I was there).

What do you think the reaction would have been, in 1965, as a bunch of us scrambled around on our hands and knees on the poster-board littered floor of someone's apartment, lettering those signs, had we been told that our work products would be honored and eventually displayed along with relics of Jefferson and Lincoln and King? It still hasn't fully sunk in.

We have arrived to an extent far beyond anything conceivable in our wildest dreams of back then and even much later. There is still very much to be done, our enemies have organized, the battles ahead will be formidable, and some of the losses will be bitter, but the symbolism of victory of this afternoon is truly impressive beyond words. Jefferson, Lincoln, King—and Kameny and Gittings and company. Let the nutty fundamentalists gainsay that!!! We have arrived irreversibly.

A year later, the Library of Congress became home to more than 70,000 items from Kameny's personal archives—his gay rights letters, speeches, photographs, even bumper stickers. Kameny enjoyed a standing ovation at the ceremony marking the arrival of his papers. "Things have changed," he said. "How they have changed. I am honored and proud that that is so."[19]

With his new status as a legendary patriotic American, Kameny found himself standing next to President Obama when he signed an administrative memorandum extending select benefits to same-sex partners of federal employees—yet another victorious moment for the man who had once pleaded for the Kennedy administration just to acknowledge his letters.

Several weeks later, John Berry, director of the Office of Personnel Management (OPM), offered Kameny a written apology for the way that the government had treated him in 1957. "In what we know today was a shameful action," Berry wrote, "the United States Civil Service Commission in 1957 upheld your dismissal from your job solely on the basis of your sexual orientation."

> With the fervent passion of a true patriot, you did not resign yourself to your fate or quietly endure this wrong. With courage and strength, you fought back. And so today, I am writing to advise you that this policy, which was at odds with the bedrock principles underlying the merit-based civil service, has been repudiated by the United States Government, due in large part to your determination and life's work, and to the thousands of Americans whose advocacy your words have inspired.
>
> Thus, the civil service laws, rules and regulations now provide that it is illegal to discriminate against federal employees or applicants based on matters not related to their ability to perform their jobs, including their sexual orientation.
>
> Furthermore, I am happy to inform you that the Memorandum signed by President Obama on June 17, 2009 directs the Office of Personnel Management—the successor to the CSC—to issue guidance to all executive departments and agencies regarding their obligations to comply with these laws, rules, and regulations.
>
> And by virtue of the authority vested in me as Director of the Office of Personnel Management, it is my duty and great pleasure to inform you that I am adding my support, along with that of many other past Directors, for the repudiation of the reasoning of the 1957 finding by the United States Civil Service Commission to dismiss you from your job solely on the basis of your sexual orientation. Please accept our apology for the consequences of the previous policy of the United States government, and please accept the gratitude and appreciation of the United States Office of Personnel Management for the work you have done to fight discrimination and protect the merit-based civil service system.[20]

Berry read the letter aloud at a ceremony in which Kameny also received the OPM's Theodore Roosevelt Award for his defense of merit-based principles. As the audience erupted in applause, giving him a standing ovation, Kameny shouted: "Apology accepted!"

The last major transformation Kameny witnessed occurred in December 2010, when President Obama signed legislation repealing "Don't Ask, Don't Tell" (DADT), a law permitting gays to serve in the military as long as they hid their sexuality. Proudly displaying his World War II medal, Kameny was in the audience at the signing ceremony. He later recounted his own enlistment in the Army. "They asked, and I didn't tell," he stated, "and I resented for 67 years that I had to lie."[21]

Franklin Edward Kameny died at home at the age of eighty-six on October 11, 2011. He had experienced heart problems before that night, and the medical examiner listed the cause of death as arteriosclerotic cardiovascular disease.[22] Less than a year earlier, Yale Law professor William Eskridge Jr. had said, "Frank Kameny was the Rosa Parks and the Martin Luther King and the Thurgood Marshall of the gay rights movement."[23]

Like Parks, King, and Marshall, Kameny was a demonstrator for decency, a civil and human rights leader, and a legal activist pleading for equal justice under law. At last, though, Frank Kameny was just himself— a visionary and tactical genius relentlessly dedicated to the proposition that gays, like other minorities in the United States, deserve the rights and privileges of first-class citizenship right here and now. From 1957 until his death, Kameny devoted his life to making U.S. society enshrine that proposition in federal laws and regulations. And his dedication paid off: With help from countless others in the gay and lesbian rights movement, Franklin Kameny helped to change society, just as he promised he would.

Notes

▶

Location of Letters

▶

Index

Notes

Introduction: Making Society Change

1. Kameny to Rae Kameny, June 3, 1972, Frank Kameny Papers (FKP), Library of Congress, Washington, DC, box 1. I will use simply "Kameny" when citing his letters.

2. Bart Barnes, "D.C. Will No Longer Prosecute Private, Adult Homosexual Acts," *Washington Post*, May 31, 1972.

3. B. D. Cohen, "Soliciting Statute Overturned," *Washington Post*, June 2, 1972.

4. Kameny to Rae Kameny, June 3, 1972.

5. Kameny to Rae Kameny, June 3, 1972.

6. The language here reflects Kameny's choice of words. He did not use the phrase "gay rights" very often in his early letters.

7. Kameny to Jack Nichols, April 24, 1975, FKP, box 7.

8. Some of the main groups at this point included the Mattachine Society (founded by Harry Hay in Los Angeles in 1951) and its various branches; ONE, Inc. (founded in Los Angeles in 1952); and the Daughters of Bilitis (a lesbian organization founded in San Francisco in 1955). For an excellent account of the early homophile movement, see John D'Emilio, *Sexual Politics, Sexual Communities: The Making of a Homosexual Minority in the United States* (Chicago: University of Chicago Press, 1983).

9. For just a few examples, see Michael Bronski, *A Queer History of the United States* (Boston: Beacon Press, 2011); Leigh Ann Wheeler, *How Sex Became a Civil Liberty* (New York: Oxford University Press, 2013); Craig M. Loftin, *Masked Voices: Gay Men and Lesbians in Cold War America* (Albany, State University of New York Press, 2012); *Letters to One: Gay and Lesbian Voices from the 1950s and 1960s*, edited by Craig M. Loftin (Albany: State University of New York Press, 2012); C. Todd White, *Pre-Gay LA: A Social History of the Movement for Homosexual Rights* (Urbana: University of Illinois Press, 2009); Martin Meeker, *Contacts Desired: Gay and Lesbian Communications and Community* (Chicago: University of Chicago Press, 2006); and Marcia M. Gallo, *Different Daughters: A History of the Daughters of Bilitis and the Rise of the Lesbian Rights Movement* (New York: Seal Press, 2006).

10. "You are as shrill in writing as you are in person." This was part of Lieutenant General Daniel Graham's written reply to Kameny's earlier letter defending gays against

337

the charge that they are security risks. See Daniel Graham to Kameny, July 17, 1989, FKP, box 129.

11. Kameny to Rae Kameny, August 2, 1975, FKP, box 1.

12. For this point and several others in this section, I am relying on "Frank Kameny," in *The Gay Crusaders*, ed. Kay Lahusen and Randy Wicker (New York: Arno Press, 1975), 89–134. I am also drawing from early autobiographical statements penned by Kameny (FKP, box 43).

13. "Frank Kameny," *Gay Crusaders*, 90.

14. Lou Chibbaro Jr., "The Scientific Activist," *Washington Blade*, July 12, 2002, http://www.washingtonblade.com/2002/07/12/the-scientific-activist/.

15. In a 2003 interview, Kameny spoke of "some experiences with a very close friend of mine who, in the end, was not gay, back when we were camp counselors, and . . . we were 15 or 16." See "Interview with Franklin Kameny (1/8/2003)," http://lcweb2.loc.gov /diglib/vhp/story/loc.natlib.afc2001001.05208/transcript?ID=mv0001. The interview was conducted by Lara Ballard, the coordinator of the Veterans History Project of the American Veterans for Equal Rights.

16. "Gay Is Good: How Frank Kameny Changed the Face of America," interview by Will O'Bryan, *Metro Weekly*, October 5, 2006, http://www.metroweekly.com /feature/?ak=2341.

17. "Interview with Franklin Kameny (1/8/2003)."

18. "Interview with Franklin Kameny [1/8/2003]."

19. Chibbaro Jr., "The Scientific Activist," July 12, 2002.

20. "Frank Kameny," *Gay Crusaders*, 91.

21. "Gay Is Good," *Metro Weekly*, October 5, 2006.

22. "Frank Kameny," *The Gay Crusaders*, 92.

23. "Gay Is Good," *Metro Weekly*, October 5, 2006.

24. "Frank Kameny," *The Gay Crusaders*, 91.

25. "Gay Is Good," *Metro Weekly*, October 5, 2006.

26. Kameny to Commanding Officer, Army Map Service, December 20, 1957, FKP, box 43.

27. Kameny, "Summary of Relevant Facts Regarding My Case Against the Government," unpublished document, no date, included in letter from Kameny to Penelope L. Wright, December 16, 1958, FKP, box 43. Kameny's summary did not include all of the important details of the arrest—for example, his physical response to his partner in crime. Kameny later stated that he had touched the stranger. "Where I made the mistake is that I responded," he eventually conceded. See Joyce Murdoch and Deb Price, *Courting Justice: Gay Men and Lesbians v. the Supreme Court* (New York: Basic Books, 2001), 51.

28. Kameny, "Summary of Relevant Facts," no date.

29. Kameny, "Summary of Relevant Facts," no date. For Kameny's explanation of the AMS and CSC charges, see Frank Kameny to The Mattachine Society, Inc. (New York), May 5, 1960, FKP, box 44.

30. David K. Johnson, *The Lavender Scare: The Cold War Persecution of Gays and Lesbians in the Federal Government* (Chicago: University of Chicago Press, 2004), 9.

31. See full document at presidency.ucsb.edu; quoted, too, in Johnson, *The Lavender Scare*, 123.

32. Kameny to Neil McElroy, June 1, 1959, FKP, box 42.

33. John W. Hanes Jr., to Kameny, November 7, 1960, FKP, box 42.

34. Kameny to Harris Ellsworth, no date (Fall 1958), FKP, box 42.

35. His visit to ONE headquarters is reported in Murdoch and Price, *Courting Justice: Gay Men and Lesbians v. the Supreme Court*, 54. I am indebted to Murdoch and Price for their account of Kameny's court battles, as well as to William Eskridge Jr., "January 27, 1961: The Birth of Gaylegal Equality Arguments," *NYU Annual Survey of American Law*, http://www.law.nyu.edu.

36. Kameny to *ONE* magazine, August 27, 1960, ONE Inc. Records, ONE Archives, Los Angeles, California, box 29.

37. All following quotations from the petition come from *Franklin Edward Kameny v. Wilber M. Brucker, Secretary of the Army et al.,* Respondents, Petition for Writ of Certiorari, no. 676, U.S. Supreme Court, 1960. Page numbers of the quotations will be cited parenthetically. Kameny's copy of this petition can be found in FKP, unprocessed files, accession number 24084.

38. On the historical context of Kameny's claim that homosexuals constituted an oppressed minority, for example, see Johnson's *The Lavender Scare*: "On the West Coast Harry Hay had articulated a similar philosophy in founding the Mattachine Society. And Buell Dwight Huggins of Mattachine's Washington chapter had likened the federal treatment of gays and lesbians to racial discrimination" (18). So, too, did Donald Webster Cory, *The Homosexual in America: A Subjective Approach* (New York: Greenberg, 1951). Cory was the pen name of Edward Sagarin. This introduction will discuss Cory at a later point.

39. For helpful details of the denial, see Murdoch and Price, *Courting Justice*, 58–59.

40. Kameny to John F. Kennedy, May 15, 1961, White House Central Name File, Kameny, Franklin, box 1418, folder: Kameny, Franklin, John F. Kennedy Papers [JFKP], John F. Kennedy Presidential Library, Boston, Massachusetts.

41. His 1968 resume shows that he worked at five laboratories in the ten-year period following his debarment from federal employment. He did not work this entire ten-year period, either; he was often unemployed, relying on financial gifts and loans from family members and friends. The resume can be found in FKP, unprocessed files, accession number 24084.

42. Eric Marcus, *Making Gay History: The Half-Century Fight for Lesbian and Gay Equal Rights* (New York: HarperCollins, 2002; 1992), 81.

43. Marcus, *Making Gay History*, 81.

44. James T. Sears, "Jack Nichols," in *Before Stonewall: Activists for Gay and Lesbian Rights in Historical Context,* ed. Vern L. Bullough(New York: Harrington Park Press, 2002), 223.

45. Cory, *The Homosexual in America*, 3, 13–14; quoted in part in D'Emilio, *Sexual Politics, Sexual Communities*, 33. Appendix A in Cory's book even included copy of a CSC letter on the federal employment of homosexuals (169).

46. Cory, *The Homosexual in America*, 46.

47. Marcus, *Making Gay History*, 82.

48. "Constitution of the Mattachine Society of Washington," excerpt included in Kameny to President John F. Kennedy, August 28, 1962, White House Central Name File, box 1418, JFKP. Kameny included this excerpt in August 28 mailings to many top officials in the U.S. government. See, too, "Statement of Purpose," No date [1962], FKP, box 85.

49. See, for example, Franklin Kameny, "Civil Liberties: A Progress Report," in *Great Speeches on Gay Rights*, ed. James Daley (New York: Dover Publications, 2010), 33.

50. See Kameny to L. Craig Schoonmaker, October 9, 1972, FKP, box 9: "I am fundamentally integrationist in regard to homosexuals for a number of reasons, among which are that it is the only practical course; that most gays want it that way, and I am not going to be prescriptive for my fellow gays; and I am very far from convinced of its unworkability."

51. Kameny coined this phrase in 1968. See chapter 6.

52. I am not, of course, suggesting that writing letters was the only way he sought to change society. As the letters themselves indicate, Kameny relied on a wide variety of methods to transform social attitudes and practices. Still, I believe that he devoted most of his early years to typing thousands of letters in support of gay rights.

1. "The Winds of Change Are Blowing": 1958–1962

1. Kameny, "Summary of Relevant Facts Regarding My Case Against the Government," unpublished document, no date, included in Letter from Kameny to Penelope L. Wright, December 16, 1958, FKP, box 43. Kameny's summary did not include all the important details of the arrest. He later stated that he had touched the stranger. "Where I made the mistake is that I responded," he eventually conceded. See Joyce Murdoch and Deb Price, *Courting Justice: Gay Men and Lesbians v. the Supreme Court* (New York: Basic Books, 2001), 51.

2. Kameny to The United States Civil Service Commission, February 14, 1958, FKP, box 43.

3. For more on Kameny and the industrial security clearance program, see William N. Eskridge Jr., *Gaylaw: Challenging the Apartheid of the Closet* (Cambridge, MA: Harvard University Press, 1999), 70.

4. "Testing Civilian Loyalty," *Washington Post*, October 30, 1958.

5. Kameny's letters to President Eisenhower and his staff have been removed from their files at the Eisenhower Library. But synopses of the letters can be found in White House Central Files, Alphabetical File, box 1639, folder "KAM," Dwight D. Eisenhower Presidential Library, Abilene, Kansas. Kameny wrote the president and his staff several letters. Staff members Sherman Adams and Rocco Siciliano informed Kameny that they could not assist him.

6. Kameny also continued to pursue the "information" that the CSC investigators allegedly had in their possession. As he later recalled this:

> I then decided that if I were going to be hanged, I was going to know what I was being hanged for. I went back to the CSC, saw one of the lesser officials in the Investigations Division, had him get out my record, and demanded to know what evidence they had against me, and upon what they based their charge of immoral conduct. I was told that this could not be revealed, since they had to protect their informants. I asked the official who his superior in this matter was, and where his office was located. I went to see the superior, my record following behind me. This procedure was repeated—and again—and again, until I had worked myself up almost to the top of the investigations division. Finally, I was informed that, aside from the San Francisco incident and the "tone and tenor, but not the gist and substance" of my remarks to the CSC interrogators, there was *nothing* in the record. This official (and others to whom I spoke later) was much upset by my expressed attitude that my personal, out-of-working-hours life was of no proper concern to the CSC—or any employer (Kameny to the Mattachine Society, Inc., May 5, 1960, FKP, box 43).

7. Kameny is referring here to a statement provided for his case by Benjamin Karpman, a psychotherapist at St. Elizabeth's Hospital in Washington, DC, and an expert on homosexuality from a psychiatric perspective. Kameny's letters suggest that the statement assured the government that he, although a homosexual, posed no security risk to the U.S. government.

8. John W. Hanes Jr. to Kameny, November 7, 1960, FKP, box 42.

9. John F. Kennedy, "The New Frontier," July 15, 1960. This is the acceptance speech Kennedy delivered at the 1960 Democratic convention. For a copy of the text, see http://www.jfklibrary.org/Asset-Viewer/Archives/JFKPOF-137-003.aspx.

10. Inaugural Address, January 20, 1961, Washington, DC, jfklibrary.org.

11. Remarks at GWU upon Receiving an Honorary Degree, May 3, 1961, Washington, DC, jfklibrary.gov.

12. State of the Union Address, January 30, 1961, Washington, DC, jfklibrary.gov.

13. This is an abridged quotation. For the full quotation, see Thomas Jefferson to Samuel Kercheval, July 12, 1816, Thomas Jefferson Papers, loc.gov.

14. Kameny complained about the lack of response in Kameny to Kennedy, July 15, 1961, White House Central Name File, Kameny, Franklin, box 1418, JFKP, John F.

Kennedy Presidential Library (JFKP JFKL); and in Kameny to Kennedy, March 5, 1963, White House Central Name File, Kameny, Franklin, box 1418, JFKP, JFKL.

15. See "Macy Urges Saving of Manpower," *Washington Post*, May 13, 1961.

16. See Jerry Kluttz, "The Federal Diary: Civil Service Chief Outlines Objectives to Personnel Heads," *Washington Post*, June 2, 1961.

17. John Macy Jr. to Kameny, June 22, 1961, FKP, box 41.

18. SAC, Washington Field Office, to FBI Director, August 8, 1961, the Mattachine Society File, FBI Papers (FBIP), Federal Bureau of Investigation, Washington, DC.

19. On Kameny and the ACLU, see my explanation following Kameny to Admiral Laurence Frost, August 28, 1962, in this chapter.

20. The Supreme Court ruled in *NAACP v. Alabama* 357 US 449 (1958) that it was unconstitutional for Alabama to demand that the NAACP make public its membership lists of branches within the state. The demand to publicize the lists was ruled to be in violation of the NAACP's right to freedom of association.

21. Mr. DeLoach to D. C. Morrell, July 9, 1962, the Mattachine Society File, FBIP: see also FKP, box 82.

22. Kameny to Hugo Black, July 18, 1962, FKP, box 81.

23. Frances M. Lamb to Kameny, July 25, 1962, FKP, box 81.

24. George Sokolsky, "These Days: 20th Century Morals," Syndicated by King Features, Inc., published in *Washington Post*, July 27, 1962. Kameny mentioned the column in a letter to Randy Wicker, August 21, 1962, Randy Wicker Papers, New York Public Library, New York, New York, box 1.

25. Joe B. Parker to J. Edgar Hoover, August 21, 1962, the Mattachine Society File, FBIP. Parker sent the copy "for your information."

26. Kameny to Randy Wicker, August 21, 1962, Randy Wicker Papers, New York Public Library, New York, New York, box 1.

27. Osgood Caruthers, "War Threat Seen: Security Agency Men Decry Flights Over Alien Airspace," *New York Times*, September 7, 1960.

28. "Walter Critical on 2 Code Clerks," *New York Times*, September 7, 1960.

29. Julius and Ethel Rosenberg were executed in 1953 after being convicted on charges of espionage; prosecutors alleged the two had stolen classified atomic bomb information from the United States. Morton Sobell was convicted with the Rosenbergs, and served eighteen years in prison for a conviction related to non-atomic spying.

30. Kameny to Robert McNamara, August 28, 1962, FKP, box 82.

31. Kameny to Demophil Center, November 22, 1962, FKP, box 81.

32. Kameny to The Mattachine Society, San Francisco, November 22, 1962, FKP, box 82.

33. Paul Johnson to Kameny, no date, FKP, accessed at kamenypapers.org.

34. Charles Chamberlain to Kameny, August 30, 1962, FKP; accessed at kamenypapers.org.

35. Joe M. Kilgore to J. Edgar Hoover, September 17, 1962, the Mattachine Society File, FBIP.

36. SAC, Baltimore, to J. Edgar Hoover, October 5, 1962, the Mattachine Society File, FBIP.

37. Kameny to the Mattachine Society, San Francisco, November 22, 1962.

38. Kameny to Demophil Center, November 22, 1962, FKP, box 81.

39. Kameny to the American Civil Liberties Union, May 15, 1962, FKP, box 75.

40. Kameny to Demophil Center, November 22, 1962, FKP, box 81.

2. "Genocide Is the Word That Must Be Used": 1963–1964

1. "Johnson Spurs Job Equality for All Minorities," *Washington Post*, May 2, 1963.

2. The Mattachine Society of Washington, "Discrimination Against the Employment of Homosexuals," February 28, 1963, Presented to the Subcommittee on Employment, D.C. Advisory Committee of the U.S. Civil Rights Commission, FKP, box 86. This statement also landed on Hoover's desk at the FBI; see SAC, WFO to J. Edgar Hoover, August 7, 1963, the Mattachine Society File, FBIP.

3. The picketing is referred to in Ernest A. Lotito, "Picketing of White House Old but Aimless Practice," *Washington Post*, October 27, 1963: "Picketers have asked Presidents to bring back prohibition, end the draft, give homosexuals better treatment."

4. "Johnson Spurs Job Equality for All Minorities," *Washington Post*, May 2, 1963.

5. Kameny to Lewis Hershey, March 31, 1963, FKP, box 81.

6. Kameny to Lewis Hershey, June 4, 1963, FKP, box 81.

7. SAC, Washington Field Office, to J. Edgar Hoover, June 10, 1963, the Mattachine Society File, FBIP.

8. Dan Wakefield, "The Gay Crusader," *Nugget* (June 1963): 51.

9. See Robert F. Kennedy Jr., "Address by Honorable Robert F. Kennedy, Attorney General of the United States," Meeting of the University of South Carolina Chapter, American Association of University Professors, Columbia, South Carolina, April 25, 1963, justice.gov/ag/rfkspeeches.

10. For similar parallels drawn between Negroes and homosexuals, see Kameny to Paul Welch of *Life* magazine, April 11, 1964, FKP, box 7.

11. Charlie Hayden to Kameny, July 1963, FKP, box 81. Hayden legally changed his name to Randy Wicker in the early 1960s.

12. J. Edgar Hoover to Robert F. Kennedy, September 11, 1963, the Mattachine Society File, FBIP.

13. J. Edgar Hoover to Robert F. Kennedy, September 5, 1963, the Mattachine Society File, FBIP.

14. One of the men reported being called a "queer" and a "cocksucker." The affidavits of the arrested men are located in FKP, unprocessed files, accession number 24084.

15. "Gay Is Good: How Frank Kameny Changed the Face of America," interview by Will O'Bryan, *Metro Weekly*, October 5, 2006, http://www.metroweekly.com/feature/?ak=2341.

16. Bruce Schuyler to the Editors of *One*, August 23, 1963, FKP, box 82.

17. Milton Berliner, "Group Defends Collecting Role," *Washington Daily News*, August 9, 1963; clipping in the Mattachine Society File, FBIP.

18. Bruce Schuyler to the editors of *One*, August 23, 1963.

19. The National Capital Area Civil Liberties Union sent about 100 telegrams to members of the House in an effort to defeat the bill ("Fundraising Bill Target for ACLU," *Washington Post*, March 9, 1964), and a *Post* editorial denounced the bill as "something of a paragon among bad bills" ("Legislating Morality," *Washington Post*, August 8, 1964).

20. The decision to march resulted partly from Jim Nichols's earlier work on the Mattachine Society's statement of purpose. Nichols insisted that the Society actively support other minority groups in their quest for civil rights.

21. The rules of the March did not target gays but called for all groups to march just for jobs and freedom—the goals of the March.

22. "How the Militant Movement Began: Frank Kameny, Interviewed by Amin Ghaziani," *Gay and Lesbian Review Worldwide* 19, no. 1, http://www.glreview.com/article.php?articleid=1054.

23. See J. Louis Campbell III, *Jack Nichols, Gay Pioneer: "Have You Heard My Message?"* (New York: Routledge, 2007), 74.

24. Edmund Bergler, *Homosexuality: Disease or Way of Life?* (New York: Collier Books, 1962), 26. This edition is the paperback version of the 1956 edition published by Hill & Wang, Inc.

25. See a helpful summary of Ellis's work as well as Bergler's in *Homosexuality and American Psychiatry: The Politics of Diagnosis* ed. Ronald Bayer (Princeton, NJ: Princeton University Press, 1987; repr., 1981), 67–100. Ellis described his assessment of homosexuality for the homosexual community in articles he penned for the *Mattachine Review*. See Ellis, "On the Cure of Homosexuality," *Mattachine Review*, November–December 1955; and "The Use of Psychotherapy with Homosexuals," *Mattachine Review*, February 1956.

26. Quoted in Marc Stein, *City of Sisterly and Brotherly Loves* (Chicago: University of Chicago Press, 2000), 200; for primary source, see Ken Travis, "Confidential Reporter Attends First Homosexual Convention in U.S. History," *Confidential*, January 1964, 26–27, 48–51. Stein's excellent account of the ECHO convention can be found in *City of Sisterly and Brotherly Loves*, 219–25.

27. Warren Adkins (Jack Nichols) to MSW Executive Board, October 14, 1963; quoted in John D'Emilio, *Sexual Politics, Sexual Communities*, 2nd ed. (Chicago: University of Chicago Press, 1988, [1983]), 163.

28. DeLoach to Jones, December 23, 1963, the Mattachine Society File, FBIP.

29. W. C. Sullivan to D. J. Brennan, December 24, 1963, the Mattachine Society File, FBIP; Hoover's undated notation appears at the bottom of this memorandum.

30. The Whitehall scene is nicely captured in Martin Duberman, *Stonewall* (New York: Dutton, 1993), 81–82.

31. M. A. Jones to Mr. DeLoach, August 7, 1964, the Mattachine File, FBIP.

32. M. A. Jones to Mr. DeLoach, October 9, 1964, the Mattachine File, FBIP.

33. Max Frankel, "President's Aide Quits on Report of Morals Case: Jenkins Was Arrested Last Week in Capital Y.M.C.A.—Is Sent to Hospital," *New York Times*, October 15, 1964.

34. Tom Wicker, "Jenkins Cleared of Security Slip in F.B.I. Report: No Evidence Is Uncovered that Ex-Presidential Aide Compromised Nation," *New York Times*, October 23, 1964.

35. Elsie Carper, "Shipley, Rauh Clash in Debate Over Walter Jenkins Case," *Washington Post*, October 21, 1964.

36. Kameny to Carl L. Shipley, October 25, 1964, FKP, box 128.

37. SAC, WFO to J. Edgar Hoover, October 29, 1964, the Mattachine File, FBIP.

38. "How to Handle a Federal Interrogation." Included with SAC, WFO to Hoover, October 29, 1964.

39. Kameny to R. Daniel Newhouse, No date (March 1973), FKP, box 42.

40. Kay Tobin and Randy Wicker, *The Gay Crusaders*, 101.

41. "Federal Job Corps to Exclude Youths Having Police Records," *New York Times*, November 21, 1964.

42. Sargent Shriver to Kameny, December 23, 1964, FKP, box 106.

43. Kameny to Kay Lahusen, November 12, 1965, Papers of Barbara Gittings and Kay Lahusen, box 6.

3. "We Have Outgrown the 'Closet-Queen' Type of Approach": 1965

1. Frederick Brown Harris, "About the YOU in You," *Washington Star*, March 7, 1965.

2. Irving Bieber et al., *Homosexuality: A Psychoanalytic Study of Male Homosexuals* (New York: Basic Books, 1962), 18. I am deeply indebted to Richard Bayer, *Homosexuality and American Psychiatry* (New York: Basic Books, 1981) for his work on Freud, Bieber, Evelyn Hooker, and many other psychiatrists at this point in U.S. history.

3. Bieber, *Homosexuality*, 173.

4. Bieber, *Homosexuality*, 220.

5. "Homosexuals Need Help," *Science News Letter*, February 13, 1965.

6. Evelyn Hooker, "The Adjustment of the Male Overt Homosexual," *Journal of Projective Techniques* 21 (1957): 18; quoted in Bayer, *Homosexuality and American Psychiatry*, 51.

7. Kameny to Barbara Gittings, March 13, 1965, Papers of Barbara Gittings and Kay Lahusen, box 6.

8. Kameny to Dick Leitsch, November 25, 1965, FKP, box 6.

9. David Goldberger to MSNY members, May 12, 1965; quoted in John D'Emilio, *Sexual Politics, Sexual Communities: The Making of a Homosexual Minority in the United States, 1940–1970* (Chicago: University of Chicago Press, 1983), 166. I am indebted to D'Emilio's excellent study for, among so many other things, its detailed description of this electoral battle.

10. Kameny to Barbara Gittings, May 30, 1965, Papers of Barbara Gittings and Kay Lahusen, box 6.

11. On April 15, *El Mundo*, the Castro government's newspaper in Havana, published an article stating that "no homosexual represents the movement, which is a movement of he-men." The article added that the government would use "revolutionary social hygiene" to undermine the "positions, procedures, and influence" of homosexuals in Cuba. According to reporter Paul Hoffman, "This was understood as a warning that homosexuals would be rounded up and sent to labor camps" ("Cuban Government Is Alarmed By Increase in Homosexuality," *New York Times*, April 16, 1965). The picketing in Washington, DC, was organized partly by Frank Kameny, and the picketing in New York was organized in part by Randy Wicker. For an oral history of this, see Marcus, *Making Gay History*, 105–6.

12. See Kameny to Del Shearer, June 14, 1965, FKP, box 9.

13. See News Bulletin of the Mattachine Society of Washington, No date, FKP, box 108.

14. Kameny is referring here to a lone activist named Warren Scarberry.

15. Warren D. Adkins (Jack Nichols) and Dennis Livingston, no title, *Eastern Mattachine Magazine*, June 1965, 6.

16. Adkins and Livingston, no title, June 1965, 7.

17. Kay Tobin and Randy Wicker, *The Gay Crusaders* (New York: Arno Press, 1975), 101.

18. Barbara Gittings, "The Earliest Gay Pickets: When, Where, Why." This one-page document can be found in various archived collections, but it is most easily accessible at http://vimeo.com/album/1891770.

19. David Eisenbach, *Gay Power: An American Revolution* (New York: Carroll & Graf, 2006), 40.

20. Kameny to Del Shearer, June 14, 1965.

21. This account draws from the historical sketch in Donald Kuhn, *The Church and the Homosexual: A Report on a Consultation* (San Francisco: Council on Religion and the Homosexual, 1964); and "Agenda for the Consultation on Church and the Homosexual," no date (1964), LGBT Religious Archives Network (lgbtran.org). This excellent website posts founding documents of the Council on Religion and the Homosexual (CRH).

22. "Clergy Shatter Another Taboo," *Christian Century*, December 23, 1964, 1581.

23. Kameny is referring to Edward Sagarin (Donald Webster Cory).

24. See Gloria Emerson, "Parliament to Study Reform of Penalties for Homosexuals," *New York Times*, May 13, 1965.

25. Anthony Lewis, "Commons Adopts a Bill to Modify Penalty for Adult Homosexuality," *New York Times*, July 5, 1967.

26. "Homosexuals Picket U.S. Civil Service Commission," *Eastern Mattachine*, August 1965, 22. See also Kameny to John Macy Jr., June 14, 1965, FKP, box 41; and Kameny to John Macy Jr., June 21, 1965, FKP, box 41.

27. Franklin E. Kameny, "Homosexuals Picket in Washington and Philadelphia," *Eastern Mattachine*, September and October 1965, 20. The woman was screaming "perverts," "criminals," and other negative words. See Kameny to Richard Schlegel, Jul 17, 1965, FKP, box 107.

28. Kameny, "Homosexuals Picket in Washington and Philadelphia," 21.

29. Kameny to John W. Macy Jr., August 15, 1965, FKP, box 41.

30. See footage of Rusk's remarks in the documentary *Before Stonewall* (produced by Robert Rosenberg, John Scagliotti, and Greta Schiller; directed by Greta Schiller; and codirected by Robert Rosenberg), First Run Features, 1984. Rusk had been informed about the pickets by the FBI. See SAC, WFO, to J. Edgar Hoover, August 26, 1965, the Mattachine File, FBIP.

31. Quoted in Tobin and Wicker, *The Gay Crusaders*, 103.

32. "Fads: The Short & the Long of It," *Time*, October 1, 1965.

33. Bill Mauldin to Kameny, October 11, 1965, FKP, box 7.

34. "Eastcoast Homophile Organization Demonstration in Front of White House, October 23, 1965," October 25, 1965, the Mattachine File, FBIP.

35. SAC, WFO, to J. Edgar Hoover, October 23, 1965, the Mattachine File, FBIP.

36. Tobin and Wicker, *The Gay Crusaders*, 104.

37. "*HOMOSEXUALS*," FKP, box 83.

38. John W. Sweeterman to Kameny, December 21, 1965, FKP, box 83.

39. Richard Conger, "Editorial," *ONE*, November 1965, 4.

4. "The Lunatic Fringe": 1966

1. Kameny sent a similar letter to *Washington Post* columnist Mary Haworth. See Kameny to Mary Haworth, April 9, 1966, FKP, box 128.

2. Kameny is quoting from her response to "Odd Man Out," which he read in her January 4, 1966 column printed in the *Washington Daily News*.

3. Ann Landers to Kameny, January 13, 1966, FKP, box 123.

4. Warren Scarberry, *American Homosexual Activities* 1, no. 1 (May 15, 1965): 3.

5. See SAC, WFO to J. Edgar Hoover, April 1, 1965, the Mattachine File, FBIP; and J. Edgar Hoover to Nicholas Katzenbach, April 2, 1965, the Mattachine File, FBIP.

6. See Warren Scarberry to President John F. Kennedy, March 18, 1963, White House Central Name File, box 2468, Folder "Scarb-Scarbor," JFKPL: "In June of 1962, I found my room mate [*sic*] to be a security risk. Being that he was a government employee, and I knowing the government policy concerning Homosexuality, I reported him to the F.B.I. though he is my best friend, who in turn reported it to the Department of Commerce where he is employed." Scarberry wrote the president asking for help evidently because he believed that the FBI "now has me down on their records as being Homosexual because I reported my room mate."

7. Macy is quoting the document submitted by MSW and drafted by Kameny ("Federal Employment of Homosexual American Citizens," November 15, 1965, 17, FKP, box 42). For a summary of the statement that MSW provided to CSC, see "Summary of MSW Statement to Civil Service Commission," *The Homosexual Citizen: News of Civil Liberties and Social Rights for Homosexuals*, May 1966, 8.

8. Rae Kameny to Kameny, February 4, 1966, FKP, unprocessed files, accession no. 24084.

9. Michael Francis Itkin to Kameny, June 29, 1966, FKP, box 6.

10. "The Homosexual," episode of *FYI*, WTVJ, Miami, Florida, April 1966.

5. "We Are People; We Are Not Specimens or Inanimate Objects": 1967

1. Michael Schofield, *Sociological Aspects of Homosexuality: A Comparative Study of Three Types of Homosexuals* (Boston: Little, Brown, 1965).

2. Kameny is suggesting that Wicker tend to Bieber's belief that it was problematic for the federal government to characterize all homosexuals as security threats.

3. Warren D. Adkins (Jack Nichols), "The Washington-Baltimore TV Circuit," *The Homosexual Citizen* (May 1967): 6–7.

4. Kameny to Robert A. Martin Jr., January 7, 1967, FKP, box 7.

5. Kameny to Robert A. Martin Jr., February 27, 1966, FKP, box 7

6. Kameny to Robert A. Martin Jr., February 26, 1967, FKP, box7.

7. Franklin E. Kameny and Barbara Gittings to All Homophile Organizations and Others Interested, no date, FKP, box 57.

8. Carl T. Rowan to Kameny, FKP, May 22, 1967, FKP, box 128.

9. Jean M. White, "Center to Treat Homosexuals Urged," *Washington Post*, September 25, 1967.

10. Drew Pearson, "Drew Pearson Says: Gov. Reagan Faces His First Acid Test; Homosexuals Discovered in His Office; His Staff Consider Themselves Certain to Serve in White House," October 30, 1967, Dell-McClure Syndicate; access at American Universities Library, Special Collections, Washington, DC.

11. Julius Duscha, "Reagan Says 'There Is No Truth' to Report of Homosexual Aides," *Washington Post*, November 1, 1967.

6. "Gay Is Good": 1968

1. Richard Harwood, "J. Edgar Hoover: A Librarian with a Lifetime Lease," *Washington Post*, February 25, 1968.

2. The Beatles' "All You Need Is Love" had peaked at number 1 on the record charts in the United States in the previous July.

3. Hal Call was part of a team that took over the Mattachine Society after founder Henry Hay lost his leading role in 1953. Far less militant than Hay, whose radical politics favored the creation of a homosexual minority with its own culture and ethic, Call favored a stance that would accommodate gays to existing social institutions and assist established psychologists and scientific organizations in their study of homosexuality (see John D'Emilio, *Sexual Politics, Sexual Communities*, 81). The result of relying on established psychologists is that Call and others were reluctant to adopt Kameny's firebrand approach to drawing from gay experience to conclude that homosexuality is a personal and social good.

4. John Stuart Mill, *On Liberty* (New York: Longmans, Green, and Co., 1913), 3.

5. William Sloane Coffin Jr., "Civil Disobedience, the Draft and the War," *Christianity and Crisis*, February 5, 1968.

6. Abe Fortas, *Concerning Dissent and Civil Disobedience* (New York: Signet Books, 1968), 18.

7. Randy Wicker to Kameny, October 2, 1968, FKP, box 10.

8. Marin Weil and Paul W. Valentine, "Dissenting Priests Warned by O'Boyle," *Washington Post*, September 3, 1968.

7. "Without Our Demonstrations . . . Stonewall Would Not Have Happened": 1969

1. "Legalized Prostitution," *Washington Star*, January 10, 1969.

2. Martin Hoffman, *The Gay World* (New York: Basic Books, 1968).

3. Gene Damon, "Lesbiana," *Ladder*, December 1968–January 1969, 34–35.

4. Barbara Grier to Kameny, February 14, 1969, FKP, box 4.

5. Kameny to the Editor, *Playboy*, March 1969, 46. Kameny used the letter to criticize behavior therapy designed to transform gays into heterosexuals and to announce that "gay is good."

6. Chapter 2 discusses the case of Bruce Scott.

7. *Scott v. Macy et al.*, 402 F.2d 644 (1968).

8. "The Homosexual Patient," *Medical World News*, March 14, 1969, 40.

9. "The Homosexual Patient," 41.

10. "Nixon on Smut," *Washington Star*, May 6, 1969.

11. See comments by Ray "Sylvia Lee" Rivera in Eric Marcus, *Making Gay History*, 127.

12. Martin Duberman, *Stonewall* (New York: Dutton, 1993), 210.

13. Kameny to Craig Rodwell, July 11, 1969; quoted in Toby Marotta, *The Politics of Homosexuality: How Lesbians and Gay Men Have Made Themselves a Political and Social Force in Modern America* (Boston: Houghton Mifflin Company, 1981), 165.

14. See Eisenbach, *Gay Power*, 108.

15. Duberman, *Stonewall*, 211.

16. *Gay Pioneers.* Documentary coproduced by WHYY and Equality Forum. Directed by Glenn Holston, Produced by Malcolm Lazin, Emily Topper, and Trudi Brown, 2004.

17. Dal McIntyre, "National Homophile Conference to Meet in Houston," *Los Angeles Advocate*, August 1969.

18. Foster Gunnison Jr. to Kameny, July 31, 1969, FKP, box 5.

19. Dick Leitsch to Barbara Gittings, June 24, 1969, FKP, box 6.

20. Carolyn Hagner Shaw, "Modern Manners: Lack of Respect Is Unpardonable," *Washington Star*, October 5, 1969.

21. See "Hostile Crowd Dispersed Near Sheridan Square," *New York Times*, July 3, 1969.

22. Marcus, *Making Gay History*, 133–34.

23. Marcus, *Making Gay History*, 136.

24. John Marchi was the Republican nominee, and Mario Procaccino the Democratic nominee, in the 1969 mayoral race in New York City.

25. Kameny is referring to the National Homophile Clearing House. Founded in 1966, the NHCH published a newsletter informing the homophile movement of news, organizations, and events across the country. Copies of the newsletter can be found in FKP, box 70.

26. Kameny is quoting from Barbara Grier to Kameny, October 23, 1969, FKP, box 4.

27. Barbara Grier to Kameny, October 31, 1969, FKP, box 4.

28. Nancy L. Ross, "Homosexual Revolution," *Washington Post*, October 25, 1969.

29. Kay Lahusen to Kameny, November 9, 1969, Papers of Barbara Gittings and Kay Lahusen, box 6.

30. Kay Lahusen to Kameny, November 9, 1969.

31. Kameny to Friends, Colleagues, and Others, December 1, 1969, Advocate file on Kameny, *ONE* archives.

8. "Psychiatry Is the Enemy Incarnate": 1970–1971

1. Dick Leitsch to Kameny, February 13, 1970, FKP, box 6.

2. Kameny to Foster Gunnison Jr., January 9, 1969, FKP, box 5.

3. See "The Homosexual: Newly Visible, Newly Understood," *Time*, October 31, 1969; and *The Same Sex: An Appraisal of Homosexuality*, ed. Ralph Weltge (Philadelphia: Pilgrim Press, 1969).

4. Kameny to Anthony Grey, May 6, 1970, FKP, box 4.

5. Kameny to Anthony Grey, May 6, 1970, FKP, box 4.

6. David Reuben, *Everything You Always Wanted to Know about Sex, But Were Afraid to Ask* (New York: David McKay Company, 1969), 181–82.

7. See Peter Tatchell, "Obituary: Martin Corbett," *Independent*, July 17, 1996.

8. See Lacey Fosburgh, "Thousands of Homosexuals Hold a Protest Rally in Central Park," *New York Times*, June 29, 1970. The "new pride" quotation comes from a speech delivered by Michael Brown, a founder of GLF in New York.

9. Tobin and Wicker, *The Gay Crusaders*. 105.

10. G. H. Rood to Kameny, February 25, 1971, FKP, box 49.

11. Bayer, *Homosexuality and American Psychiatry*, 96.

12. Quoted in Bayer, *Homosexuality and American Psychiatry*, 105.

13. Bayer, *Homosexuality and American Psychiatry*, 107.

14. "Fairness for Homosexuals," *Washington Post*, February 2, 1971.

15. Sanford J. Ungar, "Suit Backs Jobs in Defense of 4 Homosexuals," *Washington Post*, January 27, 1971.

16. "Fairness for Homosexuals," *Washington Post*, February 2, 1971.

17. Kameny to Richard Farr, April 4, 1970, FKP, unprocessed files, accession number 24084.

18. Kameny to the Screening Board of the Industrial Security Clearance Review Division, Department of Defense, July 20, 1969, FKP, unprocessed files, accession number 24084.

19. Kameny thought at the time that he was also the first openly gay person ever to run for public office in the United States, but in 1961 Jose Sarria, a drag queen and homosexual rights activist, had run for the office of city supervisor in San Francisco. Sarria lost the election but garnered 6,000 votes along the way.

20. Bart Barnes, "Kameny Stresses Personal Freedom," *Washington Post*, March 13, 1971.

21. Kameny commented on home rule, welfare, the Vietnam War, crime, drugs, the freeway system, inflation, and many other issues. See his campaign documents in FKP, box 106, and at http://www.rainbowhistory.org/html/kameny_for_congress.html.

22. William L. Claiborne, "Candidate Seeks End to Homosexual Ban," *Washington Post*, March 10, 1971.

23. Bart Barnes, "Candidates Enter Stretch Drive in District Delegate Race," *Washington Post*, March 21, 1971.

24. See David Boldt, "Fauntroy Sweeps Delegate Race," *Washington Post*, March 24, 1971.

25. Kameny to Ira Lavey, November 25, 1972, FKP, box 1.

26. Kameny to Ian Dunn, April 4, 1971, FKP, box 3.

27. http://www.rainbowhistory.org/html/gayactivistsalliance.html.

28. http://www.rainbowhistory.org/html/gayactivistsalliance.html.

29. Dudley Clendinen and Adam Nagourney, *Out for Good: The Struggle to Build a Gay Rights Movement in America* (New York: Simon & Schuster, 1991), 124.

30. Nancy Tucker, "Campaign Center Opened by Kameny," *Advocate*, March 31–April 13, 1971.

31. Dick Leitsch to the Editor, *Advocate*, August 4–17, 1971.

32. Dick Michaels to Kameny, August 16, 1971, *ONE*.

33. See Thomas W. Lippman, "Judge Limits U.S. Check of Homosexuals," *Washington Post*, September 14 1971.

34. Kameny to Barbara Gittings, October 1, 1971, the Papers of Barbara Gittings and Kay Lahusen, box 6.

9. "The Ground Rules Have Changed": 1972

1. Robert Hampton to Kameny, June 15, 1972, FKP, box 41.

2. See M. Louise McBee to Dean Suthern Sims, November 11, 1971, lgbtcenter.uga.edu.

3. Carl Bernstein, "Homosexual Ousted from Marine Corps," *Washington Post*, March 22, 1972.

4. Kameny to John Chaffee, March 31, 1972, FKP, box 49. Chaffee did not reply, and Kameny followed up in December 1972 with new Navy Secretary John Warner (Kameny to John Warner, December 4, 1972, FKP, box 49). The Bureau of Navy Personnel offered Kameny the following reply: "The Chief of Naval Personnel is of the opinion that the present policy with respect to disposition of personnel who have been homosexually involved is sound and written in the best interest of the Unites States Navy" (D. H. Evans to Kameny, February 5, 1973, FKP, box 49).

5. Kameny to Anthony Mondello, May 15, 1972, FKP, box 41.

6. Bart Barnes, "D.C. Will No Longer Prosecute Private, Adult Homosexual Acts," *Washington Post*, May 31, 1972.

7. Irna Moore, "School Board Ends Bias to Homosexuals," *Washington Post*, May 24. 1972.

8. "'Gay Life' Teachers Approved," *Washington Afro-American*, May 28, 1972.

9. B. D. Cohen, "Soliciting Statute Overturned," *Washington Post*, June 2, 1972.

10. The sodomy law remained in the DC code.

11. Remarks of Franklin Kameny, Representing the National Coalition of Gay Organizations, Before Subcommittee II—Human Rights and Responsibilities of the Resolutions (Platform) Committee of the Republican National Committee, August 16, 1972, FKP, box 124.

12. *Democratic Party Platform of 1972*, July 10, 1972, http://www.presidency.ucsb.edu/ws/index.php?pid=29605.

13. Kameny's particular target was Joe Conwell of New York City. Conwell had complained about the plank in an earlier letter to *GAY*. See the full text of his letter in *GAY*, September 18, 1972.

14. McGovern issued a position paper on gay rights on February 2, 1972. For more on this and the killing of the gay rights plank, see Dudley Clendinen and Adam Nagourney, *Out for Good: The Struggle to Build a Gay Rights Movement in America* (New York: Simon & Schuster, 1999), 141.

15. Kameny to John Thomas, September 11, 1972, FKP, box 10.

16. "All About the New Sex Therapy," *Newsweek*, November 27, 1972, 72.

17. George Weinberg, *Society and the Healthy Homosexual* (New York: St. Martin's Press, 1972).

10. "VICTORY!!!! WE HAVE BEEN 'CURED'!": 1973

1. Kameny to Robert F. Drinan, April 13, 1974, FKP, box 3.

2. Kameny to Cade Ware, February 25, 1973, FKP, box 10.

3. Kameny is referring here to the founding of the Mattachine Society in California in 1951.

4. Boyce Rensberger, "Psychiatrists Review Stand on Homosexuals," *New York Times*, February 9, 1973. For a narrative of this meeting, see Bayer, *Homosexuality and American Psychiatry*, 115–21.

5. The individuals listed by Kameny in this sentence—psychiatrists Judd Marmor, Richard Green, and Robert Stoller, and GAA member Ronald Gold—all favored deleting homosexuality from the manual.

6. Kameny to Marvin Mandel, June 16, 1973, FKP, box 24.

7. Franklin E. Kameny, "Report from Honolulu," no date, FKP, box 10.

8. Burt sent a copy of his letter to the *Advocate*, which printed it in full ("Doctor Hits Landers' Labels," April 25, 1971), and Kameny is responding to this version.

9. Kameny to Johannes Werres, July 31, 1973, FKP, box 10.

10. Kameny is referring to the 1972 court stipulation stating that the DC sodomy law "does not apply and cannot be applied to private consensual acts involving adults." See Bart Barnes, "D.C. Will No Longer Prosecute Private, Adult Homosexual Acts," *Washington Post*, May 31, 1972.

11. Bill Gold, "It Goes Beyond 'Dirty Tricks,'" *Washington Post*, August 27 1973.

12. Again, Kameny errs here. See chapter 8.

13. Kameny had sent the same letter to Harold Titus Jr. and Frank Murphy.

14. American Psychiatric Association Press Release, December 15, 1973, FKP, box 122; quoted in Bayer, *Homosexuality and American Psychiatry*, 137.

15. American Psychiatric Association Press Release, December 15, 1973, FKP, box 122; quoted in Bayer, *Homosexuality and American Psychiatry*, 137.

16. Kameny to Ralph Temple, Dennis Flannery, and Chick Lister, December 16, 1973, FKP, box 122.

17. Kameny to Mary Howell, August 31, 1974, FKP, box 5.

18. This quotation is from founding member Howard Brown. See Dudley Clendinen and Adam Nagourney, *Out for Good: The Struggle to Build a Gay Rights Movement in America* (New York: Simon & Schuster, 1999), 195.

11. "So Much to Feel Satisfied, Content, Victorious, and Enthusiastic About": 1974

1. Ann Landers, "Love," syndicated by Field Enterprises, Inc., published in the *Washington Post*, January 9, 1973.

2. Ann Landers to Kameny, January 9, 1974, FKP, box 123.

3. Ann Landers, "No Cure," syndicated by Field Enterprises, Inc., published in the *Washington Post*, January 8, 1974.

4. Ann Landers, "Generalities," syndicated by Field Enterprises, Inc., published in the *Washington Post*, January 13, 1974.

5. At one point Kameny had begun to apply for membership in the high IQ society called Mensa but evidently became distracted by other pressing matters and never completed the application. See Kameny to Rae Kameny, January 10, 1973, FFP, box 1.

6. Kameny erred here. The number of those who had cast ballots was 10,091.

7. Kameny to Jack Nichols, April 13, 1974, FKP, box 7.

8. Kameny to Jerry V. Wilson, November 21, 1973, FKP, box 113.

9. See Ethel Payne, Commentary for *Spectrum*, CBS Radio Network, June 13, 1974, FKP, box 129.

10. William Safire, "Don't Slam the Closet Door," *New York Times*, April 18, 1974.

11. See "Text of President's Message," *New York Times*, August 13, 1974.

12. See "National Gay Task Force—White House Meeting—March 26, 1977," FKP, box 125.

13. Monroe Neuman, "The Bisexuals," *Washington Post*, September 1, 1974.

14. Kameny to Irwin Starr, no date (September 1974), FKP, box 123.

12. "I Have Brought the Very Government of the United States to Its Knees": 1975

1. Kameny to —, June 26, 1975, FKP, box 11.

2. "Frank Kameny," in Kay Lahusen and Randy Wicker, *Gay Crusaders*, 127.

3. Kameny to L. Craig Schoonmaker, February 3, 1973, box 9.

4. Larry of Greatest Is Love to Kameny, no date (1974, 1975), FKP, box 84.

5. See Kameny to David Jenkerson, January 19, 1975, FKP, box 6.

6. David Wilkerson, with John and Elizabeth Sherrill, *The Cross and the Switchblade* (New York: Berkeley, 1962).

7. David Wilkerson, *Jesus Person Maturity Manual* (Glendale: Regal Books Division, G/L Publications, 1971), 47.

8. Wilkerson, *Jesus Person Maturity Manual*, 49.

9. Jack Nichols to Dear Friends, February 22, 1975, FKP, box 7. Nichols wrote more about Clarke's death in "Lige Clarke (1942–1975)," in *Before Stonewall: Activists for Gay and Lesbian Rights in Historical Context*, ed. Vern L. Bullough (New York: Harrington Park Press, 2002), 239–40.

10. See letter content in Randy Shilts, *Conduct Unbecoming: Gays and Lesbians in the U.S. Military* (New York: St. Martin's Press, 1993), 203.

11. Shilts, *Conduct Unbecoming*, 204.

12. Kameny is referring partly to a VD clinic for gay men. In order to fund the clinic, the city council decided to stop funding the police department's vice squad.

13. Walter Washington, a Democrat, served as DC mayor from 1967–1975.

14. Leon Dash, "'Deep Throat' Ruled Obscene," *Washington Post*, March 28, 1975.

15. Stephen Green, "Homosexuals Win Job Right," *Washington Post*, July 4, 1975.

16. The new rules stated that "a person may be dismissed or found unfit for federal employment where the evidence establishes that such person's conduct affects job fitness." They added that such "infamous or notoriously disgraceful conduct" was "shameful in nature . . . and talked of in a scornful manner" ("Homosexuals Win Job Right," *Washington Post*, July 4, 1975).

17. "Homosexual Gets Security Clearance," *Washington Post*, February 2, 1975.

18. Lesley Oelsner, "Homosexual Is Fighting Military Ouster," *New York Times*, May 26, 1975.

19. Kameny to Rae Kameny, August 2, 1975, FKP, box 1.

20. Wayne King, "Homosexual G.I.'s Ouster Is Recommended by Panel," *New York Times*, September 20, 1975.

21. "Notes on People: Air Force Discharging Sergeant," *New York Times*, October 22, 1975.

22. Martin Duberman, "The Case of the Gay Sergeant: Leonard Matlovich's Strange Trial Betrayed a Profound Shift in American Attitudes—and Not Only Toward Sexuality," *New York Times Magazine*, November 9, 1975.

23. Robert Spitzer to the Editor of *Psychiatric News*, published in *Psychiatric News*, October 15, 1975. In the beginning of the letter, Spitzer criticizes Robert J. L. Waugh's definition of a mental disorder.

> According to Dr. Waugh, a mental disorder is any condition "which can prevent an individual from functioning at his or her own potential optimum level." To me such a definition defines mental health in utopian terms and thereby makes virtually all of humanity mentally ill. . . . Who decides what is optimal? What are the implications of labeling all homosexuals, introverts, vegetarians, and celibates as mentally ill just because many of us believe that these conditions represent less than *optimal* functioning.

24. See Benedict Carey, "Psychiatry Giant Sorry for Backing 'Cure,'" *New York Times*, May 18, 2012.

25. Kameny to *The Gay Blade*, October 27, 1975, FKP, box 113. Five years earlier Kameny had written Ronald Ziegler, press secretary to President Richard Nixon, after he had allegedly made disparaging remarks about gay marriage. See Kameny to Ronald Ziegler, no date (1970), FKP, box 69.

26. "A Public Scandal," *Catholic Standard*, July 17, 1975, 6.

Conclusion: Jefferson, Lincoln, King—and Kameny

1. "Loony left" is a phrase that Kameny used. See June 3, 1992, letter cited in the text of the conclusion.

2. Kameny to the editor of *Newsweek*, October 24, 1976, FKP, box 128. He refers to "Homosexuals and the Law," *Newsweek*, October 25, 1976.

3. Kameny to George Will, draft, no date (May 1977), FKP, box 128. Kameny refers to George Will, "How Far Out of the Closet?" *Newsweek*, May 30, 1977.

4. Kameny to Anita Bryant Poll, May 22, 1977, FKP, box 106. Bryant's efforts in Dade County succeeded; by a 2–1 margin, voters repealed the ordinance protecting homosexuals from discrimination in employment, housing, and public accommodations. See B. Drummond Ayres Jr., "Miami Votes 2 to 1 to Repeal Law Barring Bias Against Homosexuals," *New York Times*, June 8, 1977.

5. Kameny to Barbara Gittings, March 7, 1981, FKP, box 4.

6. Kameny to the Conservative Caucus, June 16, 1981, FKP, box 3. This year, 1981, saw Kameny shift to an electric typewriter. Kameny wrote a similar letter to Associate Justice William Rehnquist, suggesting that the justice's call for less government regulation in the lives of citizens conflicted "with your support of state laws regulating private, consensual sexual conduct among adults." See Kameny to Associate Justice William Rehnquist, April 29, 1981, FKP, box 43.

7. Kameny to the editor of *Newsweek*, November 16, 1981, FKP, box 128. Kameny refers to Jerry Falwell, "The Maligned Moral Majority," *Newsweek*, September 21, 1981.

8. Kameny to William Casey, March 27, 1983, FKP, unprocessed files, accession number 24084.

9. See Susan Okie, "AIDS Sufferers Buying Hope," *Washington Post*, April 2, 1988.

10. Kameny to Admiral James Watkins, April 8, 1988, FKP, box 122.

11. Kameny to CIA General Counsel Elizabeth Rindskopf, June 14, 1990, FKP, box 57. A year later Kameny wrote on security clearances in the FBI in a letter to FBI Director William Sessions. See Kameny to William Sessions, June 19, 1991, FKP, box 57.

12. The platform called for "an end to discrimination and violent oppression based on actual or perceived sexual orientation, identification, race, religion, identity, sex and gender expression, disability, age, class, AIDS/HIV infection." See "Platform of the 1993

March on Washington for Lesbian, Gay and Bi Equal Rights and Liberation," http://queerrhetoric.com/tag/march-on-washington-1993/.

13. Kameny to the Executive Committee and the Platform Committee of the March on Washington, June 3, 1992, FKP, box 107.

14. David H. Hackworth, "Clinton Can Undo Damage to the Military," *Newsweek*, June 28, 1993.

15. Kameny to David Hackworth, June 23, 1993, box 49. Hackworth replied that his extensive experience left him convinced that homosexuals in the military would "degrade combat readiness." "Appreciate your insight," he added, "but was all the hostility necessary?" See David Hackworth to Kameny, August 2, 1993, FKP, box 49.

16. Tom Brokaw, *Boom! Voices of the Sixties: Personal Reflections on the '60s and Today* (New York: Random House, 2007).

17. Kameny to Tom Brokaw, Gina Centrello, and Kate Medina, November 26, 2007, http://kamenypapers.org/boomleter.htm.

18. Todd S. Purdum, "Clinton Ends Ban on Security Clearance for Gay Workers," *New York Times*, August 5, 1995,

19. Gail Fineberg, "Activist and Archivist: Library Acquires Papers of Gay-Rights Pioneer," *Library of Congress Information Bulletin*, November 2006, http://loc.gov/loc/lcib/0611/kameny.html.

20. John Berry to Kameny, June 24, 2009, http://www.opm.gov/mediacenter/videos/OPM-Media-Center/Dr-Frank-Kameny.aspx. This OPM link includes video of a ceremony in which Berry reads from the original of his letter.

21. Sheryl Gay Stolberg, "Obama Signs Away 'Don't Ask, Don't Tell,'" *New York Times*, December 22, 2010.

22. Certificate of Death, Government of the District of Columbia, Department of Health, file date: November 2, 2011, FKP, unprocessed files, accession number 24084.

23. "Gay Rights Papers Shown at US Library," Associated Press, May 8, 2011. See copy of this article at www.kamenypapers.org.

Location of Letters

1. "The Winds of Change Are Blowing": 1958–1962

Kameny to CSC Chairman Harris Ellsworth, no date [1958], Frank Kameny Papers (FKP), Library of Congress, Washington, DC, box 44.

Kameny to Chief Justice Earl Warren and Associate Justices, April 6, 1959, FKP, box 43.

Kameny to Defense Secretary Neil McElroy, June 1, 1959, FKP, box 43.

Kameny to President John F. Kennedy, May 15, 1961, White House Central Name File, box 1418, folder: Kameny, Franklin, John F. Kennedy Presidential Library (JFKL), Boston, Massachusetts; and FKP, box 125.

Kameny to CSC Chairman John Macy Jr., June 5, 1961, FKP, box 41.

Kameny to Attorney General Robert F. Kennedy, June 28, 1962, FKP, box 82.

Kameny to the Director of the U.S. Public Health Service, August 3, 1962, FKP, box 83.

Kameny to Admiral Laurence Frost, August 28, 1962, FKP, box 81.

2. "Genocide Is the Word That Must Be Used": 1963–1964

Kameny to Vice President Lyndon B. Johnson, May 4, 1963, FKP, box 82.

Kameny to Theodore Sorensen, June 21, 1963, White House Central Name File, box 1418, folder: Kameny, Franklin; and FKP, box 83.

Kameny to Chief of Police Robert Murray, June 26, 1963, FKP, unprocessed files, accession number 24084.

Kameny to Randy Wicker (Charles Hayden Jr.), September 8, 1963, FKP, box 81.

Randy Wicker (Charles Hayden Jr.) to Kameny, no date (September 1963), FKP, box 81.

Kameny to Randy Wicker (Charles Hayden Jr.), September 25, 1963, FKP, box 81.

Kameny to Army Secretary Stephen Ailes, May 27, 1964, FKP, box 80.

Randy Wicker (Charles Hayden Jr.) to Kameny, no date [1964], FKP, box 10.

MSW to the FBI, October 1, 1964, FBI Papers, Mattachine File (FBIP), the Federal Bureau of Investigation, Washington, DC.

Kameny to the Editors of *Washington Daily News*, October 25, 1964, FKP, box 128.

Kameny to OEO Director Sargent Shriver, November 28, 1964, FKP, box 106.

3. "We Have Outgrown the 'Closet-Queen' Type of Approach": 1965

Kameny to U.S. Senate Chaplain Frederick Brown Harris, March 13, 1965, FKP, box 128.

Kameny to the Editors of *Science News Letter*, March 13, 1965, FKP, box 9.

Kameny to Edward Sagarin, April 7, 1965, FKP, box 9.

Kameny to Barbara Gittings, April 17 section of letter dated April 12, 1965, FKP, box 3.

Kameny to the Editors of *Christian Century*, April 18, 1965, FKP, box 128.

Kameny to the Daughters of Bilitis, June 8, 1965, FKP, box 69.

Kameny to Sir Cyril Osborne, June 20, 1965, FKP, box 4.

Kameny to Hendrik Ruitenbeck and Richard McConchie, July 7, 1965, FKP, box 107.

Kameny to Richard Inman, September 2, 1965, FKP, box 5.

Kameny to William Mauldin, September 29, 1965, FKP, box 7.

Kameny to President Lyndon B. Johnson, October 23, 1965, FKP, box 108.

Kameny to John Sweeterman, December 14, 1965, FKP, box 83.

Kameny to *ONE*, December 22, 1965, FKP, box 70.

4. "The Lunatic Fringe": 1966

Kameny to Richard Inman, January 5, 1966, FKP, box 5.

Kameny to Ann Landers, January 6, 1966, FKP, box 123.

Kameny to Larry Littlejohn, January 8, 1966, FKP, box 6.

Kameny to Robert Walker, February 10, 1966, FKP, box 10.

Kameny to Dick Leitsch, February 14, 1966, FKP, box 6.

John Macy Jr., to the Mattachine Society of Washington, February 25, 1966, FKP, box 41.

Kameny to Rae Kameny, March 2, 1966, FKP, unprocessed files, accession number 24084.

Kameny to Don Slater, April 3, 1966, FKP, box 9.

Kameny to Theodore Winston, May 1, 1966, FKP, box 2.

Kameny to Richard Inman, June 25, 1966, FKP, box 5.

Kameny to Evelyn Hooker, September 17, 1966, FKP, box 17.

Kameny to Harry Morgan, November 25, 1966, FKP, box 129.

5. "We Are People; We Are Not Specimens or Inanimate Objects": 1967

Kameny to Randy Wicker (Charles Hayden Jr.), January 21, 1967, FKP, box 10.

Kameny to Robert Martin Jr., May 11, 1967, FKP, box 7.

Kameny to Carl Rowan, May 17, 1967, FKP, box 128.

Kameny to Governor Claude Kirk, Jr., July 14, 1967, FKP, box 5.

Kameny to Nevin Richardson, August 31, 1967, FKP, unprocessed files, accession number 24084.

Kameny to the Editors of *Washington Post*, October 9, 1967, FKP, box 129.

Kameny to Drew Pearson, November 5, 1967, FKP, box 8.

6. "Gay Is Good": 1968

Kameny to the Editors of *Washington Post*, February 25, 1968, FKP, box 129.

Kameny to Robert Martin, Jr., May 8, 1968, FKP, box 7.

Kameny to Robert Martin, Jr., May 18, 1968, FKP, box 7.

Kameny to the Editors of *Washington Post*, June 3, 1968, FKP, box 129.

Kameny to Dick Leitsch, June 19, 1968, FKP, box 6.

Kameny to the Mattachine Society of New York, July 10, 1968, FKP, box 78.

Kameny to William Scanlon, July 27, 1968, FKP, box 45.

Kameny to Randy Wicker and Peter Ogren, August 23, 1968, FKP, box 10.

Kameny to the Editors of *Washington Daily News*, September 4, 1968, FKP, box 128.

7. "Without Our Demonstrations . . . Stonewall Would Not Have Happened": 1969

Kameny to the Editors of *Washington Star*, January 14, 1969, FKP, box 129.

Kameny to Barbara Grier (Gene Damon), February 5, 1969, FKP, box 4.

Kameny to Barbara Gittings, March 10, 1969, FKP, box 4.

Kameny to Barbara Grier, March 26, 1969, FKP, box 4.

Kameny to Barbara Grier, April 25, 1969, FKP, box 4.

Kameny to the Editors of *Medical World News*, April 28, 1969, FKP, box 123.

Kameny to Louis Crompton, May 29, 1969, FKP, box 2.

Kameny to Hobart Bissell, May 30, 1969, FKP, box 2.

Kameny to Arthur Warner, May 31, 1969, FKP, box 10.

Kameny to the Editors of *Washington Star*, June 1, 1969, FKP, box 129.

Kameny to Dick Michaels, July 20, 1969, FKP, box 1.

Kameny to Rona Barrett, July 25, 1969, FKP, box 81.

Kameny to Foster Gunnison Jr., August 1, 1969, FKP, box 127.

Kameny to Potential Draft Inductee, August 2, 1969, FKP, box 82.

Kameny to Foster Gunnison Jr., August 4, 1969, FKP, box 5.

Kameny to Dick Leitsch, September 4, 1969, FKP, box 6.

Kameny to Carolyn Hagner Shaw, October 6, 1969, FKP, box 128.

Kameny to Louis Crompton, October 17, 1969, FKP, box 2.

Kameny to Barbara Grier, October 26, 1969, FKP, box 4.

Kameny to Barbara Grier, October 27, 1969, FKP, box 4.

Anonymous to Kameny, no date (October 1969), FKP, box 136.

Kameny to the Editors of *Washington Post*, November 3, 1969, FKP, box 129.

Kameny to Foster Gunnison Jr., November 26, 1969, FKP, box 5.

8. "Psychiatry is the Enemy Incarnate": 1970–1971

Kameny to Dick Leitsch, March 16, 1970, FKP, box 6.

Kameny to Johnny Carson, May 26, 1970, FKP, box 128.

Kameny to Anthony Grey, July 3, 1970, FKP, box 4.

Kameny to Anonymous, October 20, 1970, FKP, box 2.

Kameny to Admiral Elmo Zumwalt Jr., December 23, 1970, FKP, box 49.

Kameny to Anthony Grey, January 12, 1971, FKP, box 4.

Kameny to President Richard Nixon, March 20, 1971, FKP, box 125.

Kameny to William Scanlon, August 5, 1971, FKP, box 45.

Kameny to the Editors of *Advocate*, August 8, 1971, FKP, box 1.

9. "The Ground Rules Have Changed": 1972

Kameny to CSC Chairman Robert Hampton, March 5, 1972, FKP, box 41.

Kameny to the Editors of *Red and Black*, March 9, 1972, FKP, box 7.

Kameny to CSC Chairman Robert Hampton, May 15, 1972, FKP, box 41.

Kameny to CSC Chairman Robert Hampton, CSC General Counsel Anthony Mondello, and CSC Personnel Investigations Director Kimball Johnson, May 28, 1972, FKP, unprocessed files, accession number 24084.

Kameny to Frank Caprio, May 30, 1972, FKP, box 122.

Kameny to Congressman Walter Fauntroy, May 30, 1972, FKP, box 111.

Kameny to Rae Kameny, June 3, 1972, FKP, box 1.

Kameny to *Gay*, September 28, 1972, FKP, box 128.

Kameny to Robert Saulsbury, November 26, 1972, FKP, box 9.

Kameny to Charles Socarides, December 1972, FKP, box 128.

10. "VICTORY!!!! WE HAVE BEEN 'CURED'!": 1973

Kameny to the Washington Area Peace Action Coalition, January 12, 1973, FKP, box 107.

Kameny to Cade Ware, February 25, 1973, FKP, box 10.

Kameny to Kay Lahusen, March 27, 1973, FKP, box 4.

Kameny to Governor Marvin Mandel, April 6, 1973, FKP, box 84.

Kameny to John LaMonthe, April 23, 1973, FKP, box 6.

Kameny to —, June 10, 1973, FKP, box 6.

Kameny to the Editors of *Advocate*, July 5, 1973, FKP, box 128.

Kameny to Harold Titus Jr., September 9, 1973, FKP, box 108.

Kameny to William Berzak, September 13, 1973, FKP, box 41.

Kameny to Bill Gold, September 14, 1973, FKP, box 128.

Kameny to —, October 13, 1973, FKP, box 6.

Kameny to Chief of Police Jerry Wilson, November 6, 1973, FKP, box 113.

Chief of Police Jerry Wilson to Kameny, November 8, 1973, FKP, box 113.

Kameny to Contributors to Honolulu Trip, December 15, 1973, FKP, box 122.

Kameny to Rae Kameny, December 23, 1973, FKP, box 1.

Kameny to NGTF Board of Directors and Staff, December 25, 1973, FKP, box 97.

11. "So Much to Feel Satisfied, Content, Victorious, and Enthusiastic About": 1974

Kameny to Ann Landers, January 3, 1974, FKP, box 123.

Kameny to Ann Landers, January 29, 1974, FKP, box 123.

Kameny to Edna Lavey, February 26, 1974, FKP, box 1.

Kameny to Barbara Gittings, April 8, 1974, FKP, box 122.

Kameny to Robert Henle, April 23, 1974, FKP, box 84.

Kameny to Ethel Payne, August 31, 1974, FKP, box 129.

Kameny to William Safire, no date (April 1974), FKP, box 130.

Kameny to John Paul Hudson, September 10, 1974, FKP, box 5.

Kameny to President Gerald Ford, September 17, 1974, box 125.

Kameny to Monroe Neuman, September 17, 1974, FKP, box 128.

Kameny to WMAL-TV, September 26, 1974, FKP, box 123.

Kameny to Phyllis Schlafly, November 2, 1974, FKP, unprocessed files, accession number 24084.

12. "I Have Brought the Very Government of the United States to Its Knees": 1975

Kameny to —, no date (1975), FKP, box 11.

Kameny to Greatest Is Love, January 3, 1975, FKP, box 84.

Kameny to Jack Nichols, April 24, 1975, FKP, box 7.

Kameny to Herbert Kalin, April 24, 1975, FKP, box 6.

Kameny to Joseph Oglesby, July 5, 1975, FKP, box 41.

Kameny to Barbara Gittings, July 31, 1975, FKP, box 4.

Kameny to Sergeant Leonard Matlovich, November 9, 1975, FKP, box 53.

Kameny to Robert Spitizer, November 18, 1975, FKP, box 122.

Kameny to the Editors of *Catholic Standard*, December 4, 1975, FKP, box 128.

Index

Italic page numbers denote illustrations.

Abzug, Bella, 299–300
ACLU. *See* American Civil Liberties
Union
Addleston, David, 310
Adkins, Warren. *See* Nichols, Jack
Advocate, 194, 234–36, 269–71
Advocates, The, 295–96
African Americans: civil rights struggles
for, comparisons with homosexuals,
14, 19, 38, 50; direct-action cam-
paigns by, in civil rights movement,
21; self-loathing behaviors of, 158
Ailes, Stephen, 72–74
Alabama v. NAACP, 41
Albany Trust, 221
Alcoholics Anonymous, 66
American Astronomical Society, 8
American Civil Liberties Union
(ACLU): challenge to CSC policies,
54; Franklin Kameny's appeals for
legal assistance, 24–27; MSW part-
nership with, 48; NCACLU, 48, 50,
59, 215; on sodomy laws in Washington, DC, 1
American Psychiatric Association
(APA), 2; Bieber referendum challenge to, 293–94; challenges to diag-
nosis criteria of, 71–72; Committee

on Nomenclature, 262; diagnosis of
homosexuality as mental disorder, 4,
16, 71–72; as enemy of homosexuals,
227; Gittings and, *178*; GLF and, 227;
Franklin Kameny at annual meeting
of, 266–68; removal of homosexuality from clinical disorders, 262–63,
267–68, 278–79, 281–83; Socarides
referendum challenge to, 293–94. *See
also* health-care services
AMS. *See* Army Map Service
Annual Reminder demonstration, 93,
101–2, 192–93
anti-Vietnam War movement, homophile movement and, 130–31
APA. *See* American Psychiatric
Association
Aquinas, Thomas, 254
Army Map Service (AMS): federal court
ruling for, 12; Franklin Kameny fired
from, 25–27; Franklin Kameny's
employment at, 9–10
Associated Press, 97
Association for the Advancement of
Behavior Therapy, 263
Association of Washington Priests, 166
aversion therapy, for homosexuality,
187–88

Barrett, Rona, 196–97

Bayer, Richard, 228

Belanger, Robert, 82

Bell, Alan, 262

Bergler, Edmund, 64–65

Berry, John, 332

Berzak, William, 275–76

Bieber, Irving, 138–40; on homosexuality as mental disorder, 85–88, 267; in "The Homosexual Patient," 187–88; referendum to challenge APA decision, 293–94

bisexuality, 156, 223, 298–99

Bissell, Hobart, 189, 192

Black, Hugo (Supreme Court Justice), 42

Black Panthers, GLF and, 221

B'nai B'rith Anti-Defamation League, 53

Boom! Voices of the Sixties (Brokaw), 330

brainwashed homosexuals, 142, 147

Brass, Ronald, 124–25

Brill, Henry, 262

Brokaw, Tom, 330

Bronski, Michael, 23

Bryant, Anita, 326–27, 356n4

Burt, Loren, 269–71

buttons. *See* gay-friendly buttons

Cain, Arthur, 66

Call, Hal, 156, 349n3

Caprio, Frank, 244–47

Carliner, David, 50

Carmichael, Stokely, 157

Carson, Johnny, 2, 218–20

Casey, William, 328

Castro, Fidel, 91–93

Catholics: civil rights struggles for, comparisons with homosexuals, 14; communism and, 167; intellectual fascism of, 167

Catholic Standard, 323–25

Chaffee, John, 240

Chamberlain, Charles, 47–48

Chicago Sun-Times, 93, 97

Christian Century, 94–96

Christian League for Sexual Freedom, 131–32

Christopher Street Liberation Day: creation of, 193–94; "Gay Is Good" and, *177*; inaugural march on, 221

Churchill, Wainwright, 66

civil rights, for homosexuals: comparisons with other civil rights struggles, 14, 19, 38, 50, 205–7; in Democratic Party platform, 251; GLF and, 205–7; in *The Homosexual in America*, 19–20; individual needs in relation to, 121–23; irrelevancy of gender in, 207–11; Franklin Kameny's strategies for, 117–18; objectives of, 258–59; peace movement and, 162; public demonstrations in, 91–92; in Republican Party platform, 251; terminology for, 327; U.S. Supreme Court petition for, 13, 17, 27–29, 33, *170. See also* public demonstrations, for homosexual rights; same-sex marriage movement

Civil Service Commission (CSC): ACLU challenges to, 54; discriminatory policies toward homosexuals, 4, 16–17, 25–27, 72, 126–28, 237–39; Ellsworth in, 12, 24–27; employment regulations, 39–40; formal apology to Franklin Kameny, 332–33; immorality charges against Franklin Kameny, 27; investigation of Franklin Kameny arrest, 9–10, 27, 341n6; irrational policies of, 15; meetings with MSW members, 106; public demonstrations against, 103; revision of rules for, 314–17; Bruce Scott's forced resignation from, 49–50

Clarke, Lige, 91, 309

Cleninden, Dudley, 233

Coffin, William Sloane, 163

Collins, Dennis, 310–11

Come Out, 208

Commission on Civil Rights, U.S., 51–52

Commission on Human Rights, 2–3

Committee on Gay Education student group, 239

Committee to Fight Exclusion of Homosexuals from the Armed Forces, 161

communism, 167

Confidential, 68

Conger, Richard, 113–16

Congress, U.S.: Franklin Kameny as candidate for, *177*, 228–33; MSW statement of purpose to, 44–45

Conservative Caucus, 327

"conspiracy of silence," among homosexuals, 20

Constitution, U.S.: homosexual rights under, 20; sexuality as civil right under, 14–15. *See also* Fifth Amendment; First Amendment

Conwell, Joe, 353n13

Corbett, Martin, 220

Cory, Donald Webster, 19–20, 88–90, *172*; on "conspiracy of silence," among homosexuals, 20

Costanza, Margaret, 300

Council on Religion and the Homosexual (CRH), 121–23

CRH. *See* Council on Religion and the Homosexual

Crompton, Louis, 188–89, 205–7

Cross, The (Wilkerson), 308

cruising, 62, 67–68

Cruz, Vera, 309

CSC. *See* Civil Service Commission

Cuba: *El Mundo*, 346n11; jail threats for homosexuals in, 91–93, 123–25

"cures" for homosexuality, 87, 119; aversion therapy, 187–88; Hadden on, 87; hypnotism, 246–47; through religious conversion, 95, 308–9; reparative therapy, 323

DADT. *See* "Don't Ask, Don't Tell"

Damned, The, 196

Damon, Gene. *See* Grier, Barbara

Daughters of Bilitis (DOB), 337n8; criticism of Franklin Kameny, 5; FBI targeting of, 40–42; *The Ladder*, 106, 138, 182–84; religious organizations and, 94; response to picketing strategies, 96–99; withdrawal from ECHO, 98

David Susskind Show, The, 138

de Dion, Al, 20. *See also* Mattachine Society of New York

Deep Throat, 312–14

Defense Department: homosexuals as security risk for, 10, 27–29, 31–33, 162–65, 233–34; Franklin Kameny visit to, 47. *See also* Pentagon

Democratic Party, civil rights for homosexuals and, 251

Demophile Center of Boston, 93

Department of Health, Education, and Welfare, 42–44

DeWees, Curtis, 20. *See also* Mattachine Society of New York

Diagnostic and Statistical Manual of Mental Disorders: homosexuality in, 4, 16, 71–72; removal of homosexuality from, 262–63, 267–68, 278–79, 281–83

direct-action strategies: by African Americans in civil rights movement, 21; of homophile movement, 21; of MSW, 21; against sodomy laws, 189–90

Dixon, Arrington, 323

DOB. *See* Daughters of Bilitis

Donaldson, Stephen. *See* Martin, Robert, Jr.

"Don't Ask, Don't Tell" (DADT), 333

Dowdy, John, 60–61

Drinan, Robert, 257

Duberman, Martin, 320–22

Dunbar, Jeffrey, 240

Dunn, Ian, 233

Earl Warren (Supreme Court Justice), 27–29

East Coast Homophile Organizations (ECHO), 68; sponsorship of public demonstrations, 101; withdrawal of organizations from, 98. *See also* Daughters of Bilitis; Mattachine Society of New York; Mattachine Society of Washington

Eastern Mattachine Magazine, 92

Eastern Regional Conference of Homophile Organizations (ERCHO), 193, 214–15

ECHO. *See* East Coast Homophile Organizations

effeminacy, homosexuality and, 61, 107, 223

Eiger, Lewis, 79

Eisenhower, Dwight: homosexuals as security risk under, 10, 27–29, 31–33; Lavender Scare under, 10

Ellis, Albert, 65

Ellsworth, Harris, 12, 24–27

employment bans, against homosexuals: in CSC, 4, 16–17, 25–27; under Fifth Amendment, 17; for Franklin Kameny, 9–10; lack of logical arguments for, 38; within U.S. government, 11, 16–17

Equal Rights Amendment, 304–6

ERCHO. *See* Eastern Regional Conference of Homophile Organizations

Eskridge, William, 333

Esquire, 158

Everything You Always Wanted to Know about Sex but Were Afraid to Ask (Reuben), 218–20

exclusive homosexuals, 67

Executive Order 10450, 10

Falwell, Jerry, 327–28

Farr, Richard, 229–32, 317

Fauntroy, Walter, 232, 247–49

FBI. *See* Federal Bureau of Investigation

Federal Bar Association, 78

Federal Bureau of Investigation (FBI): DOB targeted by, 40–42; MSW and, 40–42, 75–77, 150–51. *See also* Hoover, J. Edgar

federal court system, U.S., 12. *See also* Supreme Court, U.S.

feminism: homosexuality and, 184–85; lesbianism and, 185–87

Fifth Amendment, employment bans under, 17

Fire Island, 8

First Amendment: postal restrictions and, 191; security clearances under, 235; sexuality as right under, 14–15

Ford, Gerald, 299–300

Fortas, Abe, 163

Fouchette, Louis, 20

French News Agency, 97
Freud, Sigmund, 85
Frost, Laurence, 44–48

Gay Activist Alliance (GAA), 177,
    221–22; DC chapter of, 233, 247; GLF
    and, 227
Gay Blade, The, 285
gay church movement, 131–32
gay culture, in Washington, DC, 8
Gayer, Richard, 228, 235–36
Gayety Buffet, police raid on, 57–58
gay families, 284–85
gay-friendly buttons, 61–62
gay identity, Franklin Kameny's accep-
    tance of, 8
gay-in, 220–21
"Gay Is Good" philosophy: "Black is
    Beautiful" as parallel philosophy,
    155–61; Gay Liberation Day and, *177*;
    Leitsch and, 155–61; Wicker response
    to, 165–66
gay liberation. *See* civil rights, for
    homosexuals
Gay Liberation Front (GLF): advertise-
    ments by, 210; alliances with other
    protest movements, 205–7; at APA
    meetings, 227; Black Panthers and,
    221; GAA and, 227; Gittings and,
    206; Franklin Kameny and, 206, 208;
    Lahusen and, 206
Gay Liberation Front of New York, 222
Gay Liberation Front of Philadelphia,
    222
Gay magazine, 251–52
Gay News, 271
Gay Pride Week, 222
Gay World, The (Hoffman), 182–83
Gay Youth, 222

Gay Youth groups, 246
Gazette newsletter, 75–76
Giles, Morgan, 101
Gittings, Barbara, 90–92, 138, 184,
    236, 263, 282, 330; at APA annual
    meeting, *178*; GLF and, 206. *See also*
    Daughters of Bilitis
GLF. *See* Gay Liberation Front
Gold, Bill, 277–78
Gold, Ronald, 262–63, 268, 282, 353n5
Goodman, Bernice, 262
government, U.S.: Department of
    Health, Education, and Welfare,
    42–44; discriminatory employment
    policies of, against homosexuals, 11,
    16–17; Lavender Scare throughout,
    10; purging of homosexuals from,
    10; unfair treatment of homosexuals
    by, 11. *See also* Constitution, U.S.;
    Defense Department
Graham, Daniel, 337n10
Great Britain, decriminalization of
    homosexual acts in, 99–101, 221
Greatest Is Love organization, 308–9
"Great Society, The" 110
Green, Richard, 267, 353n5
Grey, Anthony, 218–22, 227–28
Grey, Meredith, 96
Grier, Barbara, 182–87, 207–11
Grimm, George, 228
Gunnison, Foster, Jr., 132–33, 197–98,
    200, 213–14

Hackworth, David, 329–30
Hadden, Samuel, 85–87; on cures for
    homosexuality, 87
Halleck, Charles, 249
Hampton, Robert, 237–39, 240–44
Hanes, John, Jr., 11, 32–33

Harper's, 53, 65–66
Harris, Frederick Brown, 83–85
Harvard University, 7–8
Hay, Harry, 337n8, 339n38, 349n3
Hayden, Charles, Jr. *See* Wicker, Randy
health-care services, treatment of homosexuality by, 42–44
Henle, Robert, 294–95
Hershey, Lewis, 52
heterosexuality: homosexual conversion to, through religion, 95; mental health and, comparisons with homosexuality, 16
HIV/AIDS crisis, 326, 328
HLNY. *See* Homosexual League of New York
Hodges, Julian, 88, 90, 202
Hoffman, Martin, 182–83
Hoffman, Paul, 346n11
homophile movement: anti-Vietnam War movement and, 130–31; criticism of other organizations within, 68–69; direct-action strategies of, 21; divisions between religious leaders and, 94; financial costs of, 145; growing activism within, 98–99; Franklin Kameny's critique of strategies within, 3; NAACP as model for, 104–6; National Conference of Homophile Movement, 165; purpose of, 3; Sagarin and, 89–90; social activities within, 120–21; Wicker and, 64–65, 138–40. *See also* Kameny, Franklin; lesbians; *specific magazines; specific societies*
"Homosexual, The" (TV program), 133–34
Homosexual Citizen, The, 176
Homosexual in America, The (Cory), 19–20, 88–90

homosexuality: APA removal of, from clinical disorders list, 262–63, 267–68, 278–79, 281–83; aversion therapy for, 187–88; as badge of inferiority, 159; Bieber on, 85–88, 267; blindness as analogy for, 198; caste-like status of, 19; causes of, 132–33; code words for, 10; constitutional protection of, 20; conversion to heterosexuality through religion, 95; CSC's discriminatory policies against, 4, 16–17, 25–27, 72, 126–28, 237–39; cures for, 87, 119; dishonorable discharges from military for, 73; effeminacy and, 61, 107, 223; feminism and, 184–85; under Fifth Amendment, 17; as First Amendment right, 14–15; Freudian theories about, 85; genetic determinants of, 188–89; in Great Britain, decriminalization of sexual acts, 99–101, 221; Hadden on, 85–87; health-care services' treatment of, 42–44; Kinsey studies on, 13, 15, 55; Landers' advice about, 118–20, 287–90; as mental disorder, APA diagnosis of, 4, 16; military service and, 6; as morality issue, 14–16, 26, 271; MSW challenge to APA diagnosis, 71–72, 86; Navy policies against, 224–26; percentage projections, in U.S. population, 13–14; primary psychosexual causes of, 5; promiscuity and, 62; psychiatrists as enemy of, 227; as psychological condition, 147; religious leaders' response to, 83–85; Safire definition of, 297; self-loathing and, 66–67, 70; Socarides on, 146–48, 267; as sociological problem, 220; as source of sexual outlet, 67, 71; stereotypes about, 107; terminology for,

143–44; as threat to national security, 10, 27–29, 31–33, 162–65, 233–36; U.S. government treatment of, 11, 16–17. *See also* "cures" for homosexuality; gay identity

Homosexual Law Reform Society, 221

Homosexual League of New York (HLNY), 52–53, 93

homosexual mafia, 136–37

"Homosexual Patient, The," 187–88

homosexual rights. *See* civil rights, for homosexuals

homosexuals: banned from government employment, 11, 16–17; brainwashed, 142, 147; caste-like status of, 19; civil rights struggles for, comparisons with other minority populations, 14, 19, 38; "conspiracy of silence" among, 20; constitutional rights of, 20; CSC's discriminatory policies against, 4, 16–17, 25–27, 72, 126–28, 237–39; in Cuba, jail threats for, 91–93, 123–25; entertainment needs of, 122; exclusive, 67; in federal agencies, 48; genocide of, 80; in Great Britain, decriminalization of sexual acts between, 99–101, 221; lack of heterogeneity among, 16; latent, 85, 142; mainstream integration of, 22; as oppressed minority, 14; picketing of White House, 54, 56–57, 108–11, *174*; police harassment of, in DC, 57–80; public image of, 60–64, 68–69; as second-class citizens, 50; as security risk, under Eisenhower, 10, 27–29, 31–33; Selective Service System and, confidentiality of personal information for, 52; self-loathing by, 66–67, 70; social needs of, 122; spiritual issues for, 122; U.S.

military service for, 6, 46–47, 73, 240–43. *See also* police harassment, of homosexuals

"Homosexuals, The" (TV program), 136–37

Homosexuals Intransigent of City University of New York, 222

Hooker, Evelyn, 86, 134–36

Hoover, J. Edgar, 44; on homosexuals picketing White House, 54, 56–57; Jenkins investigated by, 77–79; on MSW in FBI, 150–51; PCI reports to, 52–53; Scarberry and, 124

House Un-American Activities Committee (HUAC), 44

Hudson, John Paul, 298–99

Huggins, Buell Dwight, 339n38

Human Rights Law, in DC, 295

hypnotism, as "cure" for homosexuality, 246–47

identity. *See* gay identity

Inman, Richard, 103–6; financial assistance to, from Franklin Kameny, 134; in "The Homosexual," 133–34; Franklin Kameny's criticism of, 117–18

Institute for Social Ethics, 132

intellectual fascism, 167

Ireland, 8

Itkin, Michael Francis, 131–32

Jaenicke, Jon Larson, 318

Janus Society of Philadelphia, 68

Jefferson, Thomas, 36

Jenkins, Walter, 77–79

Jews, comparisons with homosexuals, 14, 19, 38

John Birch Society, 111–12

Johnson, David, 10

Johnson, Gail, 76

Johnson, Kimball, 243–44

Johnson, Lyndon B., 49–52; federal employment discrimination under, 49; "The Great Society" under, 110; Franklin Kameny's list of grievances for, 108–11

Jones, M. A., 76–77

Kalin, Herbert, 312–14

Kameny, Franklin Edward: on acceptable terminology for homosexuality, 143–44; acceptance of gay identity, 8; AMS and, 9–10, 25–27; at APA meeting, 266–68; appeal of government firing, 10; arrest of, 8–9, 24–27, 338n27; barred from federal employment, 9–10; on bisexuality, 156, 223, 298–99; on brainwashed homosexuals, 142; as candidate for Congress, 177, 228–33; challenge to military ban on homosexuals, 240–43; on civil disobedience, 256–57; combat medals for, 7; in Committee to Fight Exclusion of Homosexuals from Armed Forces, 161; communications with parents, 4; conflict with Leitsch, 216–17; counsel for arrested gays, after police raids, 175, counsel for draft inductees, 198–200; counsel for fired federal employees, 79; on countercultural sexual ethics, 252–53; criticism of leadership, 113–16; critique of homophile strategies, 3; on cruising, 62–63; CSC investigation of, after arrest, 9–10, 27, 341n6;

CSC's formal apology to, 332–33; death of, 333; defense of MSW, 150–51; DOB criticism of, 5; early sex life for, 5; economic hardships for, 11–12; embrace of homophile movement, 12; employment at AMS, 9–10; on feminism, 184–87; financial assistance to Inman, 134; firing from Commission on Human Rights, 2–3; funding campaign for legal battles, 12; gay-friendly buttons and, 61–62; on genocide of homosexuals, 80; GLF and, 206, 208; graduate education history for, 7–8; at Harvard University, 7–8, 169; on homosexuality as psychological condition, 147; immorality charges against, 27; Inman critiqued by, 117–18; integrationist philosophy of, 340n50; in Ireland, 8; Lyndon B. Johnson and, 108–11; Kinsey as inspiration for, 13; on lack of heterogeneity among homosexuals, 16; on latent homosexuals, 142; legacy as gay rights pioneer, 330–33; letters as mode of protest for, 2, 340n52; letters from Wicker, 74–75; letters to mother, 128–30, 249–51, 283–84; letter to MSNY, 161–62; on "liberal syndrome," 108; in Library of Congress, 179–80, 331; Macy as archenemy of, 171; on media representations of gays, 302–4; as mentor to young gays, 213–14; militancy of, 18–19; military service of, 6–7, 169; on "mindless Sixties," 152–55; on morality of homosexuality, 271; as MSW president, 22, 82; papers at Library of Congress, 179–80; personal background for,

5; petition to U.S. Supreme Court, 13, 17, 27–29, 33, *170*; on philosophy behind gay liberation movement, 257–62; picketing at Independence Hall, *173*; picketing of White House by, 54, 56–57, *174*; political platform of, 231–32; as political transformist, 21; on population figures for homosexuals, in U.S., 13–14; on prostitution, 181–82; public criticism of, 5; on public image of homosexuals, 60–64, 68–69; radicalization of, 18–19; reflection on political campaign, 234–36; response to creditors, 144–46; Rodwell conflict with, 193–94; as secular rationalist, 15; on sexuality as constitutional right, 14–15; on sexual morality, 14–15; on sexual revolution, 181; Shriver reply to, 81–82; at Smithsonian Institution, *180*, 330–31; Socarides as archenemy of, 146–48; on social activities through homophile organizations, 120–21; as spokesman for National Coalition of Gay Organizations, 251; as standard-bearer for social change, 2–3; strategy for civil liberties victories, 117–18, 197–98; support for McGovern, 251–52; on transsexuality, 156, 159; at University of Arizona, 7–8; use of Hooker studies, 86; on Vietnam War draft exemptions, for homosexuals, 161–62; views on Vietnam War, 256; ; visit to One, Inc., 12–13; visit to Pentagon, 47. *See also* "Gay Is Good" philosophy
Kameny, Rae, 128–30, 249–51, 283–84
Karpman, Benjamin, 341n7
Katzenbach, Nicholas, 124

Kennedy, John F., 2, 18; appeals for homosexual civil rights, 34–35; presidential run as Catholic, 277–78
Kennedy, Robert F., 40–42, 56–57
Kilgore, Joe, 48
King, Martin Luther, Jr., 21
King, Robert, 76
Kinsey, Alfred, 13, 15, 55
Koch, Leo, 74–75
Kuntzler, Paul, 233

Ladder, The, 106, 138, 182–84
Lahusen, Kay, 5–6, 262–63, 307, 330; GLF and, 206; on relevancy of reformist strategies, 214–15
LaMonthe, John, 265–66
Landers, Ann, 2, 269–71; advice about homosexuality, 118–20, 287–90
latent homosexuals, 85, 142
Laurence, Leo, 211
Lavender Scare, 10
Lavey, Edna, 249, 291–93
Lavey, Ira, 232–33, 249
League for Civil Education, 94
League for Sexual Freedom, 74–75, 93
Leitsch, Dick, 88–90, 123–25, 200–203; conflict with Franklin Kameny, 216–17; "Gay Is Good" philosophy, 155–61; MSNY and, 88; political aspirations of, 234–36
lesbians: feminism and, 185–87; *Ladder*, 106; psychiatric assessment of, 244. *See also* Daughters of Bilitis
"liberal syndrome," 108
liberation movements. *See* civil rights, for homosexuals
Library of Congress, Franklin Kameny's papers in, *179–80*, 331

Littlejohn, Larry, 120–21, 228
Lovelace, Linda, 312
Lyon, Phyllis, 94

Macy, John, Jr.: as archenemy of Frank-
    lin Kameny, *171*; letter to MSW, 125–
    28; public demonstrations against
    CSC and, 103–6; unconstitutional
    policies toward homosexuals, 37–40.
    See also Civil Service Commission
Mandel, Marvin, 263–65
March on Washington (1992), 329
March on Washington for Jobs and Free-
    dom (1963), 64
Marcus, Eric, 18
Marmor, Judd, 267, 353n5
marriage rights. *See* same-sex marriage
    movement
Martin, Del, 94
Martin, Robert, Jr., 140–42, 151–55
Martin, William, 44
Matlovich, Leonard, 310–12, 318, 320–22
Mattachine Society, in Los Angeles,
    337n8
Mattachine Society, in San Francisco, 12
Mattachine Society of Florida, 104, 117,
    133
Mattachine Society of New York
    (MSNY), 12, 20; as civil liberties
    organization, 60–61; counsel of
    arrested gays, after police raids, 195;
    elections in, 90; Franklin Kameny
    letter to, 161–62; Leitsch and, 88;
    militant strategies within, 90; picket-
    ing of White House by, 57; prohibi-
    tion of social events by, 122–23;
    public demonstration rules for, 102;
    religious organizations and, 94; War-
    ner in, 189–90

Mattachine Society of Washington
    (MSW), 20–21; ACLU partnership
    with, 48; challenges to APA diagnosis
    of homosexuality, 71–72, 86; CSC
    meetings with, 106; as democratic
    organization, 153; direct-action strat-
    egy of, 21; FBI and, 40–42, 75–77,
    150–51; *Gazette* newsletter, 75–76;
    The Homosexual Citizen, *176*; Hoover
    on mailing list for, 75–76; Franklin
    Kameny as president of, 22, 82; Macy
    letter to, 125–28; PCI in, 52–53;
    picketing of White House by, 57;
    presidency of, battles for, 82; Bruce
    Scott in, 49; Selective Service System
    and, 52; statement of purpose for,
    44–48, 344n20; support of same-sex
    marriage rights, 263–65; *Washington
    Post*'s refusal of advertisements for,
    111–13; Wicker infiltration of, 52–53
Mauldin, David, 107–8
Mauldin, William, 107–8
McConchie, Richard, 101–3
McElroy, Neil, 11, 29–32
McGovern, George, 251–52
McIlvenna, Ted, 94
McIntyre, Dal, 194
McLucas, John, 320
McNamara, Robert, 46–47
Medical World Review, 187–88
mental disorder, definition of, 355n23
mental health: heterosexuality and
    comparisons with homosexuality, 16;
    homosexuality and APA diagnosis
    for, 4, 16
Michaels, Dick, 194–96, 235
Midnight Cowboy, 196
military, U.S.: dishonorable discharges
    for homosexuality, 73; homosexuals
    serving in, 46–47; Franklin Kameny

in, 6–7; Franklin Kameny's challenge to ban on homosexuals, 240–43; lying about homosexuality and, 6; picketing of, 74–75; repeal of DADT, 333; U.S. Navy, 224–26. *See also* Selective Service System
Military Law Project, 310
Mill, John Stuart, 163
Mitch, Richard. *See* Michaels, Dick
Mitchell, Bernon, 44
Mondello, Anthony, 240, 243–44
morality, homosexuality and, 14–16, 26, 271
Moral Majority, 326–28
Morgan, Harry, 136–37
MSNY. *See* Mattachine Society of New York
MSW. *See* Mattachine Society of Washington
Mundo, El, 346n11
Murray, Robert, 57–60

NAACP. *See* National Association for the Advancement of Colored People
NAACP v. Alabama, 342n20
NACHO. *See* North American Conference of Homophile Organizations
Nagourney, Adam, 233
Narcotics Anonymous, 66
National Association for the Advancement of Colored People (NAACP), 104–6
National Capital Area affiliate of American Civil Liberties Union (NCACLU), 48, 50, 215; police harassment of homosexuals and, 59
National Coalition of Gay Organizations, 251
National Conference of the Homophile Movement, 165

National Council of Churches, 94
National Gay Task Force, 285–86, 300
National Institutes of Mental Health (NIMH), 146–48
National Peace Action Coalition, 257
National Planning Conference of Homophile Organizations, 117
National Security Agency (NSA), 44
Navy, U.S., policies barring homosexuality, 224–26; SECNAVINST 1900.9, 226; SEGNAVINSTR 1900.9, 225
NCACLU. *See* National Capital Area affiliate of American Civil Liberties Union
Neuman, Monroe, 300–302
New Frontier, during Kennedy administration, 18, 33–37
New Republic, 257
Newsweek, 155, 253, 326, 327–28
New York News, 97
New York Post, 53
New York Times, 93, 97, 318
Nichols, Jack, 19–20, *172,* 211–12, 294, 309–12; challenge to APA diagnosis of homosexuality, 71–72; denial of homosexuality as mental disorder, 86; in "The Homosexuals," 136; staging of picket lines, 91; television appearances by, 140; Wicker and, 71
NIMH. *See* National Institutes of Mental Health
Nix, Robert, Sr., 47
Nixon, Richard, 2, 228–32; obscenity restrictions under, 190–92
Noble, Elaine, 295–96
North, Fred, 48
North American Conference of Homophile Organizations (NACHO), 194, 214–15
NSA. *See* National Security Agency

O'Boyle, Patrick, 166
obscenity, postal restrictions on, 190–92
Office of Economic Opportunity (OEO), 79–80
Office of Personnel Management (OPM), 332–33
Oglesby, Joseph, 314–17
Ogren, Peter, 165
O'Leary, Jean, 262
ONE (magazine), 60–61, 113–16
One, Inc., 337n8; Franklin Kameny visit to, 12–13
"On Liberty" (Mill), 163
OPM. *See* Office of Personnel Management
Orlando Sentinel, 97
Osborne, Cyril, 99–101

Parker, Joe, 44
Payne, Ethel, 295–97
PCI. *See* potential criminal informant
peace movement, 162
Pearson, Drew, 148–49
Pentagon, 47, 103
Peurifoy, John, 10
Phillips, Howard, 327
Playboy, 184
Poland, Jefferson, 74–75
police harassment, of homosexuals, 57–60; Franklin Kameny as counsel, after police raids, *175*; MSNY counsel, after police raids, 195; NCACLU and, 59; through raids, 57–58; in Washington, DC, 57–58
Pomeroy, Wardell, 262
pornography, postal restrictions on, 190–92

postal restrictions: under First Amendment, 191; against obscenity and pornography, 190–92
potential criminal informant (PCI), 52–53
Prada, Ray, 262
Pratt, John H., 235
Proferes, James, 312
promiscuity, homosexuality and, 62
prostitution, 181–82
Protestantism. *See Christian Century*
Psychiatric News, 322, 355n23
Psychiatric Opinion, 227
psychiatry, homosexuality and. *See* American Psychiatric Association
public demonstrations, for homosexual rights, 91–93; Annual Reminder, 93, 101–2, 192–93; against CSC, 103; defense of, 114–15; DOB response to, 96–99; ECHO sponsorship of, 101; media coverage of, 92–93, 96–97, 103; by MSNY, 102; Nichols and, 91; at Pentagon, 103; through picketing, 91–92; purpose of, 114; against U.S. military, 74–75; at White House, 54, 56–57, 108–11; Wicker and, 56–57, 91
Public Health Service, U.S., 42–44
Public Health Service Form 89, 73

Queer History of the United States, A (Bronski), 23

Reagan, Ronald, 148–49
Red and Black, 239–40
Rehnquist, William, 356n6
religious conversion, for homosexuality, 95; Greatest Is Love organization and, 308–9

religious leaders: CRH and, 121–23; division between homophile organizations and, 94; gay church movement and, 131–32; response to homosexuality, 83–85
reparative therapy, 323
Republican Party, civil rights for homosexuals and, 251
Reuben, David, 218–20
Reuters News Agency, 97
Richards, Dennis, 140
Richardson, Nevin, 144–46
Rindskopf, Elizabeth, 328–29
Robinson, Kent, 227–28, 282
Rodwell, Craig, 93, 193–94
Rood, G. H., 26
Rosenberg, Ethel, 342n29
Rosenberg, Julius, 342n29
Ross, Nancy, 211–12
Rowan, Carl, 143–44
Ruitenbeck, Hendrik, 101–3
Rusk, Dean, 106
Ryan, William Fitts, 47

Safire, William, 297–98
Sagarin, Edward, 88–90, 184; as father of homophile movement, 89–90. *See also* Cory, Donald Webster
Same Sex, The, 218
same-sex marriage movement: MSW and, 263–65; prohibition of, in Maryland, 263; in Washington, DC, 323
San Francisco: Franklin Kameny arrest in, 8–9, 24–27, 338n27; Mattachine Society in, 12; SIR in, 228
Sarria, Jose, 351n19
Saulsbury, Robert, 252–53
Scanlon, William, 162–65, 233–34

Scarberry, Warren, 123–25, 328n6
Schaefers Stipulation, 274, 353n10
Schlafly, Phyllis, 304–6
Schuyler, Bruce, 60
Science News Letter, 85–88
Scott, Bruce, 49–50, 184
Scott, Byron N., 13
Scott v. Macy (1968), 184–85
SECNAVINST 1900.9, 226
security clearances, for homosexuals, 10, 27–29, 31–33, 162–65, 233–34; First Amendment rights and, 235; legal victory for, 236–37
SEGNAVINSTR 1900.9, 225
Selective Service System: confidentiality of information in, 52; Public Heath Service Form 89 and, 73
sexuality: as First Amendment right, 14–15; Kinsey studies on, 13, 15; as moral issue, 14–16. *See also* heterosexuality; homosexuality
sexual pleasure, as right, 70
sexual revolution, 181
Shaw, Bernard, 188
Shaw, Carolyn Hegner, 203–5
Shelley, Martha, 205–7
Shipley, Carl, 78–79
Shriver, Sargent, 79–82
Silverstein, Charles, 262
Sims, O. Suthern, 239–40
SIR. *See* Society for Individual Rights
Skallerup, Walter, Jr., 47
Slater, Don, 130–31
Smithsonian Institution, Franklin Kameny papers at, *180*, 330–31
Sobell, Morton, 342n29
Socarides, Charles, 141–42; on causes on homosexuality, 146–48; on homosexuality as mental disorder, 267;

Socarides, Charles (*cont.*)
in "The Homosexual Patient," 187–88; Franklin Kameny's conflict with, 253–55; referendum to challenge APA decision, 293–94; in *Washington Post*, 146–48
Society and the Healthy Homosexual (Weinberg), 254
Society for Individual Rights (SIR), 120–21; homosexual ghettos and, 157; in San Francisco, 228
sodomy laws: ACLU and, 1; direct-action strategy against, 189–90; Schaefers Stipulation and, 274, 353n10; in Washington, DC, 1, 271–75
Sokolsky, George, 42
Sorensen, Theodore, 52–57
Spectrum, 295, 304–6
Spitzer, Robert, 278, 281–82, 322–23, 355n23
Staircase, 196
Starr, Irwin, 303
Stoller, Robert, 267, 353n5
Stonewall riots, 3, 192–93
Student Homophile Leagues, 222
student occupation of universities, 151–53
Students for Democratic Society, 153
Subcommittee on Equal Employment Opportunities, 51
Supreme Court, U.S.: Franklin Kameny petition to, 13, 17, 27–29, 33, *170*; *NAACP v. Alabama*, 342n20
Sweeterman, John, 111–13
Switchblade (Wilkerson), 308

Tabler, Otis, Jr., 317–18
Tangent Group, 130
Tavern Guild, 94

Taylor, Mattie, 247
tearooms, 67–68. *See also* cruising
Time, 107, 218
Titus, Harold, Jr., 271–75
transsexuality, 156, 159
Travis, Ken, 68
Tucker, Nancy, 234

Ulrich, Otto, 228–32, 235–36
United Press International, 97
United States (U.S.), 13–14. *See also* Congress, U.S.; Constitution, U.S.; Supreme Court, U.S.
University of Arizona, 7–8
U.S. Constitution. *See* Constitution, U.S.

Vietnam War, draft exemptions for homosexuals, 161–62
Village Voice, 206; GLF advertisements in, 210
Vincenz, Lili, 207–8

Walker, Robert, 121–23
Wallace, Mike, 136
Walter, Francis, 44
Ware, Cade, 257–62
Warner, Arthur, 189–90
Warner, John, 352n4
Warren, Bacil, 314
Warsaw Pact, 166
Washington, DC: Commission on Human Rights, 2–3; GAA chapter in, 233, 247; gay culture in, 8; Human Rights Law in, 295; police harassment of homosexuals in, 57–80; sodomy laws in, 1, 271–75

Washington Afro-American, 92, 248
Washington Area Council on Religion and the Homosexual, 198
Washington Area Peace Action Coalition, 256–57
Washington Daily News, 77–79, 166–67
Washington Post, 155; defense of MSW, by Franklin Kameny, 150–51; homosexuals as security risk in, 10, 27–29, 31–33; militancy among homosexuals in, 211–12; refusal of MSW advertisements, 111–13; Socarides in, 146–48
Washington Star, 93, 97, 181–82; postal restrictions on obscenity and, 190–92
Watkins, James, 328
Waugh, Robert J. L., 355n23
Weinberg, George, 254
Welby, Marcus, M.D., 302–4
Wentworth, Benning, 228, 249
Werres, Johannes, 271
West Side Discussion Group, 222
White House: MSNY at, 57; MSW at, 57; picketing of, by homosexuals, 54, 56–57, 108–11, *174*; Wicker's response to demonstrations at, 56–57
Wicker, Randy: on "Gay Is Good" philosophy, 165–66; HLNY and, 52–53; in homophile movement, 64–65, 138–40; letters to Franklin Kameny, 74–75; media coverage of, 138–40; in MSW, 52–53; Nichols and, 71; on picketing White House, 56–57; public image of homosexuals and, 60–64, 68–69; staging of picket lines, 91
Wilkerson, David, 308–9
Wilkins, Roy, 21
Will, George, 326
Willer, Shirley, 96
Wilson, Jerry, 279–81
Winston, Theodore, 132–33
Wolfenden, John, 99–101

Young Adult Project, 94

Zumwalt, Elmo, Jr., 224–26